OnlineArbitrage.com

Thank you for your purchase of Online Arbitrage! Purchase of this book through Amazon also gives you the Kindle version FOR FREE!

Just visit http://www.amazon.com/dp/B00N70QV6M and you'll be able to download the Kindle version to your Kindle, tablet, phone, or computer!

Free Kindle copy is only available to NEW purchases from Amazon.com.

INTERNET HIGH-FIVE PLACE HAND HERE

Online Arbitrage

Sourcing Secrets!
Learn the secrets of
buying online and
have profitable
inventory delivered
right to your door!

Chris Green

PBLLC Press, Rehoboth, MA

2012

Please REGISTER this book at <u>OnlineArbitrage.com/register</u>

**You can register your book by forwarding your Amazon receipt to
<u>chris@scanpower.com</u>**

Available for NEW purchases from Amazon or from Chris Green

Online Arbitrage:

Sourcing Secrets for buying products online to resell for BIG PROFITS

For more information and exclusive offers, please visit:

OnlineArbitrage.com

Green, Christopher John

Hi, Mom!

Awesome Editor: Paine, Kimberly

Published by PBLLC Press, Rehoboth, MA 02769

First Printing, September 2014

ISBN-13: 978-1500333829

ISBN-10: 1500333824

Printed in the United States of America

The publisher does not have any control over and does not assume any responsibility for third-party websites or their contents. Many links are included that are current and active at the time of writing. EBay links are not included as they expire over time unless they are search result links.

Amazon, eBay, Craigslist, ScannerMonkey and other names are copyright trademarks of their respective owners. Other brand names are property of their respective owners.

The focus of this book is to help you source products to resell from online retail websites. The examples shown in this book are done primarily with the expectation of selling the items on Amazon.com, primarily using their fulfillment program called Fulfillment By Amazon, or FBA. You can also sell on eBay, Craigslist, or any other sales channel that you prefer.

Things change over time.

At the time of this writing, all fees, rules, and laws are represented accurately and all links are active. It is always best to check the current web pages for any changes that may have occurred between the writing of this book and when you start your business. The fees to sell on Amazon.com and eBay.com can change and will affect prices and payouts. Laws may change regarding paying and collecting sales tax.

This book builds upon the information presented in my first book titled *Arbitrage: The authoritative guide on how it works, why it works, and how it can work for you.*

If you are familiar with the FBA program and the dynamics of the Amazon marketplace, then the examples presented in this book should make perfect sense. If you are new to Amazon and FBA, then I highly recommend reviewing *Arbitrage* before reading this book.

It is available on Amazon.com as a paperback:

http://www.Amazon.com/dp/1478251891

And also on Kindle:

http://www.Amazon.com/dp/B009B3UYEO/

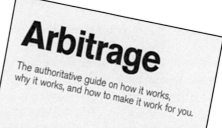

The Kindle version is FREE if you purchase the paperback version from Amazon. PS: It's only nine bucks and covers things like the Amazon Buy Box and Sales Rank.

To your success,

Chris Green

Director, ScanPower

Want to connect? Message me @ facebook.com/chris

Earnings Disclaimer

I can't make any promises as to how much money you'll make in this business. It's up to you to go out and run with this information. I can't promise that you will make a certain amount of money, or any money, or not lose money, as a result of following the information in this book. What I can do is give you as much useful and accurate information that I can and trust you to learn it and use it to the best of your ability.

I'll show you deals that we have done and the profits that we made but there is no guarantee that you will be able to replicate them exactly. With any business, your results will vary and will be based on your personal abilities, knowledge, and level of desire (among other things). Each person's results will vary.

The information provided in this book should be applied and used based on your own due diligence. By reading this book, you agree that we are not liable for your success or failure.

Basically, we can help, but it's up to you to actually run your business. ☺

The good news is that we are here and we are happy to help!

I also suggest finding a good, LOCAL certified public accountant (CPA) that can help steer you in the right direction. Many laws are state-specific so a local CPA that understands words like online seller, resale, tax-free, and NEXUS is pretty much a must. A good CPA will meet with you free of charge. Interview a few different ones and go with the one that fits your business and your personality best. Like any service, they should save you more money than they cost you. If they don't, fire them!

Post a picture with your copy of this book and leave a review on Amazon and you can schedule a 30-minute Online Arbitration consultation with Chris Green for free!

Post a picture of yourself with the book on Facebook (facebook.com/chris) or in our ScanPower Facebook group (facebook.com/groups/scanpower) and let me know that you left a review on Amazon, and we can schedule a screen share session to get all of your questions answered. Who knows, we might even find an awesome Online Arbitrage deal!

This book contains links to many UNLISTED YouTube videos. That means that only people who have bought the book can see them. To make this as easy as possible, we've placed QR codes throughout the book. They will take you directly to the videos on your phone or tablet. You can also pull them up on your PC or Mac. To use the QR codes, please download RED LASER from the Apple App Store or Google Play Store.

Try it now! When you see an image like this:

ScanPower Rap - It's All About Doin' That FBA, FBA, FBA

https://www.youtube.com/watch?v=4iKk0Be3ArE
http://bit.ly/fbarap

Just open the Red Laser app and hold your camera over the black and white square. You'll be able to quickly go to the video. LINKS (or just Google Red Laser):

iPhone/iPad: https://itunes.apple.com/us/app/redlaser-barcode-scanner-shopping/id474902001?mt=8

Android: https://play.google.com/store/apps/details?id=com.ebay.redlaser&hl=en

This is a COURSE on Online Arbitrage. It's just sold as a book. By buying the book (THANK YOU!) you get access to all of the course materials! The videos are unlisted--meaning that only people who know the links (who bought the book) will be able to see them. You also get PRIVATE SpreeCasts and webinars.

Sign up here to be notified of these private events: OnlineArbitrage.com/register

There is SO MUCH info that I wanted to put in here but it wouldn't all fit. That's why there are a ton of VIDEOS. Plus, some things are just easier to explain with videos and screen demos/walkthroughs.

ScanPower is the leader in Amazon and FBA news and content. We offer so much incredible content and information that it can be difficult to keep up. Here are the best ways to connect:

SpreeCast – Weekly LIVE video/radio shows about Amazon, FBA, and more! Special guests include online sales tax experts from TaxJar.com and deal experts from FatWallet.com.

spreecast.com/users/chrisgreen

ScanPower Monthly Magazine – Monthly publication available on Amazon in PRINT and KINDLE formats. Highlights the news around Amazon, FBA, online selling, and ScanPower.

scanpower.com/magazine

Are you on Facebook? The **ScanPower Facebook Group** is widely considered the best place to get Amazon and FBA information as well as get any questions answered by experienced online sellers. If you have a question about getting started, ask it here and get up and running.

facebook.com/groups/scanpower

YouTube – The ScanPower YouTube channel has replays of past SpreeCasts as well as demonstration videos of sourcing tips and tricks.

youtube.com/scanpowerTV

SoundCloud – Podcast audio replays of the ScanPower SpreeCasts are available for download or streaming from SoundCloud.

soundcloud.com/scanpower

ScanPower LINK – This is a dedicated app that pulls in the posts from the Facebook group, the latest YouTube videos, SoundCloud files, SpreeCasts, and ScanPower events, all on one place.

Android: bit.ly/SPLinkAndroid

iPhone: bit.ly/SPLinkiPhone

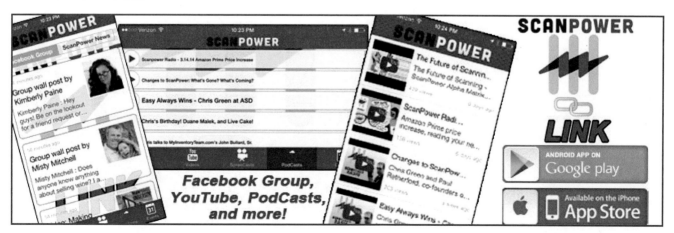

If I could give a new Amazon seller one piece of advice, it would be to read the Amazon seller guidelines, especially the details in the categories that they intend to sell in. Amazon is not very forgiving and ignorance of the rules of the Amazon seller platform is not a valid excuse for breaking them. Failure to know and follow the Amazon rules of the third party seller marketplace can be ground for termination of your Amazon selling privileges.

Selling on Amazon: www.Amazon.com/sellonAmazon (public page)
Seller Central Help: https://sellercentral.Amazon.com/hz/help/home (Seller Central login required)

Fulfillment by Amazon Revenue Calculator

Provide your fulfillment costs and see real-time cost comparisons between your fulfillment and our offering for customer orders fulfilled on Amazon.com: https://sellercentral.Amazon.com/gp/fbacalc/fba-calculator.html

Things you didn't know you needed to know to sell on Amazon.com (MUST READ):

https://sellercentral.Amazon.com/gp/help/help.html/ref=ag_200421970_cont_69034&itemID=200421970
(Seller Central login required)

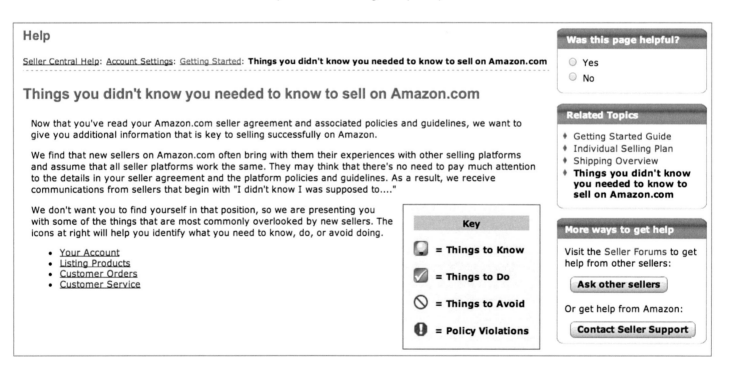

Your Account

Things to Know

When registering as a seller on Amazon.com, you create a single selling account for your business. **❶ Operating and maintaining multiple seller accounts is prohibited.**

You can help build buyer trust in your business by providing clear and detailed information about your policies.

See also: <u>Manage Returns</u>

Things to Do

Provide the business name that will be displayed on Amazon.com so that they remember your company.

Make sure your business contact information is current (e-mail & phone number if available) so that we may contact you, if necessary.

Keep credit card and bank account information current for payments and settlements

Describe the gift messaging and gift wrap services you offer

Upload your logo—your seller logo image must be exactly 120 x 30 pixels

Only enter company info specific to how you manage your business on Amazon.com

Choose shipping rate settings so buyers know what your shipping costs.

See also: <u>Manage Returns</u>

Things to Avoid

❶ Registering for multiple seller accounts.

❶ Including website URLs in product feeds, business name, or other company information that may refer buyers to your or any other website.

🚫 Assuming other sellers are doing it right. Always double-check your practices against the applicable platform policies and guidelines and the seller Help content.

Listing Products

Things to Know

- Listing products in the right categories and with the correct information is critical for good buyer experience and strong seller performance.

- You can help build buyer trust in your business by providing clear and detailed information about your policies.

- Amazon.com buyers expect their purchases to be well-packaged and to arrive on time.

- Product detail pages do not belong to any one seller. The product title, image and details must be specific to the product, not to any seller or any individual seller promotions.

- Set up your shipping charges, sale pricing, and promotions using Amazon tools; don't include any of this information in your product listing details.

- Your Amazon seller agreement requires that the price at which you list a product on Amazon.com and the other terms of your offer must be the same or better than for the same product offering on your other online sales channels.

- See also: Manage Returns

Things to Do

Product Titles

- ✓ Provide information about the specific product only
- ✓ Keep it short, but include critical information
- ✓ 100 characters maximum
- ✓ Start with the product brand where appropriate – not seller
- ✓ Include a model number, when available
- ✓ Use only plain text (no HTML formatting)
- ✓ Capitalize the first letter of each word
- ✓ Use numerals (2 instead of two)

Images

- ✓ Use white, clean backgrounds that do not distract from the product
- ✓ Create images with 300 dpi minimum; 1,000 dpi is best
- ✓ Show the entire product. It should occupy at least 80 percent of the image area
- ✓ Include only what the buyer will be receiving
- ✓ JPEG (.jpg), TIFF (.tif), or GIF (.gif) format; JPEG preferred.
- ✓ Use photographs

Things to Avoid

Product Titles

- ⊘ Marketing information ("x% off" or other marketing messages, seller URL, seller name) in product information
- ⊘ Using categories that do not match the existing Amazon.com browse tree
- ⊘ HTML code
- ⊘ ALL CAPS
- ⊘ Symbols (! * $?)
- ⊘ Promotions or other information that is not descriptiove of the product itself

Images

- ⊘ Promotional text such as "Sale" or "Free Shipping"
- ⊘ Colored backgrounds or lifestyle pictures (for the main image)
- ⊘ Borders, watermarks, text or other descriptions
- ⊘ A single image displaying multiple colors of your product together when they are sold separately
- ⊘ Line drawings or artistic representations
- ⊘ Animated images
- ⊘ URLs or seller logo/name on product images

Customer Service

Things to Know

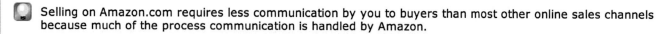

Selling on Amazon.com requires less communication by you to buyers than most other online sales channels because much of the process communication is handled by Amazon.

Amazon will provide all the order and shipping e-mails to buyers; you must not send order or shipment confirmation e-mails, to avoid conflicting messaging or confusion for the buyer.

You must not market or advertise to Amazon.com buyers, nor divert them in any way from the Amazon sales process—not even in otherwise permitted communications, such as when responding to buyer inquiries about your products or their orders.

See also: Manage Returns

Things to Do

Fulfill all orders within the promised lead time and shipping windows and ship exactly what you listed for sale.

Clearly explain your policies and processes, and provide other pertinent information. See also: Manage Returns

Learn about buyer communication policies for doing business on Amazon.com; be aware of when Amazon handles the communications to buyers and when it is appropriate for your company to communicate (or not). Generally, you will not send communications to buyers other than as necessary for order fulfillment and related customer service. Respond promptly to buyer questions about the status of their order.

Keep in mind that buyers have come to expect the same level of customer service from sellers that they receive from Amazon. If you don't meet that standard, you may have to deal with some unsatisfied buyers.

Be courteous and patient with buyers when they request information, returns or refunds.

Things to Avoid

Bribing buyers for positive feedback.

Using buyer information for online or offline marketing purposes, or directing buyers to your own or another's website.

Engaging in arguments with buyers rather than courteously working to resolve the problem.

Assuming that buyers read your policies.

Customer Orders

Things to Know

When you set up your account, you'll find information about shipping expectations that you will need to integrate into your order and fulfillment processes. You'll also see that you're required to confirm to Amazon when you have shipped your orders, so we can keep buyers informed about the progress of their orders and charge their credit cards for the purchase.

You are required to ship media products (books, music, DVD and video) within 2 business days. Non-media products must be shipped by the shipping availability date you specify in the product feed for such products.

You must confirm to Amazon that you have completed shipment in order to receive payment for an order. This confirmation will also trigger Amazon's shipment confirmation e-mail to the buyer and will set the expectation for estimated delivery date.

Things to Do

☑ Review default shipping settings and customize to fit your fulfillment model

☑ Check your account at least daily for orders

☑ Schedule order reports to ensure an authoritative report of all orders and order information

Things to Avoid

❗ Including any marketing or promotional materials with packing materials

🚫 Relying on e-mail notifications of account activity. E-mails can get lost or deleted.

60-Minute FAST TRACK to becoming an AWESOME Amazon seller!

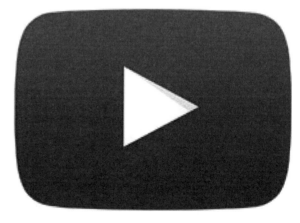

http://www.scanpower.com/fbavideos

This book will help you get up and running with profitable inventory to resell online, but there's a lot more to running a resale business than just sourcing inventory. If you're starting out and you need help, we have ScanPower University and ScanPower Coaching. Consider this the FAST TRACK way to get up and running with Amazon and FBA.

ScanPower University & ScanPower Coaching

ScanPower University is the one-stop FAST TRACK to getting started with Amazon and FBA (Fulfillment By Amazon). ScanPower University is led by Chris Green, Director of ScanPower and Duane Malek, full-time FBA seller and coach.

This course is designed to take a new Amazon seller from having little to no knowledge of Amazon and FBA to a full understanding of how it works and why it works, and helps them completely finish their first FBA shipment.

ScanPower University includes membership in a PRIVATE Facebook Group only for ScanPower University members. This means you have a dedicated place to get the answers you need about getting started with Amazon and FBA! Members also get access to monthly PRIVATE SpreeCasts with Chris and Duane as they host an ASK-ME-ANYTHING SpreeCast! This SpreeCast is PRIVATE and only for members of ScanPower University (including lifetime access to all of the past and future episodes).

The ScanPower University course outline includes step-by-step video modules to walk you through every step of learning the business of successfully selling on Amazon and using FBA including:

- Understanding Amazon rules and policies

- Taxes, business license, CPAs, and more

- Introduction to product sourcing

- Creating your first FBA shipment

Plus ongoing support to ensure your success on Amazon!

ScanPower.com/University

Once you've completed your first FBA shipment, you'll be well on your way to a successful Amazon seller experience. The first shipment will always seem like the hardest one. If you have questions and need help moving forward, we also offer ScanPower Coaching. This includes personal, one-on-one mentoring with experts in many different areas on topics like Amazon policy, Seller Central reports, wholesale sourcing information, and much more.

ScanPower Coaching courses include:

Advanced Amazon

Private Label Products

Amazon Reports

Multi-Channel Fulfillment

Wholesale Sourcing

International Expansion

Creative Bundling

To find out everything that ScanPower Coaching can offer you, please visit ScanPower.com/Coaching

This book is called SECRETS but maybe it's better as STRATEGIES. After getting some advice from Duane Malek, he said that there really are no secrets and I tend to agree with him about that. If I know about it, it's not a secret. And if I know about it, you can be sure that other people know about it. Now you may not know about it until after reading this book, but that doesn't make anything a secret. Secrets are things that nobody knows about. Strategies are what I want to share in this book to help you find more profitable inventory to resell online.

Dedicated to my loving wife, Jenn.

Without her love and support, none of this would be possible.

This book is the result of a lifetime of learning. I am very thankful for support that I've received from family and friends along the way. The last five years have been one amazing ride. Not everyone gets to work with amazing people and amazing products everyday and it is even more rewarding when those products are able to produce a positive change in so many people's lives.

FULL DEAL REVEALED

4/9/12 Disney Store email

Here is a full breakdown of a deal that I did--all the way from how I found it, to what I considered when making my buying decision, how I got the best price, and what strategies I used to set my price.

I try to stay on top of the clearance items from online retailers so that I can easily identify changes or price drops. I was keeping an eye on the clearance, or SALE section, of DisneyStore.com when they had a price drop on all SALE items.

You can see the date of 4/8/12. This was a 50% off clearance sale.

The next day, 4/9/12, I got this email:

Buy One, Get One FREE *and* a free shipping promo code! I started to like the deal more because of the branding (Disney, Pixar, and Cars).

Now I read this email on my phone, lying in bed. I had just woken up and, like most of us do, I grabbed my phone and started to check on the messages of the day (and the previous night).

Bonus Tip: Lots of promotions and price changes go into effect in the early morning hours (~4 AM EST). Online retailers do this so that they have a period of time to fix or correct anything that may not be working such as a promotional code or free shipping offer.

This is a pretty hot deal all around, whether you're buying to resell online or just buying for yourself or for gifts. Not long after this email was sent out, people started posting about it on the online deal sites (more on these later in Chapters 20, 21, and 22).

Here is the post on SlickDeals.net:

SHORT LINK: http://bit.ly/disneystoresd

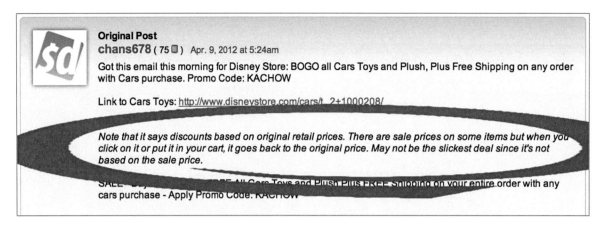

http://slickdeals.net/f/4192206-disney-store-coupon-buy-1-get-1-free-select-disney-cars-toys-mix-match-2x-die-cast-sets-from-2-2x-play-sets-from-5-2x-plush-toys-from-4-2x-rc-cars-from-30-many-more

You can see that the comments had already started to say that the deal was "dead", meaning that you could not get the deal anymore.

(More about SlickDeals later in Chapter 22)

It also hit another popular online deal site, FatWallet.com

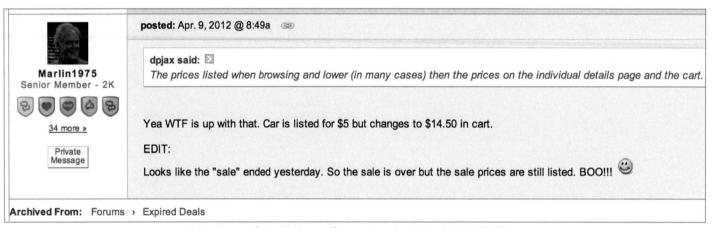

http://www.fatwallet.com/forums/expired-deals/1183260/

SHORT LINK: http://bit.ly/disneystorefw

(More on FatWallet in Chapter 21)

You can see a lot of the same comments as before. People are seeing some hot deals and good prices, but they are unable to fully check out. They can see the prices and the promos, but once they go to checkout, the website won't process the order.

Order History

Order Date	Order Number	Order Total
04/09/2012 10:48:51 AM PDT	1208061202	$207.73
04/09/2012 10:47:40 AM PDT	1208061196	$207.73
04/09/2012 07:27:41 AM PDT	1208050252	$1,015.22
04/09/2012 07:25:22 AM PDT	1208050250	$1,015.22
04/09/2012 07:23:45 AM PDT	1208050223	$1,015.22
04/09/2012 07:11:08 AM PDT	1208050063	$3,173.69

Well, it didn't stop me from placing a bunch of orders! Here's my list of online orders with DisneyStore.com. We'll break down the entire deal later. Just remember that these orders have sales tax included. The end of this book has info on not paying sales tax on products for resale. Some online retailers do it at the time of purchase. For others you have to request a refund after the fact.

The BIGGEST reason that I was able to get this deal was that I simply CALLED DisneyStore.com and asked them about the checkout issue on the site. I was polite and courteous. I'm sure I told them something like, "I want to be your biggest customer today!" All stores seem to like this line; go figure. They said that they would honor BOTH promotions (YES!). All I had to do was place the orders at the regular price online, wait about an hour for the orders to get into their system, and then call and explain the promotional glitch and ask for some refunds. So that's exactly what I did.

	☆	▷	guest.services (26)	Inbox	Your DisneyStore.com Order Is On Its Way! -
	☆	▷	guest.services (41)	Inbox	Your DisneyStore.com Order Is On Its Way! -
	☆	▷	guest.services (61)	Inbox	Your DisneyStore.com Order Is On Its Way! -

Do you get nervous when you get this many UPS shipping notifications?

Getting 94 UPS Delivery Notification Emails at one time from Disney Store Online Arbitrage

http://youtu.be/mB4NxLUG1_E
http://bit.ly/upsemails

ITEM #1 – Wasabi Mater

I placed two identical orders. The max quantity you could buy was 99, but I wanted to buy in even numbers to maximize the Buy One Get One promotion, so I ordered 98 at a time. I ended up with 196 Wasabi Mater sets. This item went through checkout as expected at $1.99, free ship, Buy One, Get One (BOGO) free.

These came in case-packs of eight toys per box. Sometimes you'll want to order in the right quantities in order to speed up the turn-around process of your FBA inventory. Open the box, put on FBA label, reseal the box.

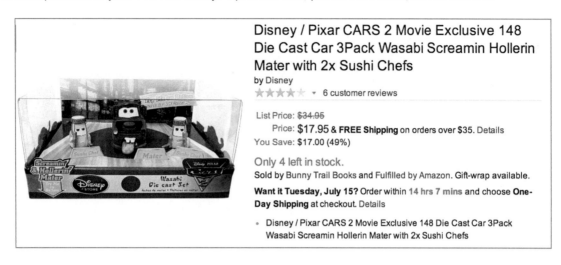

At the time of this screenshot, this item was selling for $17.95. You can see that this is a small, light-weight item. That may be something that you want to consider when making your own Online Arbitrage buying decisions. Small, light, and easy to pack is very attractive compared to big, heavy, and difficult to prep.

http://www.Amazon.com/Disney-Exclusive-Wasabi-Screamin-Hollerin/dp/B0053YRQEG/

So I sold all of mine for $11.99, which was the market price at the time. I was not always the lowest price, but I still sold them all fairly quickly. I did not want to hold these for any long period of time. The payout from Amazon at this price was $6.76.

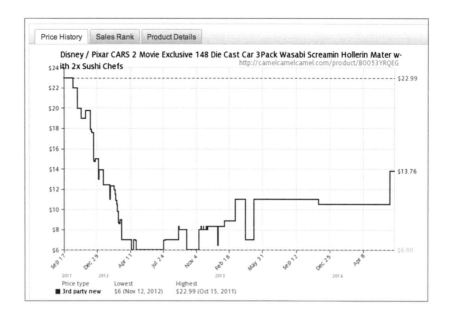

http://camelcamelcamel.com/Disney-Exclusive-Wasabi-Screamin-Hollerin/product/B0053YRQEG

Here is the CamelCamelCamel (sometimes referred to as CCC) Price History graph. You can see that it originally started out at a much higher price. After it hit its all-time lowest price, it started to come back up and now sits at $13.76 + shipping as the lower offer.

More on CamelCamelCamel later in Chapter 5, but also keep in mind that the blue price that you see on CamelCamelCamel does not include shipping.

Let's look at a full breakdown of the payouts and profits of this item:

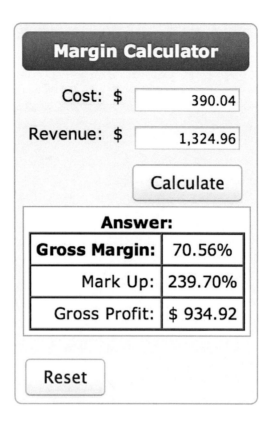

Quantity Purchased: 196

Cost/unit: $1.99

Sold/unit: $11.99

Payout/unit: $6.76

Profit/unit: $4.77

Total Revenue: $1,324.96

Total Profit: $934.92

Time: 233 days

Keep in mind that these items were all sold between December 11, 2012 and August 1, 2013.

Less than one year. 233 days divided by 365 = .638 or 63.8% of a year.

I like to think of things as YEARLY returns. Like how investing in a product yields a payout and how that payout compares to an annual interest rate at your local bank. If you deposited $390.04 on January 1st and received $1,324.96 after 233 days, what annual interest rate would that be?

To annualize these numbers, we would divide 239.70% by .638 and calculate 375.7% as a yearly return rate on the $390.04.

This is an idealized scenario of bring the items to market as soon as you purchased them. I bought these items on April 9, 2012 so my inventory dollars were tied up at that point and the clock starts ticking on my profit calculations. Start to finish on this item was 479 days, or 1.31 years. So the annualized mark up would be 183%.

Make a note of this: processed 196 units for a total profit of $934.92

Profit per unit: $4.77

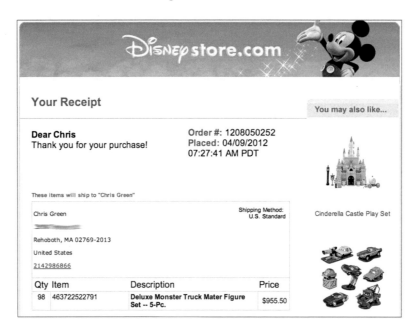

ITEM #2 – Monster Truck Mater

I placed three identical orders. Like before, the max quantity you could buy was 99, but I wanted to buy in even numbers to maximize the Buy One Get One promotion, so I ordered 98 at a time. I also ordered 98 on my largest order, making a grand total of 392 Monster Truck Mater sets. Remember, I got 50% off on these through a refund by contacting customer service, so total cost on the Monster Truck Mater sets was $4.88 each.

http://www.Amazon.com/Disney-Deluxe-Monster-Truck-Figure/dp/B004CSD3PU/

Order ID: # 102-4108639-0141021

Your Seller Order ID: # 102-4108639-0141021
Payment Information

Shipping Address:

Order Date:	September 21, 2012 3:04:16 PM PDT	**Order Totals**
Expected Ship Date:	Sep 22, 2012	Items total: $32.17
Shipping Service:	Second Day	Grand total: $32.17
Contact Buyer:		
Billing Country:	BR	
Sales Channel:	Amazon.com	
Fulfillment method:	Amazon	

Product Details	Status	Quantity Ordered	Price	Total
Disney / Pixar Cars Exclusive Monster Truck Mater Plastic Figurine Set Tormentor... Quantity: 1 SKU: Disney_08262012_013 ASIN: B004B9J5BQ Listing ID: 0826M7FCPUS Order Item ID: 62383765800218	Payment complete	1	$32.17	Subtotal: $32.17 **Total: $32.17**

	Total Charged to Buyer:	**$32.17**

Even though the Amazon Buy Box at the time of writing this book is at $25.95, I sold mine for $32.17.

According to the FBA calculator, the payout on this item at this price is $23.84.

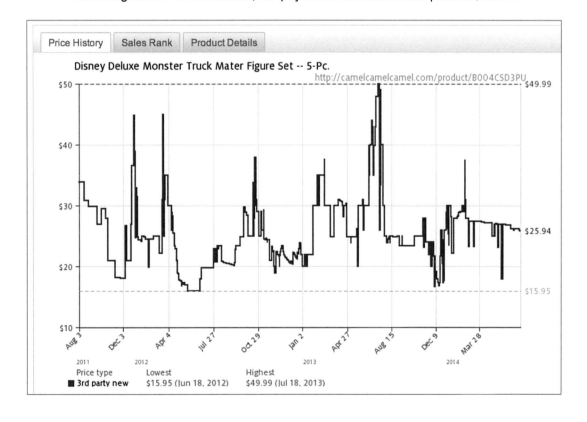

http://camelcamelcamel.com/Disney-Deluxe-Monster-Truck-Figure/product/B004CSD3PU

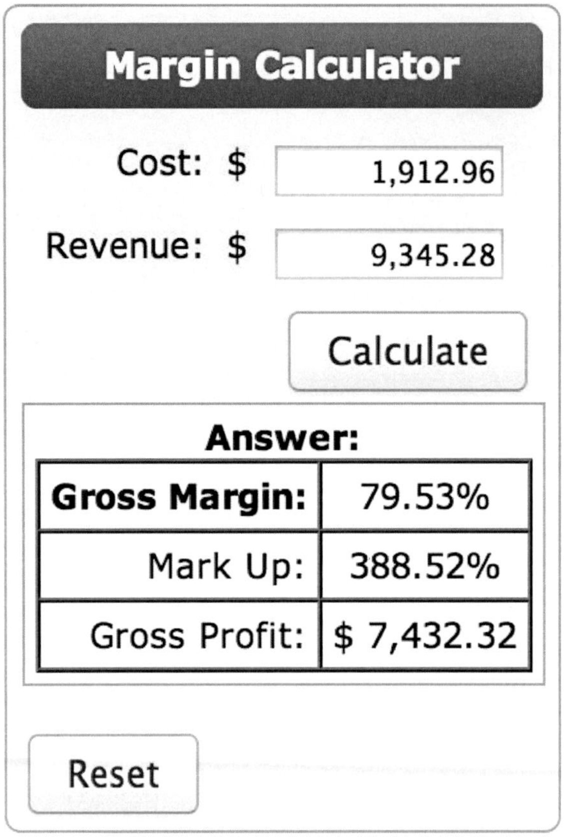

Margin Calculator

Cost: $ 1,912.96

Revenue: $ 9,345.28

[Calculate]

Answer:

Gross Margin:	79.53%
Mark Up:	388.52%
Gross Profit:	$ 7,432.32

[Reset]

Quantity Purchased: 392

Cost/unit: $4.88

Sold/unit: $32.17

Payout/unit: $23.84

Profit/unit: $18.96

Total Revenue: $9,345.28

Total Profit: $7,432.32

Time: 115 days

Keep in mind that these items were all sold between October 9, 2012 and February 1, 2013.

Less than one year. 115 days divided by 365 = .315 or 31.5% of a year.

If you deposited $1,912.96 on January 1st and received $9,345.28 after 115 days, what annual interest rate would that be?

To annualize these numbers, we would divide 388.52% by .315 and calculate 1,233.4% as a yearly return rate on the $1,912.96.

I bought these items on April 9, 2012 so my inventory dollars were tied up at that point and the clock starts ticking on my profit calculations. Start to finish on this item was 298 days, or .816 years. So the annualized mark up would be 476%.

Make a note of this: processed 392 units for a total profit of $7,432.22

Profit per unit: $18.96

EIGHT TIMES the total profit, FOUR TIMES the profit per unit, but only TWO TIMES the number of units as Example #1

I bought the last 34 of the Cars 20-piece set. I like buying the last remaining stock as it means that you know that you'll control supply (and price). Remember, I got 50% off on these through a refund by contacting customer service, so total cost on the 20-piece sets was $29.88 each.

ITEM #3 - Cars 2 20-Piece Set

Disney / Pixar CARS 2 Movie Exclusive 20 Piece Die Cast Mega Set, 1:48 scale, Includes Carla Veloso, Lewis Hamilton, Tomber Rip Clutchgoneski

by Disney

★★★★☆ ▾ 10 customer reviews

Price: **$149.99** + $7.49 shipping

Only 2 left in stock.

Ships from and sold by B'S Treasure.

- Set includes Professor Z, Grem, Acer, Mater, Finn McMissile, Holley Shiftwell, Lightning McQueen, Francesco Bernoulli, Shu Todoroki, Max Schnell, Miguel Camino, Jeff Gorvette, Rod "Torque" Redline, Nigel Gearsley, Miles Axlerod, Carla Veloso, Raoule CaRoule, Lewis Hamilton, Tomber, and an exclusive Rip Clutchgoneski figure

Click to open expanded view

CLUTCHGONESKI was exclusive. This is where product line knowledge definitely helps. At the time, this kit was the only place to get this specific car. Some kids must have really pleaded with their parents for this one at these prices.

http://www.Amazon.com/Disney-Pixar-Movie-Exclusive-Piece/dp/B006BA736M/

You can see the Amazon Buy Box price of $149.99 + shipping right now. I sold all of mine for $199.95 through FBA. The Amazon payout at this price was $162.17.

http://camelcamelcamel.com/Disney-Pixar-Movie-Exclusive-Piece/product/B006BA736M

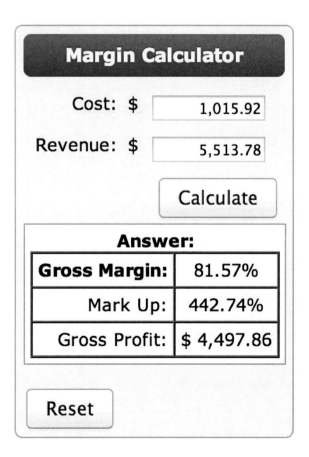

Quantity Purchased: 34

Cost/unit: $29.88

Sold/unit: $199.95

Payout/unit: $162.17

Profit/unit: $132.29

Total Revenue: $5,513.78

Total Profit: $4,497.86

Time: 229 days

Keep in mind that these items were all sold between November 24, 2012 and July 11, 2013.

Less than one year. 229 days divided by 365 = .627 or 62.7% of a year.

If you deposited $1,015.92 on January 1st and received $5,513.78 after 229 days, what annual interest rate would that be?

To annualize these numbers, we would divide 442.74% by .627 and calculate 706.1% as a yearly return rate on the $1,015.92.

I bought these items on April 9, 2012 so my inventory dollars were tied up at that point and the clock starts ticking on my profit calculations. Start to finish on this item was 458 days, or 1.25 years. So the annualized mark up would be 354.2%.

Make a note of this: processed 34 units for a total profit of $4,497.86

Profit per unit: $132.29

FIVE TIMES the total profit, TWENTY-EIGHT TIMES the profit per unit, but SIX TIMES FEWER the number of units as Example #1

60% the total profit, SEVEN TIMES the profit per unit, but almost SEVEN TIMES FEWER the number of units as Example #2

I really love this example. It nails down the importance of Average Sales Price and how it relates to margins and profits. ITEM #1 is great with its 200% mark up, but with a profit per unit of only $4.77, you have to sell an absolute ton of units to make any serious money. You see the big jump in profits going into ITEM #2. Four times the profit per unit, along with twice the number of units, and all of a sudden we're making some real good money. And the real eye-opener comes in ITEM #3. When you raise your Average Sales Price and keep your margins the same, then you're making a whole lot more money while doing a whole lot LESS work. Comparing ITEM #1 to ITEM #3 should really make you think about price, margin, and volume and let you focus and decide what kind of business you want to run.

Here's an extra little bonus tip: in my experience, most sellers stick to lower price point stuff. They shy away from spending $50 or $100 per unit on inventory. That's good news because it means that the higher price point items have fewer competitors. Go ahead and look on Amazon; do higher price point items or lower price point items have more sellers? Amazon is a very transparent marketplace. If you want to sell items with fewer competitors, you can do that with some very simple and easy searches.

So how do you know how much to buy? Where do you stop? If these deals were so good, why didn't I buy more? All great questions. As you find deals, you will have to not only decide what to buy and what not to buy, but you'll have to sometimes make decisions about how much to buy. In these examples, the products were available during a short time window at an artificially low price. I was hoping that I would be buying DisneyStore.com out on these products (meaning that I bought all of their remaining inventory). I did this on the 20-piece set by buying the last 34 units. I placed multiple orders for the other two items hoping that each order would be limited to stock on hand. When you control supply, you also have some control over price. Since this was a very transparent deal, I was very aware that other online sellers would be buying these and selling them on Amazon. However, I was very confident that no one else was able to lock in the exact same prices that I did. These deals were profitable even without the Buy One Get One Free promotion.

Factors that should go into your QUANTITY decision should include:

Available inventory funds, available storage space/capacity, ability to process inventory, expected future demand, time of the year (related to Q4), visibility of the deal (how likely is it that other sellers will have found this deal), how comfortable you are with holding inventory for a period of time (in the event that it doesn't sell as fast as expected or if you have to wait out other sellers at lower prices), and probably a few others. You may also have your own deal qualifiers.

Let this also be a lesson about deciding when to buy and hold inventory and when to get in and sell fast. I did not buy these as a long-term hold situation. I just took my time sending them in because sometimes I get lazy. On one hand, I did avoid possibly competing with other sellers who may have tried to get the same deal and undercut the prices, but all three of these items were popular and sold easily in the fourth quarter. I could have improved my financial numbers by selling faster, but I'm satisfied with the timing and the outcome. I was able to buy these items and hold them for about five to six months before sending them into FBA. Not every online seller is in a position to do that either because of space limitations or because of limited inventory dollars. Use this example as motivation to seek out and execute your own Online Arbitrage deals!

Before:

After!

One of the nicest things about ordering in bulk? Case packs! Delivered to your house, in boxes--you just open them up, re-label, and use the same boxes to send the products back in.

Here is the margin calculator that I used:

http://www.calculatorsoup.com/calculators/financial/margin-calculator.php

Calculate the gross margin percentage, mark up percentage and gross profit of a sale from the cost and revenue, or selling price, of an item.

* Revenue = Selling Price

Margin Formulas/Calculations:

- The gross profit P is the difference between the cost to make a product C and the selling price or revenue R.
    - $P = R - C$
- The mark up percentage M is the profit P divided by the cost C to make the product.
    - $M = P / C = (R - C) / C$
- The gross margin percentage G is the profit P divided by the selling price or revenue R.
    - $G = P / R = (R - C) / R$

Now, are all deals this complex, involving checking several things and asking for special pricing? Of course not. Here's a dead-simple deal that was found right on the CamelCamelCamel homepage (more on CamelCamelCamel in Chapter 5).

https://www.facebook.com/groups/scanpower/permalink/521660321269232/

Chris Green
June 27 at 11:10pm

SNATCH THESE FAST: $11.46 from AZ ATOP (ScanPower RED):

http://www.amazon.com/Targus-Versavu-Rotating-Keyboard-THZ17102US/dp/B009LENNHI

Limit 3 (otherwise I would have bought them ALL). Thanks CCC!

Targus Versavu Rotating Keyboard Case and Stand for iPad 3 and 4, Red (THZ17102US)

Transform your new iPad (3rd Generation) into the ultimate viewing and typing...

AMAZON.COM

Roll over image to zoom in

Targus Versavu Rotating Keyboard Case and Stand for iPad 3 and 4, Red (THZ17102US)
by Targus
★★★★ ⋆ · 601 customer reviews
| 12 answered questions

List Price: $99.99
 Price: **$68.99 & FREE Shipping**. Details
You Save: $31.00 (31%)

In Stock.
Ships from and sold by Amazon.com. Gift-wrap available.

Want it **Tuesday, July 8?** Order within **39 hrs 40 mins** and choose **One-Day Shipping** at checkout. Details
Color: **Red**

http://www.Amazon.com/Targus-Versavu-Rotating-Keyboard-THZ17102US/dp/B009LENNHI

Online Arbitrage - Finding Deals on the Homepage of CamelCamelCamel iPad Keyboard & Case

http://youtu.be/T41IlmoBgg8
http://bit.ly/cccipadcase

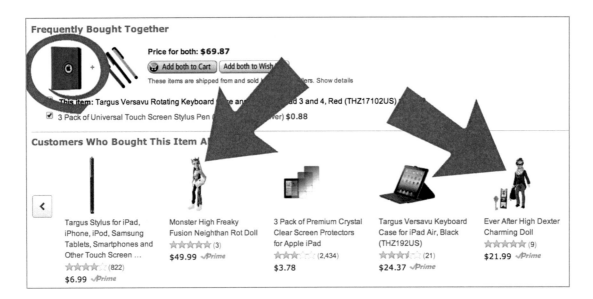

Now what are these guys doing here? Always pay attention to the items listed under Frequently Bought Together as well as Customers Who Bought This Item Also Bought. More on that in Chapter 10.

Keepa missed this price drop but CamelCamelCamel caught it and recorded it for all to see (more on Keepa in Chapter 4 and more on CamelCamelCamel in Chapter 5). So even if you missed out on this deal, you can still set up an alert at or near that previous low price in the event that history repeats itself.

And how did I find out about this deal in the first place? TOO EASY--it was posted right on the CamelCamelCamel homepage under top deals:

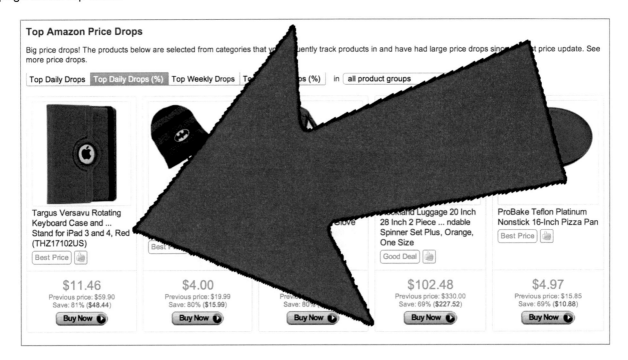

I made the arrow EXTRA BIG to indicate how easy this is to do.

There was a purchase limit of three, so I bought three and then posted the deal in the ScanPower Facebook group to share. I could also have sent the deal privately to people in a mastermind group who work together. This is one of the reasons that I strongly suggest networking with other people in a mutually beneficial relationship. If you have trouble finding people to work with, I'd encourage you to join our Facebook group and watching our SpreeCasts to meet other people who may be looking for people to work with. More about mastermind groups later in Chapter 29.

Here you can see the price drop from Amazon (green) and that it is also the all-time lowest price as tracked by CamelCamelCamel.

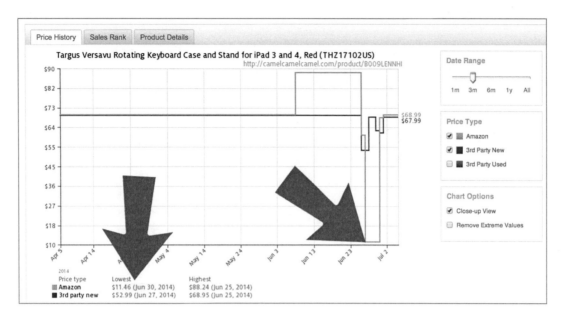

http://camelcamelcamel.com/Targus-Versavu-Rotating-Keyboard-THZ17102US/product/B009LENNHI

Big deals from rabbit trails or small deals from websites, it's all pretty much the same stuff. You may be using bookmarks, alerts, or emails, but all you're doing is using tools to find market inefficiencies and then capitalizing on them. Online Arbitrage really is easy once you know a few strategies to scout online efficiently.

As I wrote this book, I put the exact strategies into practice and ended up with this:

For full details on these deals, please visit this video link:

Online Arbitrage - Amazon Sports & Outdoors 80% Clearance Buys

http://youtu.be/j6-lo0-sx94
http://bit.ly/80percentdeals

Here is a fourth quarter 2014 prediction:

http://www.amazon.com/dp/B00JPYHRQ2

Available from Wal-Mart and Target for $89.99. You can see how easy it is to find sources thanks to some free Chrome extensions we talk about in Chapter 3). Will this item be the next Zoomer? Time will tell!

http://www.amazon.com/dp/B00DQ9RM2Q

Online Arbitrage - Dino Zoomer - Fourth Quarter 2014 Breakout Hot Toy?

http://youtu.be/McK24Mgg2sA
http://bit.ly/zoomerdino

Table of Contents

This book is pretty maxed out. 480 pages is maximum allowed. For this reason, chapters will just start on the next page and not spaced out to always start on the right-hand side of the book.

Introduction to Online Arbitrage

So you want to sell online? Great! In my opinion, there has never been a better time to sell online. More and more people are doing more and more of their shopping online, and more buyers mean more opportunity for online sellers!

More opportunity also means more competition, but don't let this worry you. If there are more opportunities to make money, then more sellers will enter the market. You should see this as a positive marker that there is definitely money to be made. If there wasn't good money to be made, would sellers, including yourself, be entering this market? Of course not!

More sellers? More competition? This may sound intimidating, and that may be the reason why you bought this book. The information contained in this book will allow you to buy smart, lower your costs, increase your margins, and source products more efficiently than your competition. Your competition will be way more scared of you than you should ever be of them after you read this book. If they are not using the techniques and strategies outlined in this book, then there is little doubt that their margins are lower than yours are, which means that they are working harder than you are (and for less money). If that trend continues, they will eventually put themselves out of business while your business continues to grow and remain highly profitable.

Knowledge is power. Never before in human history has that phrase been more accurate. What you will acquire in this book is the knowledge of how to source products online like a professional reseller.

So what does all of this have to do with product sourcing? It's been said that when you are sourcing products to sell, you make your money when you buy. This is because if you are buying smart, you are buying at a cost that is sure to maintain your margins. Do you actually 'make money' when you buy? No, of course not. But if you buy smart, while you may not always make as much money as you originally expected, you significantly reduce your risk of ever losing money on a purchase for resale.

You are using tools, apps, knowledge, strategies, and techniques that allow you to not only find great products to resell, but also to get them at the absolute lowest possible price. This can significantly lower your risk when making buying decisions, almost to the point of zero. You know that you will be able to sell the products for a profit and when you have enough margins built into the products, you will still be profitable even if you have to lower price to due to changing market conditions.

One problem that new (and existing) sellers run into is what to sell. Even if they know what to sell, they then need to know where to get it. And even if they know where to get it, they need to know the best way to make their purchases in order to source their products at the absolute lowest possible price.

This book will explain how to quickly identify products with great resale potential to buy when shopping online using tools, programs, and apps. We'll discuss many different ways to lower your final purchase price through discounts, coupons, rebates, and more.

There are really no limits as to what types of products you can source and from where you can source them. With the tools and apps available to today's online sellers, many have figured out that they do not want to discriminate in what they sell. They will sell anything that is profitable! They just need to be able to quickly identify the salability and margin of an item and then they can decide if the item fits into their individual business model.

Go With What You Know

You can make the case that if you are generally interested in a product category, that you will do better selling those types of products. This could be the Toys & Games category, the Tools & Home Improvement category, or even the Grocery &

Gourmet Food category. If you have an interest in the products, then it's more likely that you will notice the details and be more excited about product sourcing in general. So if you are having trouble figuring out where to start, go with a category that you already know something about. Maybe you are a new mom so you are familiar with the top selling items in the Baby category on Amazon.

The trick is to just get started!

There are so many options--don't think that you have to box yourself in or follow exactly what another seller is doing. There are tons of great ways to source products for resale, so evaluate your priorities, figure out what type of business you want to run, how much time you want to spend, and where you want to spend it, and then take action!

Abundance vs. Scarcity

I believe there is an absolute abundance of products out there that can be purchased and resold for a profit. What I commonly tell people who are looking to start buying products to resell online is that you will run out of time to shop or money to spend before you run out of places to go to source inventory. The limitations of the physical world will come into play. This is another reason why I encourage sellers to not psych themselves out thinking that there must be other sellers who are already doing this and that all the deals must be gone. It's simply not possible. No one person could bankroll and process all of the available deals that are presented in these inefficient markets.

DIFFERENT PRICES ON DIFFERENT SITES

http://www.ebay.com/sch/i.html?_sacat=0&_from=R40&_sop=3&_nkw=Arbitrage+%3A+The+Authoritative+Guide&LH_Complete=1&LH_Sold=1&rt=nc

These are completed listings that sold for $17.95 when you can buy them brand new from Amazon--that includes the Kindle version FOR FREE—for $8.55 delivered.

The deals are out there. First come, first served. This book will help you get there FIRST and make that money. Many of these methods help you find limited deals as well as deals that you have to execute within small windows of time.

No one can do all the deals or be everywhere at all times. You can't, either. Don't try to be. Set up systems to put yourself in the best position. Make a plan. Execute it. This isn't difficult stuff. To learn about scaling this business, see Chapter 29.

Now that I've written this book, there will be more people using the tactics and strategies outlined here to find deals. Such is the nature of business. I urge everyone to really look further and innovate; do what your competitors are not doing. Find a deal but it's sold out? Don't stop there; set up an in-stock or price-drop alert. Then look for other items from that same manufacturer. Go the extra mile. Follow the rabbit trails. Do what your competitors are not doing.

More competition? Prices never 'tank'. Prices normalize as supply moves to meet demand. I have never seen an item tank and never recover. The market bears what it will bear. Sales rank can never tank unless demand is non-existent, and in that case, items won't sell at any price (high or low).

It's a whole new world and it's wide open

The most difficult part of this book is tying it all together. There are so many strategies and tools to explain and they often work together with each other.

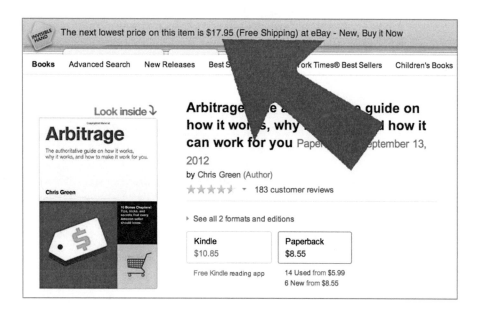

This InvisibleHand Chrome extension shows that even though my book is being sold on Amazon for $8.55, it's also available on eBay for $17.95. InvisibleHand is covered in Chapter 3.

The 3X Rule is a simple formula for identifying items with 100% margin or doubling your money. You would be looking for items that are selling for "three times" your purchase price. For example, if you scan an item that sells for $10, you want it to be selling on Amazon for $30. If you roughly estimate your Amazon FBA fees as 1/3 of your sales price, your fees on a $30 sale would be $10. So spend $10, sell for $30, give Amazon $10, and you're left with $20, effectively doubling your $10 purchase price.

I used this as a simple example to not just double your money, but to PROTECT new sellers from making bad buying decisions. If you have 100% margin built into your products, you will still be able to sell for a profit even if that $30 price comes down to $25. The 3X Rule was intended to protect new sellers as they learned the arbitrage business. It was never meant to be some kind of strict buying guideline.

As you consider products to purchase for Online Arbitrage, please consider all factors involved, not just margin/item. How fast will the items sell? How easy will the items be to process and sell? What is the overall return on investment? Don't pass up on awesome deals that will return 50% on your money in less than a month just because they don't fit the 3X Rule!

Some chapters are long (like sourcing on Amazon) and some chapters are just lists of websites. The chapters are laid out in an order to help keep things organized on this huge topic of Online Arbitrage.

One of my favorite quotes lately is from Gary Vaynerchuk. Someone said to him, "Gary, I don't work hard, I work smart." Gary got in his face and reminded him that he works hard AND smart.

So that's what I challenge anyone reading this book to do: WORK HARD *AND* SMART

The strategies in this book will help you to work smart, but only you can decide to HUSTLE and work HARD. Knowledge is nothing without follow-through. Ideas are nothing without execution. Only you can take the steps to put these strategies into a profitable business. Knowing how this works is not enough. Remember, you can OUT-HUSTLE and OUT-WORK your competition. There are things that you can't control in this world, but YOUR HUSTLE and YOUR EFFORT are all under your control.

Many things in this book may not make sense right away. Reading graphs and interpreting data may not come easy to you at first. To some, this business makes complete sense from day one, but to others, it's not intuitive. That's where this book comes in. The goal of this book is to clearly lay out the methods and strategies to use to quickly find and evaluate products sourced from online retailers for resale. YOU CAN DO THIS. From the explanations in this book along with the real examples and video demonstrations, you'll acquire a firm understanding of how this business works. If you find yourself struggling, please ask questions. My contact info is listed in this book along with links to online forums and groups. Young or old, we can all learn something new. What comes easy to some may take some time for others, but we can all learn new things.

I do believe 100% that this is truly an international opportunity. You can live anywhere on the planet and as long as you have an Internet connection, you can run a very successful and lucrative Online Arbitrage business. You can buy from anywhere and use the services outlined to receive and process your inventory. While many of the examples in this book consider the prices and demand on the US Amazon.com market, you can use the same tools to evaluate products for resale on any of the international Amazon markets. Many of them also have FBA.

There are SO MANY things to sell and sites to search. DON'T just go for the sexy stuff. Or just the clearance. Go for the low hanging fruit, but understand that your competition will be going after the same stuff. DON'T BE LAZY. Look for the other products that aren't sexy--that other sellers don't look at.

For the most part, the awesome part about Online Arbitrage is that ANYONE can buy the items to resell. Although some sites in the liquidation chapter may require a tax ID or business license, this book is not about wholesale or purchasing from suppliers, distributors or wholesalers.

You still need to know all the rules of the Amazon marketplace. There are a lot of rules. Restricted products and brands. Hazardous materials, also known as haz-mat. Which categories are gated and closed. Before you buy anything, be sure you understand the rules of selling and whether you are authorized to resell the products.

Manage your Amazon Browsing History:

Amazon keeps track of the items that you browse on their website. You may have no problem with this (it's intended to help Amazon find the best products for you as a customer), but you may also decide that you do not want that information tracked. Why? Well, if you end up looking at many of the same products that other Online Arbitrage sellers are looking at, that your browsing history is inadvertently revealing the products that you are selling. At the same time, knowing that other resellers have their browsing history turned ON can give you hints about what other products are being looked at by other online sellers.

If you want to turn your Amazon Browsing History ON and OFF, you can use this link:

https://www.Amazon.com/gp/history/cc

Your Amazon.com > Your Browsing History > Manage Your Browsing History
(If you're not Chris Green, click here.)

You're in Control

Turn off browsing history

Your Browsing History is meant to help you keep track of some of the items you've recently viewed, searches you've recently made, and product categories you've recently visited.

If you do not enjoy this feature and want to turn it off, simply click Turn Off Browsing History in the box to the left. Turning this feature off will turn it off for anyone who uses your Web browser. If you'd like to re-enable Your Browsing History for your browser, return to this page and click the Turn On Browsing History button that will appear. Because your selection is managed through HTTP cookies, if you delete these cookies or use a different browser, you will have to make this same selection again.

Online Arbitrage - Be Aware of Your Amazon Browsing History

http://youtu.be/_7me7Arah_Y
http://bit.ly/shoppinghistory

Because of the browsing history of many online resellers, you'll come across things like this. Two items Frequently Bought Together according to Amazon. While this may make you laugh, it's also revealing to potential competitors potential items to resell.

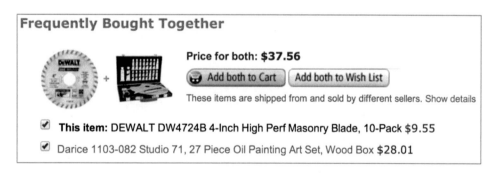

When you see weird matches like this, check the items, check the historical pricing like KEEPA and look for patterns of price drops. If you find them, set up alerts.

Chapter 1 – Retail Stores vs. Buying Online

Let's compare the similarities and differences between sourcing inventory from retail stores compared to sourcing online. The first that comes to mind is that deals made available on the Internet and visible to anyone with an Internet connection. And now that everyone has a smartphone, people don't even have to be in front of a computer to see them, either. This is important to be aware of because it's very different from a retail store where you may be in the right place at the right time in the one store in the country that is manually marking down their clearance toys by 90%. You would be the only person to know about and capitalize on that particular deal. Even if someone else knew about it, they would not be able to purchase the items because they either live in a different part of the country or they would be late to the party since you bought them all already (limited quantities as well).

Compare this to Online Arbitrage deals. An item goes on sale on a website and pretty much anyone in the world is able to order it at the same price as everyone else. And quantity limits? Sometimes there are limits, sometimes they are known, and sometimes there are no limits at all and you have to place orders with the uncertainty of how many other people are buying the same product.

This uncertainty is often made up for with the overall convenience factor of Online Arbitrage. Maybe you've driven from store to store, stood in long checkout lines, packed and unpacked your vehicle, and ended up with a garage full of retail packages. The idea of getting a large shipment from UPS already in boxes that you just have to re-label and ship back out starts to sound very attractive! No driving around means that you save gas and you can source at pretty much any time of the day instead of only when retail stores are open. Did I mention that Online Arbitrage orders often show up case-packed in boxes?

Retail Stores – Advantages

- Limited quantities (once you buy them all, your competition is out of luck).
- You can find new items that you would never have considered if you had not traveled to the stores.
- Real-world relationships can lead to increased opportunities.
- Able to get the products to market immediately.

Retail Stores – Disadvantages

- Limited quantities (when you want to buy more than they have available).
- Limitations of how many stores you can go to in a day.
- Have to physically live near them.
- Standing in lines and loading your car in the rain.

Online Arbitrage – Advantages

- Source inventory from anywhere with a computer and Internet connection.
- Inventory shows up at your location, pre-packaged.
- More sources of inventory to choose from.

Online Arbitrage – Disadvantages

- Deals are very visible and can be found by anyone.
- Margins can be lower than retail deals.
- Increased lead time to being able to offer the items for sale can mean possible price erosion.
- Honestly, it can get boring and even isolating.

Experience and knowledge are vital in this business; there are no shortcuts. Do what you can to gain experience; hit stores if you can. Retail stores and online sites can be very different. Knowing these differences is very valuable info. Some retailers have in-store exclusives and some have online exclusives. If you only source one, you may miss the other. Some stores offer in-store exclusives paired with national advertising. Well guess what? Some people don't live near stores. They see a product that they want and they want to go to Amazon first and only. You can be the one to bring that product to the Amazon marketplace (often with little to no competition).

Consider the simplicity of Online Arbitrage

When you buy online, you are not always able to buy all of the inventory so you will not know who else could be buying the product specifically for resale. It could be another seller who prices their items low and maintains slim margins. This would be bad news for you if they purchased a large quantity and you are now forced to compete against them on Amazon. Sometimes you are able to buy out the remaining stock of an online retailer so this can put you in a more favorable spot in regards to having competition. When you control the supply, you are also able to control price.

If you live in a major metro area, you'll have access to more places to source inventory than you could possibly travel to in a day, so you'll be able to truly decide what kinds of products you want to focus on. This doesn't mean that you should only focus on retail products, as there are great products that can be found online that can be resold for nice profits. You may even decide that although there are great stores all around you that you prefer to stay at home and source products online in your pajamas and be home with your kids. This book focuses primarily on sourcing products online.

If you are a seller who lives in a rural area, you may not have as many of the major retailers within a reasonable driving distance. This may force you to source certain types of products that you would not normally think of selling. It may even force you into solely sourcing products by buying online. Don't worry; we cover that extensively in this book.

Other sellers may find the same deal and show up on the listing. If this happens frequently, take note of the other sellers. They are likely resellers just like you and they source their products form the same place. If you take a look at the other items that they sell, you may just find a new source of inventory. Use Google to find out where specific items are being sold (covered more in Chapter 9).

One of the biggest things to get right with Online Arbitrage is making product matches. All the research in the world is great but if you end up matching the wrong products between a website and Amazon, all that work will be for naught. This book will show you many ways to ensure that you are matching the right products as well as ways to do this process faster and more efficiently than your competition.

There are risks with Online Arbitrage. Online retailers sometimes ship the wrong products or your shipments may arrive damaged. Sometimes your best deals will get canceled before they ever ship. Consider the risks and rewards no matter where you get your inventory.

You will find that some sites are better sources or that you simply start to prefer buying from some sites more than others. This may be because your orders consistently show up damaged or they have a difficult return policy in the event that they shipped the wrong products and you waste too much time dealing with them.

What do you do when you get items delivered in poor condition? Can you return them to a store? What if you don't live near a local store? Do you ask for discount? Credit? Process a return of the entire shipment? Do some stores do this all the time? Maybe you eventually decide to avoid certain sites altogether.

Compare & Contrast: Over-Retail Selling vs. Under-Retail Buying

There are two main models that you will encounter in this book. The first is called **"Over-Retail Selling"**. This is where you are buying products at the regular retail prices (lower prices are better of course using coupons, rebates, etc.) and selling them at prices ABOVE the normal market price. These higher prices can be the result of Amazon being sold out on popular products or items going out of production and becoming collectible.

The other model is called **"Under-Retail Buying"**. This is where you are able to acquire inventory at prices far enough BELOW the regular retail price that you are able to sell them at the market price for a profit. This may be limited quantities of clearance products or bulk quantities of products purchased using cost-reduction strategies.

Both models have their strengths and weaknesses. Over-retail selling can provide you with easy profits in a short period of time under the right market conditions, but it can also be very risky in the event that Amazon never goes out of stock again. Under-retail buying can be much safer in terms of market price stability and your ability to sell at a profit, but it can sometimes be difficult to acquire large amounts of inventory at low enough prices.

When I was a fulltime seller, I much preferred the under-retail buying model. I would either buy large quantities by hustling from store to store picking up clearanced merchandise or I would be stacking coupons, promotions, and rebates to get my final buy price low enough to sell at the market price. You'll learn some of those strategies in this book.

Ultimately, it's up to you as to how you want to run your Online Arbitrage business. I would think that most sellers would adopt a blend of both models as deals and opportunities present themselves.

Chapter 2 – Buying Online – Where to Start?

Congratulations on getting started with Online Arbitrage! Once you see some of the examples in here and get confortable with the methods and tools, I think you'll see that the world is wide open and all it will take is some hustle to make some real money.

Remember, there are no secrets in the world on Online Arbitrage. It's all out there for anyone to do. Some people do it better than others, but there is nothing stopping you from becoming an Online Arbitrage expert.

This business does require some capital to get started. If you want to sell enough products at a certain margin to make some real money, you have to support that with inventory to sell. That inventory costs money. The good news is that by using the strategies laid out in the book, the risk level of every purchases will be incredibly low. As you do more and more deals, that risk will get pretty close to zero.

Bonus Tip:

Run the numbers on your Amazon seller account and try to get an accurate estimation of your average Amazon fees as a percentage. Why? Well, if your fees average 34%, then in theory you could be purchasing ANYTHING that is selling for greater than 34% off of the Amazon price and still make money. It can give you a baseline of what products you can buy and turn around and sell for a profit.

This book has a lot of TOY examples and that's because toys are easy. I wanted to use REAL EXAMPLES in this book. Toys sell all year long, they are easy to find (even grocery stores and pharmacies carry toys), they are easy to evaluate, and they made for some great, real examples for this book. This book has tons of REAL examples, REAL screenshots with REAL numbers that you can go check yourself. Now, the market will change and so will prices so if the items are still deals at the time that you are reading this, will be out of my control. But at the time of the screenshots, you can see the real deals that were available for me to use as real examples. No theories, no maybes; all real deals that I found using the exact same tips and strategies that I lay out in this book for you.

Now because I use a lot of toys examples, don't think that you have to only do toys or that the opportunities only exist in toys. Lots of people who read this book will focus on toys. That's all well and good but I encourage everyone to do what other people don't do. Look in the categories that other sellers ignore. Sell the profitable but boring products. Everyone wants to sell the sexy products, but there is usually no money in sexy products because of the high level of competition leading to low margins.

RAW Online Arbitrage - Entire Process, Rabbit Trails, Research, Deals

http://youtu.be/Eh-tLg4U4ts
http://bit.ly/entireprocess

Bonus Tip:

A lot of this world of Online Arbitrage runs on product matches. You have to match a product at one price from one website to another website at a different price. But this only works if the products MATCH. Sometimes you just need a UPC but you're on a computer, not in a store holding physical products. Here is a site that can help you do reverse UPC searches.

Yoopsie: http://yoopsie.com

Take a look at what you get when you search for "family guy monkey". You now have the UPC!

There are sites that are some very easy places to start with Online Arbitrage. You'll get to them in the next few chapters. Use them as a guide and look at how they allow users to sort their lists and see what kind of sorting provides you with the best deals or leads.

There are sites not only monitor Amazon for price changes and drops as well as allow users to set up price alerts, they also compile lists of the price drops and post them on their websites for all to see. Some of these sites only show you one list of what they consider to be the best deals (like Keepa, Chapter 4), and some allow you more search options like dollar amount drops vs. percentage of price drops (like CamelCamelCamel, Chapter 5). They are very easy to bookmark and check several times a day.

Things to look for on each site:

Price Points: Discounts are great, but just like you saw at the very beginning of this book, low price points mean that you have to sell a whole bunch of units to make some real money. So a $4 item that is 80% off may be much cheaper per unit, is not as interesting to me as a $50 item that is 80% off that will net more actual profit.

Percentage Off: This is very important. I don't care that an $8,000 refrigerator is $800 off because that's only 10%. I am much more interested in a $80 item that is 50% off, even though $40 is a smaller discount than $800 by a factor of twenty times.

So as I glance from item to item, page to page, site to site, I'm looking for items that are NOT cheap and have a new price that is a significant discount off of the previous price. Over time, you'll get faster at this process.

ABSOLUTE vs. RELATIVE

An absolute discount or price drop means a certain defined amount. Something absolute is not tied to anything else. An item with a price drop of $100 has an absolute price drop of $100. This is the same if it's a $200 item or a $2,000 item. The difference is when you compare the RELATIVE discount or price drop. The relative price drop in a $200 item dropping $100 is 50%. When it's $100 off of a $2,000 item, it's only a 5% discount.

So sorting items by the largest ABSOLUTE price drops may find you some big discounts in terms of dollar amounts, but not in terms of RELATIVE amounts. For the most part, you will want to look at the largest RELATIVE discounts on products to resell.

Are you ready? Let's get into the world of Online Arbitrage!

Chapter 3 – Equipment & Browser Extensions

Recommended browser: Google Chrome

This is more than just a recommendation; it's pretty much a requirement.

You'll have to use Google Chrome to take advantage of the strategies explained in this book.

Download it for free here: google.com/chrome

Extensions are extra features and functionality that you can easily add to Google Chrome. By using extensions, you can customize Google Chrome with features you like, while keeping your browser free of things that you don't use.

But why use so many extensions? The simple answer is that none are perfect. Sometimes one catches something that the others miss. This may be a price drop, an in-stock alert, a coupon code, or other useful details that you want to know about. If one extension does not work well for you (for example, if you are not getting your price alerts), consider using one of the other alerts. Individual experience may vary. Don't hesitate to contact any of them with ideas, feedback, or suggestions. You may just get what you want and help improve their extension at the same time.

As far as hardware, I use Apple products. My main computer is a MacBook Pro and if I had to buy a new computer it would be another MacBook Pro. They cost a little more up front, but they have served me well. For the most part, we're just going to need the Chrome browser so using a PC will work just as well.

If buying new hardware, I'd suggest considering eBay Deals:

http://deals.ebay.com/tech-deals

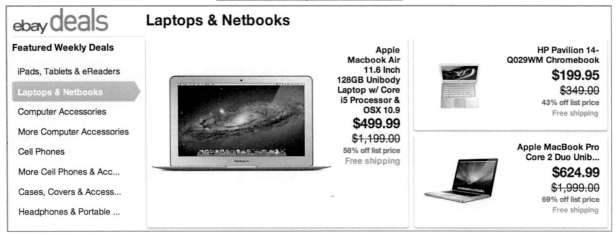

If I was in the market for a laptop for Online Arbitrage sourcing, I'd pick up one of these. $500 for a MacBook Air or $625 for a MacBook Pro? Easy decision. Remember, it just needs to be reliable and run the Chrome browser.

Definitely recommend LAPTOP for portability. There will be many times where you'll be doing a lot of online research and doing this laying on a couch will be the choice of many.

Dual Screens:

If you're not sitting on the couch, I highly recommend having a dual-screen set up. Most computers and laptops can support dual screens. Having a lot of extra screen real estate makes it easy to open several windows and compare pricing data from multiple sources. If you are unsure if your laptop or computer supports a dual-screen set up, simply contact the manufacturer or try Google.

Chrome Bonus Tip:

When you use Chrome, it saves all of your browser settings. So when you leave one computer and log into Chrome from another computer, all of your same bookmarks and settings will be there waiting for you.

ChromeBook

http://bit.ly/ArbitrageChromebook

A ChromeBook is an interesting option for Online Arbitrage. It's basically a laptop that only runs the Chrome browser. It's a fun alternative for people who do most of their computer work using a browser only (you can't install Photoshop on a ChromeBook). They are very inexpensive and some have optional 3G wireless connections meaning that you can use them in stores for mobile scanning. At the time of this writing, this ChromeBook was priced at just under $200 on Amazon.

ChromeBox

http://bit.ly/ArbitrageChromebox

The ChromeBox is another interesting alternative to a traditional laptop or desktop computer. Similar to the ChromeBook, the ChromeBox only runs the Chrome browser. All you need is a keyboard, mouse, and monitor, and you have a desktop replacement. Again, this won't run other programs that don't run in the browser. At the time of the writing, this ChromeBox was priced just under $170 on Amazon.

Below you will find a long list of Chrome browser extensions. These extensions work with Chrome to customize your browser experience. You can install some of them or all of them. As you search the Chrome Webstore, be sure to look at the RELATED extensions in case I missed any or if any new/better ones are released since the writing of this book.

You can search for any extension here: https://chrome.google.com/webstore/category/extensions

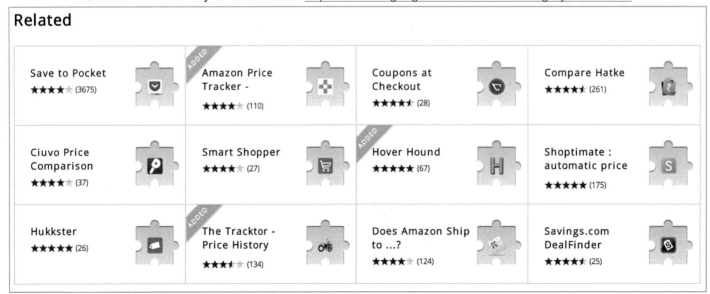

Sometimes your extensions may stop working. I don't know why this happens, but it does. First, restart your browser. If that doesn't work just uninstall them and reinstall. Also, the extensions listed in this book are independently run. This book cannot guarantee that they will continue to run or even be offered.

Section 1: Drop Down Extensions

<u>Amazon 1Button App (Amazon Browser Bar)</u>

What it does:

The Amazon 1Button App is a Chrome extension that alerts online shoppers to the current prices on Amazon.com. The intent is to remind shoppers of the Amazon price (often lower than other online retailers) and bring shoppers back to Amazon.

Why this extension is useful for Online Arbitrage:

The extension doesn't just alert online shoppers to LOWER prices. It looks for matches from the Amazon catalog and alerts online shoppers to ANY prices or offers. Sometimes these prices are much HIGHER. When you see an item being sold for a low price on one website, the Amazon 1Button App can alert you if the market price on Amazon is significantly higher (and potentially at a price where you can buy and resell for a profit). It speeds up the time it would take you to find the corresponding Amazon product page when browsing other sites.

Take a look at this example of a product from other online retailer and the simplicity of getting the Amazon pricing information on the same page automatically:

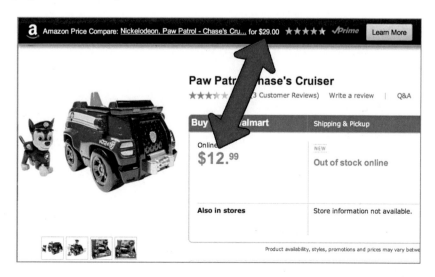

Why it's not perfect:

The Amazon 1Button App is great but it doesn't work on every site. It may be that it's not compatible or that some sites have found a way to block the extension. It's also not perfect at finding the correct Amazon product page so always double-check to be sure that the pages match before you make a purchase.

DOWNLOAD HERE:

https://chrome.google.com/webstore/detail/Amazon-1button-app-for-ch/pbjikboenpfhbbejgkoklgkhjpfogcam

EASY LINK: http://bit.ly/1buttonapp

http://www.Amazon.com/gp/BIT/AmazonBrowserBar/

Price blink

What it does:

Price Blink is an extension that alerts online shoppers to other prices from many other online retailers, including Amazon.com. Unlike the Amazon 1Button App that is designed to show the Amazon price, Price Blink works on many different sites, including Amazon.com, showing you the lowest price from across the web.

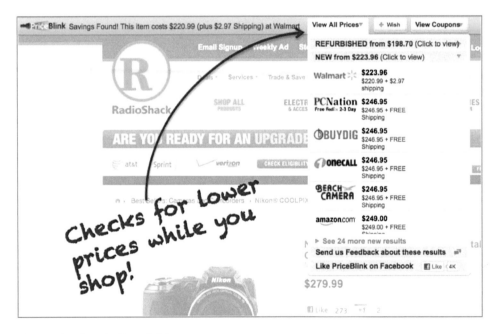

Why this extension is useful for Online Arbitrage:

When Price Blink drops down to alert you of Savings Found! you'll be able to see a list of online retailers carrying the product. This saves you huge amounts of time compared to visiting and searching many different websites to find product matches and comparing pricing information. This is especially useful on Amazon.com when you're looking at an item that appears to have potential for resale and you're wondering where to get it. Price Blink can quickly tell you the online retailers carrying the products, which often correlates to local stores as well.

Why it's not perfect:

It doesn't always match the correct product so you have to visit each site to confirm product matches before making any purchases.

DOWNLOAD HERE:

https://chrome.google.com/webstore/detail/priceblink/aoiidodopnnhiflaflbfeblnojefhigh

EASY LINK: http://bit.ly/priceblink

http://www.priceblink.com/

Includes video demo: https://www.youtube.com/watch?v=xgSeAW6_MUI

InvisibleHand

What it does:

Similar to the Amazon 1Button App and Price Blink, InvisibleHand drops down in your browser when you shop online to alert you to possible lower prices from other sites. Unlike the Amazon 1Button App that is designed to show the Amazon price, InvisibleHand works on many different sites, including Amazon.com, showing you the lowest price from across the web. I find InvisibleHand to be more useful and accurate than Price Blink.

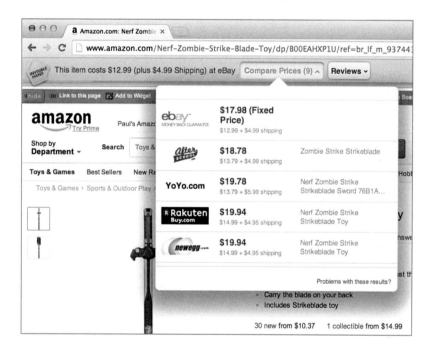

Why this extension is useful for Online Arbitrage:

When Price Blink drops down to alert you of a lower price, you'll be able to see a list of online retailers carrying the product. This saves you huge amounts of time compared to visiting and searching many different websites to find product matches and comparing pricing information. This is especially useful on Amazon.com when you're looking at an item that appears to have potential for resale and you're wondering where to get it. InvisibleHand can quickly tell you the online retailers carrying the products, which often correlates to local stores as well. In addition to displaying lower prices, InvisibleHand also shows available coupons for various online retailers as well as free shipping offers.

Why it's not perfect:

It doesn't always match the correct product so you have to visit each site to confirm product matches before making any purchases.

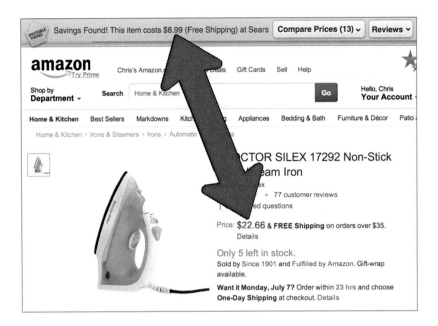

At the time of this writing, InvisibleHand works in the USA, UK, and Germany.

DOWNLOAD HERE:

https://chrome.google.com/webstore/detail/invisiblehand/lghjfnfolmcikomdjmoiemllfnlmmoko

EASY LINK: http://bit.ly/invisiblehandapp

http://www.getinvisiblehand.com/

Shop Genius

What it does:

Similar to the Amazon 1Button App, Price Blink, and InvisibleHand, Shop Genius drops down in your browser when you shop online to alert you to possible lower prices from other sites. Unlike the Amazon 1Button App that is designed to show the Amazon price, Shop Genius works on many different sites, including Amazon.com, showing you the lowest price from across the web.

Why this extension is useful for Online Arbitrage:

When Shop Genius drops down to alert you of a lower price, you'll be able to see a list of online retailers carrying the product. This saves you huge amounts of time compared to visiting and searching many different websites to find product matches and comparing pricing information. This is especially useful on Amazon.com when you're looking at an item that appears to have potential for resale and you're wondering where to get it. InvisibleHand can quickly tell you the online retailers carrying the products, which often correlates to local stores as well.

Why it's not perfect:

It doesn't always match the correct product so you have to visit each site to confirm product matches before making any purchases.

DOWNLOAD HERE:

https://chrome.google.com/webstore/detail/shopgenius/ekejkhnkppgbldboejcbcejjjamkpooa

EASY LINK: http://bit.ly/shopgeniusapp

http://www.shopgeniusapp.com/

Includes video demo: http://vimeo.com/63354353

Wal-Mart Shopper

What it does:

Similar to the Amazon 1Button App, the Wal-Mart Shopper extension is designed exclusively for one retail outlet--in this case, Wal-Mart. You can browse any online retailer, including Amazon.com, and it will work in the background to find you product matches and alert you to prices from Wal-Mart's website.

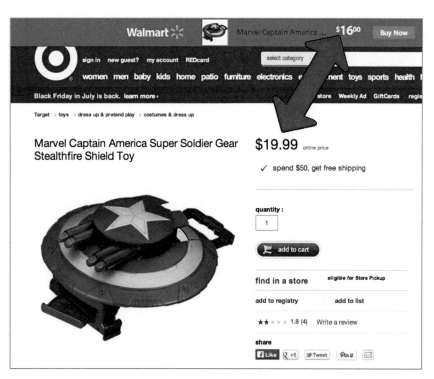

Why this extension is useful for Online Arbitrage:

This is useful for a few reasons. It will save you time trying to match up items from others sites to Wal-Mart. It will show you Wal-Mart pricing information all on one screen (sometimes lower, sometimes higher). Another reason that I like it is because it instantly shows you where to get a product being sold on Amazon.com. Instead of having to use Google to figure out where an Amazon listing is sold at retail, you'll find out right away if the product is being sold at Wal-Mart.

Why it's not perfect:

It's only comparing items to Wal-Mart and the matches are not always perfect.

DOWNLOAD HERE:

https://chrome.google.com/webstore/detail/walmart/bmelcnhnemihidpaehodijpamdaeeglh

EASY LINK: http://bit.ly/walmartbrowserapp

Price Jump

What it does:

Price Jump is a drop down similar to the others mentioned above with a little twist. They are designed to be used on Amazon.com to let you know if you are getting a good price, OK price, or bad price. They color code these as green, yellow and red.

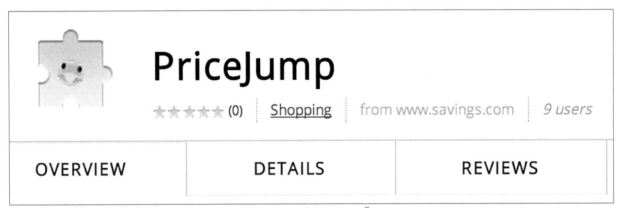

(That's right; I was their 10th user!)

Why this extension is useful for Online Arbitrage:

It is always useful to know if there are prices lower than the Amazon price. Sometimes those prices will be low enough to turn a profit using resale. You can also learn about online retailers that you may not have searched before. If they have a hot price on one item, they may have hot prices on other items.

Why it's not perfect:

Designed only for Amazon shopping. Product matches are not always perfect.

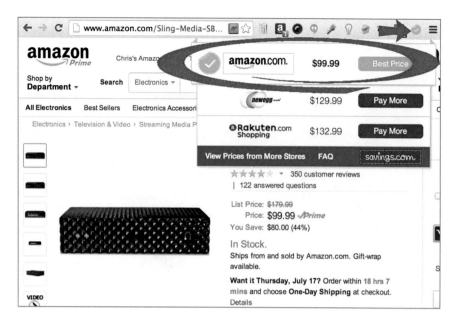

GREEN LIGHT example:
http://www.Amazon.com/Sling-Media-SB350-100-Slingbox-350/dp/B009FU8BTI/

YELLOW LIGHT EXAMPLE:
http://www.Amazon.com/GoPro-CHDHX-302-HERO3-Black-Edition/dp/B00F3F0GLU/

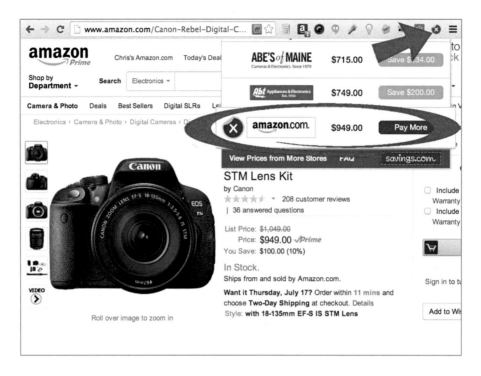

RED LIGHT EXAMPLE:
http://www.Amazon.com/Canon-Rebel-Digital-Camera-18-135mm/dp/B00BW6LX20/

DOWNLOAD HERE:

https://chrome.google.com/webstore/detail/pricejump/dblfcnaanidhgjbmcfgebdcifkaffcpb

EASY LINK: http://bit.ly/pricejump

http://www.savings.com/pricejump/extension.html

Section 2: Built-in Graphs

These Chrome Extensions will build price history graphs directly into Amazon product pages. We want to install and use multiple extensions because they are not all perfect. Some catch drops that others miss. Price drops are sometimes very brief and may even be missed entirely.

Keepa

What it does:

Keepa is easily one of the most useful extensions for Online Arbitrage. After you install this extension, Keepa will display an important and valuable pricing graph on all of your Amazon product pages. Simply visit an Amazon product page and you'll see a graph like in the image below. Keepa also includes the ability to track items and prices on Amazon.

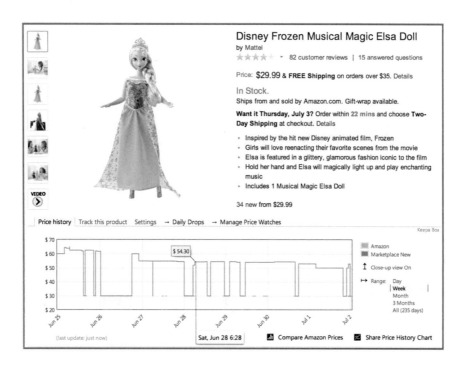

http://www.Amazon.com/Disney-Frozen-Musical-Magic-Elsa/dp/B00C6Q9688/

Why this extension is useful for Online Arbitrage:

One of the most important and valuable features of Keepa is how it differentiates between Amazon being in or out of stock on an item. In this example, when you see the ORANGE colored data points, that means that Amazon is in stock and shows the listed price ($29.99). The WHITE breaks in the orange indicate that Amazon is no longer in stock and therefore not a seller of the item at that time. Here you can see the effect on the market prices as the lowest Marketplace New price shown as the BLUE line shoots way up to the $50-$60 level. So you can see historically if Amazon has been able to stay in stock on items as well as the market prices when they are out of stock.

Consider this: If Amazon is going out of stock on an item, then it's likely a popular item. Popular items with limited supply often mean over-retail prices, which means a possible Online Arbitrage opportunity for you. You can also see all-time high and low prices including artificially low prices from Amazon.com themselves in the event they were price-matching another aggressive online retailer. Knowing that in the past Amazon has sold for a lower price is valuable information because you can then set up a price alert to be notified if Amazon lowers their price again.

Why it's not perfect:

The Marketplace New prices are the listed price (shipping not included). This often means that the deals that you'll find are even better than first glance, but I would prefer to be accurate and save the additional calculation. Some Marketplace New offers may be listed with free shipping that would then throw off mental calculations if you're expecting to add additional shipping.

DOWNLOAD HERE:

https://chrome.google.com/webstore/detail/Amazon-price-tracker-keep/neebplgakaahbhdphmkckjjcegoiijjo

EASY LINK: http://bit.ly/keepa

https://keepa.com/

Much more on Keepa later in Chapter 4.

Pricenoia

UPDATE! Pricenoia was very much in business when the first edition of this book was published. Three days later, they went out of business and shut down their site and support for their extensions. I've left the information about Pricenoia in the book for two reasons. First, they may end up back in business at some point in the future. Second, how to use the data that they had provided is still very relevant to the world of Online Arbitrage. It's possible that another new site pops up that shows similar, useful data and your knowledge of how Pricenoia worked could help you interpret their pricing data for your business.

Pricenoia is also covered in Chapter 6, which remains in this book.

What it does:

After you install this extension, Pricenoia will display an important and valuable pricing graph on all of your Amazon product pages. Simply visit an Amazon product page and you'll see a graph like in the image below.

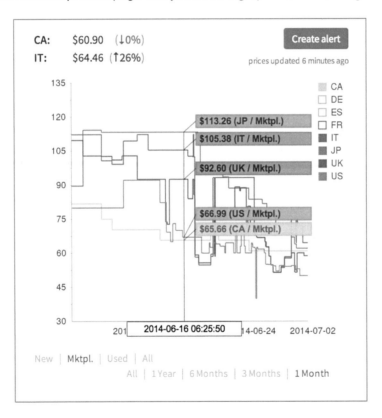

Why this extension is useful for Online Arbitrage:

While both Keepa and Pricenoia both install pricing graphs on Amazon product pages, the Pricenoia graph is clearly geared towards showing you the international market prices for the item all in one place. You can use this information to decide if you want to consider an international Amazon site for the resale of your items or even find a lower price from another Amazon site to sell on Amazon.com. Pricenoia also includes the ability to track items and prices on Amazon.

Why it's not perfect:

The prices listed do not differentiate between Amazon and Marketplace sellers. Amazon being in stock (or not) is also not tracked. Remember, Amazon's prices on all sites are LISTED FOR prices, not always representative of SELLING FOR prices. So just because an item is listed for a higher price on an international Amazon site, it doesn't necessarily mean that it is selling well (or at all). Also, consider that sales ranks from other Amazon countries will mean very different sales rates compared to Amazon.com.

DOWNLOAD HERE:

https://chrome.google.com/webstore/detail/pricenoia-compare-Amazon/ojhfdnfjggbpoakbhjdejgmncdfioafk

EASY LINK: http://bit.ly/pricenoiaapp

https://pricenoia.com/

Want to show me some love? Use this affiliate link when searching:
https://pricenoia.com/?tag=chris

Much more on Pricenoia later in Chapter 6.

TheTracktor

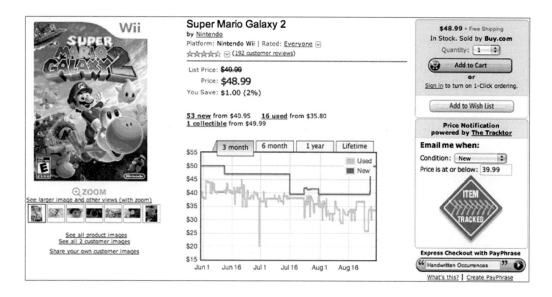

What it does:

TheTracktor is similar to Keepa and Pricenoia in that it installs a historical price graph directly on the Amazon product pages. TheTracktor also includes the ability to track items and prices on Amazon.

Why this extension is useful for Online Arbitrage:

Just like Keepa and Pricenoia, having access to historical pricing data is useful in making Online Arbitrage purchasing decisions. Since no price tracker is perfect, sometimes one will catch drops that the others miss. Check TheTracktor for low outlier prices and consider setting up price alerts.

Why it's not perfect:

From what I can tell, TheTracktor checks and updates its prices less frequently than the other price tracking extensions. However, sometimes TheTracktor will be the only one that picks up a particular price drop. A lot of this likely has to do with the random timing of prices changing and the times that the price trackers check for price changes. For this reason, I like have multiple price-tracking graph extensions installed. TheTracktor does not differentiate between Amazon being in and out of stock.

DOWNLOAD HERE:

https://chrome.google.com/webstore/detail/the-tracktor-price-histor/onajjgekdldckfgodnmoallcmdmfcfom

EASY LINK: http://bit.ly/thetracktor

http://thetracktor.com/

More on TheTracktor in Chapter 7.

Unimerc

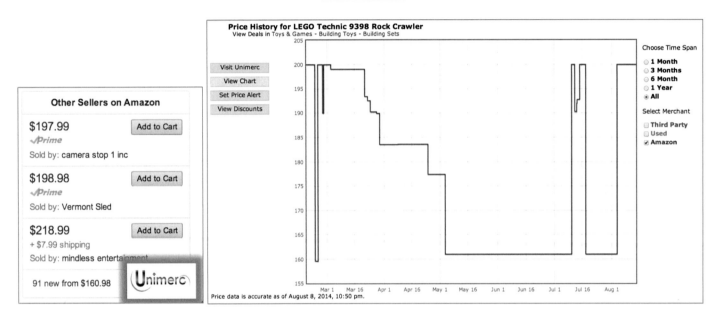

What it does:

Similar to Keepa and TheTracktor, Unimerc provides a historical pricing graph of Amazon pricing information. Unlike Keepa and TheTracktor, Unimerc does not display a pricing graph on the Amazon product pages automatically. To see the Unimerc pricing graph, you have to click on the Unimerc icon that will be present in the bottom right-hand corner of your browser. Unimerc also includes the ability to track items and prices on Amazon.

Why this extension is useful for Online Arbitrage:

Similar to Keepa and TheTracktor, Unimerc can help you identify opportunities by providing you access to historical pricing information. This information can help you set up price alerts.

Why it's not perfect:

Does not update as frequently as the other price tracking graphs. Requires an extra step to pull up information. Does not differentiate Amazon being in or out of stock.

DOWNLOAD HERE:

https://chrome.google.com/webstore/detail/unimerc-Amazon-price-trac/aodgfcodeghkkaenpamldjkobdeeojji

http://www.unimerc.com/

EASY LINK: http://bit.ly/unimerc

Section 3: Built-in Buttons

CamelCamelCamel
(sometimes referred to as CCC)

What it does:

Installing the CamelCamelCamel browser extension will install a small button at the end of your browser address bar. When you are on Amazon product page, clicking this button will open a popup window with CamelCamelCamel pricing information. It also includes a link to open the full CamelCamelCamel page in a new tab.

Why this extension is useful for Online Arbitrage:

CamelCamelCamel is one of the best and most useful sites for getting historical Amazon pricing data. Having quick, one-click access to the CamelCamelCamel pages will save you a bunch of time when evaluating products for resale. CamelCamelCamel differentiates the Amazon price from the Marketplace New price, which is very useful.

Why it's not perfect:

CamelCamelCamel does not differentiate when Amazon goes in and out of stock on a product. When Amazon is out of stock, the green line on the CamelCamelCamel graph will just be flat. Sometimes this means Amazon was out of stock but it can also mean that Amazon simply stayed at the same price: Increased fluctuations in the blue line on the CamelCamelCamel graph representing Marketplace New sellers when the green Amazon line is flat can indicate Amazon being out of stock. The popup window only shows pricing information and not historical sales rank information, which is sometimes even more valuable when gauging previous and expected demand for a product.

DOWNLOAD HERE:

https://chrome.google.com/webstore/detail/the-camelizer-Amazon-pric/ghnomdcacenbmilgjigehppbamfndblo

EASY LINK: http://bit.ly/camelcamel

http://camelcamelcamel.com/

Much more on CamelCamelCamel later Chapter 5.

FBA Calculator Widget

What it does:

Installs a button that will take you to the official Amazon FBA Calculator page from any Amazon product page with one click. It will fill in the Amazon ASIN as well as enter the current Buy Box price in order to calculate the Amazon payout.

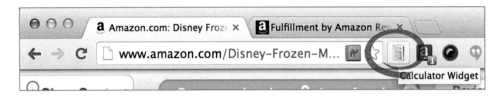

Why this extension is useful for Online Arbitrage:

Having one click access to the Amazon FBA Calculator saves you time and allows you to quickly evaluate products for potential resale based on their payouts. This is more important on items that may be oversize or overweight and thus incur addition FBA fees that might not be obvious at first glance at a product.

Why it's not perfect:

Sometimes you do not want to use the Amazon Buy Box price for evaluation. For example, you may be expecting Amazon to go out of stock and you want to know the payouts at the next lowest price (soon to be the Buy Box price). In scenarios like this, you'd have to edit the price on the FBA Calculator page.

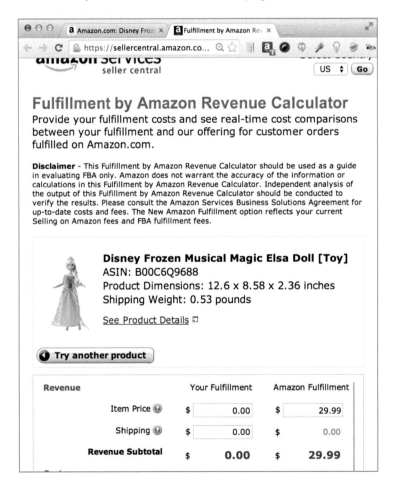

DOWNLOAD HERE:

https://chrome.google.com/webstore/detail/calculator-widget/cpplagdendnkjkiaiaijfphiflaflinc

SHORT LINK: http://bit.ly/fbacalculatorapp

https://sellercentral.Amazon.com/gp/fba/revenue-calculator/index.html

PoachIt

What it does:

Installing the PoachIt extension will add a button to your browser. When you're on a product page from any online retailer, you can click the PoachIt button and then you'll be able to add the product to your track list (public or private). They will then track the item and send you an alert if the price drops.

Why this extension is useful for Online Arbitrage:

Any extension that can track prices and send alerts can help you find opportunities for Online Arbitrage.

Why it's not perfect:

Definitely not designed with resellers in mind. No way to set alerts for only certain prices or drop amounts (for example, I don't need an alert to a $0.40 drop).

DOWNLOAD HERE:

https://chrome.google.com/webstore/detail/poachit-your-shopping-sid/ddnglgpgcjnhehalhgjaapipjkpmhimh

EASY LINK: http://bit.ly/poachitapp

https://www.poachit.com

Online Price Tracker and Mobile App - PoachIt.com

http://youtu.be/SWqjJir73u4
http://bit.ly/poachitvideo

Section 4: Functionality

Link Clump

What it does:

Link Clump is an awesome extension that allows you to open multiple links at once. Once you install this extension, you can hold down the SHIFT button and then highlight multiple links and they will all open in new tabs.

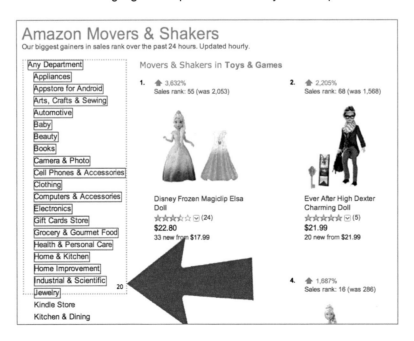

Here you can see me highlighting TWENTY of the Amazon Movers & Shakers pages at once.

Why this extension is useful for Online Arbitrage:

There are two primary places where I use Link Clump. First are the Amazon Movers & Shakers pages. I can open them all in new tabs with one click. Then I can glance for new or interesting items. If I don't see anything worth a closer look, I simply close the tab. The next tab will slide over, putting the close tab icon right where my mouse pointer was before. I can glance at the next page and decide if I want to look closer or close the tab. Closing tab after tab doesn't even require moving your mouse. You can check the top items in all of the Amazon Movers & Shakers pages in less than a minute.

Second are the category pages from Pricenoia. They list all of the departments on the left side of their website. Clicking through each one and then clicking back to choose another one is time consuming. I can do the exact same thing with Pricenoia that I did with the Amazon Movers & Shakers; Glance at the top drops and close tabs as I go. You can look at hundreds of top price drops in minutes this way.

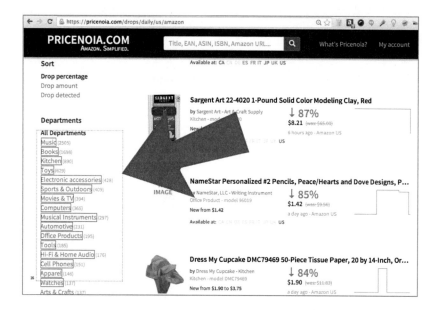

Here you can see me highlighting SIXTEEN of the Pricenoia pages at once.

DOWNLOAD HERE:

https://chrome.google.com/webstore/detail/linkclump/lfpjkncokllnfokkgpkobnkbkmelfefj

EASY LINK: http://bit.ly/linkclump

Context Search

(Thanks to Wilk Davis for this one)

What it does:

Context Search allows you to highlight any text from a web page and then choose from pre-defined search links like Amazon, Google, eBay, Craigslist, and more.

Why this extension is useful for Online Arbitrage:

Context Search will save you an incredible amount of time. No more copying titles, opening new tabs, going to Google or Amazon, then pasting and searching for product matches. This is all done in one simple step with Context Search.

31

Once you download the Context Search extension, you have to customize it. You can do this by clicking on the setting button at the top-right corner of your Chrome browser. Choose, Tools, then Extensions.

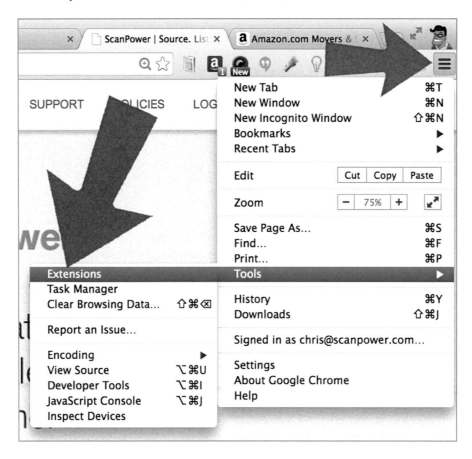

You'll then find Context Search and click on Options. You can Modify or Delete existing URLs or Add New.

Here are the ones that I use. You can add your own as well. Just find the URL or link of a search that you use and replace the search terms with "%s". You can see some examples below:

Amazon: http://www.Amazon.com/s/field-keywords=%s

EBay Completed: http://www.ebay.com/sch/i.html?LH_Complete=1&LH_Sold=1&_nkw=%s&_sop=16

EBay Active: http://www.ebay.com/sch/i.html?&_nkw=%s

Craigslist: http://southcoast.craigslist.org/search/sss?query=%s&sort=rel

(Replace 'southcoast' with your Craigslist location)

Yoopsie: http://yoopsie.com/query.php?query=%s&locale=US&index=All

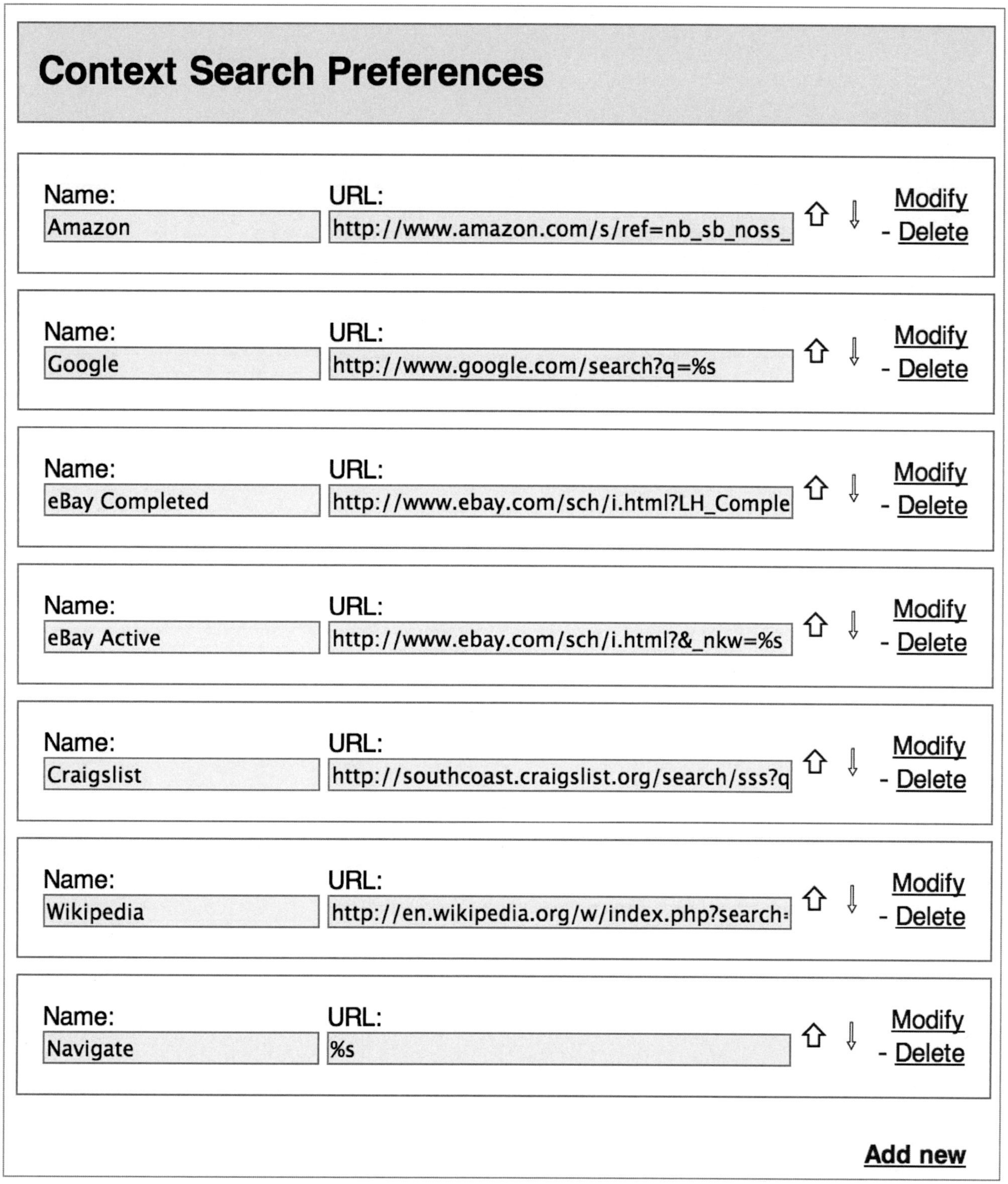

Context Search Preferences

Name:
Amazon

URL:
http://www.amazon.com/s/ref=nb_sb_noss_

⇧ ⇩

Modify
- Delete

Name:
Google

URL:
http://www.google.com/search?q=%s

⇧ ⇩

Modify
- Delete

Name:
eBay Completed

URL:
http://www.ebay.com/sch/i.html?LH_Comple

⇧ ⇩

Modify
- Delete

Name:
eBay Active

URL:
http://www.ebay.com/sch/i.html?&_nkw=%s

⇧ ⇩

Modify
- Delete

Name:
Craigslist

URL:
http://southcoast.craigslist.org/search/sss?q

⇧ ⇩

Modify
- Delete

Name:
Wikipedia

URL:
http://en.wikipedia.org/w/index.php?search=

⇧ ⇩

Modify
- Delete

Name:
Navigate

URL:
%s

⇧ ⇩

Modify
- Delete

Add new

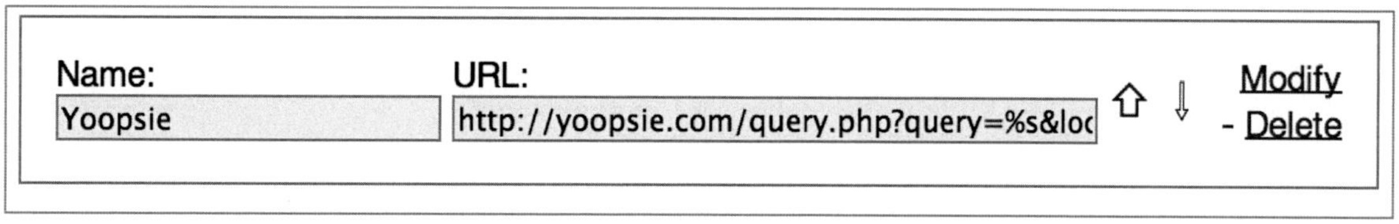

Name:
Yoopsie

URL:
http://yoopsie.com/query.php?query=%s&loc

⇧ ⇩

Modify
- Delete

Say you wanted to use Google to try to find what retailers carried this product. You can highlight the text and choose Google from the drop down menu.

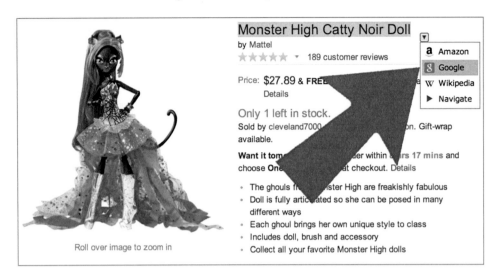

In one step, you'll end up at this page where you can quickly see that this item is sold at Toys R Us. What used to take several steps can now be done in one step.

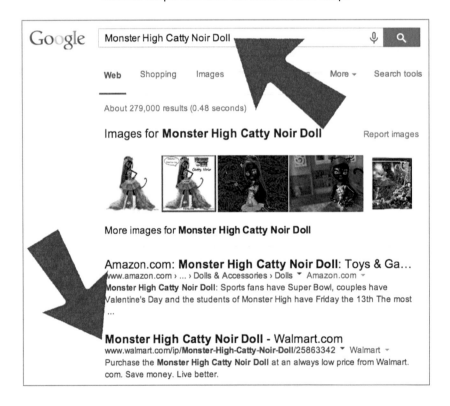

You can also use Context Search to go from other online retailers back to Amazon. Take a look at this example:

Highlight the product title and choose Amazon from the Context Search drop down menu.

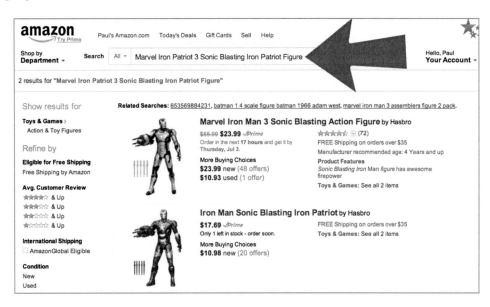

In one step, you're taken to the Amazon site with the search results for the highlighted text. You can then choose the correct match and compare pricing information.

DOWNLOAD HERE:

https://chrome.google.com/webstore/detail/context-search/dbpfafcplnjmakknnonpegphpmpmhjhj

EASY LINK: http://bit.ly/contextsearch

Switcher

What it does:

Switcher is a Chrome extension manager. It allows you to quickly see what extensions you have installed, toggle them on and off, and edit their settings.

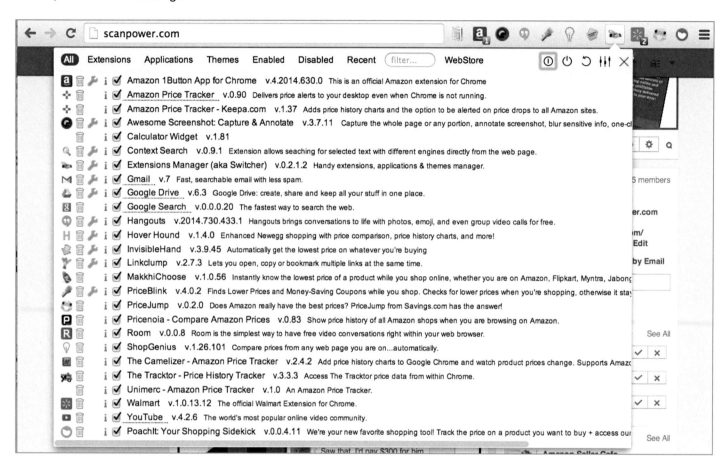

Why this extension is useful for Online Arbitrage:

Some extensions will be more useful to you than others. You may find that some extensions interfere with others. Sometimes you'll want to turn extensions off or uninstall them altogether. Switcher lets you do all of these things easily.

DOWNLOAD HERE:

https://chrome.google.com/webstore/detail/extensions-manager-aka-sw/lpleipinonnoibneeejgjnoeekmbopbc

EASY LINK: http://bit.ly/switcherapp

Section 5: Using Chrome Extension on iPad

Eventually you may be able to use Chrome and all of these extensions on an iPad, but at the time of this writing, you cannot. Using an iPad for Online Arbitrage would be awesome because of portability and ease of use. Until you can get the full Chrome experience on iPad, there is an option called Virtual Chrome.

http://www.virtualchrome.com/

Virtual Chrome is available for iPhone and iPad. I can't see using this on an iPhone screen, but you can try it if you want. This app is not free and the interface is a little clunky on the iPad, but it works.

Here you can see Price Jump and Keepa working on the iPad. Just search for Virtual Chrome in the Apple App Store.

iPad download: https://itunes.apple.com/app/id434541320?mt=8

Chapter 4 – Using Graphs – Highlight: KEEPA

We installed Keepa in the previous chapter, but Keepa does so much that it deserves its own chapter. Remember the one Keepa flaw; Keepa shows Marketplace New offers as price without shipping included. This means that prices from third party sellers are often actually even higher.

Online Arbitrage - Example of using KEEPA.com to quickly find and evaluate deals

http://youtu.be/xwTlhLx0lfs
http://bit.ly/keepavideo

There are TWO things that I'm primarily looking for using Keepa:

1. The marketplace price when Amazon is out of stock

Not all items are sold at inflated, over-retail prices when Amazon is out of stock, but some are. Some are sold at very high prices when Amazon is out of stock. Sometimes Amazon is out of stock for a short period of time, a long period of time, or they simply no longer carry the item at all.

Here is a random Keepa graph. The item doesn't matter; this is what you are looking for: The ORANGE means that Amazon is in stock. In this example, Amazon was selling at $16.99. But when Amazon is out of stock, price jumped up to $34.99 + shipping (so a safe estimate of $40+). Amazon is now in stock. This could be an item that you consider buying from Amazon at $16.99, expecting to sell for $40+ when they are out of stock. This graph shows the past three months but the item has over 1,200 days of pricing history. Before making a buying decision, I would look back at the 1,200 days to see if there is a pattern to how often Amazon goes out of stock.

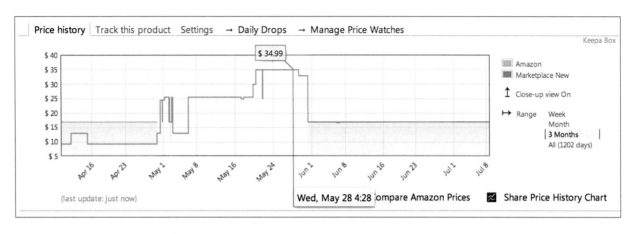

2. Historical, artificially low Amazon prices

I am very interested to know when Amazon previously dropped the price on item to a price that could be bought and resold for a profit. Maybe they price-matched another retailer or dropped their price for some other reason. Knowing that Amazon dropped their price to $30 on an item that normally sells for $80 is valuable information. If it happened before, it could happen again. That's why we set up price and in-stock alerts.

Take a look at this example. It has a steady price of $29.99 from Amazon, but for one small period of time, Amazon dropped the price to $14.99. They were likely matching another online retailer that was running a sale.

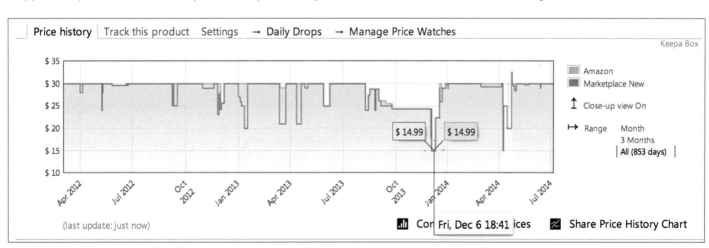

When you find items like this, simply set up a price alert at $14.99

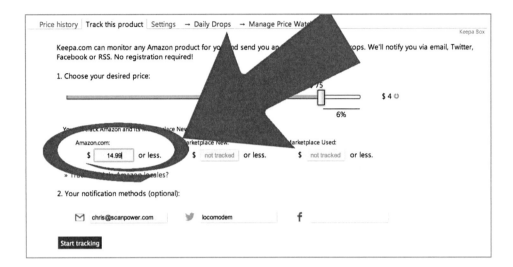

Here is another example of an item that sells pretty steadily from Amazon in the $45-$55 range. For a few days, Amazon dropped price to $16.99. Again, probably matching another online retailer.

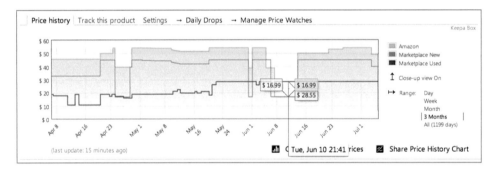

This is so easy to do. You know the price that Amazon dropped to before. Will they drop again? Who knows, but if they do, you'll be ready by setting up your pricing alert at $16.99.

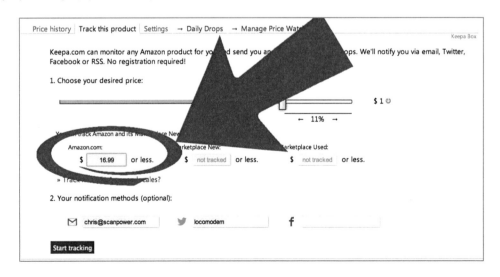

I also like to know about low prices from third party sellers, but that is a less-reliable source of inventory. First, it's much more likely that a third party seller will cancel an order sold for an artificially low price (could be an error on their part). Second, you have less assurance of the legitimacy of the supply chain from third party sellers compared to purchasing directly from Amazon.

Keepa Tip:

The Keepa default display is three months (unless being tracked for less than 3 months). If you want to use Keepa to find original MSRP when being sold by Amazon on an item that is only available from third party sellers, click on ALL DAYS and go back in time to when Amazon was still in stock.

How to use www.keepa.com to identify Online Arbitrage opportunities on Amazon.com

https://www.youtube.com/watch?v=eusWj8Gm74s
http://bit.ly/keepavideo2

Keepa: Deals

Keepa has a page where they list all of the biggest prices drops.

https://keepa.com/#deals ←BOOKMARK and check frequently

Keepa Deals are sorted by highest RELATIVE price drop. You can sort by Amazon offers, New offers, and Used offers. You can choose to show price drops for Today only, or the past Week, or the past Month. You can choose any specific Amazon category. You can also choose the size of the images (small, medium, and large).

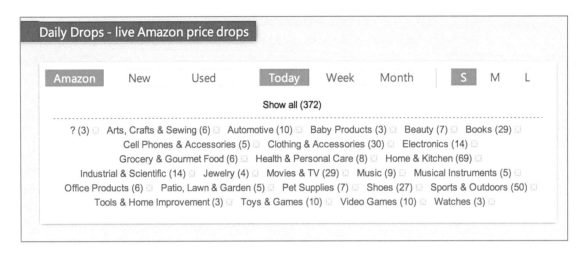

I'm primarily interested in Amazon offers as they are much more likely to actually ship in the event that it's a price error, although if the price from a third party seller is attractive enough, I'd purchase.

If you are checking frequently, you'll want to just check Today and keep track of new items. If you have been away and have not checked this page in a few days, then you may want to also check the Week to see the biggest drops that you may have missed and that would not be present on the Today list. This can be a great way to find deals that are still available but that others are missing because they are only checking the Today page. Same goes for Month. S M and L stand for Small, Medium, and Large and are for how large the item previews are. I prefer S for Small to get more of them on the screen. Use whatever you prefer here.

Let's take a closer look at some items from the Keepa Deals page: https://keepa.com/#deals

It is sorted by percentage off the previous price and it also shows the before price and the current price. When I am browsing this page, I am looking for not just the big drops in RELATIVE price, but also in ABSOLUTE price. I want a big

drop (%) but also I want the item to have a good average sales price. From the example above, the third item is 65% off. This is great but it's on a $10.93 item. You would have to buy and sell a ton of these to make any real money.

You also see a small preview of the Keepa price history graph. This can also give an indication if the price is a sudden recent drop on an item that has been listed at a higher price for some time, or if an item has traditionally been listed at a lower price, was subject to a short term price increase, and has now come back down. While this would still trigger a price drop with a high percentage, it's not necessarily a true indication of an item being sold at a short-term low price that requires action.

Let's look at the first item as an example:

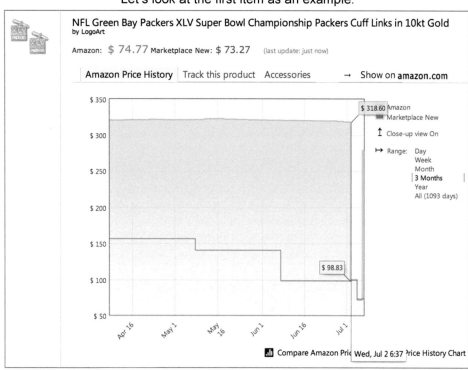

As the mini preview graph suggested, this item was low, then high, then low again, but it also shows that it was high for a long time before. There are some signs that would point to this being a great deal from Amazon, but there is more to consider. The Marketplace New price (blue line) has been consistently LOWER than Amazon the entire time. Take a look at that BLUE LINE. When I see a graph that has such a huge difference between the top orange line and the bottom blue line, it is not a deal in most cases. Think about it; while many customers prefer Amazon, even at a higher price, are they really going to spend $318.60 when they can get it for $98.83? If the Marketplace New price had been in line with the Amazon price, then this item would look much more attractive. It appears that Amazon has decided to drop their price to compete with this merchant fulfilled seller at the sub-$100 price point. As it looks now, I would strongly suspect that this item has a VERY high sales rank in it's category indicating that it has not sold in a very long time. You can also see that the BLUE line (Marketplace New price) has been much lower than Amazon for the entire time. It's true that Amazon buyers will often pay more to get the exact same items from Amazon vs. a third party seller, but there is a limit. This strongly indicates that the Amazon price is non-competitive and any sales on this item are more likely coming from third party merchants at the Marketplace New price.

Product Details

Product Dimensions: 1 x 1 x 1 inches ; 0.2 ounces

Shipping Weight: 0.8 ounces (View shipping rates and policies)

Shipping: This item is also available for shipping to select countries outside the U.S.

ASIN: B004LCBIHW

Item model number: NFL45PACCL-10K

Average Customer Review: Be the first to review this item

Amazon Best Sellers Rank: #2,507,716 in Sports & Outdoors (See Top 100 in Sports & Outdoors)

Discontinued by manufacturer: Yes

Checking the Amazon sales rank confirms that the rank is very high indeed at 2,507,716 in Sports & Outdoors.

Also going against this deal is the fact that this item is from a specific sports event. A seller would have to hope that a buyer came along that really loved the Green Bay Packers and really wanted to relive Super Bowl XLV with these specific gold cufflinks.

Why Amazon offered this particular product for such a long time at a price so much higher than their closest competitor is a mystery to me. It would appear to be a non-competitive price.

Clothing items are not exciting for the most part because clothing is a gated category that requires approval and clothing also requires that items be purchased form distributors, not bought from retailers and resold. For the most part you'll ignore clothing items on hot deal lists but if you can find some sweet deals and have a way to resell them for a profit, by all means go for it.

The fourth item on this list is awesome.

Turtle Beach TBS-2052 Ear Force Z2 Professional Grade PC Headset (Black)
by Turtle Beach

★★☆☆☆ ▾ 156 customer reviews

List Price: ~~$69.95~~

Price: **$17.99** & **FREE Shipping** on orders over $35.
Details

You Save: $51.96 (74%)

In Stock.

Ships from and sold by Amazon.com. Gift-wrap available.

Want it Tuesday, July 8? Order within **19 hrs 40 mins** and choose **One-Day Shipping** at checkout. Details

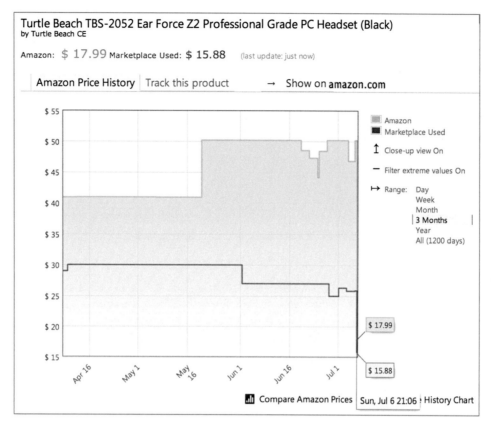

The Keepa price history mini preview graph shows on recent drop. A closer look shows a consistent price around $40 and then a more recent price of around $50. Be sure to look at the details here. The second line is Marketplace Used, not New as you saw in the cuff link example. New products command a premium price over Used. This price drop just recently happened and is barely visible on the Keepa graph. You can click on the 'Show on Amazon.com' link to go to the Amazon product page to gather additional information.

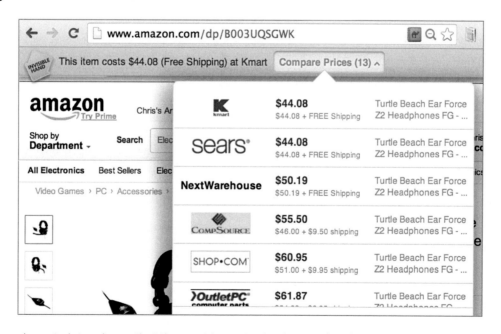

InvisibleHand drops down to let us know that the next lowest price is over $44 for a couple of online retailers.

I like seeing this on the Amazon offers page! Next lowest price over $50 on an item that is being sold by Amazon for $17.99.

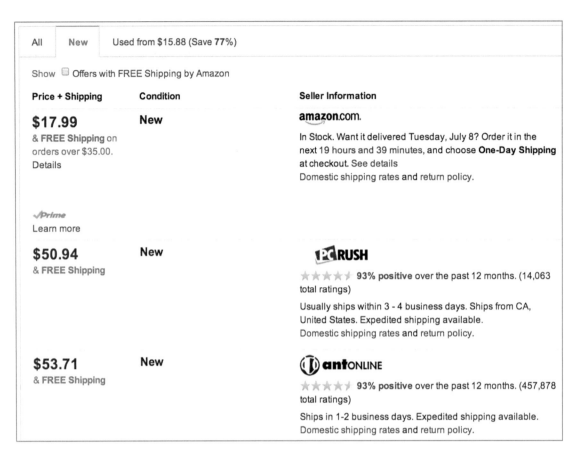

Product Details

Product Dimensions: 9 x 4 x 11 inches ; 9.4 ounces

Shipping Weight: 15.2 ounces (View shipping rates and policies)

Shipping: This item is also available for shipping to select countries outside the U.S.

ASIN: B003UQSGWK

Item model number: TBS-2052-01

Average Customer Review: ★★⯪☆☆ ☑ (156 customer reviews)

Amazon Best Sellers Rank:

    #10 in Electronics > Computers & Accessories > Game Hardware > Accessories > **Headsets**

    #39 in Electronics > Accessories & Supplies > Computer Accessories > **Headsets & Microphones**

Date first available at Amazon.com: July 4, 2010

We want to check the sales rank but it's in the Electronics category where many items do not have an overall sales rank, only sub-category sales ranks that are more difficult to decipher.

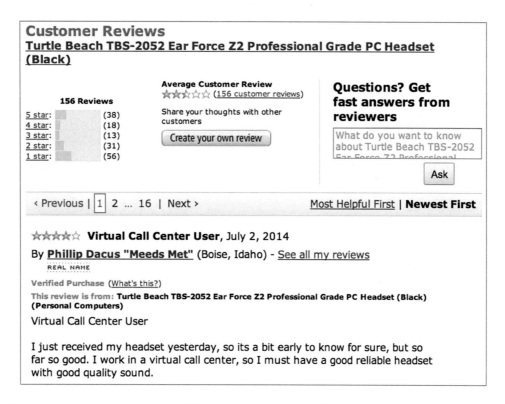

The alternate plan is to check for recent reviews. There we can see that it does have a very recent review indicating several recent sales.

So maybe you found some interesting items but you missed out on the hot price. No problem; if you can see a historic price drop from Amazon (recently or way back), you can set up a price alert to get notified when the item lowers to that price again! If you missed this deal either because Amazon raised their price back up or because they sold out, just pull up the Keepa tracker and enter $17.99 and sit back and be patient.

Here is the Keepa tracker:

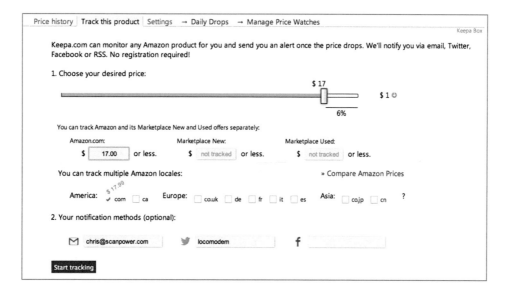

Here is what you see when you click on Compare Amazon Prices:

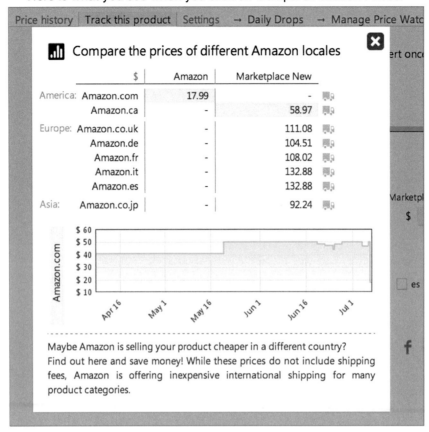

You can look for opportunities where an item is being sold a lot cheaper on other Amazon sites **OR** look to buy from one country and resell on another! Prices are shown in equivalent US dollars. When considering this strategy, remember that Amazon sales ranks are relative to each country.

Manage your Keepa tracks:

https://keepa.com/#manage

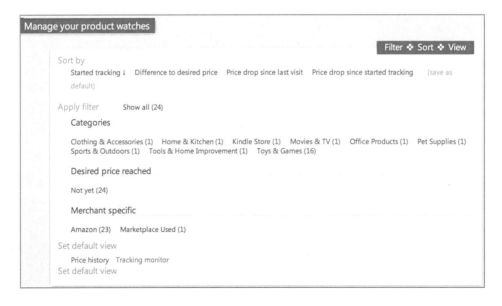

If you track a lot of items, you may find a benefit to monitoring this page for items that trigger under "Desired price reached." For those looking to pounce/capitalize on very brief price drops, you're more likely going to rely on the alert systems to know when you want to take action.

There are three ways to get direct alerts from Keepa:

1) Email: Straightforward

When Keepa detects a price at or below your trigger price, you'll get an email. The email will contain the product link for easy verification and purchase. Use this option if you are more of an email user compared to Twitter or Facebook.

2) Twitter: Requires set up

This is important to get correct. My Twitter ID is locomodem. So even though you may sometimes type @locomodem, you don't do that here otherwise tweets will be sent to @@locomodem. Also, don't put your email address here otherwise Keepa will send messages to @chris@scanpower.com which of course won't work. Don't put http://twitter.com/locomodem or twitter.com/locomodem. These won't work, either. I've seen so many Keepa users set this up incorrectly. Not only does it stop them from getting their alerts, it also then publicly shows everyone what they are tracking. For the most part, Keepa is used by people looking to save money on their stuff and not by people reselling products online, but if you want to be secretive, using Twitter Keepa alerts is NOT the way to go.

BONUS Keepa Twitter secrets:

Bookmark and follow/check: https://twitter.com/keepa_notifier

In case anyone sets up their Keepa alerts incorrectly, you'll get their alerts. You'll also get alerts for general shoppers who are just looking for good deals. Some of these deals may be resalable. Keepa messages sent out properly will not show up as Keepa alerts even if you follow @Keepa_notifier. To see all of the Keepa tweets, you need to check this page that includes their tweets AND replies:

https://twitter.com/Keepa_Notifier/with_replies

The only problem with this page is that it includes all countries when you may only be interested in specific countries. If you want to filter this page to only see items from US or Canada, use CTRL or Command F to FIND in Google Chrome. Then enter $. If you want to see items in Euros, press Option + Shift + 2. Yen, press Option Key + Y. British Pound, Option + 3. The right-hand side of the browser will give you markers where the matches can be found for quick access. [These shortcuts are only good for Mac users. Got a Windows option?]

Secret link to check on: https://twitter.com/Keepa_Notifier/with_replies

You'll see all of the incorrectly formatted Keepa alerts. Use this to see what other people are tracking and possibly find BOLOs or get ideas for additional items to track.

3) Facebook (private vs. public)

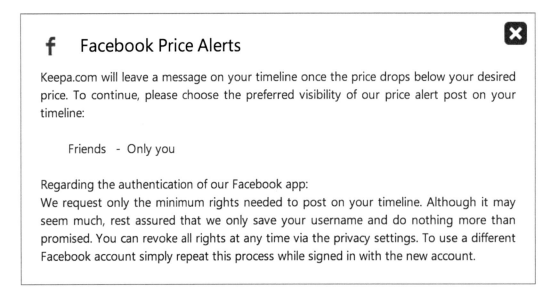

I expect that Keepa will eventually do Facebook private messages, which would be an improvement, privacy-wise.

Do you want to see what happens when people don't set up their Keepa twitter alerts properly? I got a whole bunch of alerts from people with the extra @ in their Twitter ID that were tracking this item:

http://www.Amazon.com/LEGO-6089500-Ghostbusters-Ecto-1-21108/dp/B00JRCB3HQ/

Check it out:

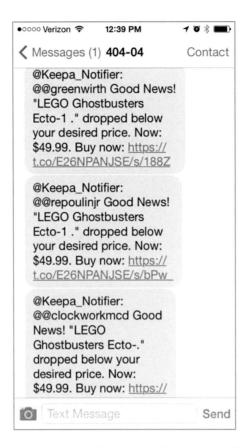

Now if I'd been living under a rock and had not noticed this item on the Amazon Movers & Shakers lists (or FatWallet and other deal sites) or monitored popular, new Lego releases, I may just decide that this is something that I should also be tracking. The Twitter alerts were at $49.99. Price Jump and the Wal-Mart Shopper quickly show me that this item is available for at Target.com and Wal-Mart.com for $49.99 and a Google search shows shop.lego.com for $49.99 as well.

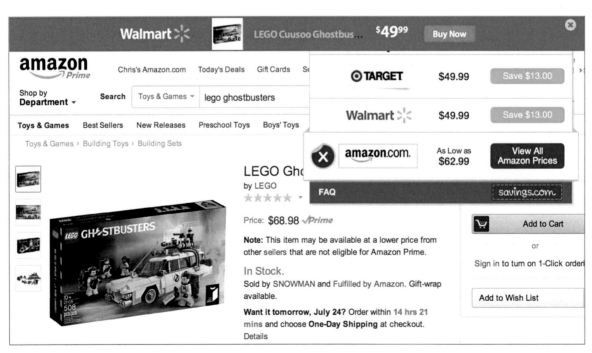

And of course the Keepa alert and graph itself reveal that the price from Amazon was $49.99. Looking more closely at the Keepa graph, you can see that it has not been in stock very often and each time has quickly sold out. These dynamics may lead you to want to set up your own Keepa alert at $49.99 to track this item for possible resale.

Now if I go back in time using Keepa, I can see what happened at launch. I can see the date that it was first in stock on Amazon, the price, how long it was in stock, and the price that it was sold at once Amazon was sold out. Use this info as valuable research.

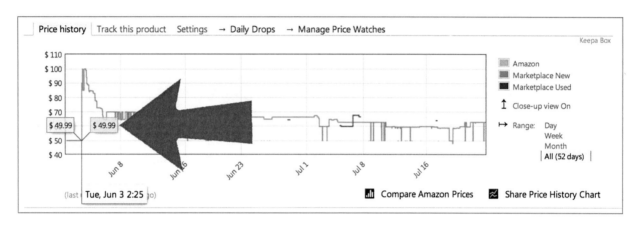

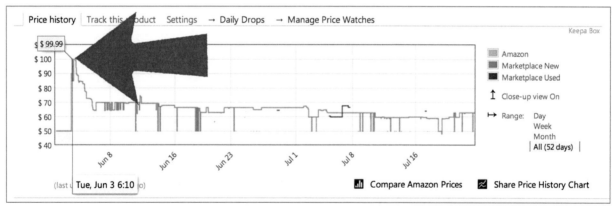

As soon as the first batch was sold out on Amazon, the price jumped to $99.99 + shipping from third party sellers.

Chapter 5 – Using Graphs – Highlight: CamelCamelCamel

CamelCamelCamel is easily one of the best and most useful sites and extensions for Online Arbitrage. Become familiar with this site and its features. One of the biggest pieces of useful data from CamelCamelCamel is the sales rank tracking. Looking at historical sales rank can help you determine previous demand for products.

CamelCamelCamel: Top Price Drops

http://camelcamelcamel.com/top_drops

CamelCamelCamel gives you a lot of customization options. You can choose to see the top drops for any Amazon category as well as choose between the biggest ABSOLUTE and RELATIVE price drops. You can sort these results for the past day all the way up to the past seven days. You can also choose the most RECENT price drops and further refine those results with a qualifier of absolute or relative price drops. For example, you could choose to view the most recent price drops with an ABSOLUTE price drop of $50 or you could choose to view the most recent price drops with a RELATIVE price drop of 50%.

Don't get too excited when you see $650 cell phones for $0.00. Those prices are with a new contract--although I do click through sometimes in the event that I might catch an Amazon pricing error. The third item, the Hitachi battery charger, is the item that we are going to look at more closely. At the time, it was the #3 top price drop detected by CamelCamelCamel at 86% off the previous price (was $49.06, now $6.77).

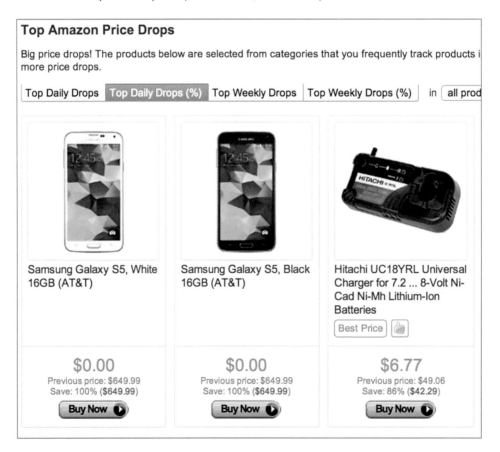

http://www.Amazon.com/dp/B000K8AS9K

The product detail page shows seven left in stock from Amazon.com (with more on the way).

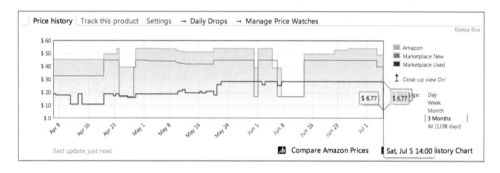

https://keepa.com/#product/1-B000K8AS9K

The Keepa graph shows a historical price of $45-$55 from Amazon with Marketplace sellers coming in a little below that. It also shows a week of time where Amazon lowered the price under $20 before going back up in price. The $6.77 price is right at the very end, meaning we've caught this deal just as it happened.

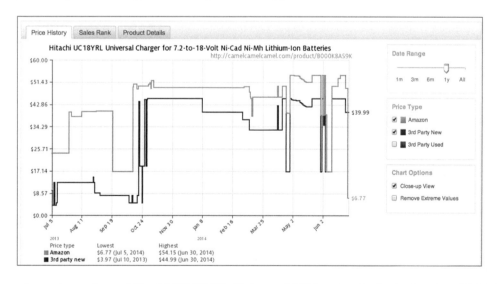

http://camelcamelcamel.com/Hitachi-UC18YRL-Universal-Lithium-Ion-Batteries/product/B000K8AS9K

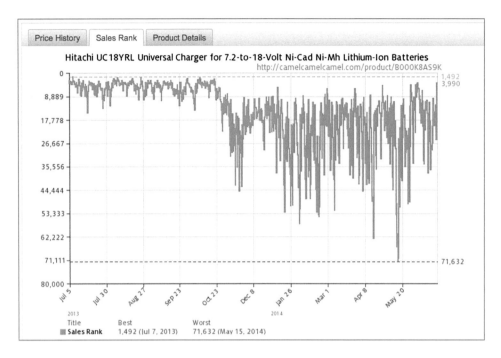

Doing our due diligence, we check the CamelCamelCamel historical prices as well as the sales rank history. We can see that the price has held pretty steady along with the sales rank.

Additional Information

ASIN	B000K8AS9K
Customer Reviews	★★★★☆ ☑ 72 reviews 4.3 out of 5 stars
Best Sellers Rank	#2,213 in Home Improvement (See top 100) #10 in Home Improvement > Power & Hand Tools > Power Tool Accessories > Battery Packs & Chargers > Charger & Converters > Battery Chargers
Shipping Weight	1.9 pounds (View shipping rates and policies)
Shipping	Currently, item can be shipped only within the U.S.
Date First Available	August 17, 2005

The current sales rank is better than the average sales rank due to the increased sales at the artificially low price. You want to double check this to be sure that an item has a sales history and not just recent sales due to the lower price. You can also check to see if sales are trailing off because of a higher market price.

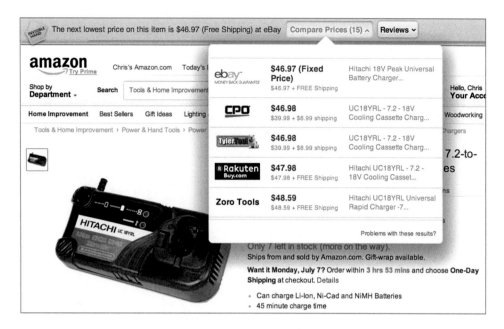

The InvisibleHand extension pops up on the Amazon product page to show prices from other sites including eBay. Sometimes eBay is a viable option such as if the product you are looking at is listed in a restricted category.

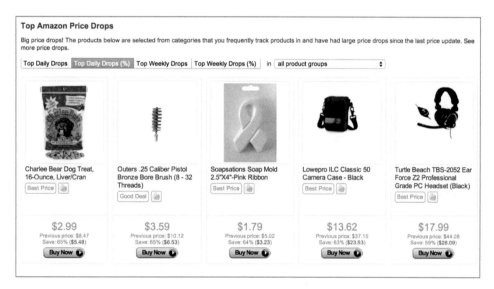

You can see that CamelCamelCamel also picked up the price drop on the Turtle Beach headphones from the Keepa chapter.

International CamelCamelCamel:

We briefly mentioned international Online Arbitrage opportunities earlier in this book. The biggest thing to consider when comparing Amazon sites is how sales ranks correlate from each one. If you're looking to compare the USA (.com) and Canada (.ca) Amazon sites, a great site to use is CamelCamelCamel's .CA site. They track sales rank on Amazon.ca and you can then compare the sales rank graphs to estimate sales volumes form each site.

http://ca.camelcamelcamel.com/

Later in this book in Chapter 16, we'll show you an example of using CamelCamelCamel Canada on a Lego kit.

Social:

Follow their Twitter account for deal alerts: https://twitter.com/camelcamelcamel

You can also get Twitter messages for price alerts by using their Camel Concierge service:

https://twitter.com/camelconcierge

More information at: http://camelcamelcamel.com/concierge

Here's a video walkthrough of CamelCamelCamel:

Online Arbitrage - CamelCamelCamel walkthrough for resellers, tracking

http://youtu.be/iDy63FxRLUs
http://bit.ly/camelvideo

Bonus Tip: Did you know that they had a separate site just for tracking BestBuy.com?

http://camelbuy.com/

Chapter 6 – Pricenoia & International

Pricenoia: Daily Drops

https://pricenoia.com/drops/daily/us/Amazon

(Be sure to use the Link Clump Google Chrome Extension here and choose Hide Fake Drops as explained in Chapter 3)

Pricenoia allows you to sort by deals from the past hour, past 24 hours, past week, and past month. You can choose from the different international Amazon sites. You can choose from four different conditions: All conditions, Amazon New, Amazon Marketplace, or Amazon Used. You can sort by Drop Percentage, Drop Amount, and Drop Detected (meaning the most recent drops). Finally, you can sort by any Amazon category and they show you in advance how many price drop listings there are for each category.

This is an affiliate link for doing searches on Pricenoia if you want to give me a virtual high-five:

https://pricenoia.com/**?tag=chris** or use this one: http://pricenoia.com

Be sure to check the box for 'Hide fake drops'. When enabled, it only shows price drops from the previous lowest price in the last 30 days.

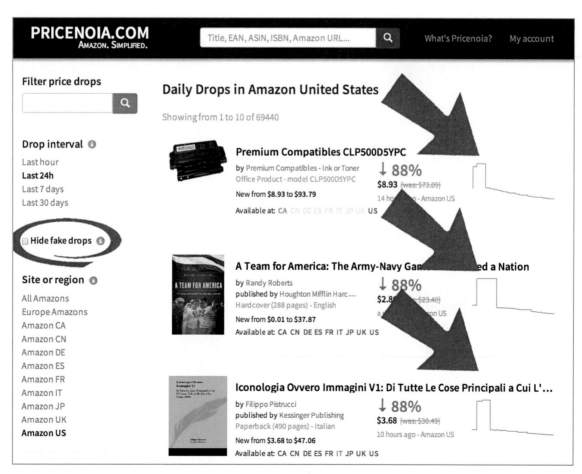

You can see the differences in the price graph reviews when you check the box for Hide Fake Drops:

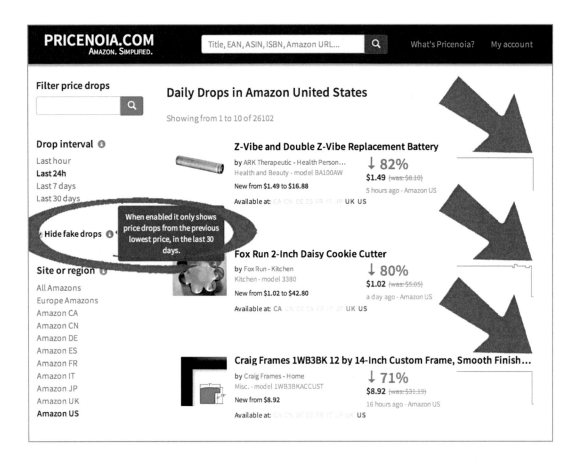

Pricenoia is my favorite place to use the Link Clump extension that you should have installed from Chapter 3. Just choose ALL of the categories at once to open them all up in new tabs. Browse the items and close the tabs when you're through.

Some categories have 'false positives' like Kindle listings and Books & Media items. Also, be careful with categories that you are not approved to sell in. Just because an item has dropped in price, it does not mean that it was actually selling at the previous high price.

When I'm looking at Pricenoia pages, I'm looking for a big drop first, a good graph second. If the top drop is not a big percentage, I'm pretty much closing the tab right away. I'm also looking for items that are NOT selling for a super-low price point such as $4 items that are 75% off selling for $1. I like the 75% off, but you would have to process and sell way too many units to make a substantial profit.

Pricenoia caught the headphones as well. #1 deal/drop on the electronics page:

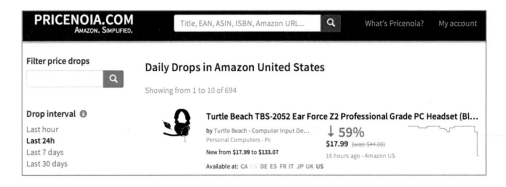

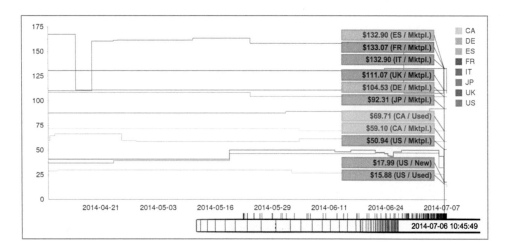

This is where Pricenoia is a little different than the other sites. In one place, you can see the prices on all of the Amazon international sites. You may find a country where an item sells for much more. Do some additional homework to see if that's an opportunity that you want to explore.

		Shipping to ☰ United States (USD) (change)				
Amazon New ①	Marketplace ⑦		Used ②	All ⑩		
Amazon	**Original**		**Your currency**	**Shipping**	**Total**	
.com (used)	$12.91	Good Price	$12.91	$3.99	$16.90	Go »
.com (new)	$17.99	Good Price	$17.99	$3.99	$21.98	Go »
.ca (mktpl.)	C$62.85	Good Price	$59.10	$9.38	$68.48	Go »
.ca (used)	C$74.14	Good Price	$69.71	$9.38	$79.10	Go »
.co.jp (mktpl.)	¥9421	Good Price	$92.31	$14.70	$107.01	Go »
.fr (mktpl.)	€79.51	Good Price	$108.04	$11.55	$119.59	Go »
.de (mktpl.)	€76.93	Good Price	$104.53	$20.78	$125.31	Go »
.co.uk (mktpl.)	£64.79	Good Price	$111.07	$14.54	$125.61	Go »
.es (mktpl.)	€97.81	Good Price	$132.90	$15.16	$148.06	Go »
.it (mktpl.)	€97.81	Good Price	$132.90	$16.52	$149.42	Go »

Pricenoia has the ability to refresh prices. So be sure to check when the last time prices were updated:

Pricenoia also has an alert system. You can set price alerts by price point, by percentage drop, and even for specific countries.

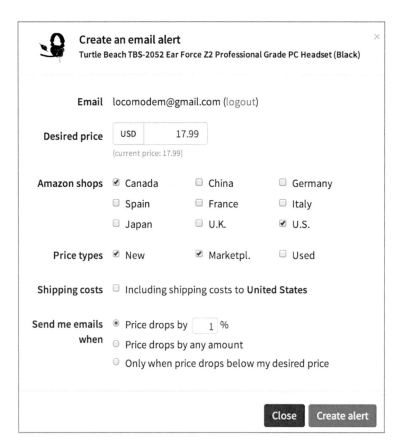

Here is an example of a price drop on Pricenoia.

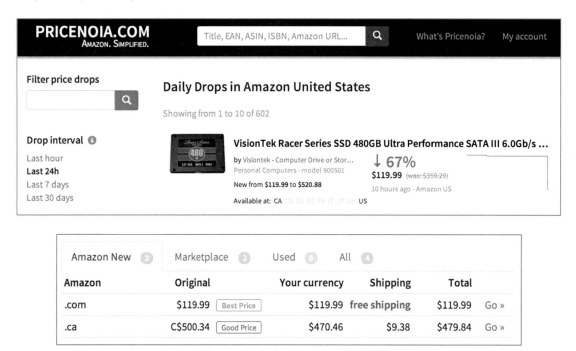

You'll see that the $119.99 price is labeled by Pricenoia as a 'Best Price'. This can be a clue to a low price but it is not always on items that are truly all-time low prices.

Checking the Amazon product page, you can see that the item is backordered and not shipping for 1 to 3 months.

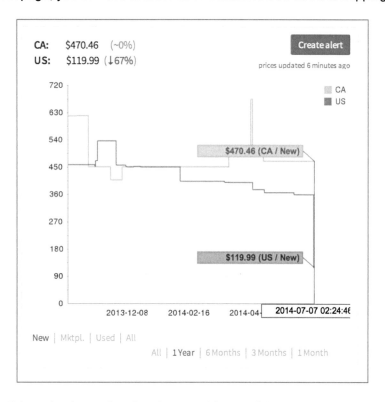

The price history tracked by Pricenoia shows that they have no history of Amazon dropping to this price before. This is a good indication that this is an outlier low price and not something that has happened many times before.

The Keepa price history also shows a very steady price of around $400 with a sharp drop to the current offer of $119.99.

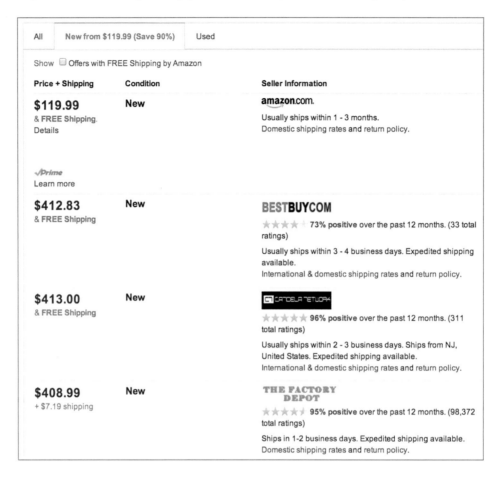

Comparing the offers on the Amazon page shows a consistent price from third party sellers. This is a good indication of the actual market price, but it is not an absolute certainty. Many sellers will list items at inflated prices on Amazon because it is free to add their listings and they just hope that they get a sale. Not all prices on Amazon are necessarily competitive.

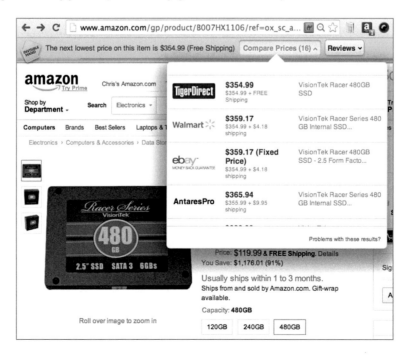

InvisibleHand confirms the prices from other online retailers. This is useful to check because if there are other online retailers listed at a lower price, it could indicate that the prices listed on Amazon are non-competitive.

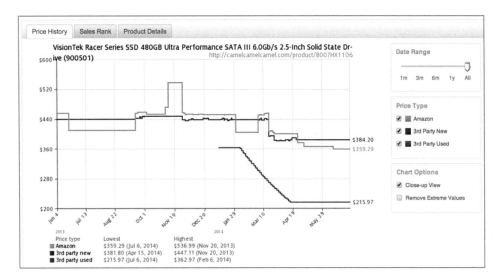

CamelCamelCamel had not even registered the drop yet. That can be good sign that you are one of the first to see the price drop.

Chapter 7 – TheTracktor Movers

TheTracktor: Movers http://thetracktor.com/movers/

Check the default list of Price Change, which is the list of the largest ABSOLUTE price drops detected, but the better list is the Percent Change, which is the list of the largest RELATIVE price drops detected. TheTracktor also lets you sort between Amazon New and Amazon Used and lets you choose your Amazon category.

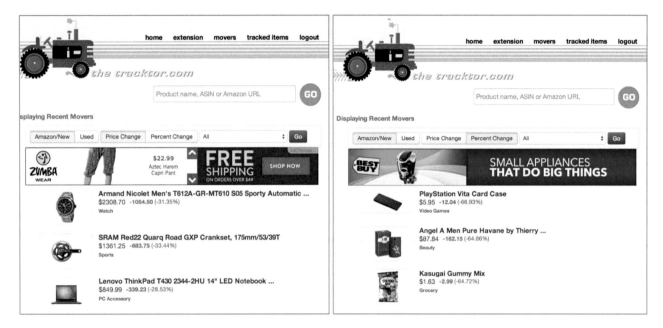

Online Arbitrage - TheTracktor.com, finding deals, quickly evaluating them, setting up alerts

https://www.youtube.com/watch?v=mNuCedHyplo
http://bit.ly/tracktorvideo

Generally, I would say that TheTracktor provides the least amount of truly relevant information when compared to the other sites and extensions, but just because it's not always a winner, it doesn't mean that good deals can't be found using TheTracktor (and deals that are missed by the others). It's so EASY to check these sites that you might as well get in the habit of checking them. It only takes one really good deal to make the effort pay off.

Here is an example from their Movers page:

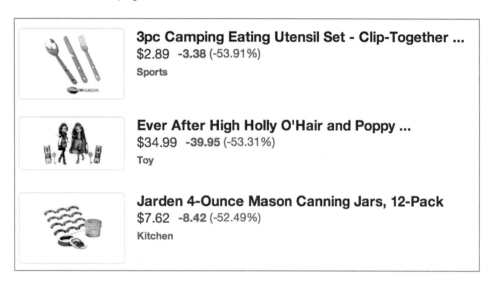

This Ever After High Holly O'Hair and Poppy doll set is showing a significant discount compared to its previously listed price.

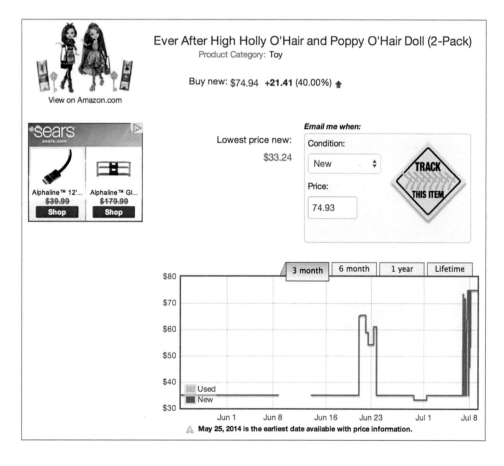

TheTracktor detail page shows definite spikes in price above the $35 price point in the last three months. The previous page showed a price of $34.99 while this page shows an all-time lowest price of $33.24. I would prefer to see the current price MATCHING that price. Remember, even though it's not clearly labeled as such, that price is the all-time lowest price on Amazon according to TheTracktor's records. When they match, it's a sign that it's a great deal. Seeing this information, it's worth a closer look on Amazon:

http://www.Amazon.com/gp/product/B00IVFCESW

You can see that it's offered for sale from Amazon at $34.99 although it is not currently in stock. The Invisible Hand browser extension instantly alerts us that this item is being sold at Wal-Mart for $34.97 with free shipping.

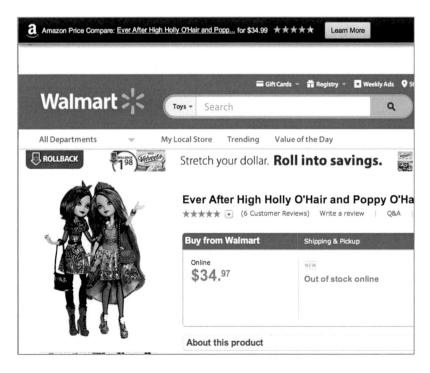

Checking the Wal-Mart website, we find that it is out of stock online but may be available in stores. You'll also notice that the Amazon 1Button App kicks in to remind us of the price on Amazon.com.

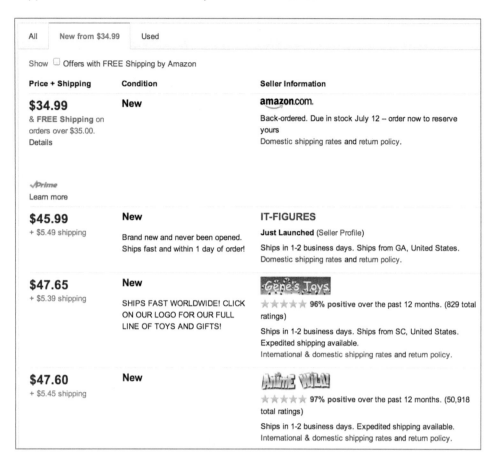

Next step is to take a look at the pricing information on Amazon. You can see from the offers page that the other third party sellers on Amazon are all priced significantly higher than Amazon. This is a great sign that this item has gone out of stock in the past and may go out of stock in the future as many sellers are listed at a non-competitive price. The only reason that they would do this is in anticipation of Amazon going out of stock.

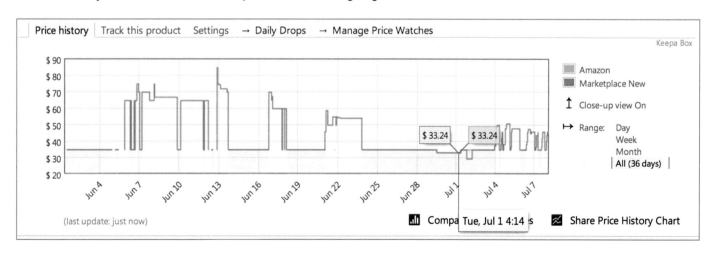

This is confirmed by looking at the Keepa graph. The BLUE spikes in the graph indicate the higher prices from third party sellers when Amazon goes out of stock (represented by the white breaks in the orange on the graph). You can see in the previous month that the item was listed for over $80. In the past week, you can see that Amazon has come in and out of stock frequently. The prices in June were much better than the prices in July, so this deal may have seen better days. Even if you don't find a way to make money on this particular item, I would strongly suggest following the rabbit trails on items like this. See what items are purchased together as well as the items that customers who bought this item also viewed. Take it to the next level and learn this line using the strategies explained in Chapter 10.

From this example, you can start to see how you can use all of the Chrome extensions together to gather the relevant pricing and sales data that you need to make a buying decision (TheTracktor, InvisibleHand, Wal-Mart app, and Keepa).

BONUS TIP

Each sort has it's own custom web address (URL) which means that you can easily bookmark your most useful pages. Make a whole list of bookmarks in Chrome and open them all up at once using Chrome -> Bookmarks -> Open All Bookmarks. If you set up links for the most recent price drops that you find yourself refreshing constantly looking to be first to act on a newly detected price drop, consider using a program that detects changes or updates to web pages or hiring someone to write a program to do this for you. Or you could hire a virtual assistant to monitor websites as one of their daily tasks and email, call, or text you with important deals, updates or news.

Lots more information about this in Chapter 29 - Scaling to help you outsource repetitive tasks and grow your Online Arbitrage business.

Chapter 8 – Social Media (Follow & Search)

There is no denying that social media is more than just a fad; it's now a part of our lives. Now even if you aren't an active social media user, there is no reason that you shouldn't understand how it works in terms of finding deals for Online Arbitrage. People are posting pictures of pretty much everything these days and that includes CLEARANCE DEALS.

Get Notifications from Facebook Pages:

We'll talk more about individual deal sites later in Chapters 20, 21, and 22, but I wanted to show you how to not just LIKE Facebook pages, but to truly follow them using something called Get Notifications. The way Facebook Pages work is that you can LIKE something and then you'll see updates form them in your Facebook Newsfeed. But because Facebook charges people and businesses to promote their posts and their pages to their fans, you won't see everything that the pages that you LIKE actually post. In fact, you'll probably only have about 10% of a page's posts show up in your Facebook Newsfeed. You can get around this and tell Facebook that you want to see everything from a Facebook Page by first LIKING a page and then hovering your mouse over the LIKED button and then clicking on Get Notifications. This will send everything that the page posts to your Facebook Newsfeed. You have to do this process from a full browser, not on a mobile device. Here is an example of what this looks like (more on Ben's Bargains later in Chapter 20):

Bonus Tip:

Look at what other pages Facebook recommends based on your LIKES. You may find pages that you had not heard of before as well as some new sites that no one has heard of yet. These are the Facebook Pages recommended to me when I LIKED Ben's Bargains page:

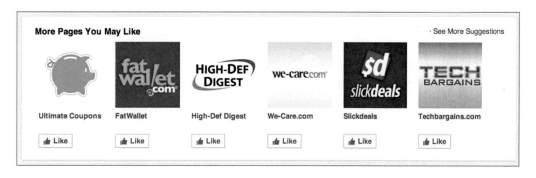

71

Following People on Twitter:

Following people on Twitter is pretty straightforward. Be sure to consider following the Twitter accounts recommended to you based on the accounts you currently follow. You'll likely find some great suggestions of Twitter accounts that you had not thought of.

On Twitter, it's a little bit different to get all notifications, including on mobile, but you can set your account up to be sure that you never miss alerts from certain Twitter accounts.

First, you want to enable your Twitter account to receive MOBILE notifications. To do this, you need to add your cell phone number to your Twitter account and then under Mobile Settings, check the box for 'Tweets from people you've enabled for mobile notifications'.

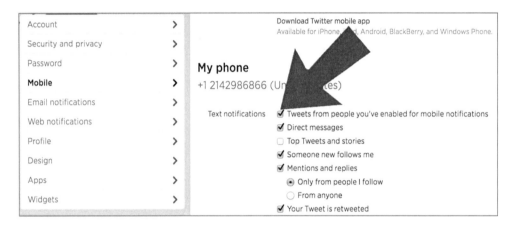

Then, when you go to a Twitter account that you want to follow AND get mobile notifications from, click on the GEAR to see the settings and then click on 'Turn on mobile notifications.'

Use this method for ANY Twitter account that has alerts that you want to know about via text message! Time is a huge factor in Online Arbitrage so getting relevant, actionable tweets FAST can mean the difference between cashing in on a deal and missing a deal.

Remember, even if you miss a deal, knowing about a previous price drop is still very valuable information. Use it to set up price alerts in the event that the price drops again.

Another way to get mobile notifications from Twitter accounts is to simply send text messages to the number 40404.

For example, you can get mobile alerts from Keepa (@Keepa_notifier) by texting **follow @keepa_notifier** to 40404. If you have free or unlimited text messages then this won't cost anything. If you pay for incoming text messages, then this will not be free.

While you're doing this, you might as well follow ScanPower on Twitter the same way.

Just text **follow @ScanPowerNews** to 40404 to get alerts from ScanPower about SpreeCasts, promotions, new features and releases.

https://twitter.com/ScanPowerNews

Just a warning: If you use your personal Twitter account to do this, all your friends (or competitors) will see who you follow. For this reason, you may want to set up a second Twitter account just for following deal sites. All you need is an active email address to set up an additional Twitter account. Here's a trick to keeping multiple accounts under one email address: If I'm using chris@scanpower.com for my Twitter account and I want to make a second Twitter account without using another email address (that I'd have to check), I can use the email address chris+secondtwitter@scanpower.com as my email address. Any email sent here will still go to chris@scanpower.com. You can add +ANYTHING to your email address this way. Twitter will see this as a new, unique email address. You can use this strategy on any site that requires a unique email address for multiple accounts.

Here is Twitter's page on their SMS Notifications:

https://support.twitter.com/groups/34-apps-sms-and-mobile/topics/153-twitter-via-sms/articles/14020-twitter-for-sms-basic-features

There are a lot of tricks that you can use with Twitter that most people don't know about.

SEARCH - Twitter

https://twitter.com/search

Twitter search is ridiculously powerful in seeing what people are talking about online. It's 100% free and is a marketer's dream come true. You can search for and see what individuals are talking about at any time. This includes products, toys, and brands, as well as stores and websites. The trick is to search for information relevant to your Online Arbitrage business. But what types of searches would those be?

Well it's certainly no secret that pumpkin spice flavor has been added to more and more products. Given this popularity, there are bound to be new products coming out and some of those products may represent Online Arbitrage opportunities.

A simple search in Twitter for search term 'pumpkin spice' brings up suggested searches. These are based on trending topics and search volume; therefore, they are the most relevant results. Use these results to your advantage to see what people are talking about.

A quick Google search for 'pumpkin spice oreos' brings up this article about their impending release:

http://consumerist.com/2014/08/18/pumpkin-spice-oreos-this-could-really-be-happening/

You could now monitor a few websites to see if they will get them in stock and you can be first to market. If you are unsure about a product, you can do a search for other variations on products, use Google to figure out when they came out, then cross reference Amazon pricing information using Keepa or CamelCamelCamel. See what worked in the past as well as what didn't. You can even try to spot patterns in the market prices coming to equilibrium. Did prices start high and trail off over a period of months? Days? There is so much historical data at your fingertips and all you have to do is use it to help you make better buying decisions.

This is just one example of searching for trends on Twitter. Search for popular toys such as the ones on Amazon's Movers & Shakers, Bestsellers, New Releases, and Most Wished For. See what people are talking about and gain valuable insight about the current state of the market.

SEARCH - Instagram

Well, we all know that people love to talk about themselves and that everyone loves a good deal. Put those things together with a little bit of social media like Instagram, and you have people bragging online, posting pictures, and using hashtags like #toysrus, #walmartclearance, and #90percentoff (same types of searches on Twitter, too).

Searching Instagram using the Instagram website is unfortunately not useful. Thankfully, there are other sites that will allow you to do this.

You can also search Instagram on your mobile phone right through the app. The coolest part is that Instagram will auto-suggest additional search terms based on whatever you enter.

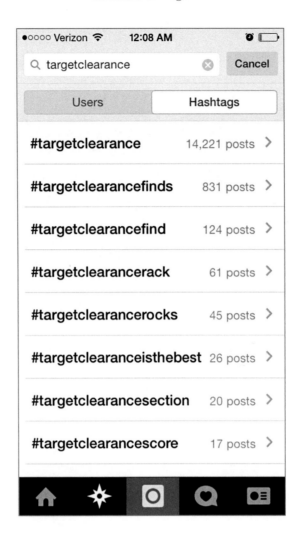

So you may have a good search term, but realize there may be other terms that are better or even more refined to find exactly the types of posts that you are looking for.

The app also shows you how many posts have used that hashtag. Searching using these other search terms may help you find pictures and posts that no one else finds if they are only searching for the most obvious or generic hashtags.

Another searchable Instagram site is IconoSquare: http://iconosquare.com

Here is an example search: targetclearance

http://iconosquare.com/viewer.php - /search/targetclearance

Just like we saw on the mobile app search, you'll get suggestions for other hashtags that you may not have thought to search for.

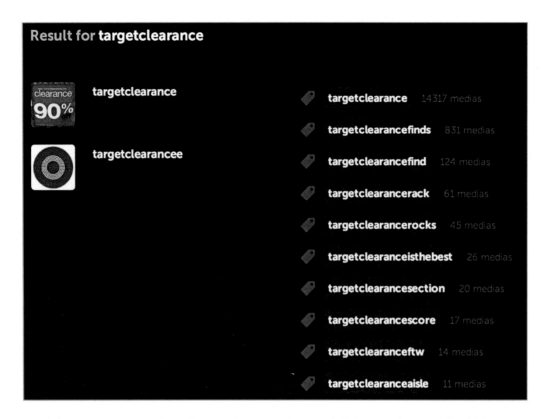

Here's an example of an Instagram post for a Target clearance item: a $70 item being sold for $20 in stores. Knowing that this item is on clearance in the stores, you may want to check www.target.com to see if this item is sold online and if the price is the same. If not, you may add it to your shopping list for the next time you go to Target.

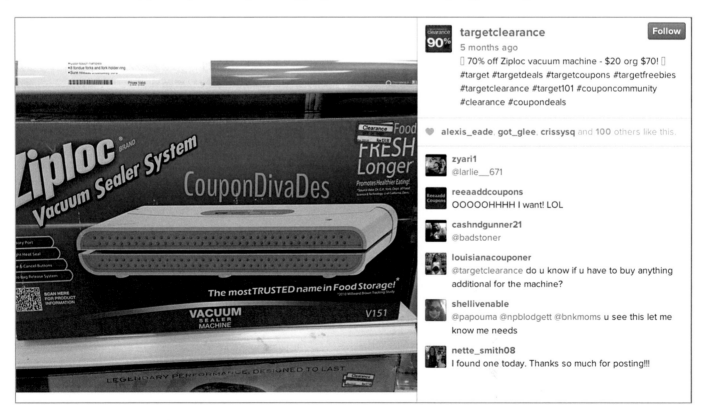

Also, be sure to look at the OTHER hashtags that the poster used to get ideas for other terms that you want to search for.

Here is another site that can be used to search Instagram: http://www.gramfeed.com

Example used: walmartclearance:

http://www.gramfeed.com/instagram/tags - walmartclearance

GramFeed also shows you related/recommended search terms, but they also show you a map so that you can see exactly where people are using these hashtags. The more people using a hashtag, the more popular that hashtag is.

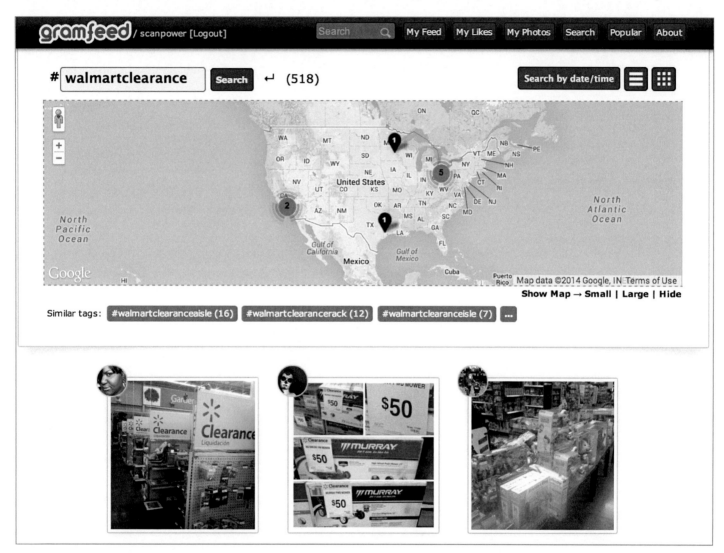

Want to learn an awesome way to use your phone to virtually "scan" pictures of items and find their Amazon prices? There is an app called Amazon FLOW. More about how this works later in Chapter 37.

I could do the same types of searches for any social media site (including Facebook). You should, too. ☺

We'll talk more about scaling, outsourcing, and hiring virtual assistants (VAs) later in Chapter 29. These types of searches would be an excellent task to outsource.

Chapter 9 – Google is your Friend

Google is an amazing resource to do Online Arbitrage research from the comfort of your own home.

Google advanced search filters: https://support.google.com/mail/answer/7190

NOT ROCKET SCIENCE TIP:

Find popular items on Amazon that are on the Best Sellers or the Movers & Shakers pages. Use Keepa to see items that Amazon goes out of stock on. Find the manufacturer from the Amazon product pages. Google them. Contact them to become a distributor.

Simple Google Search #1:

Just take the Amazon product name and click Search.

Simple Google Search #2:

"product name" + "retailer" (where 'product name' is from Amazon and 'retailer' is Target, Wal-Mart, Toys R Us, etc.)

Simple Google Search #3:

"product name" + "vendor or manufacturer" (where 'product name' is from Amazon and 'vendor' is the company that makes the item.) This is usually listed on the Amazon product pages. Or you can also look on the physical packaging of the product. Sometimes Google will find this all by itself.

This is an example of a difficult search that was solved with a couple of Google tricks. It was posted in the ScannerMonkey® Facebook Group and shared here with permission:

https://www.facebook.com/groups/ScannerMonkey®/permalink/325963077581880/

For whatever reason, this item was not showing up on Amazon by UPC or title search. Amazon FLOW (Chapter 37) also did not find this item. But it's Google to the rescue!

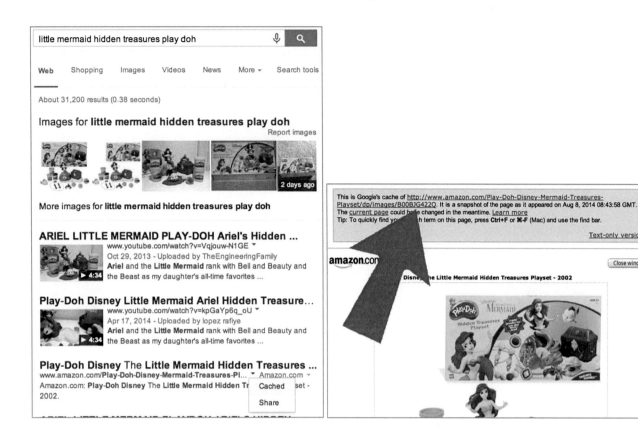

You can see that Google still had a cached copy of an old Amazon image page (not even an actual product page). From this page, you can find the ASIN and if you can find the ASIN, you can find the Amazon product page!

Bonus Tip: Amazon links can always be formatted as simply http://www.amazon.com/dp/B00BJG422Q where B00BJG422Q can be any ASIN.

For more information about ScannerMonkey®, please visit http://ScannerMonkey®.com/why-join/ and check out Chapter 38 near the end of this book for information about BOLOs and the BOLO Exchange.

Google Image Search: http://images.google.com/

If you are having trouble finding a matching product using Google with keywords, consider trying a Google Image Search. Save an image from the Internet or grab an image using screen capture software. Then, instead of entering search terms, you upload an image by clicking on the camera icon in the search bar on the Google home page. Google then compares the image to images in search. Sometimes you can find old Amazon product pages this way.

If you need a screenshot program for Chrome, try Awesome Screenshot:

http://awesomescreenshot.com/

https://chrome.google.com/webstore/detail/awesome-screenshot-captur/alelhddbbhepgpmgidjdcjakblofbmce?hl=en

EASY LINK: http://bit.ly/awesomescreenshot

Google Shopping: https://www.google.com/shopping

Google Shopping is a filtered Google search result focused on shopping. For this reason, it can be a useful place to check results. If you are having trouble finding matching retailers using the regular Google search because of generic search terms, Google Shopping may help you find what you are looking for. WARNING: currently Google Shopping does NOT return Amazon listings in their Google Shopping search results.

Amazon to Google + IMAGES

Let's walk through how sometimes you can even use Google Image Search to find the correct product matches.

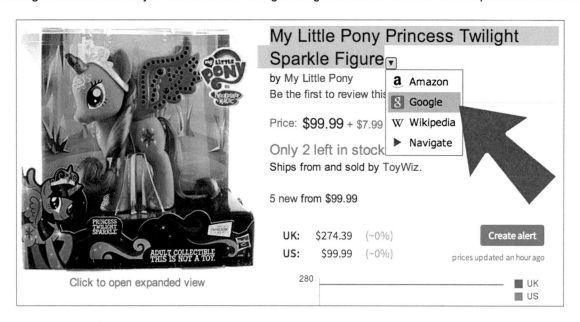

Using Context Search, we highlight the product title and choose Google form the drop down menu.

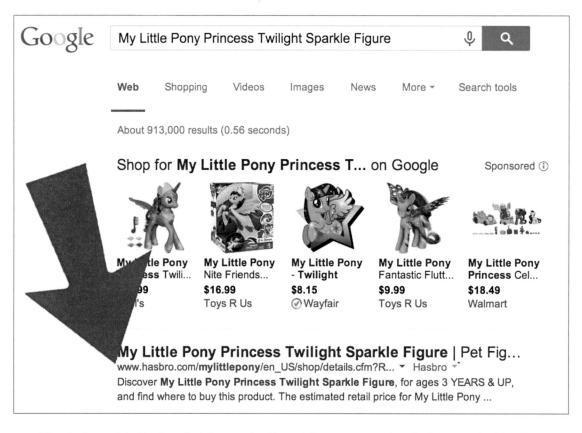

The first result is Hasbro, but the product is not the same version that we are looking for.

So instead of a regular Google search, click on the Images link.

And you can quickly see a matching image and the site that the image is from. This is important because we want to find sites that are selling this item, not just reviewing or talking about this item.

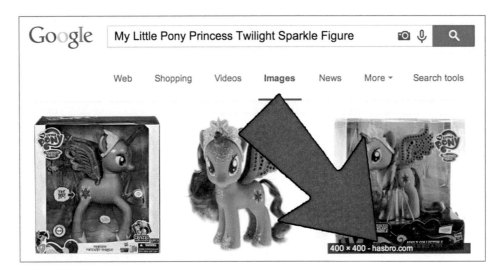

Clicking through to the website shows us the correct product match from Hasbro

The Hasbro site is even kind enough to give a link for Where To Buy this item. Clicking through and entering our zip code, we see the results of Target, Wal-Mart and Kmart. With phone numbers and addresses listed, you can contact the stores ahead of time to verify inventory as well as map out the most efficient route.

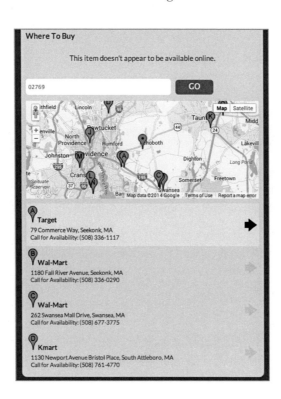

<u>Learning more about My Little Pony toys from Toys R Us, Target, Amazon, and Hasbro</u>

<u>https://www.youtube.com/watch?v=l1w-XifxJDQ</u>
<u>http://bit.ly/ponyvideo</u>

Chapter 10 – Sourcing on Amazon.com

This is going to be a long chapter. There is A LOT that can be done on Amazon.com in terms of sourcing as well as product research. Knowing how Amazon works and how you can search can give you the upper hand on your competition.

First things first: You can't use your Amazon Prime benefits for resale!

https://www.facebook.com/groups/scanpower/permalink/506189276149670/

 Bryan Young Update:

I just got off the phone with a member of the Amazon Executive Team (not sure what that means, but it sounds very authoritative), and this is what he said. First off, he apologized for any confusion, and acknowledged that they're aware that some of their reps have been giving conflicting information. Amazon Prime benefits are to be reserved for personal use only. If you buy something and you intend to use it for personal reasons, but then decide to sell it later on Amazon this is ok. But, if you buy something with the intent to resell it on Amazon, this is in violation of the Prime Membership Terms & Conditions.

Karin Isgur Bergsagel, Chris Green and others were right! Sorry to "Stir-the-pot", but I'm glad that this issue has been resolved. Thanks Karin for all the info and correspondences that you have been providing over the last week.

May 28 at 3:58pm · Like · 👍 2

To purchase items from Amazon that you intend to resell, you should open up a NEW Amazon account that does NOT have Amazon Prime benefits. Use this account to make your purchases. Simple as that. If you use your Amazon Prime account to buy things for resale, and you lose your Amazon Prime privileges for doing so, please do not come crying to me.

Bonus Tip:

When buying from Amazon for resale, you'll often encounter quantity limits. This can happen when an item has shown recent popularity. I'm not sure exactly what triggers this restriction from Amazon, but there are often no quantity limits early on before an item becomes popular and ends up on deal sites. It's very advantageous to find deals early for this reason. The catch-22 to this is that by buying items from Amazon in quantity, you may be triggering the item to have quantity limits.

You might as well use Amazon Smile to support a charity organization using your Amazon Online Arbitrage purchases:

http://smile.Amazon.com/

Suppressed Buy Box:

Sometimes you'll see items that do not have a Buy Box (the big yellow 'Add to Cart' button on Amazon product pages). This happens when the offers are priced ABOVE the MSRP (manufacturer's suggest retail price). In this example, you can see that Amazon even tells customers that the MRSP is only $34.99 even though the lowest priced offer is $49.97.

What can we learn from this simple information? We now know that the prices on Amazon are inflated, over-retail prices. The next logical step for the Online Arbitrage seller is to find out where to get these items and then sell them on Amazon for a profit. Use the Chrome extensions you installed to do this (as well as Google).

Here is a short video explaining this in additional detail:

Online Arbitrage - Amazon Suppressed Buy Box

http://youtu.be/jb6YzdGGidk
http://bit.ly/suppressedbuybox

The TWO Amazon Windows:

Just like with Keepa, where we were looking for two types of circumstances (Amazon sold out with third party sellers selling at higher prices, and Amazon selling at a very low price), we are looking for those same types of scenarios when sourcing products form Amazon.com.

Window #1:

Amazon is OUT OF STOCK. In this scenario, price is set by the supply and demand of the third party marketplace. When a product has high demand and low supply (both factors backed up by Amazon selling out), then there exists a WINDOW of time where sellers can sell their inventory to meet the demand at an inflated, over-retail price. This price is often very profitable. The window can close quickly when Amazon gets more inventory in stock with no guarantees that they will go out of stock again. In these scenarios, it is important to SELL while the price is high. Over time, price will normalize back to MSRP as supply catches up with demand. Windows like this are also very attractive to other sellers and if there are profits to be made, competition will find the items.

This window also represents an opportunity to buy inventory FROM Amazon when they are in stock.

Window #2:

Amazon is selling at an artificially low price. In this scenario, Amazon has decided to drop their price to a level where the item can be bought, turned around, and sold for a profit (sometimes at the market price).

One reason that you can sometimes buy products from Amazon at these low prices is because Amazon will break MAP (Minimum Advertised Price) to price match another online retailer who broke MAP first. Amazon will not break MAP first but they will break MAP in a heartbeat if a competitor breaks MAP.

Bonus Tip:

Report Lower Prices to Amazon

Why does Amazon drop price to silly low prices? Prices low enough to turn a profit? Often they are price matching a competitor who is breaking MAP pricing. Use Google Shopping to find these. If you catch them first, report them to Amazon in hopes that they drop price as well. Then you can also buy from the other map breaker to resell on Amazon.

In the Product Details section of any Amazon Product Page (where the sales rank is usually located), there is a link to tell Amazon about a lower price. Click on it to report a website or local store selling the item for less. Sometimes you can trigger an Amazon price drop yourself.

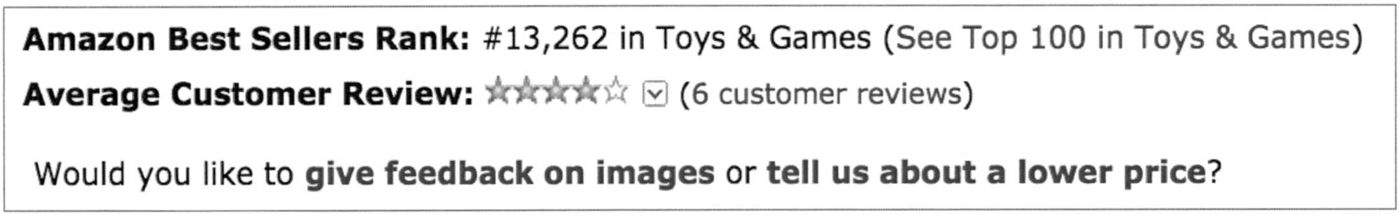

Amazon Best Sellers Rank: #13,262 in Toys & Games (See Top 100 in Toys & Games)
Average Customer Review: ★★★★☆ ☑ (6 customer reviews)

Would you like to **give feedback on images** or **tell us about a lower price?**

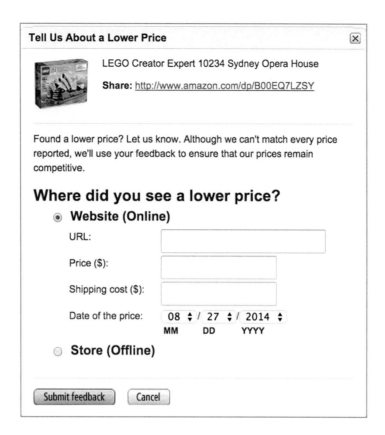

Amazon Top 100 Lists:

Amazon has several Top 100 lists that can provide online sellers with amazing information. Each of these lists is available in the different Amazon categories. We'll take a close look at the ones for the Toys & Games category, but be sure to look at the pages for the other categories as well.

Movers & Shakers

http://www.Amazon.com/gp/movers-and-shakers/toys-and-games/

The biggest gainers in sales rank over the past 24 hours. Updated hourly.

Why I like this list:

This list is really awesome. The Movers & Shakers list shows items that have a spike in sales. Two things can cause this: a surge in demand (maybe a new movie just came out), or a drop in price. Sometimes these price drops are low enough to purchase items for resale.

The bad part about Movers & Shakers is that often by the time an item hits the Movers & Shakers, the best part of the deal is over. Maybe the item currently has a great sales rank because of the surge in recent sales but it's no longer available at the lower price that caused that surge. No worries--use the price trackers to find the low price that sent the item up the Movers & Shakers page and then set up your price alerts in the event that the item comes back in stock.

Best Sellers

http://www.Amazon.com/Best-Sellers-Toys-Games/zgbs/toys-and-games/

The most popular products based on sales. Updated hourly.

Why I like this list:

Knowing which items are the best selling items on Amazon is very valuable information. Amazon is pretty good at forecasting demand and keeping items in stock, but they are not perfect. Which items do you think Amazon may run out of stock on? Often it's the best sellers. When Amazon is out of stock, you may have an opportunity to sell those items, sometimes at an over-retail price.

I also like this item for complementary product research. If remote control helicopters are spending a long time on the Best Sellers list, then that should give you a huge clue over what customers are searching for and buying.

Also check this list for items with a suppressed Buy Box and then set up price alerts.

New Releases
http://www.Amazon.com/gp/new-releases/toys-and-games/

The best-selling new and future releases. Updated hourly.

Why I like this list:

It's important to know the newest product in any category. To be in the business long term, you have to truly learn the business and the products. Knowing about a product or a line of product months ahead of your competition is an awesome advantage. Check for the newest items, check the price history graphs to see if Amazon is able to stay in stock or not.

Most Wished For

http://www.Amazon.com/gp/most-wished-for/toys-and-games/

The products most often added to Wishlists and Registries. Updated daily.

Why I like this list:

Knowing which items have strong demand from customers is always valuable information when deciding what types of products to sell on Amazon. While adding an item to a wishlist isn't the exact same as actually buying the item, it can be a great indicator of items that will see a spike in sales, especially around gift giving times (not just Christmas either; think Valentine's Day, Mother's Day, etc.).

They also have pages for **Most Gifted**

http://www.Amazon.com/gp/most-gifted/toys-and-games/

And for **Top Rated Items**

http://www.Amazon.com/gp/top-rated/toys-and-games/

Amazon DEALS:

Amazon has several types of 'deals' that they promote regularly. They include Gold Box, Lightning Deals, Daily Deals, and others. At the time of this writing, only Lightning Deals are listed as NOT for resale by Amazon (this could change).

No Lightning Deals for resale!

http://www.Amazon.com/gp/help/customer/display.html/ref=gb1h_rsa_c-2_1842_?nodeId=201134260

Lightning Deals are nontransferable, not for resale, and not redeemable for cash.

EASY LINK: http://bit.ly/AmazonDealsResale

Here is an Amazon Lightning Deal that was posted on FatWallet:

http://www.fatwallet.com/forums/expired-deals/1370022/

Some people voted this down RED either because they were trying to hide the deal from others by making people not click on it because they'd think it was not a good deal, or because they had trouble placing orders and getting them to go through. Comments in the FatWallet thread can be very useful as well. They can let you know of available coupons or free shipping codes.

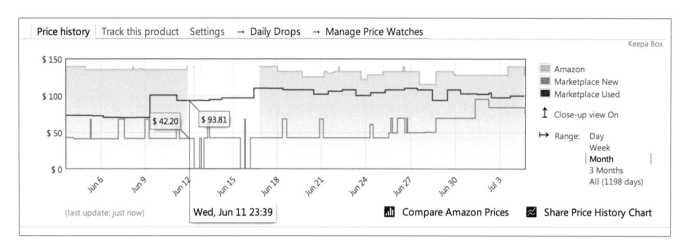

Amazon Gold Box and Lightning Deals: http://www.Amazon.com/gp/goldbox

Movers & Shakers, Keepa, Alerts, Frustration Free Packaging, Oversize, and MORE

http://youtu.be/OSKkJbjYsuU
http://bit.ly/dealexample

If you find one item that has dropped in price, there are likely others. Check for products in the same line or the same category. Rarely will one random item be marked down.

Understanding Frustration Free Packaging, ASIN Variations

Check out these examples: http://www.Amazon.com/Fisher-Price-Jake-Never-Land-Pirates/dp/B00DYM5R40/

Check out the variations on the AZ page showing FF and retail packaging:

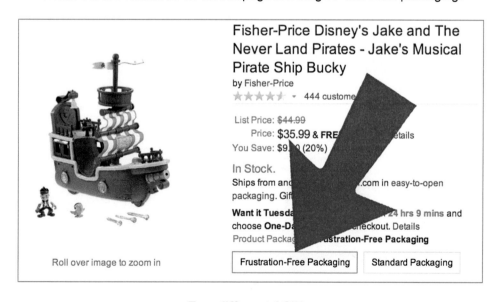

Two different ASINs:

Frustration-Free Packaging: B00DYM5R40

Retail Packaging: B0077NCEWA

Two different ASINs = two sales rank = two Keepa graphs so if you want to check historical prices on the toy in general, you have to check BOTH.

Frustration-Free Packaging is the default on search if there is a qualifying offer. This is a powerful position to be in. Many customers won't even see competitive offers from retail packaged sellers.

Frustration-Free Packaging Keepa price history graph:

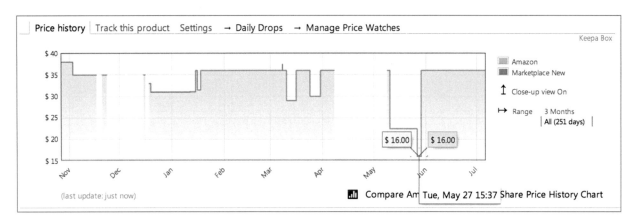

Retail Packaging Keepa price history graph:

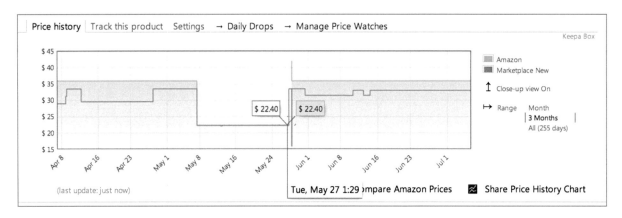

Frustration-Free Packaging CamelCamelCamel price history graph:

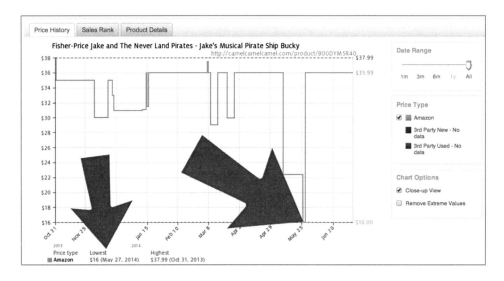

http://camelcamelcamel.com/Fisher-Price-Jake-Never-Land-Pirates/product/B00DYM5R40

Retail Packaging CamelCamelCamel price history graph:

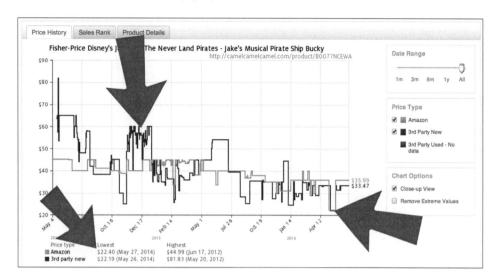

http://camelcamelcamel.com/Fisher-Price-Disneys-Jake-Never-Pirates/product/B0077NCEWA

Frustration-Free Packaging Certification Requirements

http://www.Amazon.com/gp/help/customer/display.html?ie=UTF8&nodeId=201221950

The Amazon Frustration-Free Packaging (FFP) program allows sellers who manufacture and sell their own branded products on Amazon.com to have their products evaluated by Amazon's packaging certification lab for FFP compliance. Movers & shakers and learning a product line

Online Arbitrage - Quickly evaluating items from the Amazon Movers & Shakers list – TOYS

http://youtu.be/-2XGQYhc5Dl
http://bit.ly/quicktoys

Bonus Tip:

Amazon Movers & Shakers to Buy Box Suppression Deals

Here's an item ranked number three on the Amazon Movers & Shakers page.

Taking a close look, we can see that Amazon is often out of stock on this product. When they are in stock, they sell for $14.95. When Amazon is out of stock, The market price had been jumping up to ~$80 + shipping.

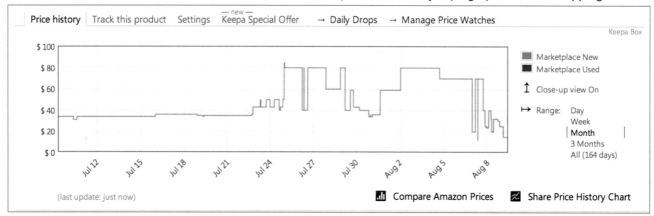

This is confirmed by CamelCamelCamel.

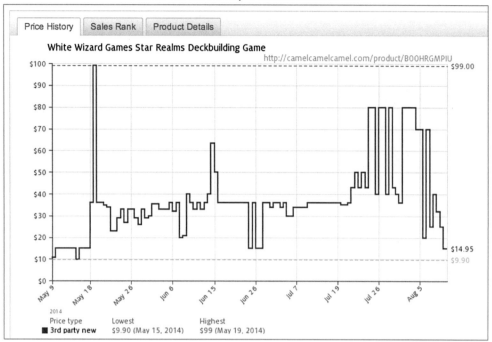

Despite the inflated, over-retail price, the item has a great sales rank.

Now that we have found one item that sells for an over-retail price when Amazon is out of stock, we should take a look at products listed under 'Customers Who Bought This Item Also Bought'.

If there is no price under the item, this means that there is no Buy Box. This is a huge clue. Items with a suppressed Buy Box are often selling for prices well above their MSRP. Once you find them, you can then search to find out where you can get them or you can set up price alerts for when Amazon comes back in stock at the MSRP.

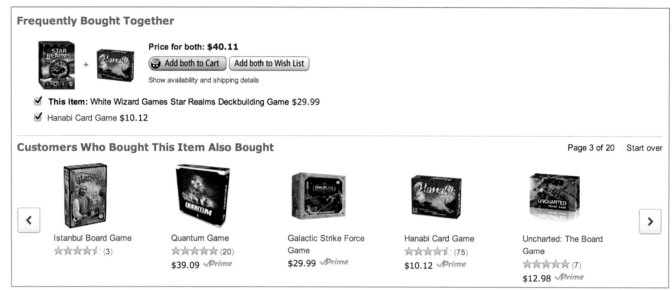

Frequently Bought Together

Price for both: **$40.11**

Add both to Cart   Add both to Wish List

Show availability and shipping details

☑ **This item:** White Wizard Games Star Realms Deckbuilding Game $29.99
☑ Hanabi Card Game $10.12

Customers Who Bought This Item Also Bought

Page 3 of 20   Start over

| Istanbul Board Game ★★★★½ (3) | Quantum Game ★★★★★ (20) $39.09 ✓Prime | Galactic Strike Force Game $29.99 ✓Prime | Hanabi Card Game ★★★★½ (75) $10.12 ✓Prime | Uncharted: The Board Game ★★★★★ (7) $12.98 ✓Prime |

We easily find an item with a suppressed Buy Box.

Istanbul Board Game
by Alderac Entertainment Group
★★★★½ ▾ 3 customer reviews

Note: This item is only available from third-party sellers (see all offers.)

Available from these sellers.

- Highest quality components with wooden bits and beautiful red ruby pieces
- Created by famed game designer Rudiger Dorn
- Gorgeous artwork by Andreas Resch

6 new from $79.99

http://www.amazon.com/Alderac-Entertainment-Group-5809-Istanbul/dp/B00IVF4UK2

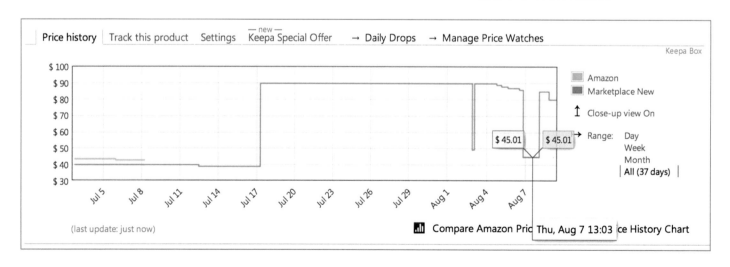

The Keepa price history graph clearly shows that Amazon is out of stock more often than being in stock on this item. When they are in stock, they sell for $45.01. When they are out of stock, the item sells for $90 + shipping.

96

Amazon Movers & Shakers - NERF Toys on sale

http://youtu.be/ajXWvlU4pyw
http://bit.ly/nerfsale

In this example, we take a look at the steps to follow when a new item shows on the Amazon Movers & Shakers page.

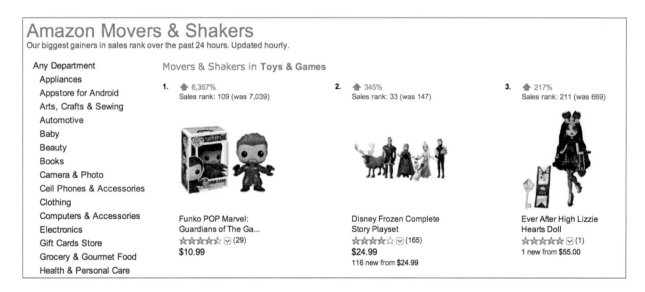

This item deserves a closer look for a few reasons. First, it's shot up to #3 on the Amazon Toys Movers & Shakers page. Second, it has a suppressed Buy Box. Compare it to the Frozen set that has TWO prices showing. Remember, suppressed Buy Box strongly indicates that the item is being sold significantly higher than MSRP. Once you know this, you just have to find out where to get them.

Ever After High Lizzie Hearts Doll
by Ever After High

★★★★★ ▾　1 customer review

Note: This item is only available from third-party sellers (see all offers.)

Available from these sellers.

- Lizzie Hearts, daughter of the Queen of Hearts, is excited about her destiny and a member of the Ever After Royals
- The posable doll is dressed in a spellbinding outfit that takes a modern spin off her mother's legacy
- Her exquisite outfit has rich details, luxe fabrics and spellbinding sparkling accents
- A love-ly heart theme is carried through her queenly accessories
- She also comes with a doll stand, doll hairbrush and bookmark that tells her side of the story

1 new from $55.00

Roll over image to zoom in

The Amazon product page confirms that there is no Buy Box.

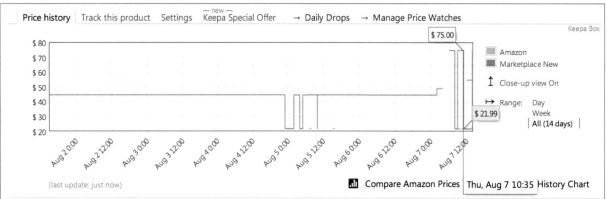

Keepa shows us that Amazon has had this in stock (although very infrequently) at $21.99. The Marketplace price when Amazon is out of stock was pretty steady around $45 + shipping and as high as $75 + shipping more recently.

So what are the next steps? Set up price alerts from Amazon at $21.99 using Keepa alerts (or any other price tracker) as well as Google the product title to see if you can find what retailers carry this product. Also, look at other products in this line to see if the entire line is hot or just certain figures. THIS IS REALLY JUST THIS EASY.

This is how easy it is to spot hot toys using the Amazon Movers & Shakers pages. This one hits #3.

Checking the Amazon product page and InvisibleHand pops up telling me that this item sells for $12.97 and $12.99 from Wal-Mart and Target, both online and in stores.

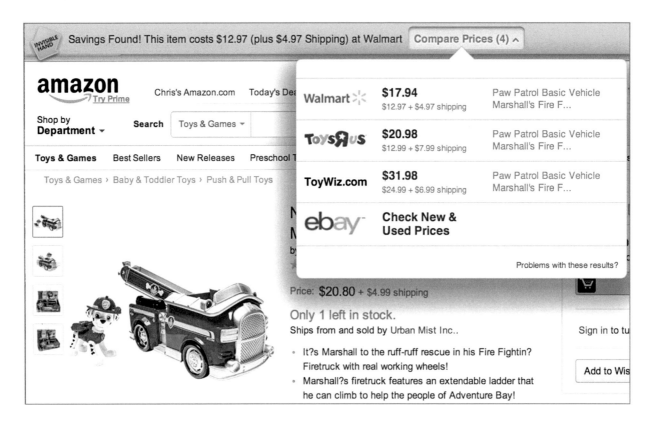

You can also check the Keepa data to see that Amazon recently had it in stock at $12.99. This is very likely what sent it up the Movers & Shakers list. A lower price will always lead to increased sales.

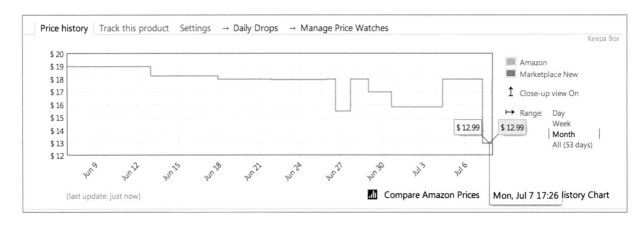

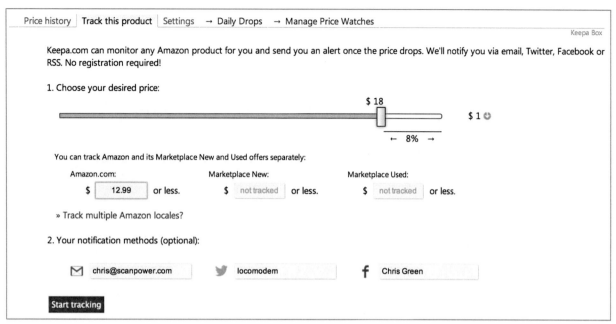

So set up your price alerts at $12.99 from Amazon if this is an item that you would want to purchase at the Amazon price.

Actually pretty easy, huh? Next steps? How about checking the Frequently Bought Together items:

Along with the Customers Who Bought This Item Also Bought items:

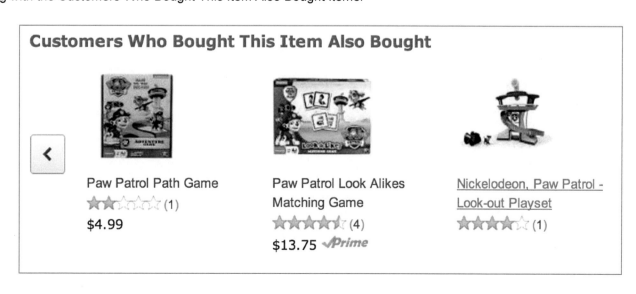

And what do we see here? An item with a suppressed Buy Box. You know we're going to take a closer look at that!

No Buy Box indicates that the prices from third party merchants are significantly higher than MSRP. Now we just have to figure out what MSRP is along with where this item can be purchased (and if Amazon has sold it).

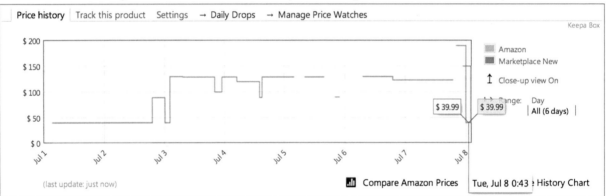

Keepa gives us everything that we need in one place. You can see that Amazon has been out of stock on this item, but when they are in stock, they sell this item for $39.99.

By now, setting up price alerts for when Amazon comes back in stock should become standard procedure.

Product Details

Product Dimensions: 10.5 x 15.5 x 14.5 inches ; 2.2 pounds

Shipping Weight: 3.4 pounds

Shipping: This item is also available for shipping to select countries outside the U.S.

Shipping Advisory: This item must be shipped separately from other items in your order.

ASIN: B00J3LXLNA

Item model number: 6022481

Manufacturer recommended age: 36 months - 8 years

Batteries 3 Nonstandard Battery batteries required. (included)

Amazon Best Sellers Rank: #13,195 in Toys & Games (See Top 100 in Toys & Games)
#66 in Toys & Games > Baby & Toddler Toys > **Push & Pull Toys**

Of course you want to do your due diligence and check the Amazon sales rank before buying any significant quantity of inventory. Here you can see that it has a great sales rank.

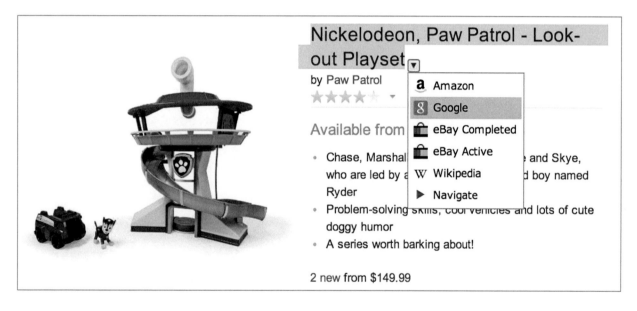

Nickelodeon, Paw Patrol - Look-out Playset
by Paw Patrol
★★★★

Available from

- Chase, Marshal   e and Skye, who are led by a   d boy named Ryder
- Problem-solving skills, cool vehicles and lots of cute doggy humor
- A series worth barking about!

2 new from $149.99

Amazon
Google
eBay Completed
eBay Active
Wikipedia
▶ Navigate

Now if we want to see where else this item is being sold, we can use Context Search to highlight the keywords in the title and then choose Google from the drop down menu.

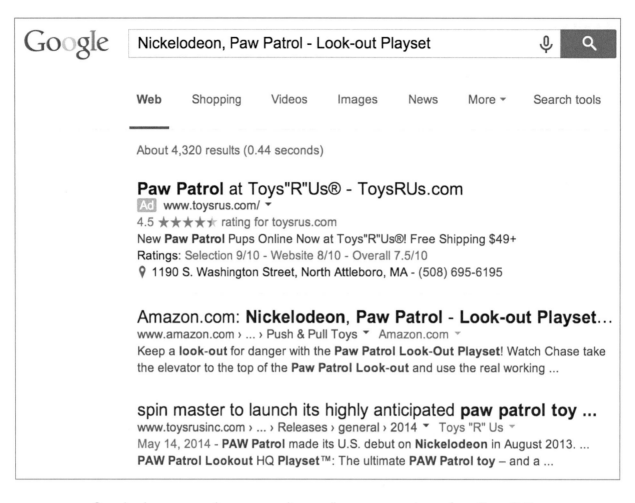

Google shows us an Amazon result as well as a press release from Toys R Us.

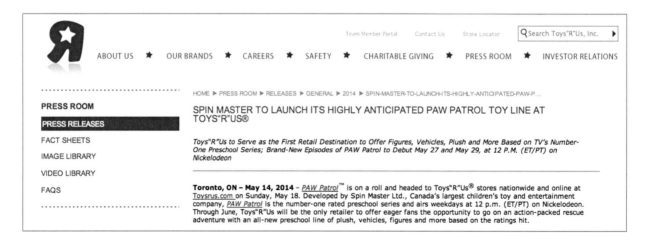

Reading this press release gives us some great information about the release of Paw Patrol toys at Toys R Us.

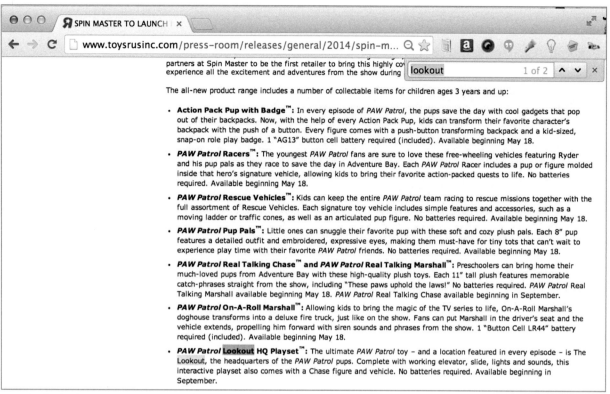

A quick way to find what you are looking for on pages with a lot of text is to press COMMAND – F or CTRL – F to open the 'FIND' function in the browser. Then enter the keywords that you are looking for. In this case, I wanted to see if there was anything about the LOOKOUT playset. I was able to find it quickly without having to read the entire page.

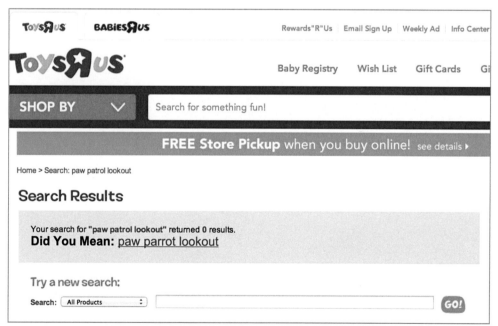

Knowing now that Toys R Us is going to be selling the Paw Patrol Lookout Playset, you can go to their website and search. At the time, there were no search results. But you could certainly bookmark this page and check it frequently so that you would know right away when they were made available for order. In Chapter 28 we talk about tools to monitor webpages for any types of changes. This would be a good example of something that you would be interested in tracking.

UPDATE

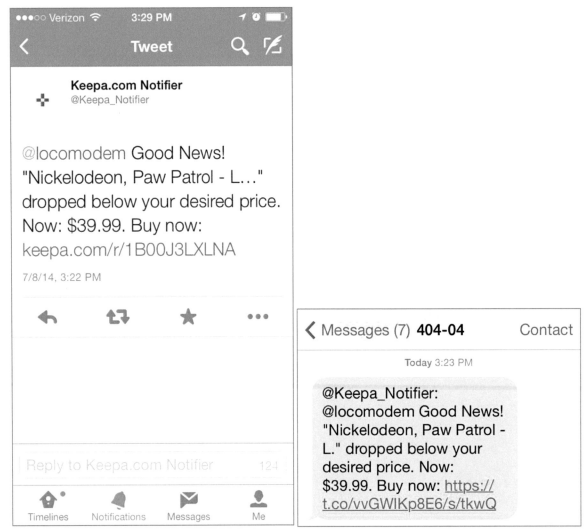

So I had previously set up my Keepa price alert to send me a Tweet when Amazon came in stock at $39.99 on the Paw Patrol Lookout Playset. And because I set up my Keepa Tweets to also be sent as SMS text message, I got a text at the same time.

Checking the Amazon product page shows the set available from Amazon.com (although not for immediate shipment).

Take a look at your current competition before making a large purchase. You can see that the prices are still significantly higher than the Amazon price (selling at MSRP).

But how many does Amazon have in stock? How many should you buy? A simple trick is to add the item to you cart, then edit the quantity to 999. Amazon will edit your cart to show the maximum allowed.

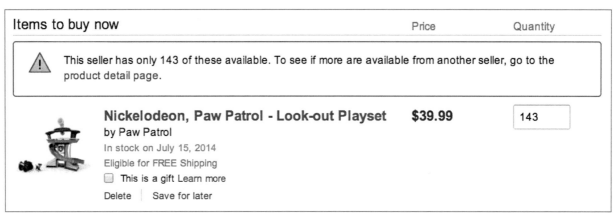

Remember, Amazon does not always have purchase limits on items until AFTER they have ended up on the Movers & Shakers pages or have been purchased in large quantities by resellers. No one knows exactly what triggers have to go off for Amazon to start enforcing quantity limits. If you can spot deals early, you can often make larger purchases and tie up quantity before Amazon imposes these quantity limits. This is a HUGE advantage over your potential competition. Once Amazon enforces purchase limits, you'll be limited to ordering two per week (unless Amazon changes this).

 Important messages about items in your Cart:

1 item has been moved to the Saved for Later section of your Cart.
The following items are no longer available from the seller you selected. We have moved the following items to the saved Items section of your Shopping Cart:

- Nickelodeon, Paw Patrol - Look-out Playset ▾

What happens if you don't act fast on the 143 items in your cart? They get bought by someone else and when you refresh your cart you get this message!

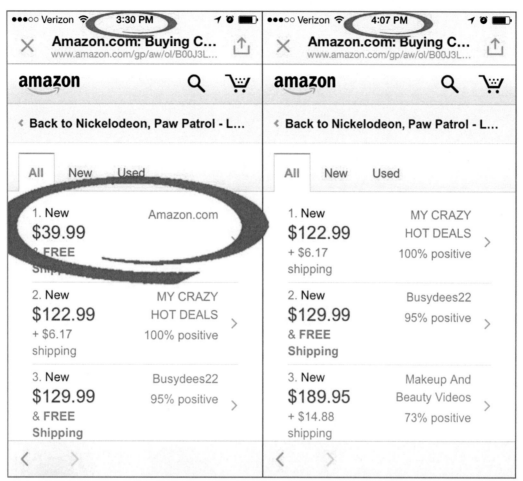

This is why ALERTS are so important. You have short windows of time to act. You could bookmark this and check all the time, or you could set up alerts. Get the alert, make your purchase, move on. Going back, you can see that I got my text message at 3:23 PM and this item was sold out by 4:07 PM. So unless you were refreshing this product page during those 44 minutes, you'd miss out on this deal.

Updated: Back in stock!

But check the TIME on this one. 12:25 AM. This was the email sent to me by IFTTT from the RSS feed for the Movers & Shakers page. More on IFTTT in Chapter 27 and more on RSS in the Vendor Spotlight at the end of this book.

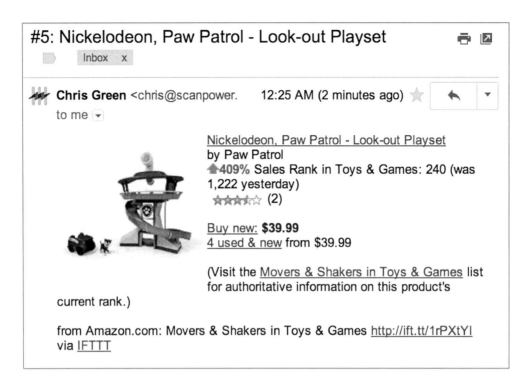

Getting alerts at weird hours like this is actually really awesome because it's more likely that other resellers (your competition) have gone to bed or are not actively paying attention to price and in-stock alerts. This means that you have more time to make your purchases and it also means that the deals will likely be available for a longer period of time because fewer people will be buying them up. So even if you can't place your order right as the alert comes in or you don't see the alert right away, it's more likely that the deal will still be there later.

Paw Patrol Research and Alerts from Amazon Movers & Shakers Pages

http://youtu.be/w7n9Y9obRc0
http://bit.ly/pawpatrolvideo

Look at this perfection! All six of these toys on the Movers & Shakers list are money-makers. Go back and check the Keepa data to confirm. This is how easy it is to find product to research. Online Arbitrage is EASY!

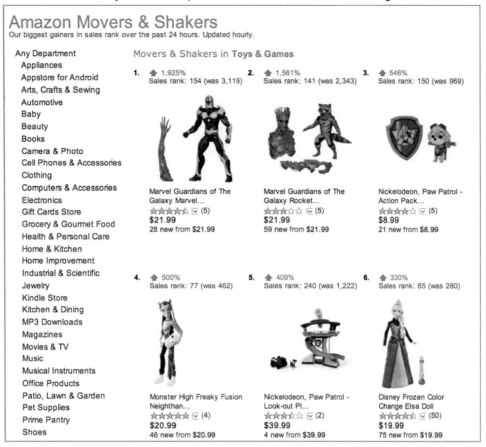

Let's follow the rabbit trail on this next one. #1 on the Amazon Movers & Shakers

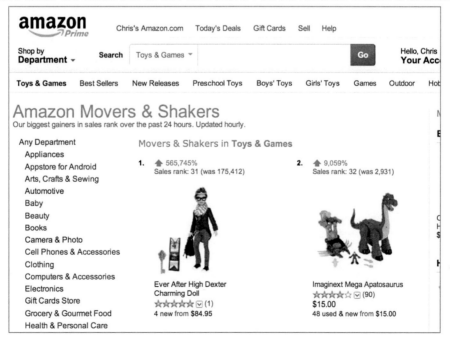

http://www.Amazon.com/gp/movers-and-shakers/toys-and-games/

You should notice now that the item has a suppressed Buy Box on the Movers & Shakers page along with on the Amazon product detail page.

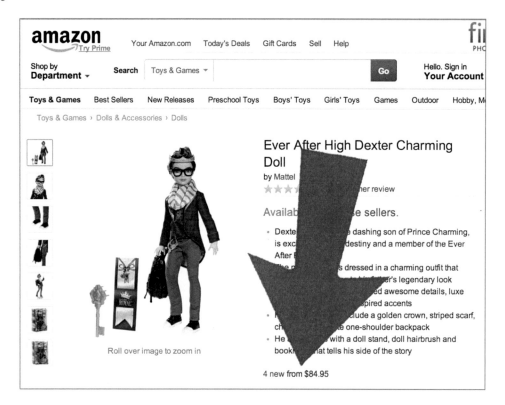

http://www.Amazon.com/Ever-After-High-Dexter-Charming/dp/B00J0RZKE0/

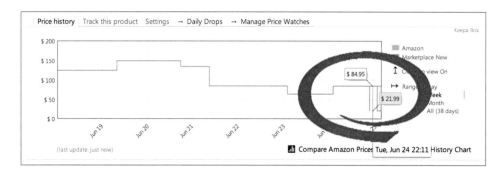

Keepa shows us the Amazon price is $21.99 when they are in stock.

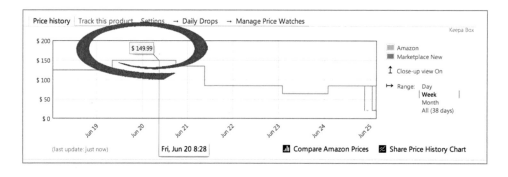

Keepa also shows us that this item was being sold for a high price of $149.99 + shipping a few months ago.

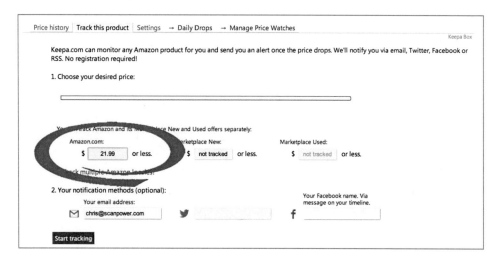

Set your price alerts at $21.99 from Amazon and sit back and wait. Be ready to pounce. You can see from the Keepa history that when Amazon comes in stock, they are not in stock for very long. This indicates that you'll want to act fast.

Let's do it all again:

In this example, the Buy Box is NOT suppressed even though you may already know that this is not a $60 doll. This indicates that the product listing does not have a list price or MSRP entered. This is good for sellers as it will help the item sell by having a Buy Box, although Amazon's motivation for suppressing the Buy Box and informing customers of the MSRP is to improve the customer experience. Because of how Amazon product details pages work, any seller at any time could enter a list price or MSRP and the Buy Box would become suppressed. So while this type of listing is more attractive than one with a suppressed Buy Box, it's not something that you can rely on long term.

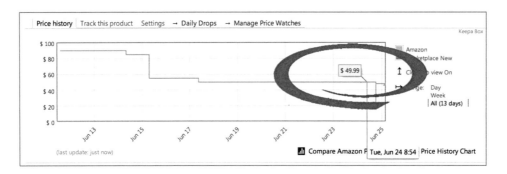

This time Keepa does NOT have any record of Amazon selling this item. So we still do not know the MSRP in order to calculate potential profit.

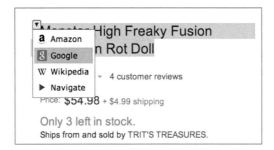

So let's use the tools at our disposal to do some more research. Highlighting the product title with Context Search, we can then choose Google from the drop down menu.

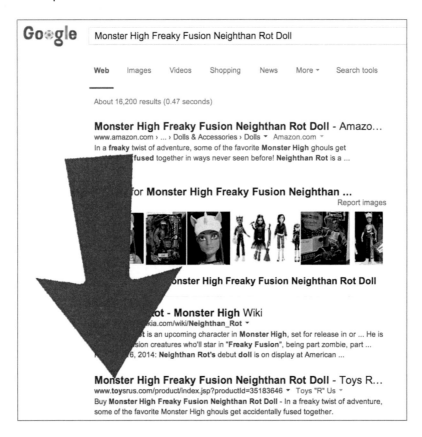

And one simple Google search later, we can see that this item sells at Toys R Us.

So now we know two important pieces of information: This item sells at Toys R Us (online and in stores) and the MSRP is $19.99. The Toys R Us page shows that it can't be ordered online but it does have an alert system to send an email when it's available.

Easy enough to enter your email address here:

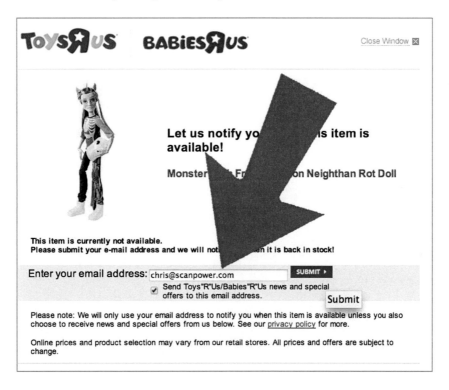

Now even though Amazon has not had this item in stock yet, now that we know the MSRP is $19.99, we can set up an alert at $19.99. It's easy enough to do.

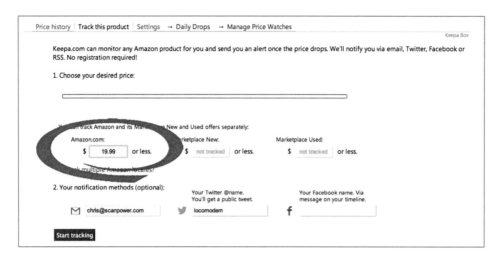

Most of the time, you can gather the information that you need from the first page of the Movers & Shakers lists. By the time you get to the end of page one, the items that you will see are items that already sell well, and are just selling a little better. Like an item ranked #90 and then is updated to #63 and gets a boost of 60% in sales rank. Sometimes Amazon will run a sale or promotion that will send a lot of one type of product to the Movers & Shakers lists that were not there previously. When this happens, you may miss the more random price drops that get pushed to page two of the list, so consider checking page two from time to time.

Here is an example of something that I would have missed if I had not checked page two of the Amazon Movers & Shakers Toy section. Starting with #26:

25. ⬆ 60%
Sales rank: 143 (was 230)

Crayola Colored Pencils, Assorted Col...
★★★★☆ ☑ (57)
$5.29
61 used & new from $1.21

26. ⬆ 56%
Sales rank: 379 (was 592)

Nickelodeon, Paw Patrol - Action Pack...
★★★★☆ ☑ (7)
$6.99
60 new from $4.48

Looking at the product detail page, InvisibleHand pops up to show us that this item also sells for $6.99 from Toys R Us.

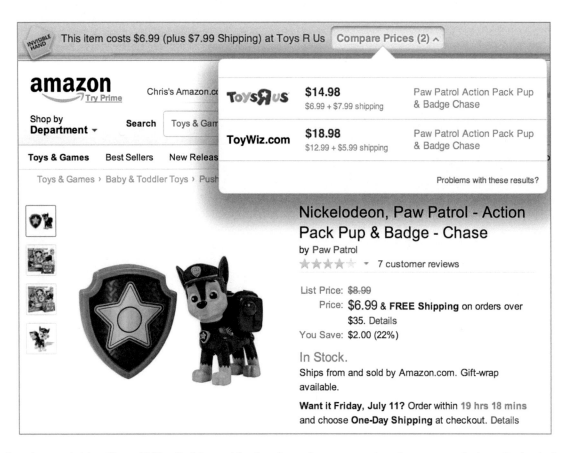

So Amazon is price matching Toys R Us. But free shipping from Amazon makes it an easy choice of who to buy from. The inflated price from ToyWiz is also a clue (more about ToyWiz in Chapter 13).

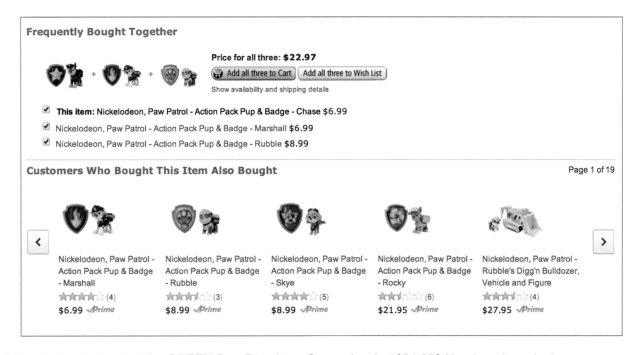

Now follow the leads. Look at the GREEN Paw Patrol toy. Same size, but $21.95? Needs a closer look.

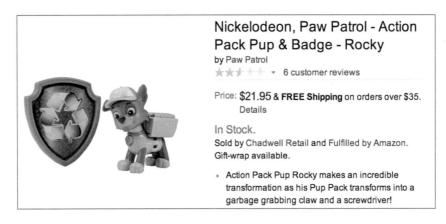

Nickelodeon, Paw Patrol - Action Pack Pup & Badge - Rocky
by Paw Patrol
★★☆☆☆ ▾ 6 customer reviews

Price: **$21.95** & **FREE Shipping** on orders over $35.
Details

In Stock.
Sold by Chadwell Retail and Fulfilled by Amazon.
Gift-wrap available.

- Action Pack Pup Rocky makes an incredible transformation as his Pup Pack transforms into a garbage grabbing claw and a screwdriver!

You already know that this line of toys sells for $6.99 - $8.99. Maybe this one is harder to find. Use the tools to FIND IT.

What else do you see? How about that three-pack with no price underneath? Remember, this means that the Buy Box is suppressed or there are no offers at all.

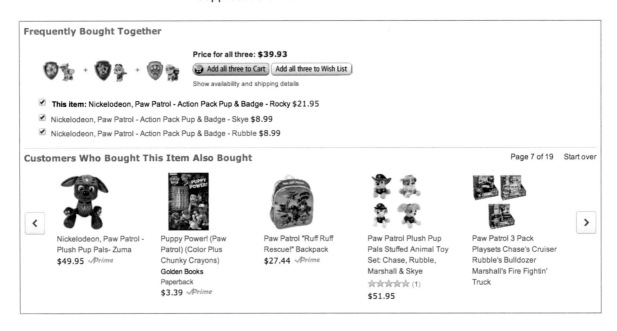

Frequently Bought Together

Price for all three: **$39.93**
[Add all three to Cart] [Add all three to Wish List]
Show availability and shipping details

- ☑ **This item:** Nickelodeon, Paw Patrol - Action Pack Pup & Badge - Rocky $21.95
- ☑ Nickelodeon, Paw Patrol - Action Pack Pup & Badge - Skye **$8.99**
- ☑ Nickelodeon, Paw Patrol - Action Pack Pup & Badge - Rubble **$8.99**

Customers Who Bought This Item Also Bought   Page 7 of 19   Start over

| Nickelodeon, Paw Patrol - Plush Pup Pals- Zuma $49.95 ✓Prime | Puppy Power! (Paw Patrol) (Color Plus Chunky Crayons) Golden Books Paperback $3.39 ✓Prime | Paw Patrol "Ruff Ruff Rescue!" Backpack $27.44 ✓Prime | Paw Patrol Plush Pup Pals Stuffed Animal Toy Set: Chase, Rubble, Marshall & Skye ★★★★★ (1) $51.95 | Paw Patrol 3 Pack Playsets Chase's Cruiser Rubble's Bulldozer Marshall's Fire Fightin' Truck |

Let's take a closer look. You can see that there are NO offers at all. This may be an item that you want to track down and sell. But we need to find out what prices it was selling at before as well as the historical sales rank to be sure it was actually selling.

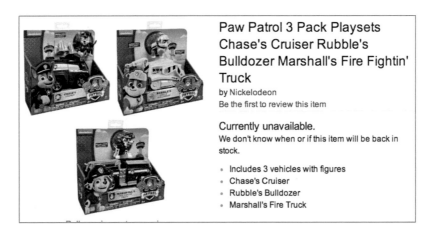

Paw Patrol 3 Pack Playsets Chase's Cruiser Rubble's Bulldozer Marshall's Fire Fightin' Truck
by Nickelodeon
Be the first to review this item

Currently unavailable.
We don't know when or if this item will be back in stock.

- Includes 3 vehicles with figures
- Chase's Cruiser
- Rubble's Bulldozer
- Marshall's Fire Truck

Keepa shows recent prices from Marketplace sellers in the $70 - $90 range. Looks attractive!

A sales rank of 25,303 in Toys even with NO offers at all. This is very strong evidence that this item was selling at those $70 - $90 prices.

Product Details

Product Dimensions: 12 x 10 x 12 inches

Shipping Weight: 3.2 pounds

Origin: Imported (China)

ASIN: B00KH78AJO

Manufacturer recommended age: 3 years and up

Amazon Best Sellers Rank: #25,303 in Toys & Games (See Top 100 in Toys & Games)

Average Customer Review: Be the first to review this item

So what do you do? Go find those three items! Find out where they are sold. Find their MSRPs and set up alerts if they are currently only available at over-retail prices.

And it just goes on and on. I'm not going to do this one for you. ☺ What steps would you take once you see these items for the first time at #1 and #2 on the Amazon Movers & Shakers page?

What do you do?

Doing Product Research on Amazon:

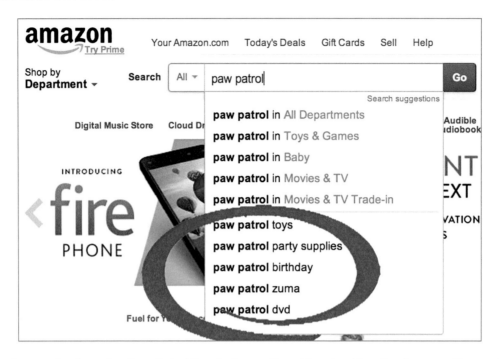

We just saw a lot of examples from the Paw Patrol line that were found by checking the Amazon Movers & Shakers page. If we want to proactively do some research on the Paw Patrol line, how would we do that? Let's take a look.

First, a basic Amazon search for keywords 'paw patrol' will show some suggested search results from Amazon. These suggestions are very relevant. They are based on customer searches and trends. Pay attention to them! Consider 'party supplies.' If customers are searching for 'paw patrol party supplies' but there are not many search results or in stock listings, then that may be something that you want to bring to the Amazon marketplace yourself. If you know what people are searching for, you can sell it to them!

Now, I want to look for hot toys that are so hot that they are out of stock. If out of stock, they won't show on Amazon's search results (because Amazon is consumer-facing, and showing out of stock items serves no real purpose since the customers wouldn't be able to buy them anyway). But we are resellers doing product research so we want to know what items are out of stock. Here is how to do that.

First, you have to do a search and choose a Department. You can't SORT until you choose a Department.

Once you choose the Toys & Games Department, you'll see that there are 155 search results. You'll also be able to sort by Price: High to Low.

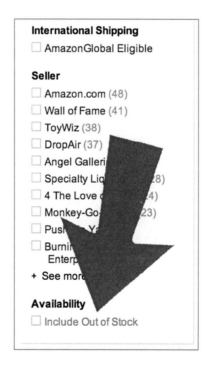

Here's the little secret. Scroll way down and on the left hand side you can check the box under Availability: Include Out of Stock. Now, even if an item is out of stock (possibly because it's awesome and selling for an over-retail price when it's in stock), it will show up in the search results.

Now you can see that there are 173 search results instead of 155. Now it may be that not all of those additional results are even Paw Patrol items, but we'll see what we get.

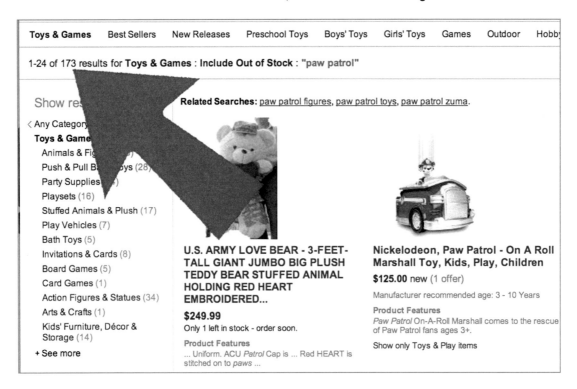

173 items – 155 = 18 additional items related to Paw Patrol in toys. Now we have to find them. That's why we sorted by price; just go the end of the list.

Scroll down and go through the pages of search results.

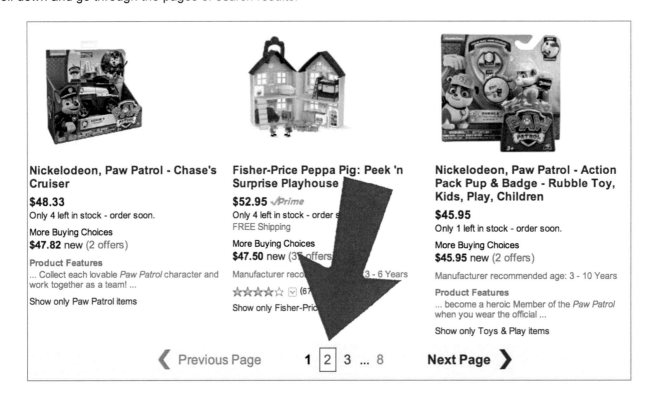

You know that there are eight pages of search results. That's not that many to click through. But if you have a TON of pages, you can shortcut your way to the end by editing the URL.

http://www.Amazon.com/s/ref=sr_pg_2?rh=n%3A165793011%2Ck%3Apaw+patrol%2Cp_n_availability%3A1248837011&page=2&sort=price-desc-rank&keywords=paw+patrol&ie=UTF8&qid=1405394786

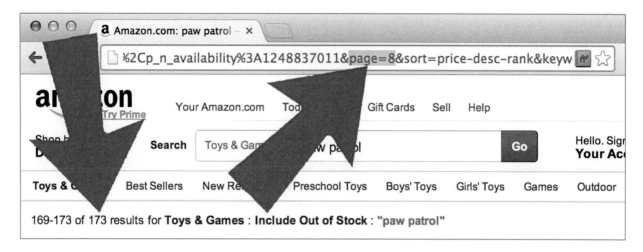

And here we go! We've successfully found the out of stock Paw Patrol items on Amazon with just a few simple search methods and tricks. These would be the items that I would be checking against Keepa history for in stock rates and previous offer prices.

Paw Patrol Inspired Chase Earrings

Currently unavailable

Product Features
Paw Patrol Chase Children Earrings

Show only Twiltz Giftz items

NEW Teenage Mutant Ninja Turtles Movie Backpack & Lunch Box! Back to School Set!

Currently unavailable

Show only Nickelodeon items

Nickelodeon, Paw Patrol - Action Pack Pups 3pk Figure Set Chase, Rocky, Zuma

Currently unavailable

Manufacturer recommended age: 3 - 8 Years

Product Features
The *Paw Patrol* Action Pack Rescue Team is made for kids ages 3+.

Show only Paw Patrol items

Nickelodeon, Paw Patrol - Action Pack Pups 3pk Figure Set Marshal, Skye, Rubble

Currently unavailable

Manufacturer recommended age: 3 - 8 Years

Product Features
The *Paw Patrol* Action Pack Rescue Team is made for kids ages 3+.

Show only Paw Patrol items

Nickelodeon, Paw Patrol - Real Talking Chase Plush

Currently unavailable

Manufacturer recommended age: 3 - 8 Years

Product Features
... Real Talking Chase is made for *Paw Patrol* fans ages 3+ and includes 1 LR ...

Show only Paw Patrol items

Nickelodeon, Paw Patrol - Rocky's Recycling Truck

Currently unavailable

Manufacturer recommended age: 3 - 8 Years

Product Features
... Collect each lovable *Paw Patrol* character and work together as a team! ...

Show only Paw Patrol items

❮ Previous Page   1 ... 6 **7** 8   Next Page ❯

Once you find an item that looks interesting, pull up the Amazon product page. There is still some research to be done.

Nickelodeon, Paw Patrol - Rocky's Recycling Truck
by Paw Patrol
Be the first to review this item

Currently unavailable.
We don't know when or if this item will be back in stock.

- It's Rocky to the rescue in his Paw Patrol Recycling Truck with real working wheels!
- Rocky's Recycling Truck features a forklift for heavy lifting and storage area in the rear of the truck!
- Collect each lovable Paw Patrol character and work together as a team! Marshall, Zuma, Skye, Chase and Rubble all have transforming vehicles!
- The Paw Patrol Rocky's Recycling Truck comes to the rescue of Paw Patrol fans ages 3+.
- 1 Rocky Figure, 1 Vehicle

Roll over image to zoom in

http://www.Amazon.com/Nickelodeon-Paw-Patrol-Rockys-Recycling/dp/B00ITOAYV4

It may seem counter-intuitive, but I want to do an Amazon search on this item on Amazon. I want to be sure that this is NOT a duplicate listing. This is easy to do with the Context Search app. Just highlight the title and then choose Amazon from the drop down menu.

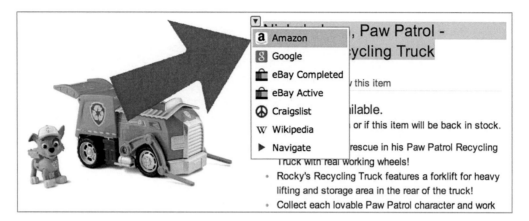

The search results show that there is no other match for this item. We do this to prevent buying items that you may end up listing against the incorrect Amazon product page.

Now we do the same Context Search but this time we choose Google.

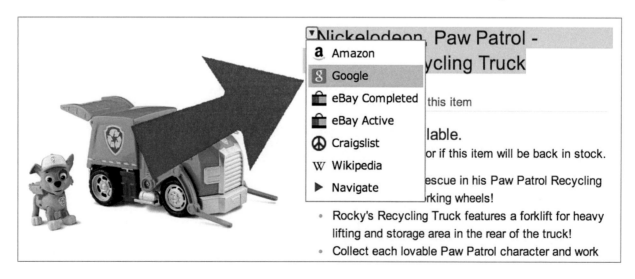

And our one-step, simple Google search shows us that this item sells at Target. Online Arbitrage is easy!

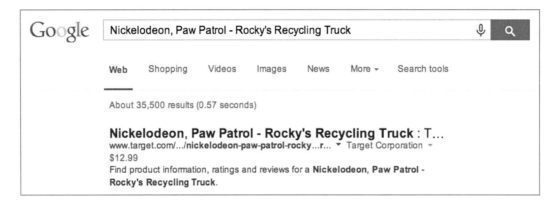

Available from Target although out of stock. Bookmark and check.

Additionally, a general Google search for 'paw patrol toys' shows that the number two result is Wal-Mart.

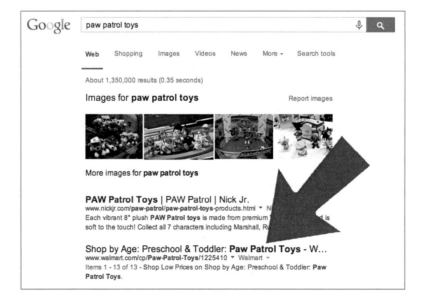

A quick check of their website shows that Wal-Mart also sells this item (although out of stock online).

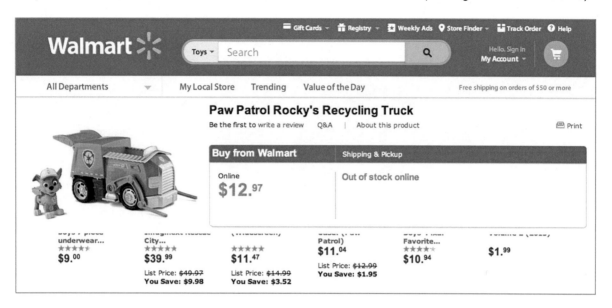

Searching for Out Of Stock (OOS) Paw Patrol Toys on Amazon.com for Online Arbitrage

http://youtu.be/7rZSQmjxEYM

http://bit.ly/pawpatrolvideo2

Learn to SEARCH and SORT on Amazon

Example: Media, DVDs, box sets (higher average sales price)

A word of caution: if purchasing DVDs or Blu-Ray discs to resell on Amazon, I strongly recommend only buying from Amazon and making yourself familiar with restricted items. You can check if you are restricted by attempting to list the item before even buying it. Some media items are restricted so please do your homework and confirm that you can resell the items before making a purchase. You may also consider reselling on eBay if the item makes sense.

127

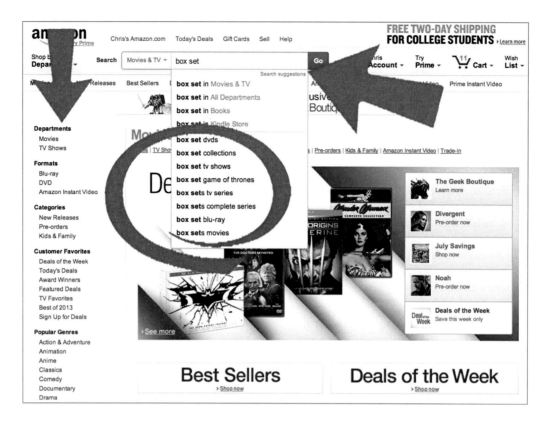

You see the same type of information that we saw with our Paw Patrol search. Amazon suggested search terms that may come in useful for other research. Be sure to choose a department in order to enable sorting.

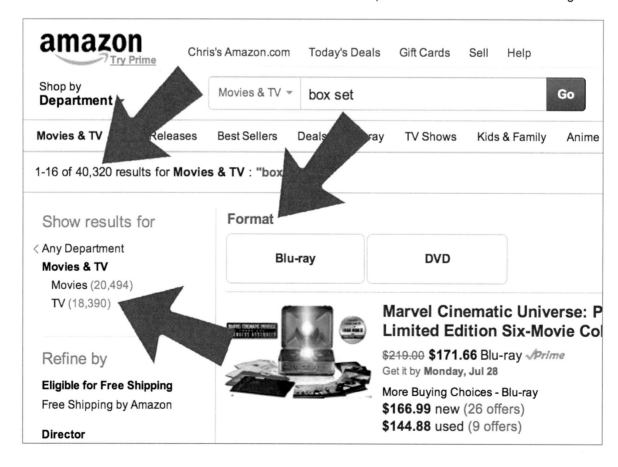

You'll then have lots of choices on the left hand side to further refine your search.

Once you choose a category, there are a few things that we want to look for.

1. The Buy Box price (the larger, prominently featured price) to be EQUAL to the lowest New price.

If it's higher than the lowest New price, then that means that there is an offer at a price EVEN LOWER than the Buy Box price. It is much less likely that the Buy Box is being sold at a low enough price in cases like this.

2. You want the Buy Box price AND the lowest New price to be LESS THAN the lowest Used price. This indicates that the Buy Box offer is not only the lowest price in New condition, but that the price is so low that it is in fact LOWER than even the Used offers.

In this example, we see that condition #1 is met but #2 is not.

Twilight Forever: The Complete Saga Box Set [DVD + UltraViolet Digital Copy) 2013 PG-13

~~$64.98~~ **$39.96** DVD *Prime*

Get it by **Monday, Jul 28**

More Buying Choices - DVD
$39.96 new (28 offers)
$31.94 used (11 offers)

★★★★☆ ☑ (632)

Starring: Kristen Stewart, Robert Pattinson, et al.

FREE Shipping

Trade in this item for an Amazon.com Gift Card

In this example, we see that #2 is met, but #1 is not.

Terminator Anthology (The Terminator / Terminator 2: Judgment Day / Terminator 3: Rise of the Machines / Terminator... 2013 R

~~$49.99~~ **$34.73** Blu-ray *Prime*

Get it by **Monday, Jul 28**

More Buying Choices - Blu-ray
$29.73 new (45 offers)
$35.95 used (10 offers)

★★★★☆ ☑ (173)

Runtime: 8 hrs 5 mins
Starring: Various
Directed by: Various

FREE Shipping with your current order

Trade in this item for an Amazon.com Gift Card

In this example, we see that both qualifiers are met. Let's look at the product details.

The Dark Knight Trilogy: Ultimate Collector's Edition (Batman Begins / The Dark Knight / The Dark Knight Rises... 2013 PG-13

~~$99.97~~ **$38.99** Blu-ray *Prime*

In stock on July 28, 2014

More Buying Choices - Blu-ray
$38.99 new (46 offers)
$39.97 used (20 offers)

★★★★☆ ☑ (1,969)

Runtime: 7 hrs 38 mins
Starring: Christian Bale, Michael Caine, et al.
Directed by: Christopher Nolan

FREE Shipping

Trade in this item for an Amazon.com Gift Card

$38.99 from Amazon but not in stock. I like the 61% off as a relative price drop. You can still place your orders and lock in the price. Looking at the other offers, you can see the large price jump from Amazon's $38.99 price going up to the next lowest offer of $68.15.

So why is Amazon selling for this price? Who knows, but they are. Maybe they are price matching another online retailer. You'll often see that with InvisibleHand or another Chrome extension.

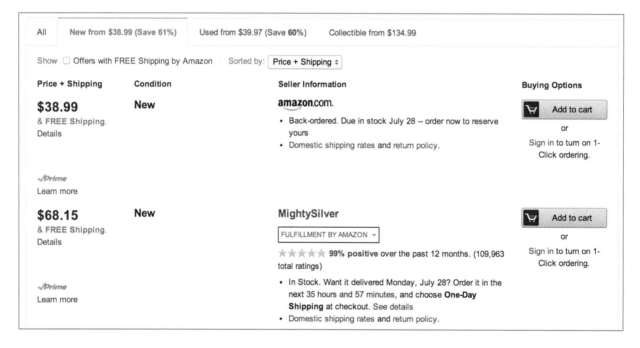

Checking CamelCamelCamel price history on this item shows that the current price is the all-time lowest price. You can also see the prices that Amazon has been selling at recently. This can give you an idea of where the price will return to in the event that this is a temporary price drop from matching another online retailer.

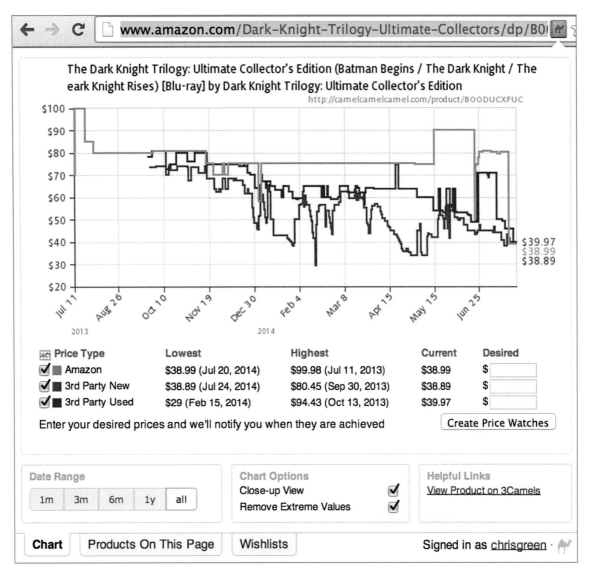

The Dark Knight Trilogy: Ultimate Collector's Edition (Batman Begins / The Dark Knight / The eark Knight Rises) [Blu-ray] by Dark Knight Trilogy: Ultimate Collector's Edition

http://camelcamelcamel.com/product/B00DUCXFUC

Price Type	Lowest	Highest	Current	Desired
✔ Amazon	$38.99 (Jul 20, 2014)	$99.98 (Jul 11, 2013)	$38.99	$
✔ 3rd Party New	$38.89 (Jul 24, 2014)	$80.45 (Sep 30, 2013)	$38.89	$
✔ 3rd Party Used	$29 (Feb 15, 2014)	$94.43 (Oct 13, 2013)	$39.97	$

Enter your desired prices and we'll notify you when they are achieved

Create Price Watches

Date Range	Chart Options	Helpful Links
1m 3m 6m 1y all	Close-up View ✔ Remove Extreme Values ✔	View Product on 3Camels

Chart | Products On This Page | Wishlists   Signed in as chrisgreen ·

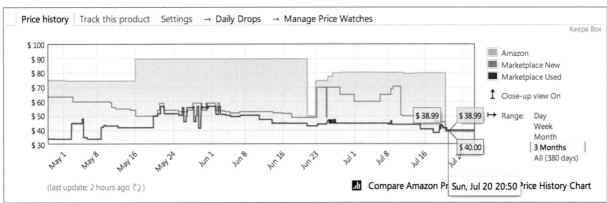

Keepa confirms that CamelCamelCamel pricing history and also shows that despite the aggressive pricing, Amazon has not gone out of stock on this item. That is an important piece of data. I like this item less not knowing if Amazon will ever go out of stock.

Clint Eastwood: 20 Film Collection [Blu-ray] 2013 R

~~$129.95~~ **$91.99** Blu-ray *Prime*

Get it by **Monday, Jul 28**

More Buying Choices - Blu-ray
$91.99 new (18 offers)
$110.28 used (5 offers)

★★★★☆ ☑ (14)

Runtime: 8 hrs 38 mins
Starring: Various
Directed by: Various

FREE Shipping

Trade in this item for an Amazon.com Gift Card

Here's the next example. #1 and #2 both pass. What I don't like from what I see is the lower savings in relative terms. 29% off is a lot less than what we saw with Batman at 61% off.

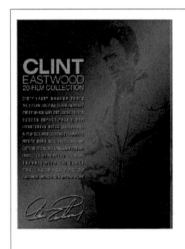

Clint Eastwood: 20 Film Collection [Blu-ray] (2013)

<u>Various</u> (Actor), <u>Various</u> (Director) | Rated: R | Format: Blu-ray

★★★★☆ ☑ (<u>14 customer reviews</u>)

List Price: ~~$129.95~~

Price: **$91.99** & **FREE Shipping**. <u>Details</u>
You Save: $37.96 (29%)

In Stock.
Ships from and sold by **Amazon.com**. Gift-wrap available.

Want it Monday, July 28? Order within **35 hrs 51 mins** and choose **One-Day Shipping** at checkout. <u>Details</u>

<u>18 new</u> from $91.99   <u>5 used</u> from $110.28

Look at the offers prices, we see that the second lower offer is really not that much cheaper than Amazon, leaving no room for potential profit.

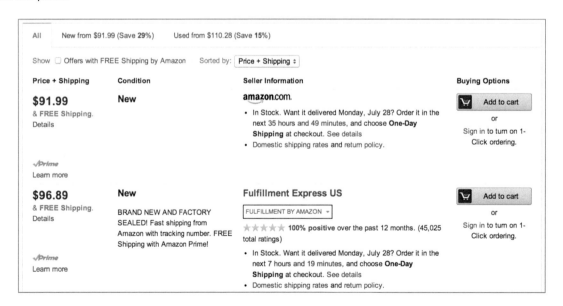

Here's where CamelCamelCamel comes in really handy. While we are looking at this item we can quickly check historical pricing information using the CamelCamelCamel Chrome extension. In it, we can see that the all-time lowest price from Amazon happened on December 22, 2013 at $56.99.

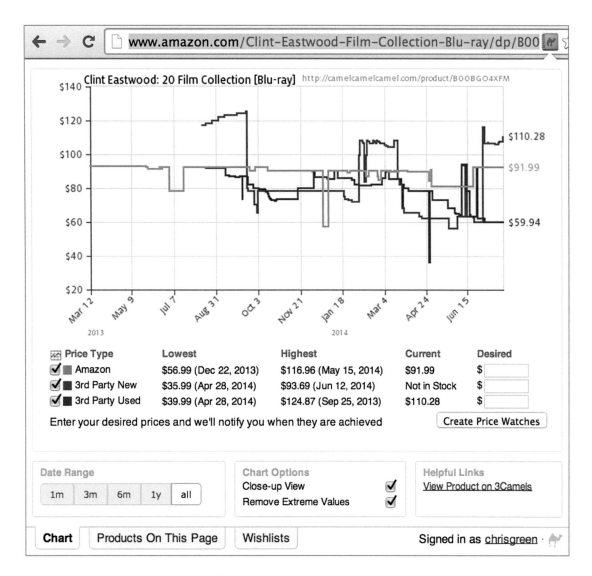

Now that's a much more interesting price than $91.99 so we can set up pricing alerts to be notified if Amazon drops the price again on this item. And remember to always set your alerts just a little bit higher than previous low prices just in case the price drop is not exactly like the previous price drops.

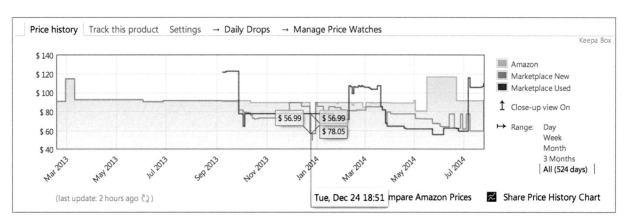

Here is a deal that I posted in the ScanPower Facebook Group:

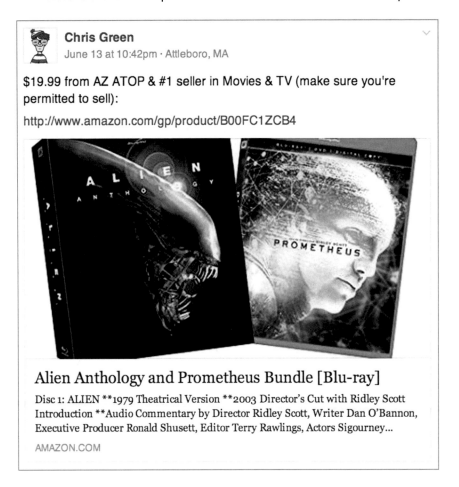

https://www.facebook.com/groups/scanpower/permalink/515937088508222/

http://www.Amazon.com/gp/product/B00FC1ZCB4

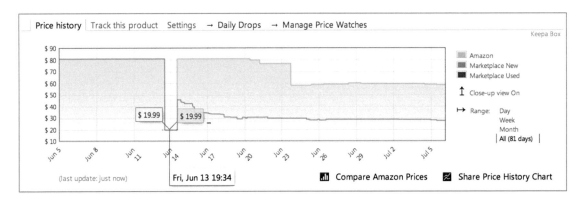

You know the drill by now; set up alerts at $19.99. Amazon was probably price matching another online seller like Wal-Mart or they offered this item as a Gold Box Deal. Finding graphs like this are awesome, but there is no guarantee that Amazon will drop to the previously low price again (they haven't on this item other than the one time recorded by Keepa). You know what to set your alerts for as well as the price that Amazon likes to be at most of the time. What I don't like about this item is the consistently lower prices from Amazon Marketplace sellers. Buyers will often pay a premium to buy from Amazon (I do) as well as from FBA sellers. These customers want their items fast and they are not as sensitive about price. But how much of a premium price are they willing to pay? That is a true unknown.

Amazon rank search past 100

The Amazon Best Sellers page is awesome to see what the most popular items are on Amazon, but what if you want to search PAST that top 100? Here I'll show you how.

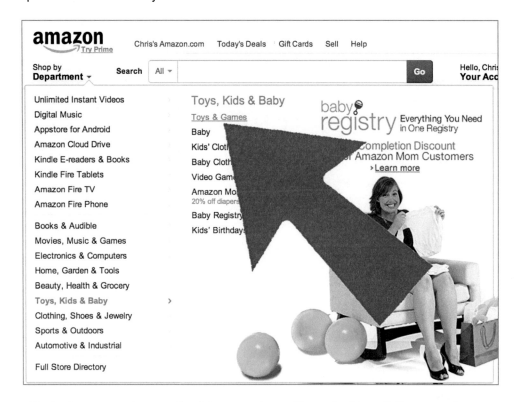

First, choose a category. For this example, we'll use the Toys & Games category.

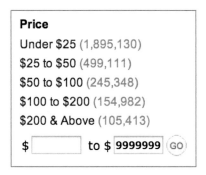

On the left hand side, choose a price range and enter a max price of 9999999.

You'll now see the total number of listing in the category. In this case, 2,884,035 results.

135

For this type of search, we want to sort by New and Popular.

This type of search isn't perfect because Amazon mixes in items from other categories. Here you can see items from the Baby category as well as Video Games. Just keep this in mind as you view the search results.

Refine by

Boutique

☐ Specialty (59,728)

☐ Geek (6,416)

Featured Characters & Brands

Magic the Gathering (58,175)

Yu-Gi-Oh! (50,052)

Pokemon (32,691)

Star Wars (23,621)

Barbie (17,593)

Hello Kitty (12,894)

Disney Princess (9,905)

+ See more

Interest

Animals & Nature (251,333)

Anime & Manga (7,675)

Comics (3,247)

Fantasy & Sci-Fi (118,541)

Fashion (56,025)

Learning (58,839)

Music (30,188)

Occupations (56,392)

Sports (60,921)

Transportation (157,441)

TV & Movies (15,193)

Video Games (676)

Show results for

Age Range

☐ Birth to 24 Months (284,339)

☐ 2 to 4 Years (460,223)

☐ 5 to 7 Years (364,549)

☐ 8 to 13 Years (543,718)

☐ 14 Years & Up (332,595)

Gender

Boys (910,755)

Girls (812,000)

Eligible for Free Shipping

Free Shipping by Amazon

Featured Brands

☐ Cards Against Humanity LLC. (3)

☐ Nintendo (2,272)

☐ Baby Banana (1)

☐ Cards Against Humanity (9)

☐ Baby Einstein (99)

☐ Frozen (107)

☐ SUPERSOAKER (41)

+ See more

Packaging Option

☐ Frustration-Free Packaging (384)

Avg. Customer Review

★★★★☆ & Up (268,392)

★★★☆☆ & Up (321,748)

★★☆☆☆ & Up (342,554)

★☆☆☆☆ & Up (362,233)

Certifications

Amazon Frustration-Free (2)

International Shipping

☐ AmazonGlobal Eligible

Price

< Any Price

$ [   ] to $ 9,999,999 (GO)

Discount

10% Off or More (927,998)

25% Off or More (704,491)

50% Off or More (142,373)

70% Off or More (49,365)

Seller

☐ Little Troopers (271,045)

☐ Vision Store (148,546)

☐ Amazon.com (139,319)

☐ Okinawa Japan (138,990)

☐ World Market JPN (120,480)

☐ EKATOMI (110,734)

☐ EnvyDeal (98,270)

☐ NuVur (94,595)

☐ JAPAN SELECT (92,540)

☐ Rich World Japan/ (83,209)

+ See more

Availability

☐ Include Out of Stock

Here are all of the additional ways to sort the list. This is important because you want to narrow down your list to see what items are popular in each sub-category.

Let's take a look at Action Figures and Statues:

So now that we have the sort broken down to Action Figures & Statues priced from $0 to $9,999,999:

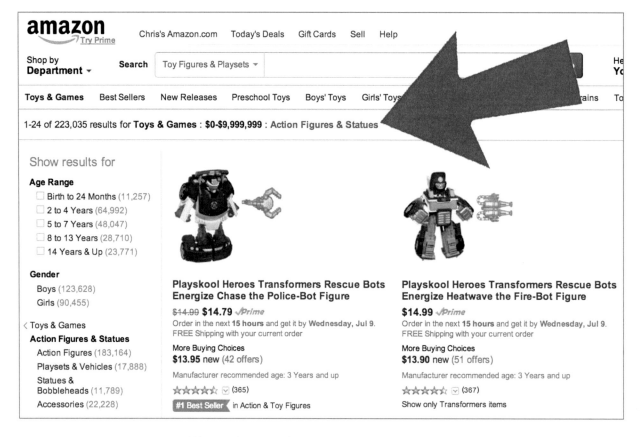

We can further refine to see just Transformers:

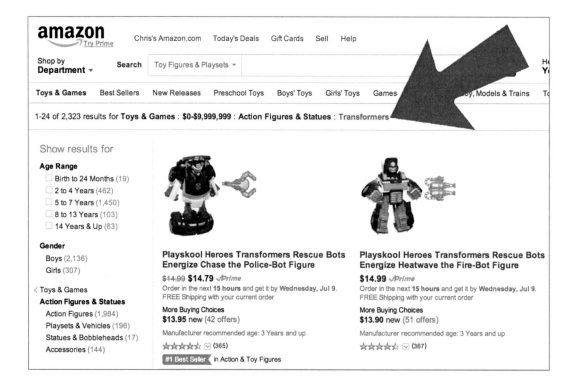

138

You'll see that this search result, while fairly narrow, still has 97 pages of products.

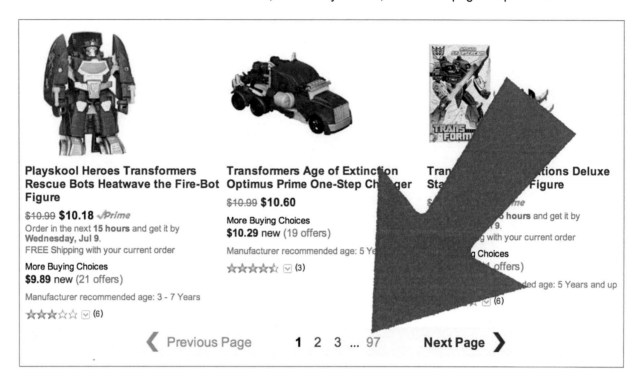

You can see that it won't let you go to page 97 by clicking but you can use the same trick that you saw earlier to skip through the search result pages (have to click to page 2 to do this trick). Then look closely at the URL and find where it says "page=". Here you see how to skip to page 74 of the 97 pages of search results.

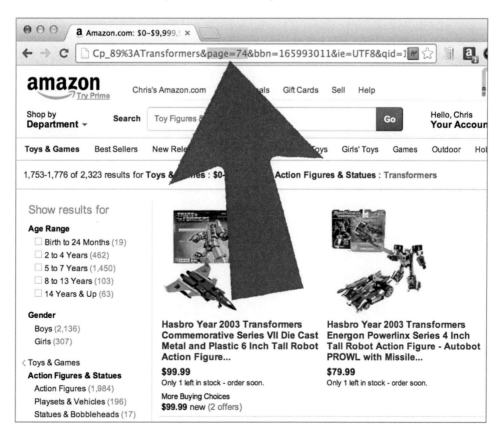

To clear the search and start researching another line of products, just click on the price. This will bring you back to the beginning of your search.

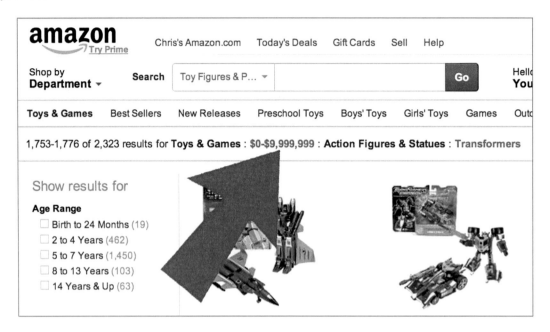

Additional search refinements may include Eligible for Prime shipping (to find FBA offers) or items being sold by Amazon.com only.

Online Arbitrage - Finding the Amazon Listing for Sold Out Amazon Items

http://youtu.be/-Dl7RcElVyo
http://bit.ly/soldoutitems

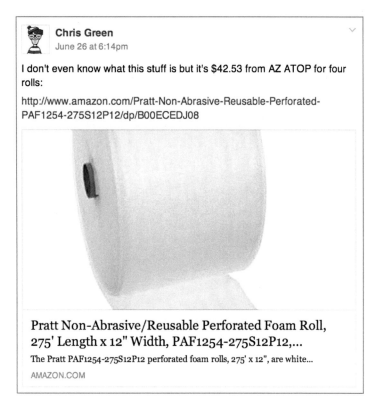

After the price drop, it returned to the $142.80 price point.

Keepa shows the price history of $120 range then a sudden drop to $42.53, then back up to $142.80.

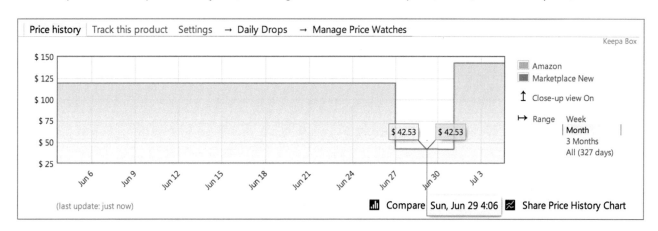

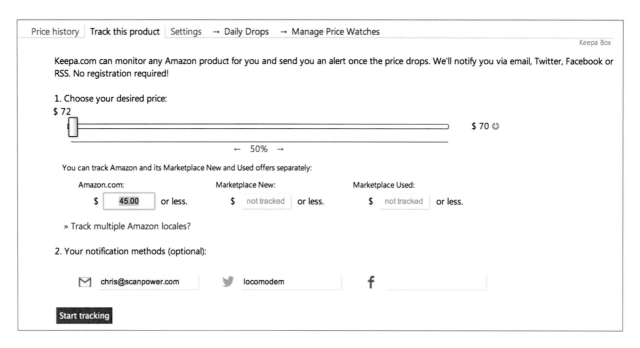

Finding random items? There may be others who are finding the same random items and leaving a trail of good deals behind. Doesn't it seem kind of strange that people who bought this roll of foam also bought all of these other items?

Start looking closely and you may like what you find.
Especially lists of items like this and items with suppressed Buy Boxes.

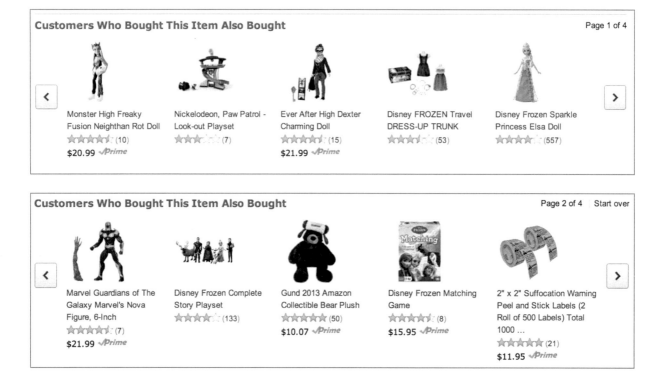

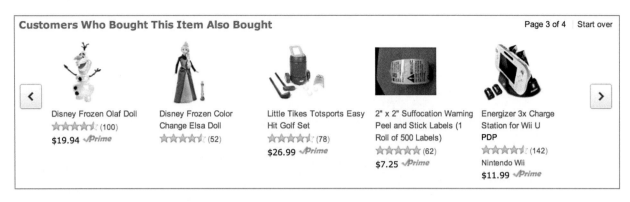

Getting ideas from your competition:

This may be an unpopular thing to do or even mention but I post it here to remind everyone of how visible Amazon sellers are. If you sell online, anyone can see what you sell. And they can use Google to see where to get it. There are no secrets. Please don't act like this is a taboo subject. Other sellers are doing it to you right now. Just be aware. Do it, don't do it. If you see the same sellers on many of your listings, guess what? They are likely sourcing products and inventory at the same places that you are! So be smart about it. Maybe you want to take a look at what else they sell.

Copy successful sellers:

Feedback quantity can indicate seller size. If you come across a seller that looks very successful, take a look at how they do things. Copy what they do well. Look at the types of items that they sell. Can you tell if they are a high volume, low margin seller? Or do they look like a Long Term Hold seller with collectible listings? Do they specialize in toys? Books? High price points or low? Long Tail inventory or Fast Turning inventory?

Being undercut is GOOD:

Now you know a new competitor. You KNOW someone who sells the same items that you sell. Maybe they get the same products from the same places that you do. Maybe you can get some new ideas about things to sell, or how to get a better price. Then look at what else they sell. If they have been sourcing at the same online sources as you, you may get new product ideas. Undercutting actually kind of backfires.

DON'T CONTACT OTHER SELLERS

This is one of the worst ideas that a seller can have. Amazon can track contact between sellers. There is really no reason to contact other sellers and any contact could be construed as price-fixing or collusion. If Amazon suspects this, your selling privilege on Amazon could be instantly revoked. Don't risk it.

Ethics and Price Mistakes: What would you do?

Take a look at this item:

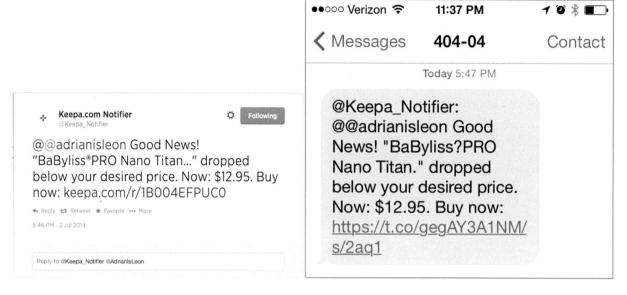

https://twitter.com/Keepa_Notifier/status/484453187739725825

I got this Keepa Tweet (and text message) because @adrianisleon set his alerts up incorrectly with an extra '@' in his settings. I didn't even know what it was, but I clicked through to take a look.

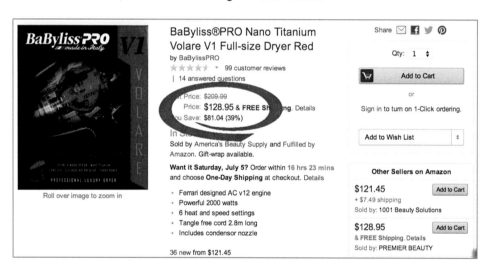

Turns out it's a ~$130 hair dryer! And a third party seller offered it for a cool $12.95.

You can see that Keepa caught this very short-term price drop.

So what would you do in this situation? Place your order and cross your fingers? Would it be different if it was from Amazon compared to a third party seller? Was it a sale or a pricing error?

If you do this long enough, you'll find products like this. Personally, this is what I would suggest that you do. Place your order. If you don't someone else will. You can wait to see if the items ship, if the seller contacts you asking to cancel the order, or if the seller cancels the order without contacting you; or you can proactively contact them to confirm the price on the order. It may be that it wasn't a price mistake and the seller has no problem shipping to you. If it was a price mistake, I would hope that everyone would be understanding, especially considering that we are also sellers and would not want to be taken advantage of ourselves. It's about treating others the way that we'd want to be treated.

In this book, you'll see a lot of examples, but everything written can be applied to every category on Amazon.

Amazon to Amazon? Or Amazon to eBay?

It's about getting the products from one market to another. Use research along the way to reduce and minimize risk.

Take a look at the following examples:

Chris Green
May 26

3 in stock @ $119.51 from Amazon ATOP. Not a great sales rank on Amazon, but 3 out of 4 listings on eBay have sold in the past two months.

http://www.amazon.com/Jardine-18-4018-723-02-Brushed-Slip-On-Exhaust/dp/B000N73KBQ

Jardine 18-4018-723-02 Brushed GP1 Slip-On Exhaust

Material: Stainless Steel Stylish, affordable and lightweight Aluminum or polished stainless steel canister with aluminum tubing/race core Installation is a breeze, requiring at the most a couple of wrenches and a screwdriver Features a...

AMAZON.COM

Here is an item being sold by Amazon at a significant discount.

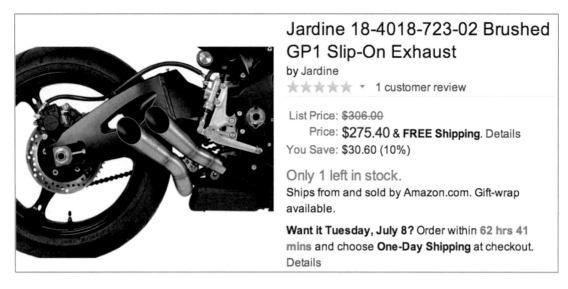

Jardine 18-4018-723-02 Brushed GP1 Slip-On Exhaust

by Jardine

★★★★★ ▾ 1 customer review

List Price: $306.00
~~$306.00~~
Price: $275.40 & **FREE Shipping**. Details
You Save: $30.60 (10%)

Only 1 left in stock.

Ships from and sold by Amazon.com. Gift-wrap available.

Want it Tuesday, July 8? Order within **62 hrs 41 mins** and choose **One-Day Shipping** at checkout. Details

Here is the Amazon product page (price had gone back up when I took the picture).

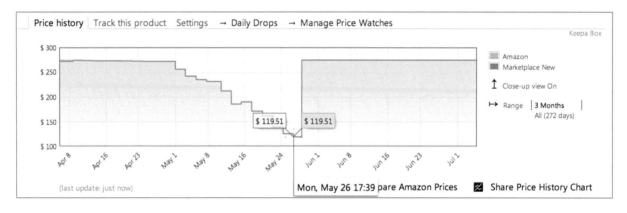

Keepa shows the price history and low price offer of $119.51.

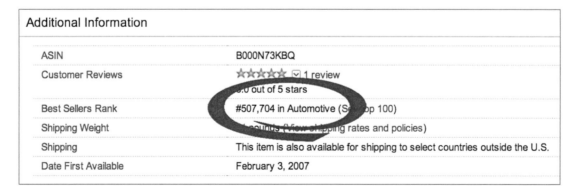

Additional Information	
ASIN	B000N73KBQ
Customer Reviews	★★★★★ ☑ 1 review
	.0 out of 5 stars
Best Sellers Rank	#507,704 in Automotive (See top 100)
Shipping Weight	(view shipping rates and policies)
Shipping	This item is also available for shipping to select countries outside the U.S.
Date First Available	February 3, 2007

The sales rank, even with a low price offer, is still pretty terrible. It's not too attractive to list and sell this item on Amazon, even if purchased at the lower price.

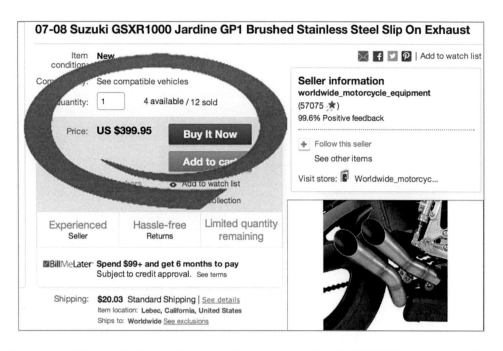

EBay to the rescue! This seller listed sixteen of this item on eBay for $399.95 and sold twelve of them!

Chris Green
June 30 at 10:19am

$179.99 from AZ ATOP (normally sells for $300 from AZ). Check Keepa graph and decide:

http://www.amazon.com/Uniden-Guardian-Advanced-Wireless-Surveillance/dp/B0091DR2NK

Uniden Guardian Advanced Wireless 7-Inch Screen Video Surveillance System with 2 Outdoor Cameras...

The Guardian G755 Advanced Wireless 7-Inch Screen Video Surveillance System...

AMAZON.COM

I posted this one in our Facebook group:

https://www.facebook.com/groups/scanpower/permalink/522682037833727/

http://www.Amazon.com/Uniden-Guardian-Advanced-Wireless-Surveillance/dp/B0091DR2NK

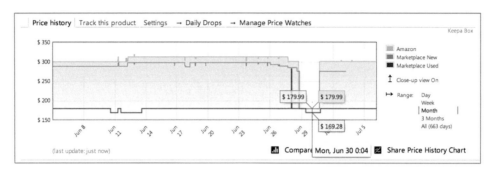

Keepa clearly shows the historical prices of $300+, the price drop to $179.99, and the price returning to the $300 level.

At $179.99 (probably price-matching another online retailer), and selling for the regular price of $299.99 would give you a payout of $260.05. This gives you a profit of $80 for processing ONE BOX.

https://www.facebook.com/groups/scanpower/permalink/519418118160119/

http://www.Amazon.com/dp/B007EIPQW8

Husqvarna H238SL 38-Inch Soft Bin
Double Bagger
by Husqvarna
★★★★½ ▾   10 customer reviews

Price: $314.95 & **FREE Shipping**. Details

Temporarily out of stock.
Order now and we'll deliver when available. We'll e-mail you with
an estimated delivery date as soon as we have more information.
Your account will only be charged when we ship the item.
Ships from and sold by Amazon.com.

- Fits all husqvarna 38-inch tractors
- 2 bins -6 bushal capacity
- Top designed for improved air flow resulting in fuller bags
- Full bag indicator
- Easy-glide bin with built-in handles

Click to open expanded view

This is not a deal for everyone. Way too big if you have no room to receive, store, and process large inventory.

Product Details

Product Dimensions: 47.5 x 24 x 25.5 inches

Shipping Weight: 46 pounds (View shipping rates and policies)

Shipping: Currently, item can be shipped only within the U.S.

You can see the monster size of this item.

Keepa clearly shows the historical $350 price point, the sudden drop to $42 (who knows on this crazy price drop) and the jump back up to $314.95.

It's also important to note that due to the size and weight of this item, it may make more sense to MERCHANT FULFILL this item vs. FBA. Use the FBA Calculator and run the numbers to see which makes the most sense to you and your business. Always consider your options and don't restrict yourself to only certain sales channels.

Bonus Tip:

Did you know that Amazon has their own built-in email alert system? If a product is completely out of stock, you can ask Amazon to email you when they are back in stock. This can be useful on popular items that Amazon can't keep in stock because of popularity or because they are selling at artificially low prices.

Take a look at this example:

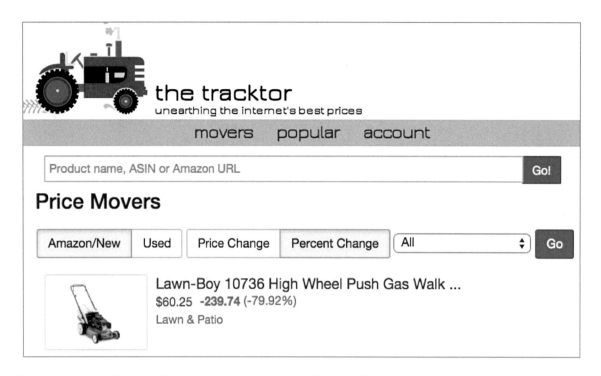

The number one item on TheTracktor Movers page (Percent Change) is a lawnmower at 79.92% off.

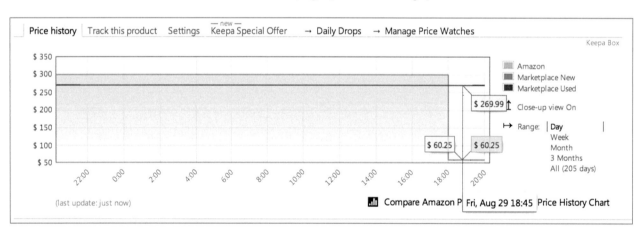

Zooming in on the Keepa graph shows that this offer was from Amazon and it was only available for a very brief time. Even with such a short period of time, this item landed at the number one Best Seller and the number three Mover & Shaker in the Patio, Lawn & Garden category on Amazon.

So when an item is completely sold out on Amazon, you'll see the option to receive an email when the item becomes available again. Just click on the big, yellow Email me button when you are logged into your Amazon account.

Lawn-Boy 10736 High Wheel Push Gas Walk Behind Lawn Mower, 21-Inch with Honda Engine
by Toro
Be the first to review this item
#1 Best Seller in Patio, Lawn & Garden

Sign up to be notified when this item becomes available.

Share ✉ 🇫 🐦 📌

Currently Unavailable
Want us to email you when this item becomes available?

Email me

Email: locomodem@gmail.com
Not Chris Green? Sign Out.

Success!

Lawn-Boy 10736 High Wheel Push Gas Walk Behind Lawn Mower, 21-Inch with Honda Engine
by Toro
Be the first to review this item
#1 Best Seller in Patio, Lawn & Garden

Sign up to be notified when this item becomes available.

Share ✉ 🇫 🐦 📌

Signed up for alert
You are signed up to receive an email when this item is available.

Email: locomodem@gmail.com
Manage my alerts

Add to Wish List   ⇕

151

Chapter 11 – Deals vs. Duds

A lot of the examples that we saw in the previous chapter were easy to identify as legitimate resale deals. But what about deals that look like winners but actually are total flops? Let's look at some examples and what you can check to keep yourself from making bad purchase decisions.

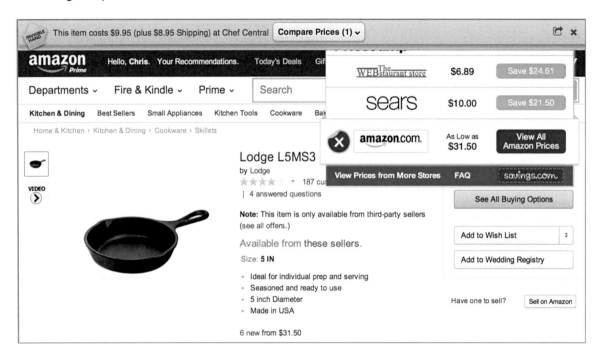

Take a look at this item. Suppressed Buy Box, No Amazon competition, InvisibleHand showing two online retailers at significantly lower prices than the power Amazon offer.

Item model number: L5MS3

Average Customer Review: ★★★★☆ ☑ (187 customer reviews)

Amazon Best Sellers Rank: #15,142 in Kitchen & Dining (See Top 100 in Kitchen & Dining)

Would you like to **give feedback on images** or **tell us about a lower price**?

The sales rank of 15,142 looks pretty good, too!

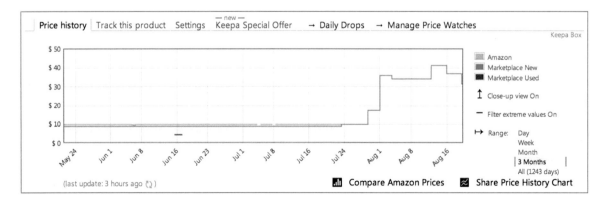

The Keepa price history shows that the price has gone up steadily ever since Amazon stopped selling the item for ~$10.

At this point, all available data pint to this being a great deal to buy from The WEBstaurant Store or Sears and sell on Amazon, right? Well, let's look at two more graphs from CamelCamelCamel:

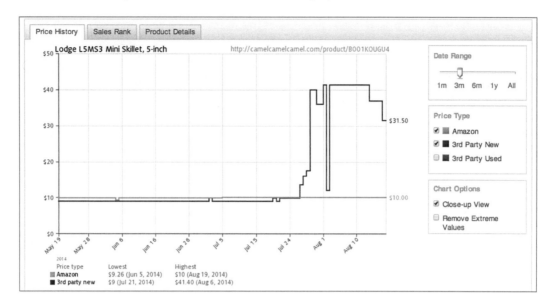

These are both THREE MONTH graphs so try to imagine them overlaid. You can see that the item used to have a GREAT sales rank when Amazon was in stock at ~$10. But when Amazon stopped selling the item and prices went up, sales rank went in the gutter. I would not be interested in this item at all because of the TRENDING sales correlating to increased price.

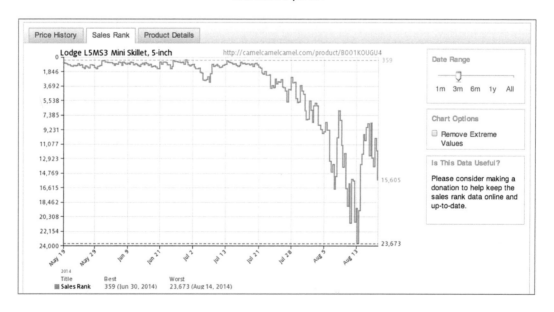

Remember that sales rank is a single point in time. One recent sale can make an item look like it has a good sales rank. Before making any kind of large purchase, do as much research as you can on previous sales, especially looking at the sales rank history from CamelCamelCamel. It can help you avoid making bad buying decisions.

Online Arbitrage - When a good deal isn't as good as you think

http://youtu.be/rA06ZixXmgI
http://bit.ly/notadeal

Here is an example where InvisibleHand returned the wrong product from another online retailer. InvisibleHand said that Fry's had this item for $19.99 + shipping, but clicking through just takes you to their Monster High Doll Assortment page. This is why you have to click through and check pages yourself. The extensions can help make you faster, but they are not without errors.

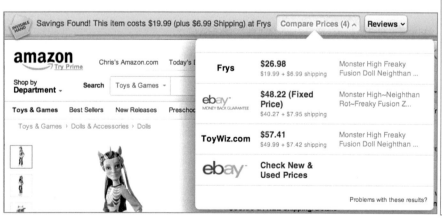

Online Arbitrage Deal Due Diligence - TheTracktor.com

http://youtu.be/xNcj02xA34M
http://bit.ly/tracktordeal

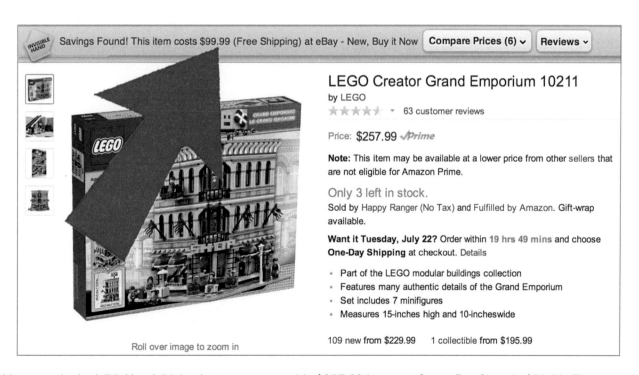

In this example, InvisibleHand thinks that you can get this $257.99 Lego set from eBay for only $99.99. That would be totally awesome, but let's go to eBay and check to be sure.

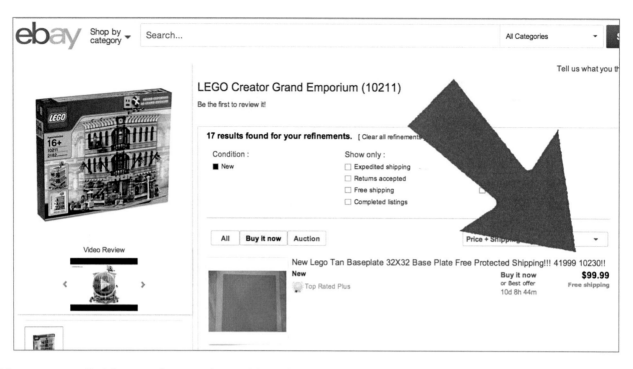

And here you see that they are incorrectly matching a listing for a single Lego baseplate piece for $99.99 on the same page as the Lego set. Even though this is not a match, it's very quick and easy to check and verify.

http://www.Amazon.com/dp/B00009ZK08/

This was a pretty crazy item that many people tried to order. I posted this deal and many people decided to place an order to see what happened. A seller listed this $129.95 knife for $10.40 + $11.95 shipping. They had 358 in stock.

Keepa did catch this very brief price drop.

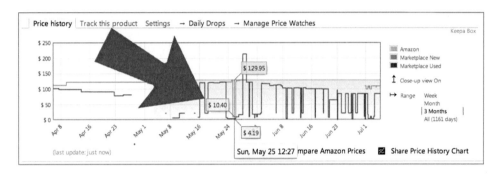

This Keepa graph is quite suspicious. It seems that while this was an anomaly in New condition, every now and then the Used offer dips way down. It's possible that a seller, maybe even Amazon Warehouse Deals, prices these things at a very low price, but it is rare to see such a pattern of aggressive pricing. In a case like this, I would set up a price alert or in-stock alert for this item in Used condition because those offers are just so far below the general market price for this item. I would be extra careful of selling them back on Amazon as well if buying from a Marketplace seller instead of Amazon. If you were able to acquire this item at those prices from third party sellers, another venue to consider selling would be eBay.

My other thought about this is that this may really represent a real opportunity because it's very unlikely that any other resellers are tracking items this way. The easy, low-hanging fruit is the stuff from Amazon, but the price points shown on this Keepa graph from Marketplace Used sellers are just too attractive to dismiss.

This did turn out to be a price mistake from the seller. I heard all orders were canceled.

Because of this low price, I did set up a Keepa price alert 'just in case', and guess what happened?

I got a Tweet and a text that the item was available for an even lower price! This time $5.97 and strangely enough from a DIFFERENT seller.

Take a look at the alerts and the order I placed right from my phone. Remember, sometimes you have to be QUICK. Sometimes you won't have time to go inside to your computer if you're outside cutting the grass.

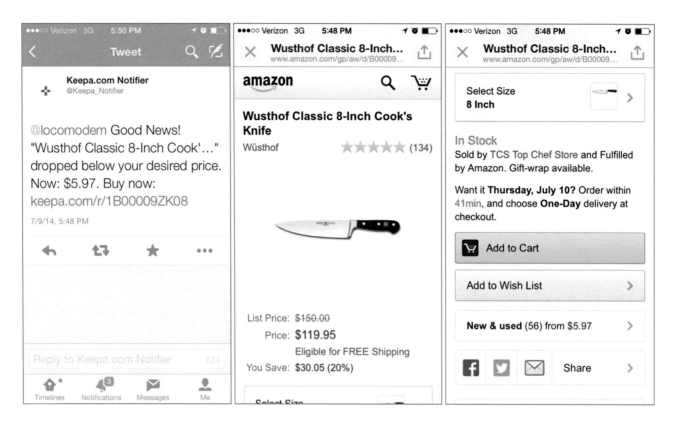

I got the alert, I clicked through, I went to the New and Used offers from $5.97, I added them to my cart, I edited the quantity but was limited to a quantity of ten.

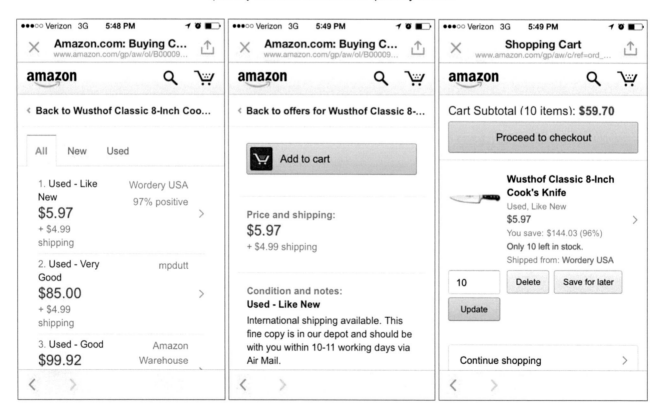

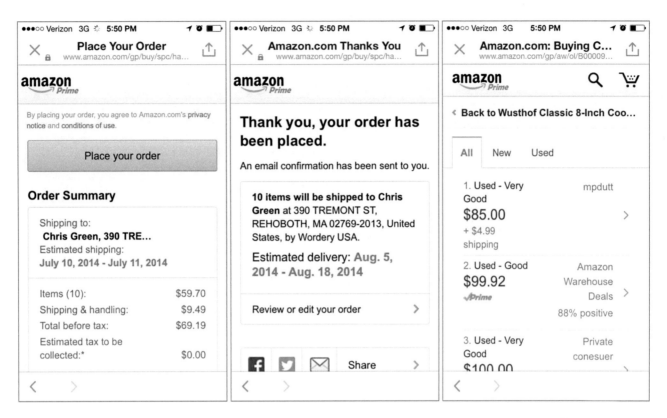

I place my order, got my confirmation, and now that $5.97 offer is no longer listed on the Amazon offers page. I did this entire process in less than TWO MINUTES of receiving the alert.

As I would have predicted (and as you may have expected), the order was canceled. No big deal. I really didn't expect it to go through. The seller did not contact me and instead just marked it as Customer Canceled.

159

I was not going to think about this deal again but as soon as I received the cancelation email, the Chrome Keepa alert pops up telling me that the item is back in stock AGAIN! Clearly what happened is that this seller canceled my order but did not adjust their price or stock levels. Once the order was canceled, the ten units went back into their inventory at the same $5.97 price.

So I click through and sure enough it's the same seller with the same price and the same quantity. At this point I feel as if I am doing them a favor by buying all ten units. Instead of having to cancel ten orders, they will only have one order to cancel.

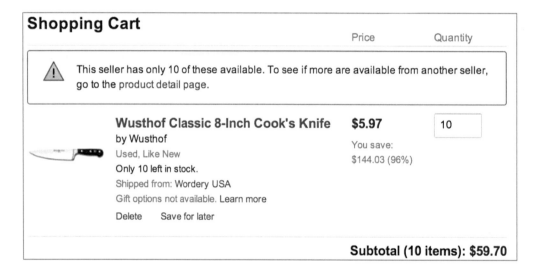

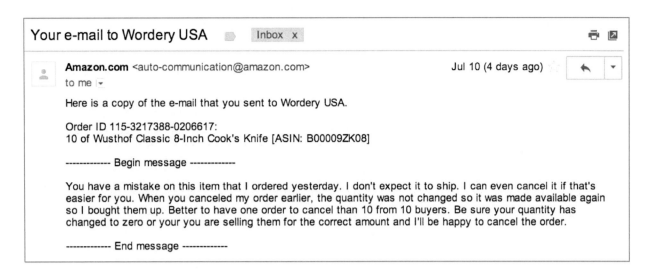

This time I send them an email explaining what is going on. I offer to cancel the order for them (this will reflect better on their metrics as a seller). I get no response but I do get another cancelation email saying that it was Customer Canceled.

Chapter 12 – Rabbit Trails

This is probably my favorite chapter. A lot of rabbit trails start with lists or deals. Track them back and see if you can figure out what triggered something. Then look for other similar deals. It's really just that easy.

In this video, we start on TheTracktor and end up buying candy.

Online Arbitrage Rabbit Trails - TheTracktor Almond Joy Candy Replenishables

http://youtu.be/fkKfUBMpKHI
http://bit.ly/rabbittrail1

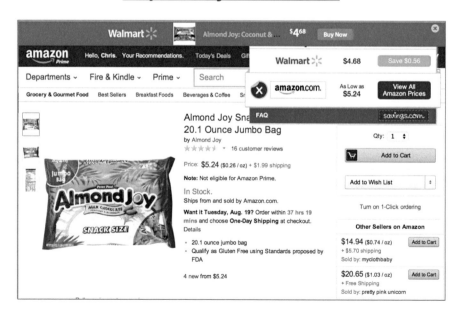

Product featured: http://www.Amazon.com/dp/B00CP3KSRU

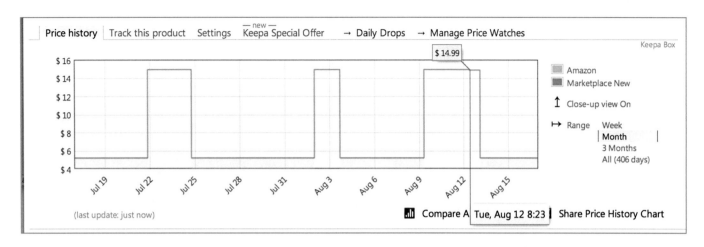

Check out this awesome Keepa graph. Love seeing the consistent pattern of Amazon going out of stock and then the lowest offer price going way up.

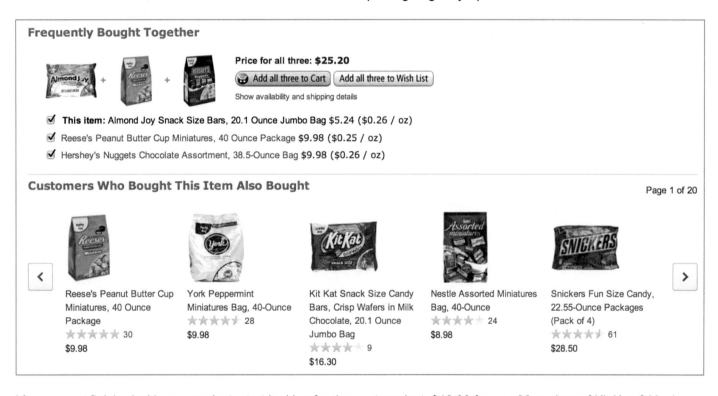

After you get finished with one product, start looking for the next product. $16.30 for one 20 oz. bag of Kit Kats? Yeah, you better go check on that. There are TWENTY pages of additional items to consider checking for possible resale opportunities. It's like they do all the hard work for you.

In this example, we start on CamelCamelCamel with a deal from their Top Price Drops and follow the rabbit trail.

Online Arbitrage Rabbit Trail - CamelCamelCamel Dog Treats

http://youtu.be/tHQE1qQnkVo
http://bit.ly/rabbittrail2

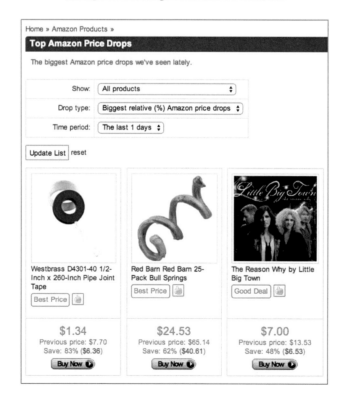

Product featured: http://www.Amazon.com/dp/B0017JFNNC

In this example, we start on Keepa and end up finding deals on candy sold at Wal-Mart.

Online Arbitrage Rabbit Trail - Keepa Deals to Wal-Mart Starburst Candy

http://youtu.be/DpU6JNNAK8U
http://bit.ly/rabbittrail3

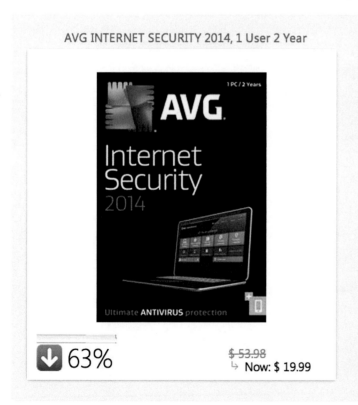

AVG INTERNET SECURITY 2014, 1 User 2 Year

↓ 63% $~~53.98~~
          ↳ Now: $ 19.99

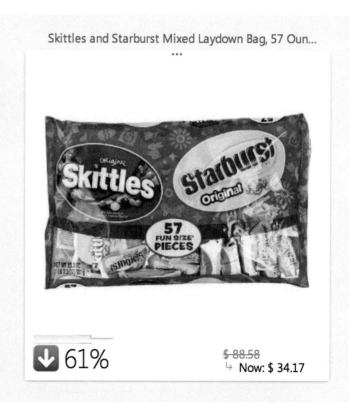

Skittles and Starburst Mixed Laydown Bag, 57 Oun...

↓ 61% $~~88.58~~
          ↳ Now: $ 34.17

Product featured: http://www.Amazon.com/dp/B00F94XO8W

In this video, we start on the Amazon Movers & Shakers page and end up on eBay searching for BOLOs.

Amazon Movers & Shakers Rabbit Trail to eBay - NERF GUNS

http://youtu.be/KQo_DvgMnkc
http://bit.ly/rabbittrail4

Product featured: http://www.Amazon.com/dp/B003H9MTJ6

In this video, we start at Pricenoia and find some How To Train Your Dragon BOLOs using tools like Keepa, CamelCamelCamel, Google, and Google Images.

Online Arbitrage - BOLO Hunting with Pricenoia, Keepa, CamelCamelCamel, Google, and ToyWiz

http://youtu.be/E1s1VFYVCh8
http://bit.ly/rabbittrail5

Product featured: http://www.Amazon.com/dp/B00DH2M6U0

This is an example of a product that was on the CamelCamelCamel Top Price Drops.

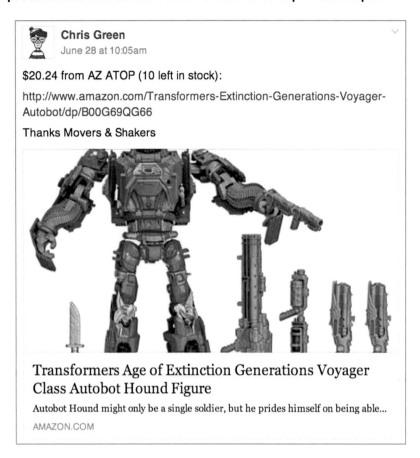

CamelCamelCamel reported a price of $20.24. Checking the Amazon product page, we can see that the Buy Box price when Amazon is out of stock is $48.99 + $4.77 shipping. People are paying over $50 for a Transformer toy! Why? Doesn't matter; you just need to figure out where to get these things.

Product featured: http://www.Amazon.com/dp/B00G69QG66/

Keepa shows that when Amazon was in stock, they sold for $26.99 before dropping to a discounted price of $20.24. This was likely Amazon price matching another online retailer.

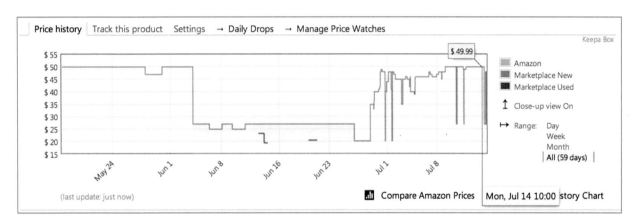

You can clearly see the prices spike when Amazon is out of stock to the $50+ levels. You could also check CamelCamelCamel to be sure that the item has a good historical sales rank, even at the $50+ price points.

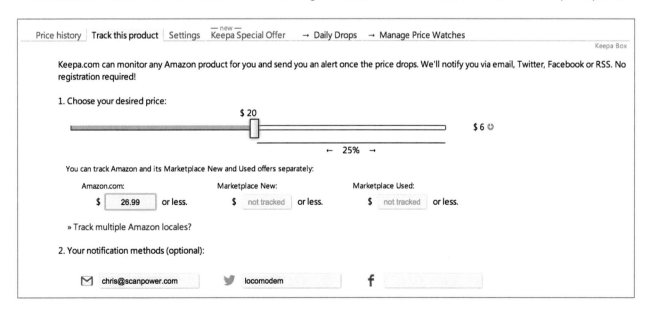

Since Amazon is out of stock, we want to set up a price alert. We set this one at $26.99 so that we catch Amazon even if they listed the item at the original MSRP OR the reduced $20.24. If we only entered $20.24, we would miss this item at $26.99, a price that would still return a profit.

But let's not stop there! Take a look at what InvisibleHand shows us on the Amazon product page:

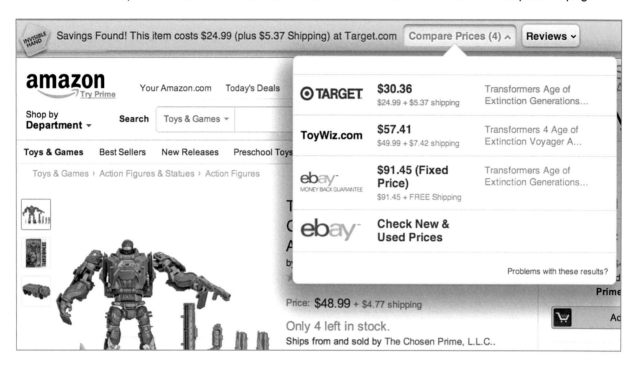

Each of these other offers is interesting. Seeing that this item sells for a very high price on eBay is a great sign that this is not just an over-retail price on Amazon. The fact that ToyWiz (more on ToyWiz later in Chapter 13) is also selling over-retail also indicates that this item is hard to get and commanding a premium price.

InvisibleHand also shows us that Target.com carries this product. One click and we're at the Target page only to find out that it is currently unavailable online. Depending how hot this item was and how desperately you wanted to know when this item comes in stock at Target.com, you could set up a webpage monitor (more info on webpage monitors in Chapter 28).

While not true Online Arbitrage, you can check the availability at your local stores. Depending on the deal, you may even venture outside, leaving the safe and secure confines of your home to pick up some deals at an actual store.

Here's a BONUS TIP for you. Make a list of several Zip Codes from across the country. Use Google Maps if you don't know anyone from certain states (pick a Wal-Mart Zip Code like Wal-Mart Denver, CO or Wal-Mart Houston, TX to get Zip Codes from anywhere in the country). Enter those zip codes in the store locator page on websites and see if the product is in stock or hard to find from other parts of the country.

Three things you can learn here. First, if a product is hard to find all across the country, that can give you some inside info about what will happen with online inventory and potential demand. Second, you may find that some parts of the country have an item in stock (even if sold out near you). You may be in a mastermind group (more on mastermind groups in Chapter 29) with someone in that area and you can pass along that information, or you may post that info in the ScannerMonkey® BOLO Exchange to trade that info for another BOLO that is more actionable to you in your area (more on ScannerMonkey® BOLO Exchange in Chapter 38).

Here is an example of a Keepa alert that I received through their Chrome Extension.

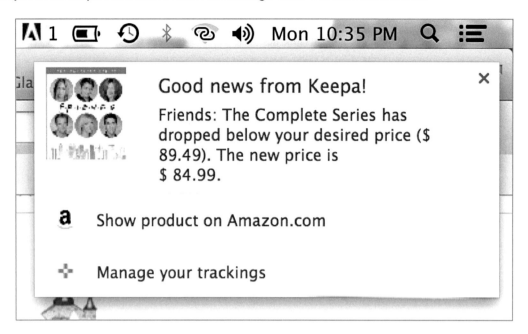

Amazon later dropped the price on this DVD box set to $76.96.

A quick check of Keepa shows that this is a very low price compared to Amazon's past prices. The 61% discount off of the $200+ List Price is another good sign.

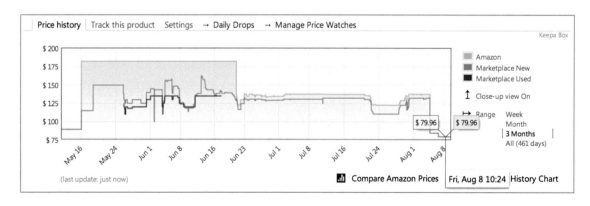

Taking a closer look at the competitive offers shows a nice price difference between Amazon and the next lowest offer.

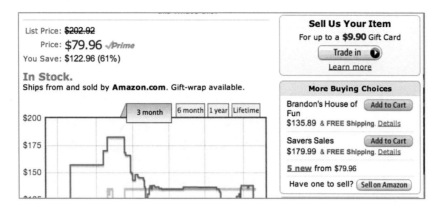

The dropdown Wal-Mart Shopper extension shows that Amazon is most likely price-matching Wal-Mart on this item. If this item is not restricted for you as a seller, you may want to consider buying it from Wal-Mart, especially if Amazon is imposing quantity limits on this item. If you are restricted from selling this item, consider eBay.

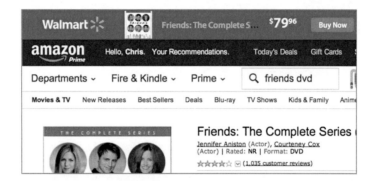

A quick check of the Wal-Mart site and the Amazon 1Button App shows what we already know: The price is the same on Amazon. But the more interesting information is in 'Other items purchased by customers who viewed this item'. If one DVD box set is on sale, it's very possible that other DVD box sets are also on sale. I want to look for big price drops relative to the original price. For example, the Friends DVD box set on Blu-Ray, Gilmore Girls, Smallville, and Gossip Girl.

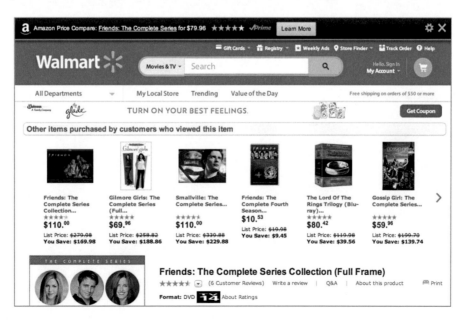

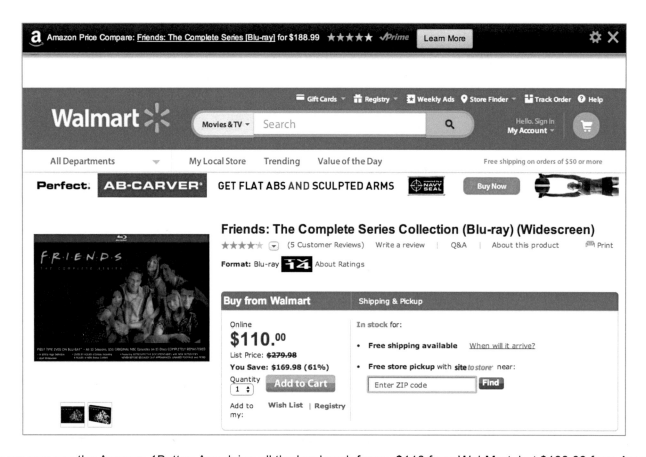

Here we can see the Amazon 1Button App doing all the hard work for us. $110 from Wal-Mart, but $188.99 from Amazon.

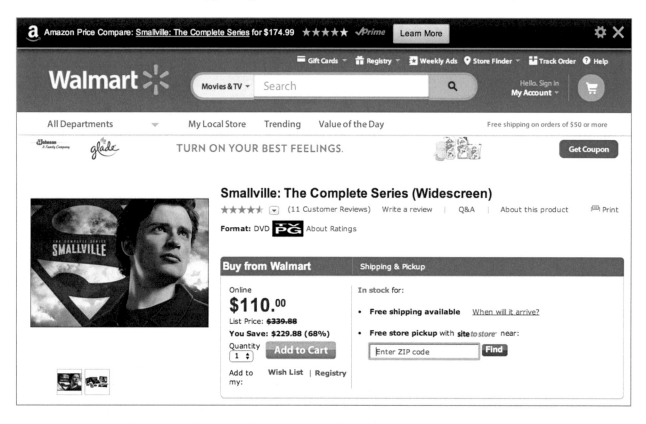

Here is another one. $110 from Wal-Mart, but $174.99 from Amazon.

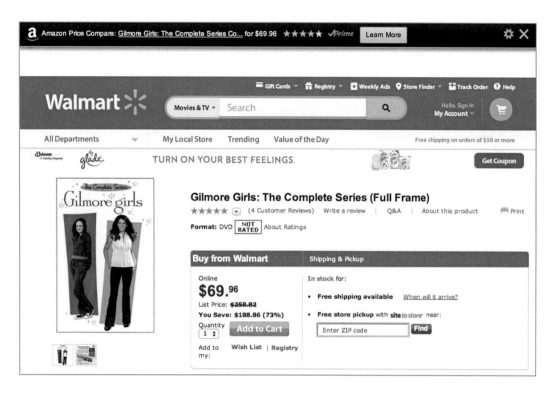

In this example, the Amazon 1Button App found the match, but Amazon has it for the same price. So is it a deal or not a deal? Let's check the data on Amazon product page (you'll see the next lower offer is $115) and use our Chrome extensions:

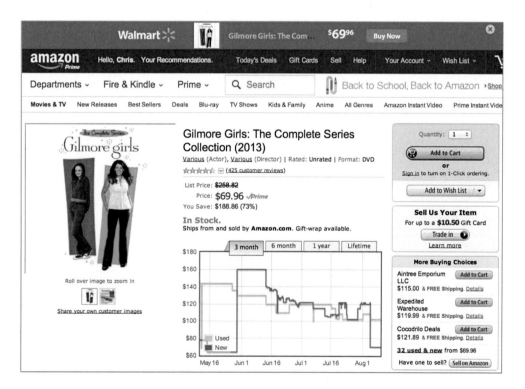

By checking all of the prices, you can see that we found this one by going backwards from Wal-Mart back to the Amazon Marketplace prices. If only looking at the Wal-Mart price and with no history of sales price, you can't gauge the actual Marketplace price and demand. Once you see the price history and the prices from other third party sellers, you can more accurately determine if the item is being sold at a price that can be resold for a profit.

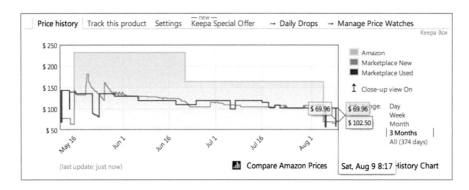

The Keepa graph shows that this is a low price from Amazon compared to their recent prices of over $150 and over $200 just a few months ago. While the Amazon price has fluctuated a lot, the Marketplace prices have stayed pretty steady. Looking back, you can see that around May 16, Amazon dropped the price very low. Checking this price may give you a clue about how to set up your price alerts.

Rabbit Trail: VTech Switch & Go Dinos

Starting at the Amazon Movers & Shakers, Related Products, Invisible Hand, Kohl's Clearance:

This next rabbit trail starts on the Amazon Movers & Shakers List at #17 with a toy that has not been on list before. It also has the $8.00 Buy Box price matching the '37 used & new from' price indicating that the $8.00 price is the overall lower offer from all sellers.

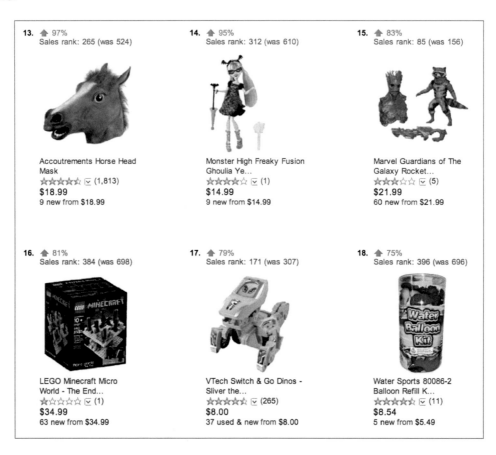

Checking the product detail page confirms that Amazon is the seller (good sign).

http://www.Amazon.com/dp/B007XVYSYI/

Comparing the other offers shows that Amazon is the lowest price by a considerable margin (next lowest offer at the time: $14.99 + $4.99 shipping).

Price + Shipping	Condition	Seller Information
$8.00 & FREE Shipping on orders over $35.00. Details ✓Prime Learn more	New	**amazon**.com. In Stock. Want it delivered Friday, July 11? Order it in the next 22 hours and 11 minutes, and choose **One-Day Shipping** at checkout. See details Domestic shipping rates and return policy.
$14.99 + $4.99 shipping	New	**Ncruzlittleshop** ★★★★☆ 100% positive over the past 12 months. (2 total ratings) Ships in 1-2 business days. Ships from NJ, United States. Expedited shipping available. Domestic shipping rates and return policy.
$15.29 + $5.99 shipping	New	**yoyo.com** ★★★★☆ 94% positive over the past 12 months. (30,888 total ratings) Ships in 24 hours. Domestic shipping rates and return policy.
$17.35 + $4.99 shipping	New *** THIS ITEM CAN ONLY BE SHIPPED TO PHYSICAL ADDRESSES IN THE CONTINENTAL US *** NO APO/FPO/DPO/PO BOX, PR, HI or AK ***	**Toys Online** ★★★★☆ 90% positive over the past 12 months. (10,124 total ratings) Ships in 1-2 business days. Expedited shipping available. Domestic shipping rates and return policy.
$22.94 & FREE Shipping on orders over $35.00. Details ✓Prime Learn more	New	**DynaBooks , LLC** FULFILLMENT BY AMAZON ★★★★★ 100% positive over the past 12 months. (92 total ratings) In Stock. Want it delivered Friday, July 11? Order it in the next 18 hours and 11 minutes, and choose **One-Day Shipping** at checkout. See details Domestic shipping rates and return policy.

The InvisibleHand extension shows where else this item can be purchased as well as the prices. $8.00 certainly seems to be the lowest price from all online retailers.

This is confirmed by the Keepa graph shows historical Amazon prices in the $12 - $16 range.

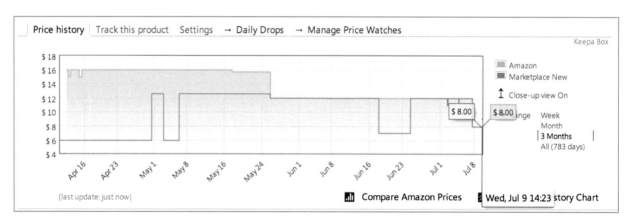

Looking back, we can see that just prior to Christmas 2013, the price was over $32 when Amazon was out of stock.

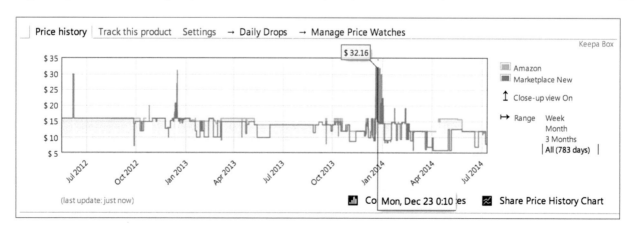

This information alone may be enough to make a buying decision on this item, but we want to follow some rabbit trails and learn a little more about this line of toys in the event that other items may be similarly reduced in price. We also want to learn a little more about other items in this line that may be selling at over-retail prices when Amazon is out of stock.

We can follow two rabbit trails for most any product on Amazon: the 'Frequently Bought Together' items as well as the 'Customers Who Bought This Item Also Bought' items.

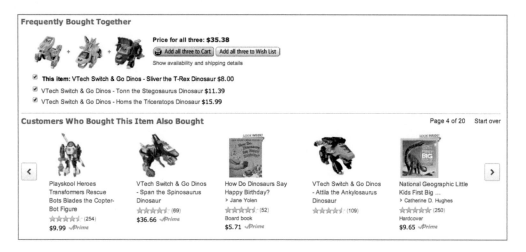

The three 'Frequently Bought Together' items do not look as interesting at first glance. The two other items that appear to be the same scale and that likely sell for the same prices are not also being sold for $8.00. But on the fourth page of 'Customers Who Bought This Item Also Bought' items we see an item that does not have a price underneath it. We all know what this means, right? This indicates an item whose Buy Box price is being suppressed by Amazon because the item is being sold at a price ABOVE the list price or MSRP. Looking at the item's product page, this is exactly what we see. $68.99 for this toy. http://www.Amazon.com/dp/B007XVYSZ2/

And the Keepa graph shows that Amazon originally sold this toy for $11.99. You can see the pricing trend on this item over time as well as noting Amazon being out of stock since May.

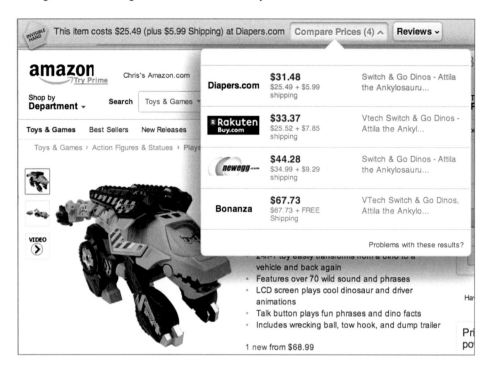

InvisibleHand pops up trying to help, but unfortunately, these links were all expired and led nowhere.

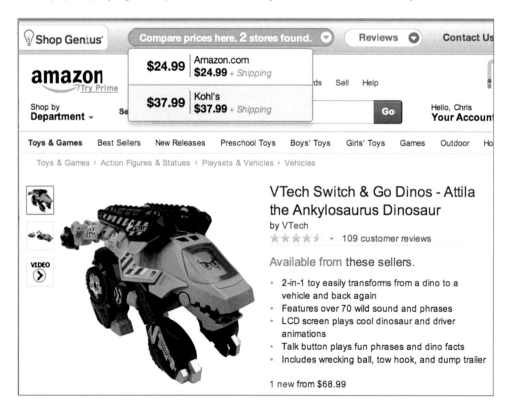

Shop Genius, on the other hand, was helpful. They show is that Amazon sells this for $24.99 (actually not true as we saw on the product page) as well as Kohl's selling this for $37.99.

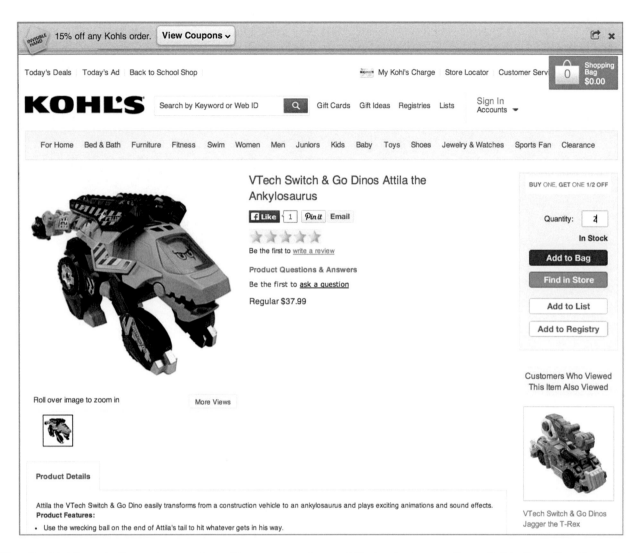

Visiting the Kohl's website, we're greeted with some good news! It's in stock as well as eligible for a Buy One, Get One 50% off sale. InvisibleHand is back and telling us about a 15% off any Kohl's order coupon (thanks!).

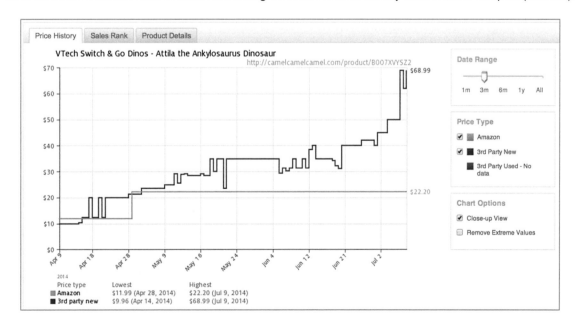

Now that we're here and things are looking pretty good, you should do some additional deal due diligence. The Keepa data looked good, but let's also check CamelCamelCamel for historical prices as well as historical sales rank. Finding an item with great margin is nice, but if it has no history of actually selling, then it won't do you any good.

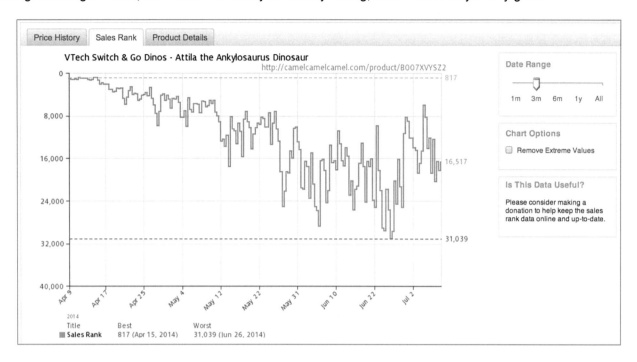

You also want to gauge sales rank and sales velocity to help you decide HOW MANY of an item to buy. You'd then relate that to the potential margin and profit. Your business model may support lower margins as long as the items sell very quickly. If the item has a large profit potential, you may be more inclined to buy items that sell more infrequently. Depending on the time of year and the sales rank history, you may be more inclined to purchase and hope to sell during the fourth quarter. Checking the past sales rank on this item shows that it does sell well (although not as well as when Amazon offered it at a much lower price).

Product Details

Product Dimensions: 4.2 x 9.4 x 3.5 inches ; 3.2 pounds

Shipping Weight: 3.2 pounds

Shipping: Currently, item can be shipped only within the U.S.

ASIN: B007XVYSZ2

Item model number: 80-132100

Manufacturer recommended age: 36 months - 8 years

Batteries 2 AAA batteries required. (included)

Amazon Best Sellers Rank: #26,808 in Toys & Games (See Top 100 in Toys & Games)
 #47 in Toys & Games > Electronics for Kids > **Electronic Pets**
 #83 in Toys & Games > Action & Toy Figures > Playsets & Vehicles > **Vehicles**

Average Customer Review: ★★★★☆ ☑ (109 customer reviews)

You may also want to check the Product Details to see the item's weight as it relates to preparation and fees. You can run this item through the FBA Calculator or ScanPower WebScout to see exact fees and payouts at different price points.

Now that you've found a good deal, you might as well look around the Kohl's website. They have a clearance section so you might as well see what's available.

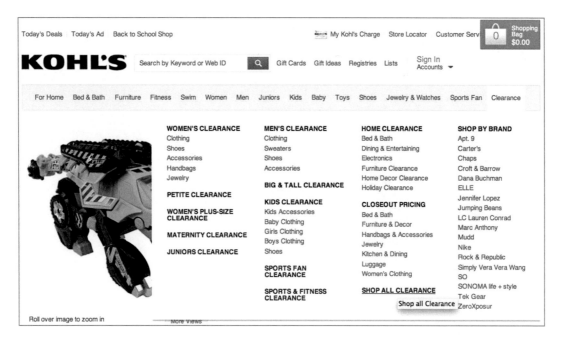

If you have been doing Online Arbitrage for a while, some items may pop out at you because you had seen them before. Experience certainly gives you an advantage. Let's take a closer look at that pirate ship.

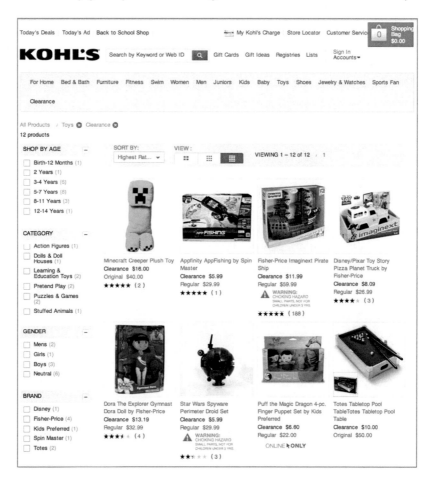

183

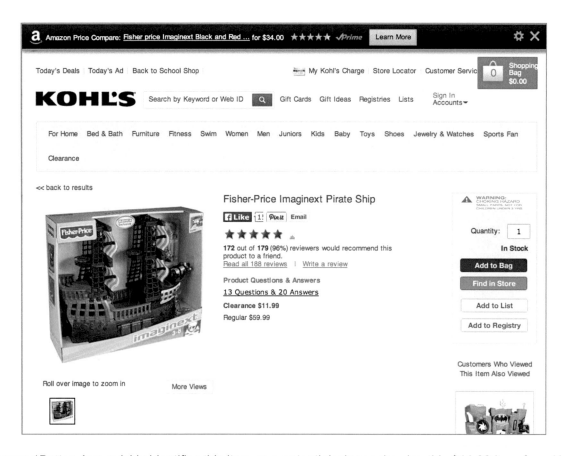

The Amazon 1Button App quickly identifies this item as a potential winner showing this $11.99 item from Kohls.com selling for $34 on Amazon.com.

Invisible Hand shows another online retailer at an even higher price. Looks like we found another item to add to our online shopping cart!

Here is the Amazon product page: http://www.Amazon.com/dp/B002LRKB36/

Keepa shows a price of ~$30 + shipping with no Amazon competition over the past two months.

Product Details

Product Dimensions: 20.5 x 5.2 x 10 inches

Shipping Weight: 7.3 pounds (View shipping rates and policies)

Origin: IMPORTED

ASIN: B002LRKB36

Item model number: R8250

Manufacturer recommended age: 36 months - 7 years

Amazon Best Sellers Rank: #2,580 in Toys & Games (See Top 100 in Toys & Games)

    #24 in Toys & Games > Action & Toy Figures > **Accessories**

    #29 in Toys & Games > Preschool > Pre-Kindergarten Toys > Pretend Play > **Toy Figure Playsets**

    #33 in Toys & Games > Action & Toy Figures > Playsets & Vehicles > **Playsets**

Average Customer Review: ★★★★★ ☑ (96 customer reviews)

The Product Details page shows a great sales rank. You could also double check CamelCamelCamel for historical sales rank.

They also have a 'Customers Who Viewed This Item Also Bought' section similar to Amazon. This is a great place to look for other deals. You may find items from shoppers who are looking for the best deals, or items that other resellers have been looking at. This may give you new ideas or show you products that you wouldn't normally have looked at.

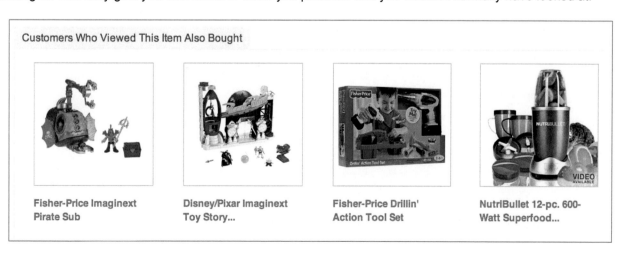

Do you even remember where this rabbit trail started? It was a new toy popping up on the Amazon Movers & Shakers list. We didn't do anything crazy or weird here; we just followed some simple and logical steps to find similar products and used tools and extensions to check prices and other sites quickly and efficiently. Truly anyone can do this business.

Canceled Orders:

Despite all your best Online Arbitrage efforts, sometimes your orders will end up being canceled anyways.

Amazon.com Customer Service <order-update@amazon.com>	Aug 16 (9 days ago)

to me ▾

Hello,

We're contacting you about order #002-5552243-0004235

002-0304033-5339443

002-2650694-5169861. Unfortunately, we recently discovered that an error caused the following item(s) to be displayed at an incorrect price:

Reusch Argos D1 Ortho Tec Junior Goalie Glove, Black/White, 5

ATEC AT7600 Remote Control for Arm Pitching Machine

ATEC AT7600 Baseball Arm Pitching Machine

In this case, we're unable to offer this item for the incorrectly posted price. Therefore, we've canceled your order for this item. We're sorry about this. At any given time, despite our best efforts, a small number of the millions of items on our site may be mispriced.

To make up for any inconvenience, we're adding a $20 Amazon.com Gift Card to your account. This balance will automatically apply to your next order at Amazon.com.

But at least you'll usually get $20 out of it.

Online Arbitrage - Rabbit Trail Deals, Lawn Mowers, and $1,000 American Flags

http://youtu.be/jY3Bf9UTxD4
http://bit.ly/rabbittrail6

Chapter 13 – Learn a Line

Learn what products in a line are going to be popular, hot, hard to find, in short supply, collectible, etc. Whatever you want to call it, knowledge is power in this game of Online Arbitrage!

Use the strategies outlined in this chapter to quickly become 90+% fluent in ANY LINE or ANY PRODUCT. And don't just think about toys. There are a lot of toys examples in this book because toys are easy, but do what other sellers don't do and you'll find that you have less competition.

REMEMBER: If you find one item that has dropped in price, there are likely others. Same line, same category, same manufacturer, same seller. Rarely will one random item be marked down.

Watch TV and take note of the commercials. Pay attention to the main aisle end caps at the major retailers. See what products are being promoted on the homepages of the major online retailers. What items are on the Amazon Best Sellers and Movers & Shakers lists. What products are being talked about in groups, forums, collector circles, fan pages?

Here we are going to look at some shortcut ways to see which products have greater potential for becoming 'hot' or in a more specific definition, hard to find, in demand, and being sold online at an inflated, over-retail price for a short window of time.

When it comes to toys, it is very valuable information to know to identify and find short packs, rare versions, chase figures, flagship products, and other toys that become HOT.

Let's look at a toy retailer that does not follow MSRP or MAP, but not in the way that you may be thinking. They don't break MAP by selling for LESS. They INCREASE their prices to sell at the market price set by supply and demand.

Go ahead and get on their email list!

Let's start with an easy example that you've already seen in previous chapters: http://www.toywiz.com/pawpatrol.html

You can see which items are being sold at retail and which ones are being marked up. Experienced sellers are already doing research like this. Why are certain toys being sold at higher prices than others? Possibly because they are short packed, the strong demand is outpacing the current supply, or for some other reason. Use their experience as a guide.

To find out the true MSRP, use Amazon or some other online retailers product pages.

Once you know the MSRP, look for markups and items that are sold out.

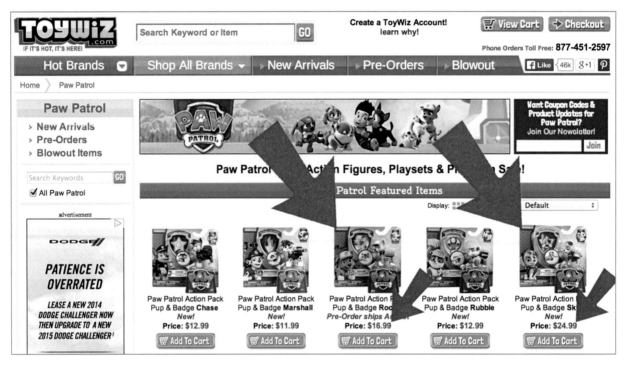

Look at all the price variations across the Paw Patrol line of plush toys.

Look at the prices for the last four items knowing that the MSRP from Amazon when in stock is $12.99. What do they know? Do they expect strong demand? Do they know they are in short supply? Whatever it is, you know it now, too.

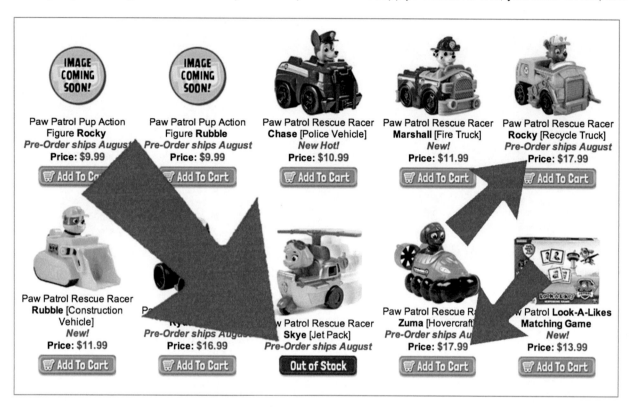

You definitely want to pay attention to the out of stock items. And guess what else is out of stock?

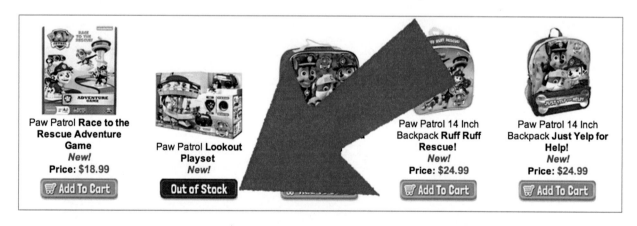

Another Amazon seller that sells toys at MSRP but also at over-retail prices is Brian's Toys.

http://www.Amazon.com/gp/node/index.html?&me=AQFDJWVWBAE1T

They also buy toys back on their website: http://www.brianstoys.com/

Learn a line – trending brands

Ever heard of Moose Toys? If you haven't, I'm sure you've heard of some of the toy lines that they make. Take a look for yourself. Have you seen any of these brands on the shelves of your local retailers? On the front pages of their websites? On the Amazon Movers & Shakers and Best Sellers pages? They should already be on your radar.

You may be familiar with some of these products. Skylanders have been popular for a few years now and you'd have to live on a different planet to have never heard of Angry Birds. Many of these products should also be familiar to anyone who has bookmarked and checked the Toys Movers & Shakers, Bestsellers, New Releases, and Most Wished For pages on Amazon. So when one toy is popular, you may think to yourself, "I wonder what other products this company makes?"

Well, the answer is just a simple Google search away. It's also printed on the packages of these toys. #NotASecret

You can see that they have a link to 'Where To Buy' where you can see at a glance all of the retailers that carry their products (so that you don't waste time looking on the wrong websites or going to the wrong stores). They have a link to 'What's New' where they also have media press releases. Reading these, you can see what they've said about toy awards and popularity of their products. You can also use this information to look back at what happened in the market, what items won awards, and what items sold well and compare that to the historical prices on Amazon using Keepa and other price tracking websites. Start to connect the dots on what worked before and use this information to predict what will work next!

http://www.mooseworld.com.au/au/about-moose/press-room/for-the-media/

This is just one example of one company. This is why it's important to stay up to date with the latest trends. Find something that works, and follow the rabbit trails.

Beados? We'll see an example of Beados later in Chapter 18.

Groups, Forums, and Fan Sites:

Maybe you see an item like this on the Amazon Movers & Shakers page:

7. ⬆ 338%	8. ⬆ 271%	9. ⬆ 179%
Sales rank: 287 (was 1,258)	Sales rank: 76 (was 282)	Sales rank: 378 (was 1,058)

Betrayal At House On The Hill - 2nd E...	Funko POP! Movies-Sharknado: Blood Sp...	Fisher-Price Ocean Wonders Soothe and...
★★★★☆ (286)	★★★★★ (1)	★★★★☆ (1,772)
$50.48	Currently unavailable	$14.99
12 used & new from $50.48		

#8 is not only up 271% in sales rank, but it's also **completely sold out**. You can click through to see the most recent price on this item as well as set up in stock and price alerts. You may even want to use this item as a clue to do a little more research on this line.

A simple Google search finds this site: http://popvinyls.com/

And a simple Facebook search finds this group: https://www.facebook.com/groups/funkotrading/

This is just an EXAMPLE. You can do these same searches for ANY PRODUCT or any line of products on Amazon. When you check the Movers & Shakers pages and the Best Sellers pages, you'll be able to keep up with new products. Then do your research. The Internet allows you to basically become 90% fluent in any category in a matter of hours.

You may have heard the phrases 'girl toy in a boy line of toys' or 'boy toy in a girl line of toys' if you've been in any of the Facebook groups or listening to our SpreeCasts and YouTube videos.

Here is an example, and we'll also walk through how to gather historical research and pricing info for this product (that you can later do yourself on any other product that you want to learn about).

The Teenage Mutant Ninja Turtle line of toys is generally targeted at boys, but this is GIRL character.

Roll over image to zoom in

Teenage Mutant Ninja Turtles April O'Neil

by Teenage Mutant Ninja Turtles

★★★★☆ ▾   59 customer reviews

Price: **$28.00** ✓*Prime*

Only 2 left in stock.
Sold by Red Wolf Collectibles and Fulfilled by Amazon. Gift-wrap available.

- April O'Neil may not fit in at school with her peers, but when it comes to the Turtles, she's all about team green
- Clever and independent, this gal's got guts to spare and a mind for mischief
- Teenage Mutant Ninja Turtles and all related titles, logos and characters are trademarks of Viacom International Inc

Product Featured: http://www.Amazon.com/dp/B008DBZC8S/

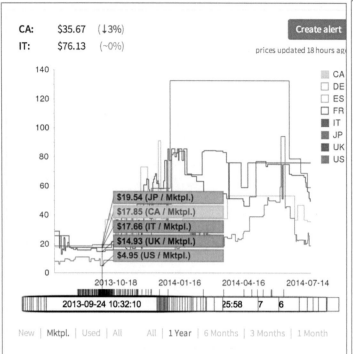

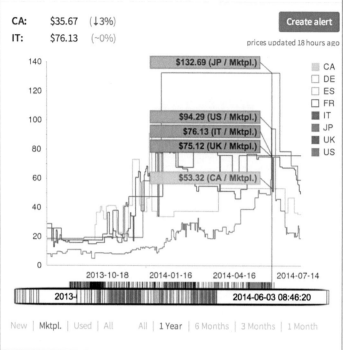

The Pricenoia graphs show much lower prices back in 2013. They clearly spiked in price in 2014. Before coming back down in price (although not back down to original retail).

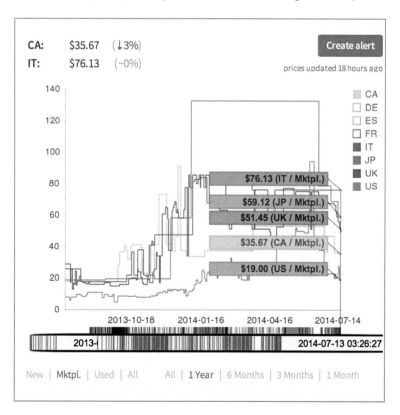

Looking at the 1-month Keepa shows us the last time Amazon was in stock (and MSRP): $11.99.

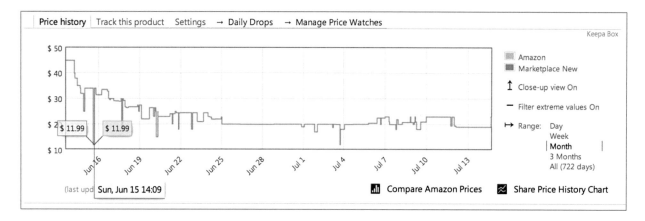

The 3-month Keepa shows us the highest historical price on Amazon of $94.29 + shipping back in June.

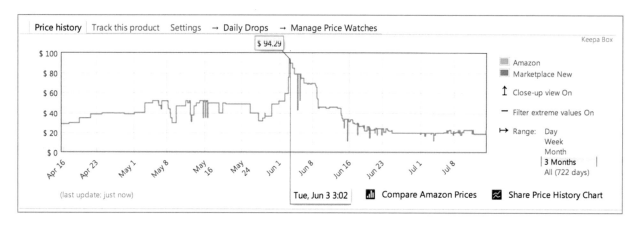

The total Keepa history shows that Amazon was even selling at a discounted $8.99 at one point.

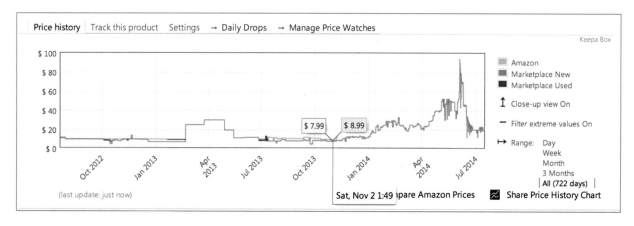

Since Keepa has been tracking this item for 722 days, it's very unlikely that any stores (retail or online) that originally sold this item would still be carrying it at the MSRP. But let's try to find them anyway as research for the next round of toys.

CamelCamelCamel confirms the all-time lowest price on Amazon from Amazon of $8.99 back on November 1, 2013.

http://camelcamelcamel.com/Teenage-Mutant-Ninja-Turtles-April/product/B008DBZC8S

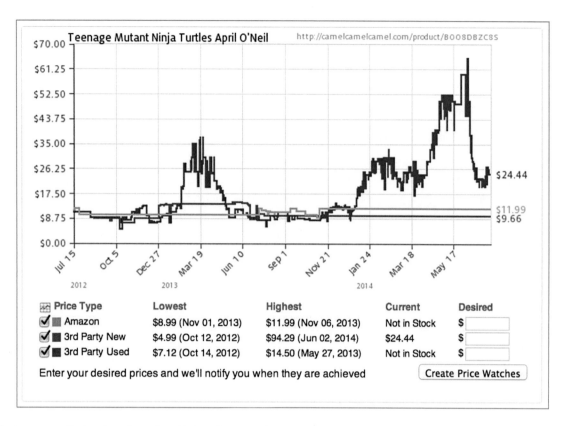

Let's see what we can find using Google. Using Context Search, we highlight the title and choose Google from the drop down menu: Teenage Mutant Ninja Turtles April O'Neil

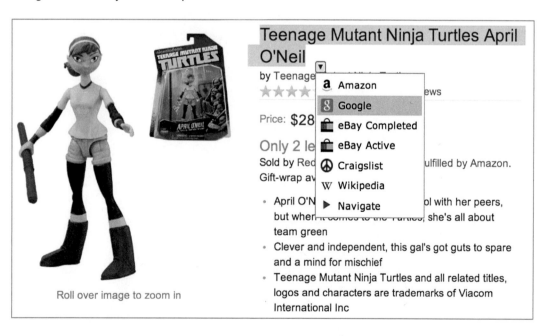

This doesn't work very well, as you may have predicted, since the title is just the character's name and the product line. Google thinks that you may be looking for information on the movie, the actress, or any other search result but not necessarily a toy or even this specific toy.

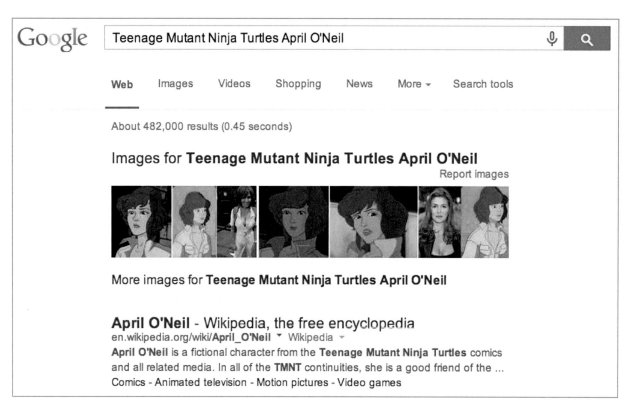

So how do we refine the Google search to get what we are looking for? Simple, let's add some additional search terms.

Looking at the packaging from the Amazon product photo, we can see that this particular product is from the Nickelodeon line of TMNT toys. So let's add key words 'nickelodeon' and 'toy' to our Google search.

Now the Google results are starting to look a little more interesting.

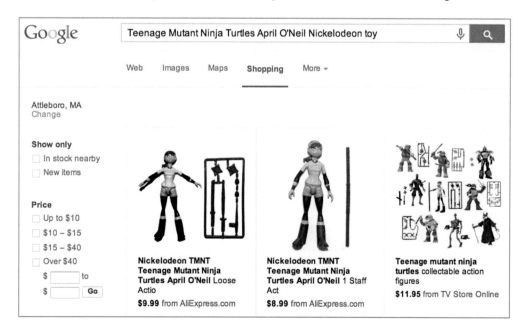

Looking at the Google Shopping results, we see a couple if images that match what we are looking for. However, this is where you need to be cautious and do your due diligence on your sources and suppliers. These items are 100% fake. If you check the details on the websites, you'll find that they are not in retail packaging, they are coming directly from China, and they don't even include all of these accessories. Please stay away from these types of items.

From the Google results, there was a toy review site that you can check:

http://www.actionfigurefury.com/toy-review/nickelodeon-teenage-mutant-ninja-turtles-april-oneil-figure-review/

Remember the Command-F and CTRL-F trick to find keywords? Use that for store names like walmart, target, toys r us, etc. You can see in the image above, we were quickly able to find that the website mentions Wal-Mart and as an added bonus we learn that at the time Wal-Mart was selling them for a discounted price of $7.77. See how easy it is to find historical pricing information as well as which stores sold specific items?

Now that we know that this item was sold at Wal-Mart, let's add search term 'walmart' to our Google search.

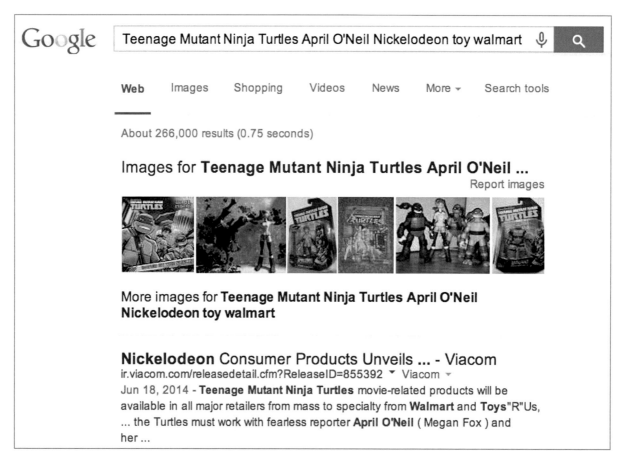

Very interesting search result. Viacom Press Release!

http://ir.viacom.com/releasedetail.cfm?ReleaseID=855392

🖶 🖨 🗎
« Previous Release I Next Release »

June 18, 2014

Nickelodeon Consumer Products Unveils Complete Merchandising Lineup for Teenage Mutant Ninja Turtles Summer Movie Blockbuster

Almost 30 New Licensees Will Launch Products Across Toys, Books, Home Décor, Apparel, Jewelry and Accessory Categories

LAS VEGAS--(BUSINESS WIRE)-- Nickelodeon today announced the full merchandising roster for the highly anticipated Paramount Pictures theatrical movie, *Teenage Mutant Ninja Turtles*, directed by Jonathan Liebesman, written by Josh Appelbaum and André Nemec and Evan Daugherty and produced by Michael Bay, arriving in theaters August 8. A full lineup of products inspired by the film will be available this summer through the holiday season, bringing to life the film's thrilling action and adventure.

Command-F or CTRL-F again and enter major retailer names such as walmart and target:

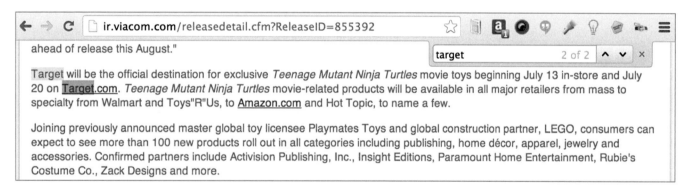

Target will be the official destination for exclusive *Teenage Mutant Ninja Turtles* movie toys beginning July 13 in-store and July 20 on Target.com. *Teenage Mutant Ninja Turtles* movie-related products will be available in all major retailers from mass to specialty from Wal-Mart and Toys"R"Us, to Amazon.com and Hot Topic, to name a few.

Joining previously announced master global toy licensee Playmates Toys and global construction partner, LEGO, consumers can expect to see more than 100 new products roll out in all categories including publishing, home décor, apparel, jewelry and accessories. Confirmed partners include Activision Publishing, Inc., Insight Editions, Paramount Home Entertainment, Rubie'sCostume Co., Zack Designs and more.

This is a great website to bookmark to check on. Press releases detailing which retailers are getting exclusive toys? Months ahead of their release? Yes, please. Be ready using these online resources. It's free research.

Online Arbitrage - TMNT April O'Neil, Google Searches, and Rabbit Trails

 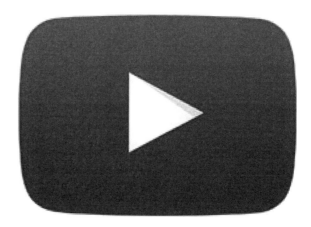

http://youtu.be/4FolvwqNt1c
http://bit.ly/rabbittrail7

So April O'Neil was an example of a toy that came out a while ago. Let's do a similar example with a more current toy.

Captain America Marvel Legends Black Widow Figure 6 Inches
by Captain america
★★★★ ⯪ ▾ 18 customer reviews

Price: $34.90 & FREE Shipping on orders over $35. Details

Only 1 left in stock.
Sold by deals2thedoor and Fulfilled by Amazon. Gift-wrap available.

Want it Friday, July 11? Order within 15 hrs 46 mins and choose **One-Day Shipping** at checkout. Details

- Get a part you need to build a mighty Mandroid figure with this cool Black Widow figure
- Figure comes with torso for Mandroid figure
- Other figures (sold separately) come with other parts
- Collect the whole Mandroid series
- Figure comes with torso part

Product Featured: http://www.Amazon.com/dp/B00G69PU2W/

The Keepa graphs show that Amazon sporadically came in stock at $21.99 and that for a while the price was as high as $60-$80 + shipping.

When on the Amazon product page, InvisibleHand shows us some useful information. In addition to alerting us that Target.com sells this for a cool $19.99, we also see that the prices from eBay, ToyWiz, and Rakuten are all over-retail. This is a great sign that the market price for this item is high everywhere, not just on Amazon.

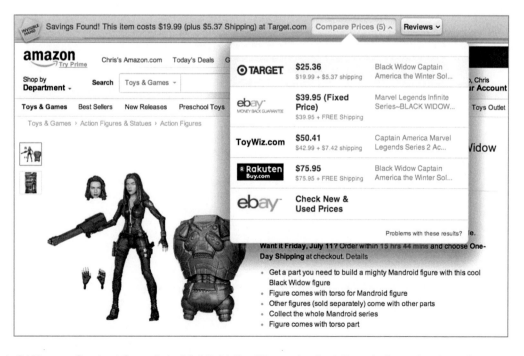

So what do we do? We use Context Search to highlight the title and select Google from the drop down menu. We want to find out where else we can buy this item to sell it on Amazon.

201

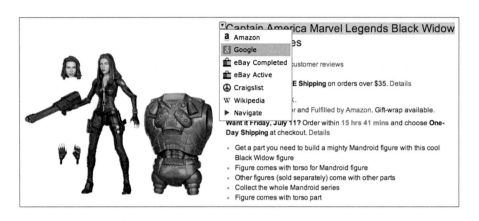

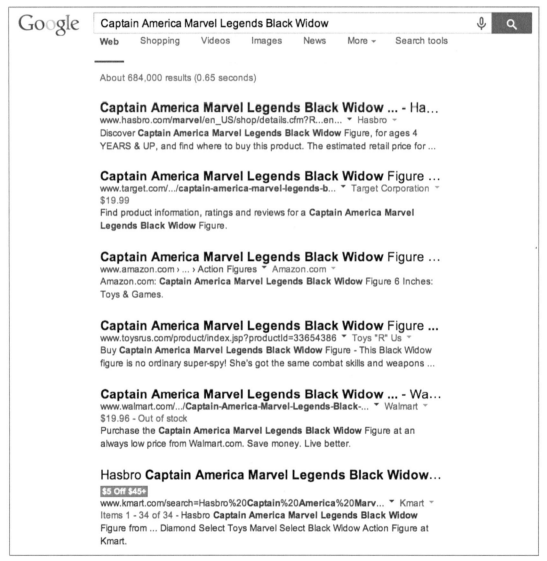

This is really just this easy. Googling the Amazon title shows us that this item is sold at Hasbro, Target, Amazon, Toys R Us, Wal-Mart, and Kmart. There really are no secrets. You can visit each site, see if they are in stock for online ordering, or maybe they are only available in stores.

The Hasbro website reveals the list rice of $19.99 and has a nice big button to direct you 'Where to Buy'.

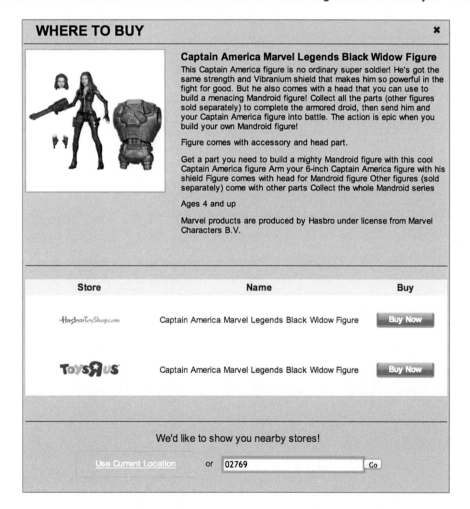

They give you direct links to buy from the Hasbro Toy Shop as well as from the Toys R Us website. You can also enter your zip code to find the item from other retailers. You get a full list with phone numbers so that you can even call ahead and make sure that the stores have stock before making a trip. This would be a great task for a virtual assistant (covered in Chapter 29)

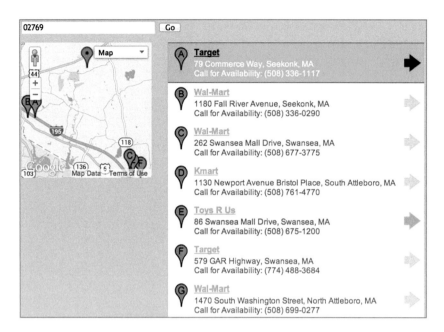

Let's take a look at what a popular movie can do to the retail prices of toys.

Example: Guardians of Galaxy.

These toys were all over the Amazon Movers & Shakers pages.

It was very easy to identify the line, start tracking each one, and try to see what's hot, what's popular, what items have unexpectedly strong demand that could be outweighing the supply, or what items were short packed.

The movie was officially released on August 1, 2014. All of these screenshots and examples were taken BEFORE the movie was in theaters.

Want to look for items where most, if not all, third party Amazon sellers are priced ABOVE Amazon when Amazon is in stock. These sellers are not priced competitively. Why not? It's very possible that they are waiting for the Amazon out of stock window.

Product featured: http://www.Amazon.com/dp/B00IJZPZLC/

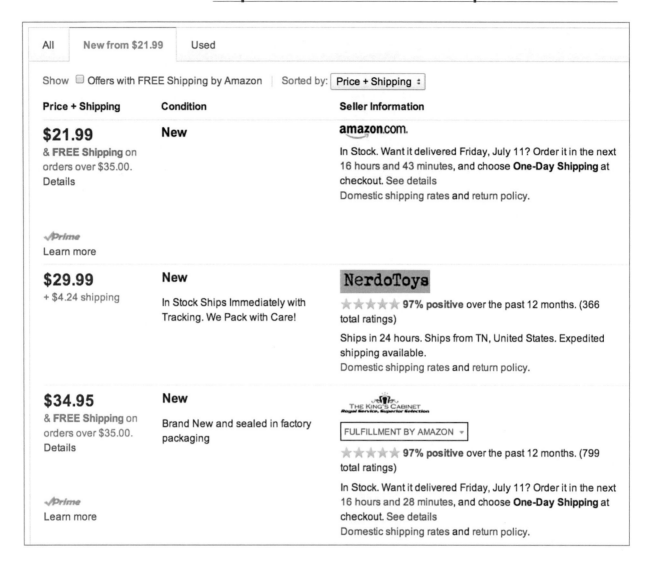

Here you can see that the other Amazon sellers of this item are not trying to compete with the Amazon price. This is a good sign that the market price will be higher if and when Amazon goes out of stock.

The Keepa graph shows that this has already happened several times. Depending on when you looked at this Keepa graph, you'd probably want to set up price alerts from Amazon at $21.99.

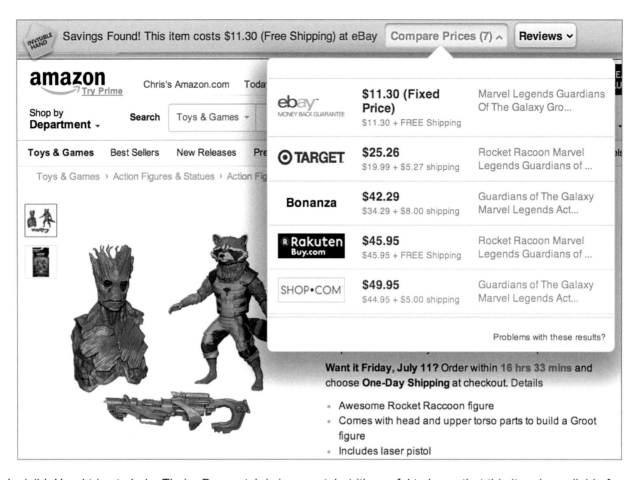

InvisibleHand tries to help. Their eBay match is incorrect, but it's useful to know that this item is available from Target.com. The other sites with higher prices confirm that the overall market price for this item is currently over-retail.

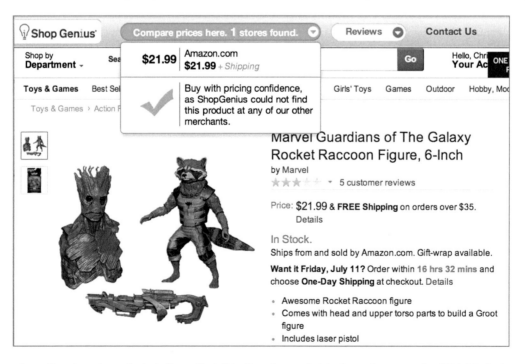

Shop Genius on the other hand wants to tell me that this item is available from Amazon for $21.99. I already know that; I'm actually on the Amazon product page right now!

Marvel Guardians of The Galaxy Marvel's Nova Figure, 6-Inch
by Marvel

★★★★⯪ ▾   5 customer reviews

Price: **$38.99** & **FREE Shipping**. Details

Only 1 left in stock.
Sold by The Captain's and Fulfilled by Amazon. Gift-wrap available.

Want it Friday, July 11? Order within **12 hrs 56 mins** and choose **One-Day Shipping** at checkout. Details

- Awesome Nova figure
- Comes with right arm part to build a Groot figure
- Other figures - sold separately - come with other Groot parts
- Collect the entire Groot series - other figures sold separately
- Figure comes with right arm part

31 new from $32.00

http://www.Amazon.com/dp/B00IJZPZM6/

Looking at one Guardians of the Galaxy item will lead you to the others in the same line. We already know that this line of figures has a MSRP of $19.99 (Target) to $21.99 (Amazon). Seeing this one at $38.99 means that it needs a closer look.

Similar to the other one, the prices were over-retail when Amazon was out of stock. Amazon only very briefly came in stock at $21.99. You may consider setting up an Amazon price alert at $21.99.

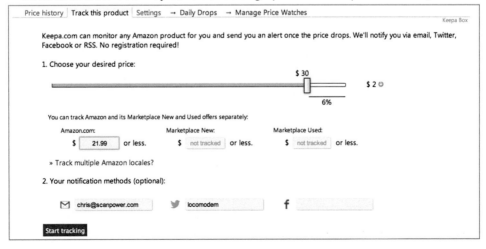

So if you want to sell items related to popular movies and try to cash in on that time frame of hysteria, I'd suggest keeping up with movie review sites like Rotten Tomatoes. Let other sites help you see what movies are popular and then decide if you want to source the products related to those movies (either before or after the movie comes out).

http://www.rottentomatoes.com/

Research COLLECTIBLE ITEMS: Monster High

In this next example, we're going to do some product research on a line of toys that has already been out for a while (compared to something currently popular and trending) so that we can see how to do historical research using Amazon.com.

First, do a search for the keywords, "monster high" on Amazon and choose a Department so that you can enable sorting.

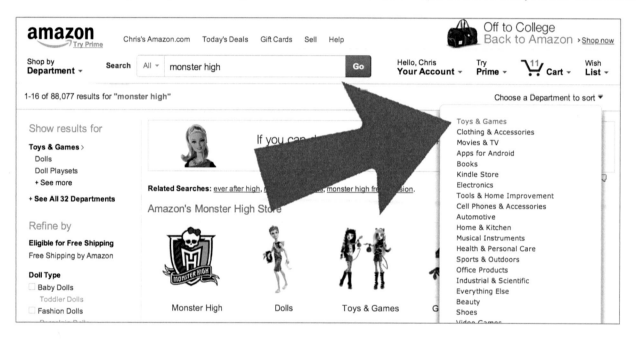

We are going to sort by Price: High to Low

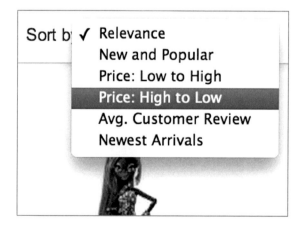

We now see all items in the Toys & Games category that come up for keyword search Monster High. Some items are not relevant either because the product page has the keywords, "monster high" somewhere in the product details, Amazon considers it a related product, or it just happens to be a different product that also has matches for keyword "monster" and keyword "high."

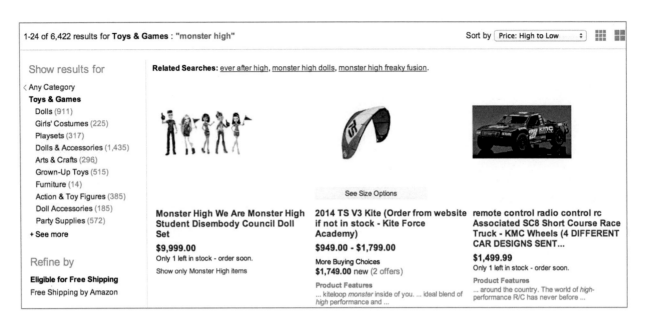

There are 6,422 items in this search. That's a lot of items to wade through, so we want to narrow it down a little bit. Some of the search results are non-competitively prices items like the first match at $9.999.00. We're going to put in a price range to get rid of those high outlier prices. For this example, we're going to put in a max price of $300. Experiment yourself with what works here. Using $300 would mean that if there were Monster High items selling for over $300, I would miss them. As you learn about other products and search other categories, try using different upper price limits.

As I glance through the search results, I'm looking for items that have ratings (more the better) and multiple sellers (more the better).

Clicking through, I want to see items with sales ranks. If an item has no ratings and only one seller, I may do a title search to see if there is a duplicate Amazon listing that is a better match. Some sellers purposefully make duplicate listings in order to list at high prices and have no competition listed and hope that customers don't notice (don't do this).

See Color Options

Monster High Skull Shores Gil Webber Doll

$279.99

Only 1 left in stock - order soon.

More Buying Choices
$195.00 new (5 offers)

Manufacturer recommended age: 6 - 14 Years

★★★☆☆ ▼ (29)

Product Features
Collect all your favorite *Monster High* Skull Shores dolls

Show only Mattel items

Power Wheels Kawasaki KFX with Monster Traction, Normal

$276.73

More Buying Choices
$276.73 new (8 offers)

Manufacturer recommended age: 3 - 5 Years

★★★★☆ ▼ (218)

Product Features
High-speed lock-out for beginers and power lock brake system.

Show only Fisher-Price items

Monster High Toralei Stripe Doll with Pet Sweet Fang

$274.99

Only 1 left in stock - order soon.

More Buying Choices
$200.00 new (22 offers)

Manufacturer recommended age: 6 - 15 Years

★★★★☆ ▼ (130)

Product Features
Collect all your favorite *Monster High* dolls!

Show only Mattel items

You'll notice here that Amazon is giving me the option to show only Mattel items. The item in the middle is Fisher Price. So I can refine these results if there are too many mismatches. If the results were not too mixed up with other items, I'd leave it so that you don't miss matches that simply do not have the manufacturer listed on the product details page.

Roll over image to zoom in

Monster High Skull Shores Gil Webber Doll

by Mattel

★★★☆ ▼   29 customer reviews

Price: **$279.99** + $19.99 shipping

Only 1 left in stock.

Ships from and sold by ToyWiz.

- Its spring break and all the ghoul kids are on an island adventure
- The students of Monster High are decked out in spooktacular swimsuits
- Even monsters love to play in the sun and go on vacation
- Doll is fully articulated and can be posed in many different ways
- Collect all your favorite Monster High Skull Shores dolls

5 new from $195.00   3 collectible from $189.99

http://www.Amazon.com/Monster-High-Skull-Shores-Webber/dp/B0060S30QC

Here is a toy that is listed for almost $300 on Amazon. Checking the Keepa price history, you can see that there was a time where Amazon sold this exact item for $12.99.

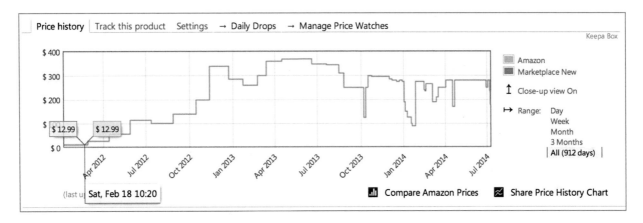

At the time of this writing: **Amazon Best Sellers Rank:** #151,250 in Toys & Games

You can easily check the CamelCamelCamel sales rank history to see how frequently the item sells. You can see from a graph like this that it does not sell often, but it does sell consistently. This sales rank graph covers six months.

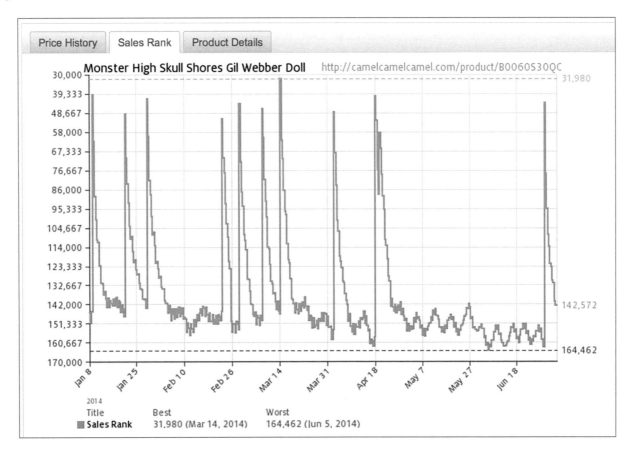

http://camelcamelcamel.com/Monster-High-Skull-Shores-Webber/product/B0060S30QC

Monster High Toralei Stripe Doll with Pet Sweet Fang

by Mattel

★★★★☆ ▾   130 customer reviews

Price: **$274.99** + $6.50 shipping

Only 1 left in stock.
Ships from and sold by Crystal Cave Toys.

- The ghouls from Monster High are freakishly fabulous!
- Toralei Stripe is the daughter of The Werecat
- Doll is fully articulated so she can be posed in many different ways
- Includes doll, pet saber-tooth tiger Sweet Fang, diary, doll stand, brush, and accessory
- Collect all your favorite Monster High dolls!

Roll over image to zoom in

22 new from $200.00   5 collectible from $75.00

http://www.Amazon.com/Monster-High-Toralei-Stripe-Sweet/dp/B0062DMB4M

Here is another one that is listed for almost $300. Keepa shows that Amazon originally sold this item for $19.99. This is obviously a girl toy so the 'boy toy in a girl line' is not the only factor that causes prices to rise on Monster High toys.

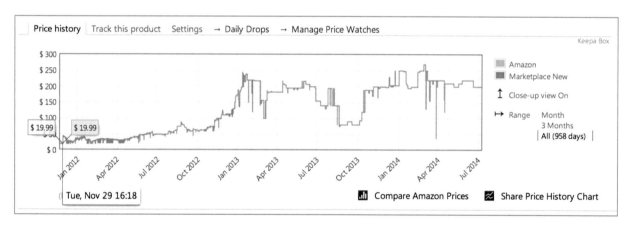

At the time of this writing: **Amazon Best Sellers Rank:** #82,347 in Toys & Games

Here is the six-month sales rank history graph from CamelCamelCamel. Just like the previous example, it may not sell often at these prices, but it sells consistently.

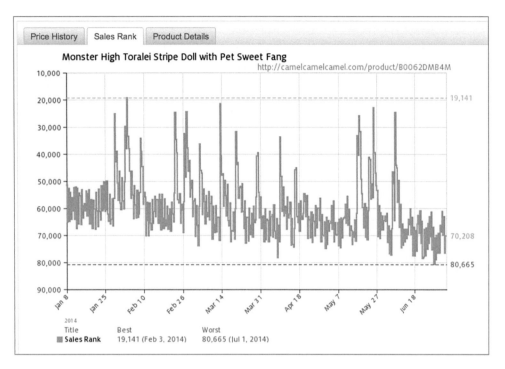

http://camelcamelcamel.com/Monster-High-Toralei-Stripe-Sweet/product/B0062DMB4M

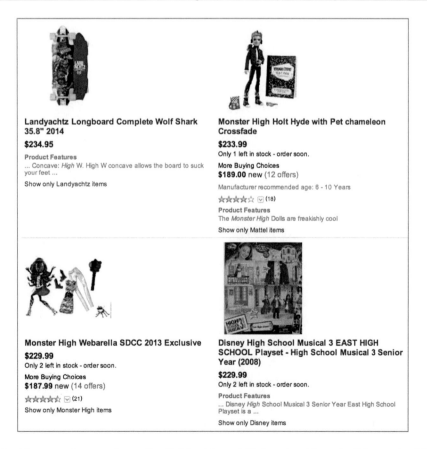

We just keep going on down the list looking at high-priced toys in this product line.

Monster High Holt Hyde with Pet chameleon Crossfade
by Mattel

★★★★☆ ▾   18 customer reviews

Price: **$233.99** + $4.99 shipping

Only 1 left in stock.
Ships from and sold by tammystunezz.

- The Monster High Dolls are freakishly cool
- Holt Hyde is the son of the infamous Dr. Jekyll and Mr. Hyde
- Coolest ghouls in school with their trendy fashions and scary cute pets
- Dolls are fully articulated so they can be posed in many different ways
- Includes doll, pet, accessory, journal, and doll stand

12 new from $189.00   4 collectible from $130.00

Roll over image to zoom in

http://www.Amazon.com/Monster-High-Holt-chameleon-Crossfade/dp/B0045VUXD4

Here is the six- month CamelCamelCamel sales rank history.

At the time of writing: **Amazon Best Sellers Rank:** #134,118 in Toys & Games

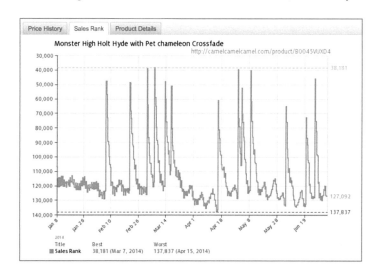

http://camelcamelcamel.com/Monster-High-Holt-chameleon-Crossfade/product/B0045VUXD4

Would it make any sense to set up price alerts on these items? You may think not, because Amazon will never get these items in stock again, but I would consider setting them up in the event a third party sellers simply misjudges the market and is happy to take a lower price. Not all low price outliers are price mistakes.

I may also want to do a Google search on these items to see if I can find out more history or background information as to why they are so popular. Exclusives? What stores were they sold at? Variants? Short packs? Was there some other reason why these particular items are prices so high while others in the same line are not? Google knows everything.

Remember, it's not always about if you can't find these specific items, but what you can learn from these historically that you can later apply to current deals.

Product Variations:

Check out this silly example. Same toy but if you want it in pink, you have to pay a premium!

Fisher-Price Little People Wheelies Rev 'n Sounds Race Track
by Fisher-Price
★★★★⯪ ▾ 98 customer reviews
| 3 answered questions

Price: $31.99 & FREE Shipping on orders over $35. Details

In Stock.
Ships from and sold by Amazon.com.

Want it Monday, July 28? Order within 26 hrs 38 mins and choose One-Day Shipping at checkout. Details

- Rev 'n Sounds Race Track unfolds to reveal an action-packed rolling race track

Roll over image to zoom in

http://www.Amazon.com/Fisher-Price-Little-People-Wheelies-Sounds/dp/B004ORV2D4/

Fisher Price Little People PINK Exclusive!! Wheelies Rev and Sounds Playset
by Wheelies
Be the first to review this item

Price: $55.98 & FREE Shipping. Details

Only 1 left in stock.
Sold by The_Smorgasbord and Fulfilled by Amazon. Gift-wrap available.

Want it Monday, July 28? Order within 26 hrs 25 mins and choose One-Day Shipping at checkout. Details

- Exclusive PINK color!

1 collectible from $45.00

Click to open expanded view

http://www.Amazon.com/Fisher-Little-Exclusive-Wheelies-Playset/dp/B008SX5SIK/

Here's another one. Same toy, but different prices and only one minor variation.

Fisher-Price My First Dollhouse (Caucasian Family)

by Fisher-Price

★★★★☆ ▾   170 customer reviews

| 19 answered questions

Price: **$42.99** & **FREE Shipping**. Details

In Stock.

Ships from and sold by Amazon.com. Gift-wrap available.

Want it Monday, July 28? Order within **26 hrs 13 mins** and choose **One-Day Shipping** at checkout. Details
Product Packaging: **Standard Packaging**

http://www.Amazon.com/dp/B003NUSGS2/

Roll over image to zoom in

Fisher-Price My First Dollhouse (African-American Family)

by Fisher-Price

★★★★☆ ▾   11 customer reviews

Currently unavailable.
We don't know when or if this item will be back in stock.

- Introduce the fun of dollhouse play with a house that's just right for little girls
- Chunky figures are easy to hold and stand
- Wide open spaces so little hands can reach
- Sweet styling to encourage early role play
- Dollhouse features 5 rooms with removable accessories

http://www.Amazon.com/dp/B003NUSGSW

At the time of this writing, there was not even an offer for the African-American version. So how did I know that the price is higher? Easy: I sold one for $92.66. At the time, I priced at to match the current Amazon price. It sold quickly.

You can also go back on Keepa and see the historical prices. Amazon was originally selling this item for $37.99. Use this info to consider buying products to resell when they are on clearance or no longer being sold by Amazon.

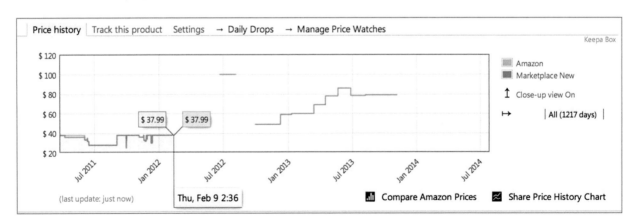

Let's take a quick look at the CamelCamelCamel price history so see how sales were affected by price and availability.

While Keepa showed a most recent price of $37.99 from Amazon on this item, CamelCamelCamel shows that the all-time lowest price from Amazon was actually $27.83 on September 10, 2011. You can see my $92.66 price as the last price offered on this item from a third party seller.

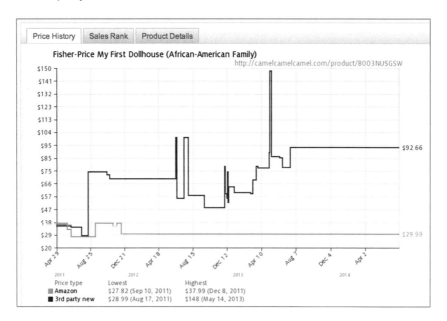

http://camelcamelcamel.com/Fisher-Price-First-Dollhouse-African-American-Family/product/B003NUSGSW

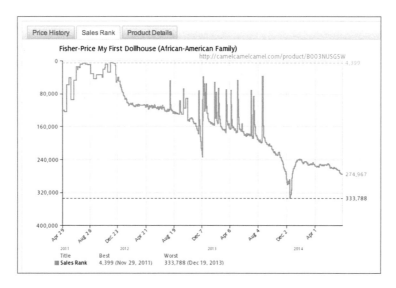

The sales rank history graph shows what happens when an item is out of stock. Consider this behavior when sourcing products that are NOT available on Amazon from any seller. The sales rank history may look terrible, but that's because no one could buy it even if they wanted to.

Bonus Tip:

Did you know that there is a section on Amazon JUST for girls' toys?

http://www.Amazon.com/Girls-Toys/b/ref=sv_t_4?ie=UTF8&node=1263207011

Chapter 14 – Learn a Line: Highlight LEGO

Speaking of new items on Amazon that sell out and are then sold at higher market prices, take a look at what showed up on the Movers & Shakers list. Three new Star Wars sets! These are all up for preorder to be released on August 1, 2014. You can see by the details that there is only one offer on #2 and #3 (Amazon's offer).

https://keepa.com/#product/1-B00JRCB3HQ

LEGO Star Wars 75054 AT-AT Building Toy
by LEGO

List Price: $109.99
Price: $95.09 ✓Prime
You Save: $14.90 (14%)

This item will be released on August 1, 2014.
Pre-order now.
Ships from and sold by Amazon.com. Gift-wrap available.

- Includes 5 with assorted weapons and an accessory: AT-AT Driver, General Veers, Snow trooper Commander and 2 Snow troopers
- Features a moving head with a cockpit for 2 and 2 spring-loaded shooters, possible legs and an opening body with switch-operated trap door
- Weapons include a blaster pistol and 3 blaster rifles Also includes an electro binoculars element
- Measures over 12" (33cm) high, 12" (32cm) long and 4" (11cm) wide
- Match against the 75049 Snow speeder (sold separately) to recreate the classic Battle of Hot!

Roll over image to zoom in

2 new from $95.09

http://www.Amazon.com/LEGO-Star-75054-AT-AT-Building/dp/B00J4S9BEA/

This one already has a two New offers so we know that there is one other seller. Let's take a closer look.

219

Also note in the last product detail: Star Wars Battle of HOTH typo.

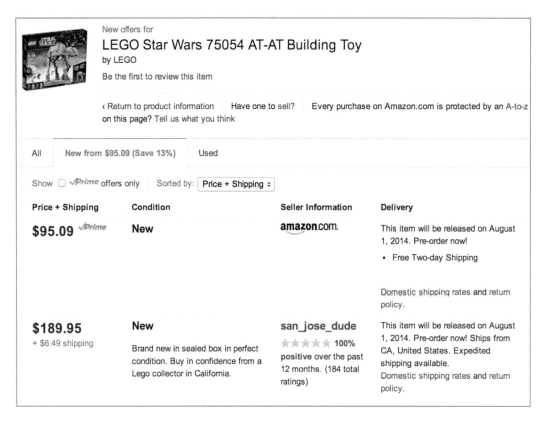

Once Amazon is sold out, third party sellers and prices take over. In this example, if Amazon sells out, this seller would be the only offer at $189.95 on a popular, new toy. Also, now that you know the Amazon price, you can set up Keepa alerts or any other alerts in the event that Amazon does sell out.

Are you wondering why would people pay a premium to buy the same product from Amazon rather than from other online sellers? Especially when the items can be bought elsewhere from other retailers like Lego.com, Target. Wal-Mart?

Well, people just simply prefer/choose to buy from Amazon (I know I do).

Take a look at the Simpson's Lego house:

http://www.Amazon.com/LEGO-Simpsons-71006-The-House/dp/B00HX14C7Q

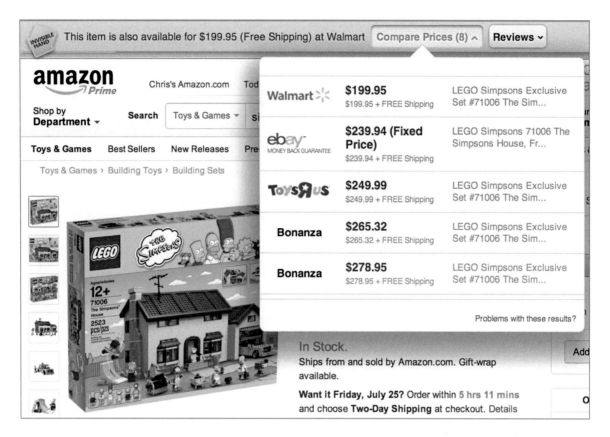

InvisibleHand clearly shows that it is available for $199.95 from Wal-Mart.

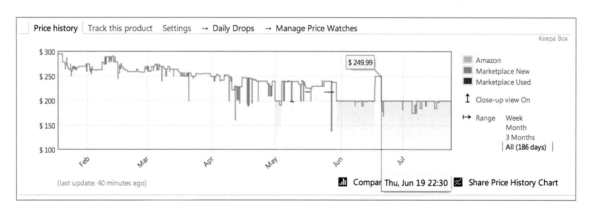

But looking at the Keepa graph, we see that the prices on Amazon go up to about $250 when Amazon is out of stock.

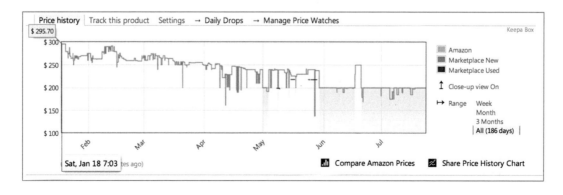

When it first came out. Amazon prices were up at the $300 level.

$199.95 from Amazon when they are in stock. But a $50 premium when Amazon is out of stock? How do you know that they are actually selling at those prices? Easy: We can check the CamelCamelCamel sales rank history graph.

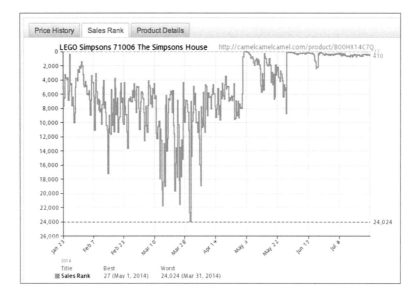

You can see that it sells very well at those prices when Amazon is out of stock. You can even buy from LEGO.com for less. Just because Amazon goes out of stock, doesn't mean other sites have.

Now it certainly sells better from Amazon and at $199.95. Part of it is the price but another boost in sales comes from being Amazon and not just another third party seller, whether the seller uses FBA or not.

So what does this mean? It means that you can use the knowledge that there are Amazon customers who want to buy from Amazon, even at a higher price. You can be the seller who is selling at those higher prices and meeting the demand of those customers.

Spotting Lego Deals: Movers & Shakers

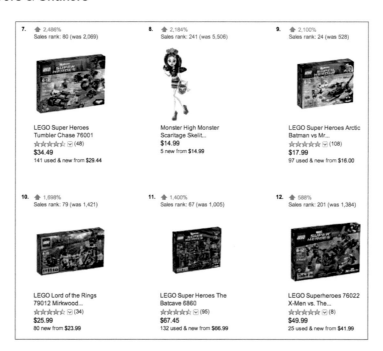

When so many new Lego kits end up on the Movers & Shakers page, you know that there is something going on. Take a look at one of the items and you'll find this promotion listed:

Buy One, Get One 40% Off Select Toys Brands

For a limited time and while supplies last, buy one select popular toy and get 40% off the second. Learn more

Clicking through the link will take you right to their Amazon promotions page that shows you all of the eligible products.

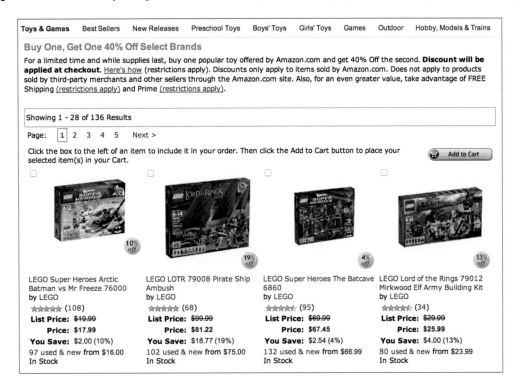

Use the items on the Movers & Shakers page as a guide to what others think are the best deals. The items that are shooting up in sales rank are not just being bought by other sellers. Lego buyers who want the best deals on the best kits are also buying them. It's more free market research right in front of us.

Anytime a Lego kit hits the Movers & Shakers page, it's normally worth a closer look.

From the Amazon page, InvisibleHand shows the other retailers so that you can quickly see if it's being price matched.

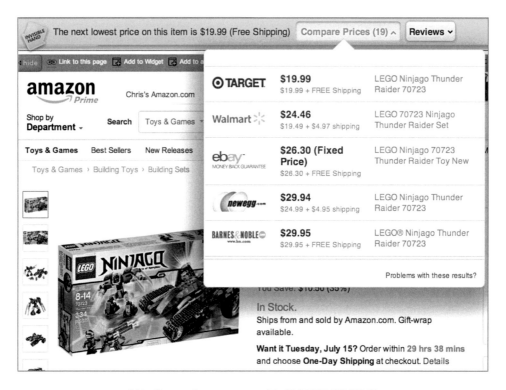

http://www.Amazon.com/dp/B00ERARO94/

You can see from the other Amazon offers that Amazon has a small discount on this item. This kit is likely moving up the Movers & Shakers page by being purchased by consumers, not resellers (the price isn't that hot).

But because it's Lego, there are actually other ways to make a profit on kits, even when their sale price is only a minor discount. Consider http://brickset.com/

http://brickset.com/sets?query=70723

Searching for this kit on BrickSet shows you the MSRP of $29.99. BrickSet is useful to find MSRP of Lego sets if you have trouble finding the MSRP elsewhere.

There is a whole other world of Lego where sellers are making money by not just buying and selling the kits as a whole, but by parting them out, piece by piece. This model may not be attractive to all sellers, but I mention it here in case anyone wants to learn more about it.

BrickLink has a website where you can estimate the Part Out Value for any set just by entering the Lego set number.

http://www.bricklink.com/catalogPG.asp

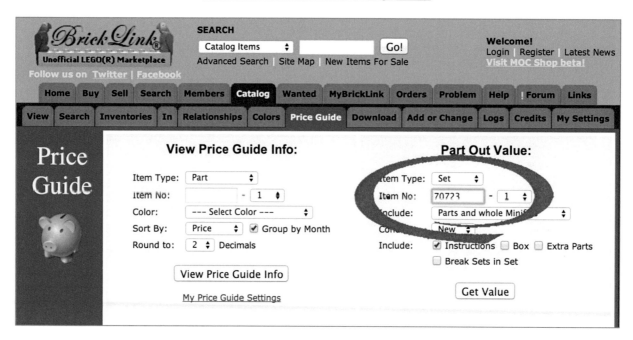

Here you can see the Part Out Value both in 'Average of the Last 6 Months Sales' as well as the 'Current Items For Sale'.

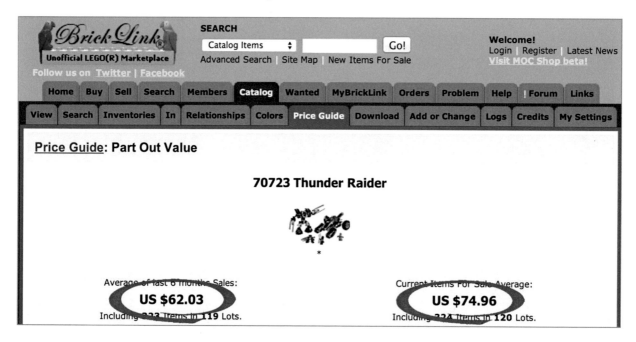

$62.03 and $74.96 respectively. Not bad! Definitely a little more work than packing up and shipping a single box to Amazon, but it's a very viable business model for those who want to learn it.

For more information about investing in complete Lego sets compared to parting them out, here is a great article from the people at BrickPicker:

http://blog.brickpicker.com/lego-investing-complete-sets-vs-parting-out/

For more information on Lego, you should LIKE BrickPicker on Facebook and subscribe to their feed:

https://www.facebook.com/BrickPicker

You'll get cool alerts in your Facebook News Feed like this one about the new Lego Batman Tumbler set.

They also give the heads up on awesome Lego sales and deals like this (so you never miss out on a deal):

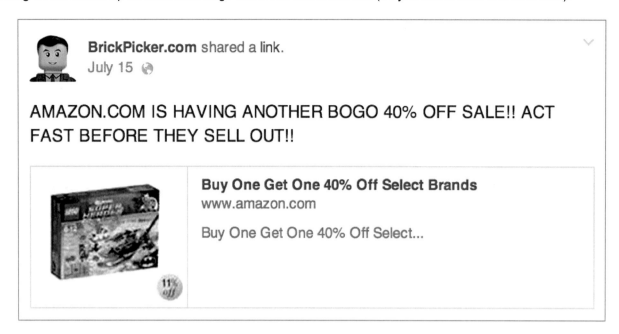

On their website, they have all kinds of information and videos about the world of Lego investing.

http://www.brickpicker.com/

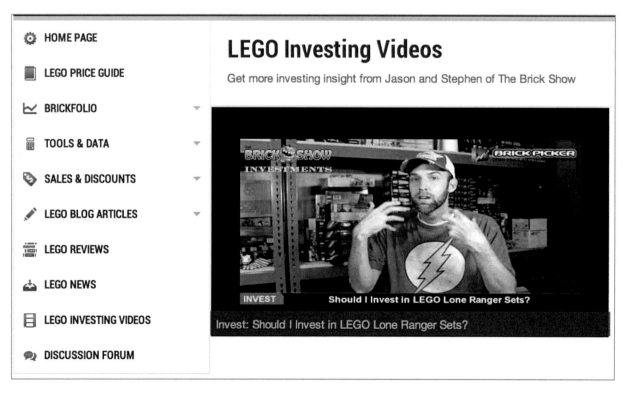

BrickPicker has pages on Lego Price Guide, a space to create your own Brickfolio, tons of Tools & Data, links to Sales & Discounts, tons of Lego Blog Articles, Lego Reviews, Lego News, Lego Investing Videos, and a Discussion Forum.

http://www.brickpicker.com/bpms/brickfolio.cfm

Let's take a quick look at what happens to the market price of Lego once it's no longer available from major retailers.

Lego Star Wars Super Star Destroyer:

LEGO Star Wars Super Star Destroyer 10221
by LEGO

★★★★★ ▾   97 customer reviews | 6 answered questions

Price: **$690.00** + $12.99 shipping

Only 1 left in stock.

Ships from and sold by HSDStore.

- Includes Darth Vader, Admiral Piett, Dengar and Bossk minifigures and also includes IG-88 figure
- Center section lifts off to reveal command center
- Includes display stand and data sheet label
- Measures nearly 50 inches (124.5 cm) long and weighs nearly 8 pounds (3.5kg)
- 3152 pieces

52 new from $679.82

Roll over image to zoom in

http://www.Amazon.com/LEGO-Star-Super-Destroyer-10221/dp/B0050R0YB8/

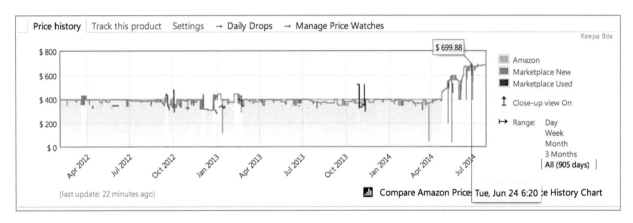

The MSRP or list price on this item was $399.95. You can see some minor bumps in prices the few times that Amazon went out of stock before, but the last part of the Keepa graph shows when the set was retired by Lego and therefore no longer available from traditional retailers. The price quickly rose from the $400 level to the $700 level.

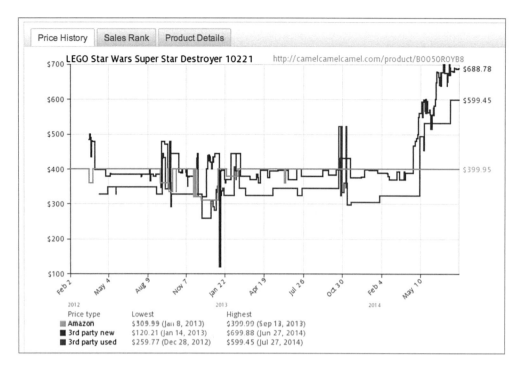

http://camelcamelcamel.com/LEGO-Star-Super-Destroyer-10221/product/B0050R0YB8

CamelCamelCamel shows that the all time highest prices are from July 27, 2014.

Keepa tracks Amazon being out of stock while CamelCamelCamel does not, but you can see a steady price from Amazon and then a rise in price from third party sellers. This can indicate Amazon is out of stock if using CamelCamelCamel instead of Keepa. Also notice that Amazon once sold this for $309.00 in 2013.

Comparing the CamelCamelCamel sales rank history graph to the price history graph, we can see that sales certainly slow down as price increases. Even so, this set continues to sell, even at the new, higher market prices.

Online Arbitrage of Lego could be a book all it's own so we won't go into more details in this book.

To learn more about reselling Lego, please join the Lego Investing Facebook Group run by full-time professional Lego seller, Amanda Moak. https://www.facebook.com/groups/legoinvesting/

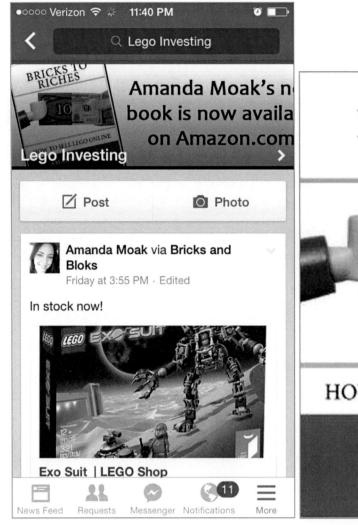

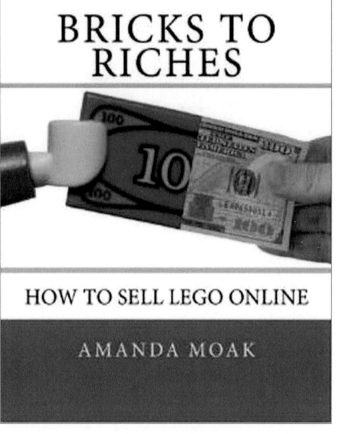

Amanda has also written a book about the business of selling Lego and it's available on Amazon here:

http://www.Amazon.com/dp/1500310220/

Chapter 15 – Stay Current: Highlight ZOOLERT

The Internet has basically allowed anyone to shorten the learning curve for any topic. This includes the topic on online selling and learning about specific products or lines of products. There are many websites out there designed to help people stay informed and up-to-date on various topics or industries. Find the ones that are related to the topics that you are interested in and use them to your advantage.

In addition to keeping people up to date on toys and other items, Zoolert is designed to track in–stock availability on items from major online retailers. If you're looking for a PlayStation 4 and they are sold out everywhere, you can set up an alert with Zoolert to be instantly notified when they come in stock.

Sign up for their email alerts but be careful that they don't end up in your spam or promotions folder in Gmail.

LIKE them on Facebook (and turn Get Notifications ON)

https://www.facebook.com/zooLertOfficial

FOLLOW them on Twitter (and get their mobile notifications).

https://twitter.com/zoolertOfficial/

You can even follow them on Google+. At the time of this writing, they only have 43 followers. I like seeing things like this. This means that hardly anyone else is following them on Google+ and any information that they post on Google+ will not be seen by very many people.

https://plus.google.com/+zooLertOfficial/

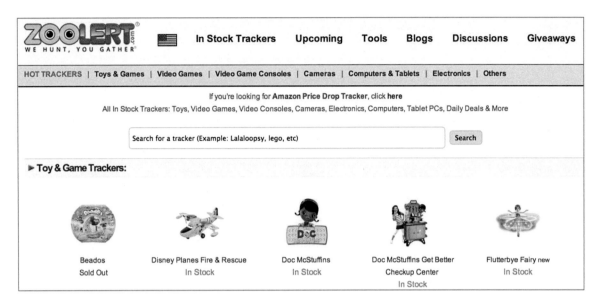

http://www.zoolert.com/alltrackers.php

Zoolert Forums:

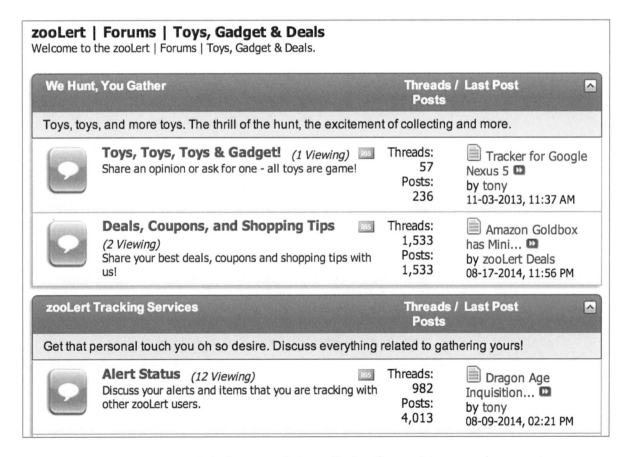

http://www.zoolert.com/forums/forum.php

Zoolert also has community-run forums where other people (some resellers, some regular buyers) can talk about deals and what's hot. If you find lots of people talking about trying to track down a particular item, it may just be the next hot toy.

They also have an Amazon in-stock tracker:

http://www.zoolert.com/habitat/

Amazon.com Price Drop Tracker And Alerts

| What Can We Help You Find? | Search |

Already have my custom Amazon Price Tracker? **Sign In**

AMAZON.COM PRICE & STOCK TRACKER

Don't keep checking for deals at Amazon. Let us do it for you!

- Search For Products.
- Set Your Price.
- We Keep Checking!
- Optional: Use it as your wish list.

When There Is A Match, You Get An Email!

See a **sample Amazon.com Price Drop Tracker Alerts**.

You can see the recently tracked items as well as the most tracked items from other people. It's almost like more free market research.

The next page shows the Top 30 Hot Trackers on their site.

I hope you can get some product ideas from the items on this list.

There is a reason that they are all being tracked. They are hard to find. If a lot of other people are looking for a way to be alerted when they come in stock, they may just be products that you would want to know a little bit more about.

TOP 30 HOT TRACKERS — 1

PlayStation 4

Xbox One

AMD Radeon R9 295X2

Fujifilm X-T1

Destiny Ghost Edition

Destiny Limited Edition

Skylanders Trap Team

Monster High Doll / Playset / Accessories

Frozen Doll / Playset / Costumes / Accessories

Zoomer / Robot

TOP 30 HOT TRACKERS — 1

new LEGO Exo Suit

new LEGO Research Institute

LEGO The Tumbler

new NVIDIA SHIELD Tablet

Flutterbye Fairy

DJI Phantom 2 Vision+

Paw Patrol

Paw Patrol Plush Pup Pals

Teenage Mutant Ninja Turtles Movie

LEGO Minecraft Micro World The End

TOP 30 HOT TRACKERS — 1

Dragon Age Inquisition Inquisitor's Edition

Assassin's Creed Unity Collector's Edition

new WWE 2K15 Hulkamania Edition

new The Witcher 3 Wild Hunt Collector's Edition

Call of Duty Advanced Warfare Atlas Pro Edition

Call of Duty Advanced Warfare Atlas Limited Edition

Titanfall Collector's Edition

Diablo III Reaper of Souls Collector's Edition

new Marvel Legends Infinite Series - Jubilee

Marvel Legends Infinite Series - Mandroid

235

Another in-stock tracker to consider is NowInStock: http://www.nowinstock.net

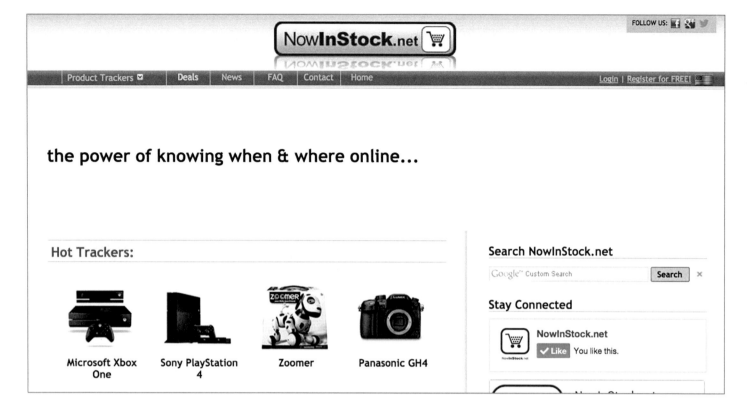

Chapter 16 – Learn Your Favorite Websites

There are so many websites out there where you can purchase products to resell for a profit. Try to learn as much as you can about them to help you spot deals, learn insider tricks, and even simply speed up your site navigation. This chapter will have a lot of Target.com references, but the same strategies can be applied to most any online retailer's website.

First off, if you want to learn as much as possible about a retailer, use Google to see if there are already websites or Facebook pages dedicated to this already. It may be that someone else has already gathered a lot of store-specific information.

When it comes to Target and Target.com, three major sites come to mind.

Read: TotallyTarget.com

Get Notifications: https://www.facebook.com/TotallyTarget

Follow with mobile notifications: https://twitter.com/totallytarget

Read: TargetSavers.com

Get Notifications: https://www.facebook.com/targetsavers

Follow with mobile notifications: https://twitter.com/targetsavers

Read: AllThingsTarget.com

Get Notifications: https://www.facebook.com/allthingstarget

Follow with mobile notifications: https://twitter.com/allthingstarget

These sites already compile deals, post and share clearance items, and even try to disclose Target pricing policies. Use their knowledge to your Online Arbitrage advantage.

When prices drop on other sites, Amazon often matches. Amazon monitors prices and breaks MAP if another online retailer breaks MAP first. If you want to buy from Amazon at the low price, you can report the lower price to Amazon.

Search & Sort:

Sorting your searching on websites is a great way to narrow down what you are looking for. Different sites have different ways of sorting search results. Some sites default to Best Selling or Relevant matches. Most will let you sort by Price, High to Low or Price: Low to High. Both have their advantages. Sorting high-priced items first can show you items that would have a higher Average Sales Price and can lead to higher revenue and profits while processing fewer units. On the flip side, looking at the lowest priced items may reveal the biggest discounts. A $100 item that's 90% off would be down to $10 and while a $15 item marked down to $10 wouldn't be as exciting to find, both $10 items could come up side by side on a low-price sort. Experiment with different sorts on different sites and see what gives you the best results.

Seeing which items are the Best Selling can sometimes quickly show you what other people are buying. If a price is super hot, the item will sell quickly, and not just to resellers. Customers making lots of purchases is a great sign that an item is being sold at an attractive price, and sometimes that price is low enough to be bought and resold for a profit.

I also want to see as many items on one page as possible. I don't want to waste time going through and opening up twelve pages of search results to view them twenty items at a time. I want to just see all 240 items loaded onto one page.

Price Drop Refunds:

Learn the policies of each online retailer. Will they refund recent price drops? If so, for how long? 30 days? If so, set some alerts after you make your purchases to go back and check the online prices. If they have lowered their prices, request a refund of the difference. Just know their policies and hold them to them.

Speed Browsing:

When I am looking at search results on an online retailer, I am trying to glance at the results as fast as I can. I don't want to individually evaluate each and every product. I want to find some products that are potential winners and then do some due diligence. To do this, I look for a few key pieces of data:

Previous Price and Current Price

I'm doing the calculations in my head, but here I want to see a large relative (percentage compared to previous price) difference. I'm not as concerned a large absolute (dollar amount) difference.

Bonus Tip:

Some stores reveal their online stock levels. Just edit your cart and change the quantity to 999. If there are only 364 units available, the shopping cart will let you know. Use this information strategically. Can you afford to buy them all? Are you comfortable with 364 units or is that too deep on one product? Knowing that no one else is able to buy the product at the same price may change the way you feel about how deep you want to buy. If you aren't buying them all, you will know how many items could possibly end up being purchased by resellers. You can also monitor this stock level to see how quickly they are selling. If you only wanted to buy 100, but you would prefer that other resellers (your competition) did not buy the other 264 units, you may consider posting it as a Hot Deal on FatWallet or SlickDeals and hope that regular customers buy them up. This can be risky and backfire, though, because some resellers monitor FatWallet and SlickDeals for possible resale deals. More information on how to use FatWallet in Chapter 21 and SlickDeals in Chapter 22.

Bonus Tip:

Some stores and websites often get products before Amazon does. This gives you a window of time to bring those products to market and sell them for higher prices before Amazon comes in stock. If doing this, SELL FAST.

Bonus Tip:

Store Exclusives

How hard is it to find store exclusives from websites? They are pretty much identified and promoted for you. You can't really miss them. Here, the Only at Target icon is shown right on the search results (you don't even have to go to the product page).

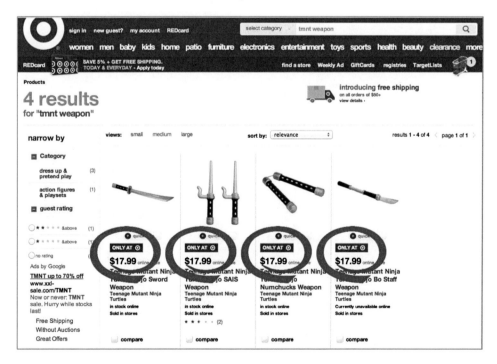

Here are four more Only at Target items on their website. Let's take a closer look at them.

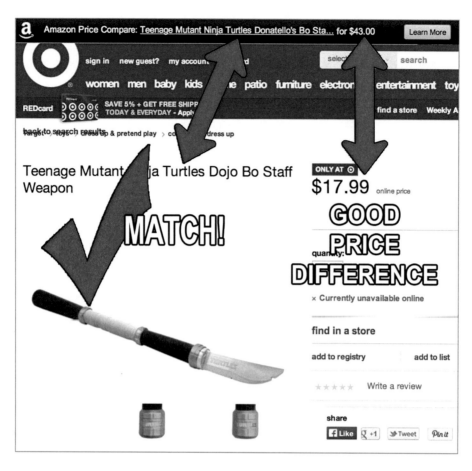

The Amazon 1Button App finds the item on Amazon and shows the lowest price. We can verify that the product is actually a match and also use this information to quickly make a buying decision.

240

At first glance, it looked like we had another winner, but a closer look shows that the Amazon 1Button App did not match the correct product. The title on Amazon shows Raphael's Sais, but the Target website shows NUMchucks (SP!)

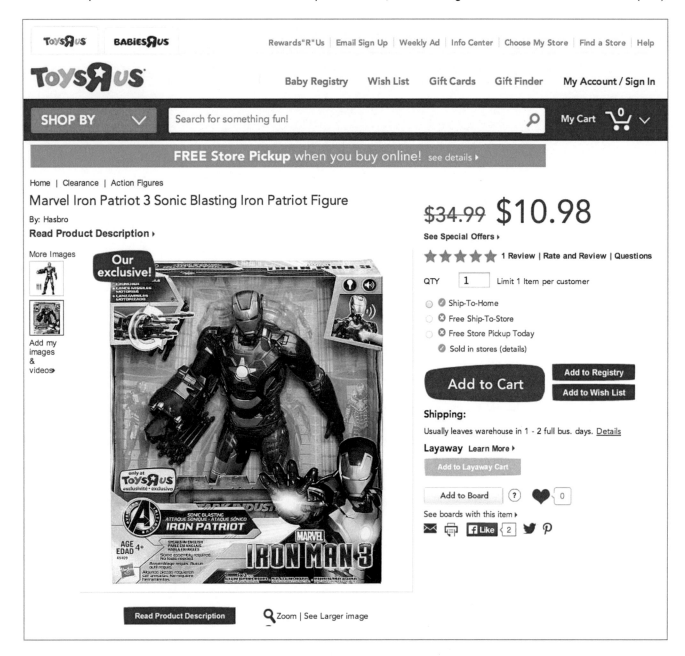

Here is an example of a store exclusive from Toys R Us. You can clearly see the Only at Toys R Us sticker on the packaging as well as the overlaid image on the top left corner of the package that says Our Exclusive!

Here is an item on Amazon. With a closer look you can see the Kmart Exclusive sticker on the package on the Amazon listing.

This item was sold for $34.99 at Kmart stores. How do I know this? Because I bought them and sold them.

I bought them to resell specifically because they were Kmart exclusives. Collectors pay a premium for these types of products. When selling these types of products, I recommend leaving the exclusive stickers on the products.

Order ID: # 105-3737447-3475435

Your Seller Order ID: # 105-3737447-3475435
Payment Information

Shipping Address:

Order Date:	October 21, 2013 2:48:42 PM PDT	**Order Totals**	
Expected Ship Date:	Oct 22, 2013	Items total:	$149.95
Shipping Service:	Second Day	Grand total:	$149.95
Contact Buyer:			
Billing Country:	US		
Sales Channel:	Amazon.com		
Fulfillment method:	Amazon		

Product Details	Status	Quantity Ordered	Price	Total
Disney / Pixar CARS 2 Movie Exclusive Playset Pit Crew Garage	Payment complete	1	$149.95	Subtotal: $149.95
Quantity: 1				Total: **$149.95**
SKU: CC_010				
ASIN: B005Q9DFU2				
Listing ID: 0711NPBXHPS				
Order Item ID: 51624853777194				

Total Charged to Buyer: **$149.95**

Here is a completed sale of this kit.

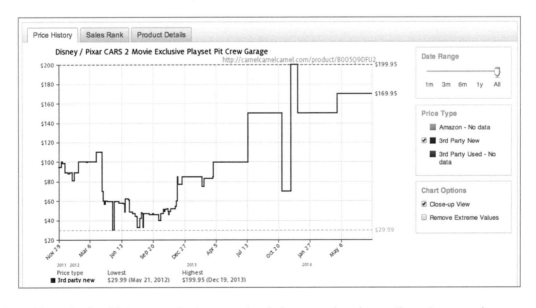

The CamelCamelCamel price history graph shows a steady increase in price as the set was no longer available from Kmart.

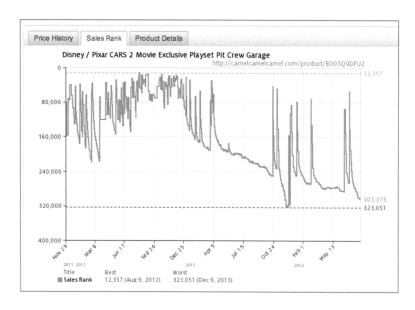

But as you can see, higher prices lead to fewer sales.

Bonus Tip:

Some brands like to partner with certain retailers. It could be a special product line or other type of promotion. Keep up with certain websites can get you the inside scoop on these types of things. Remember MISSONI at Target? A lot of people made some good money on those products. The ones who made the most were the ones who had the best information.

Knowing your favorite websites is important, and thankfully it's easy. Looking at this product, you can see the availability options. It's not available to Ship to Home, it's not available for Free Ship To Store, it's not available for Free Store Pickup Today. It's only available in stores. Knowing how Toys R Us works means that this item MIGHT be found in stores, although that's unlikely. Your best move on this product is to put it in the back of your mind in case you're in a store and you randomly find one.

Bonus Tip:

When you place orders online, do you want to do in store pickup or regular shipping?

Pickup Pros: Ability to inspect products before taking possession, acquire product faster, easy to return if damaged.

Pickup Cons: Limited to in-store, on-hand quantities, waiting in line for orders to be processed and pulled.

Delivery Pros: Just shows up at your door, additional quantities.

Delivery Cons: Possibly damaged products, delivery lead time.

TARGET EMAILS:

Most of the time, store promotional emails will not feature products that can be resold for a profit. But some emails are more interesting than others. This one warranted an additional look. 50% off, Black Friday in July, and a Lego kit in the corner. Let's take a close look.

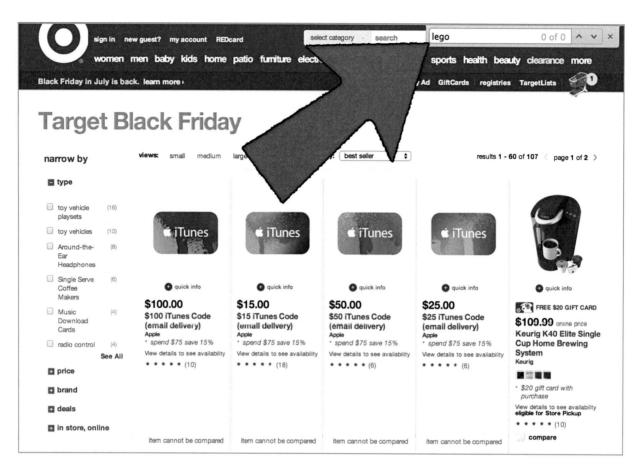

Clicking through to the promotion page shows no Lego kit. Even using Command – F or CTRL – F does not find any match for the word Lego on this page. Maybe it sold out already. If it did, I definitely want to know at what price.

Sometimes you can find the product page by search, but some sites don't give results if the item is not in stock. If this happens, you can try searching deal sites to see if it was posted with link and price.

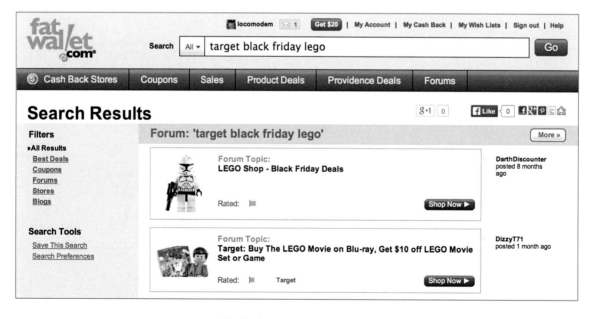

No luck on FatWallet.com

Found it on SlickDeals.net

http://slickdeals.net/f/7086600-lego-the-lone-ranger-constitution-train-chase-79111-69-99?v=1

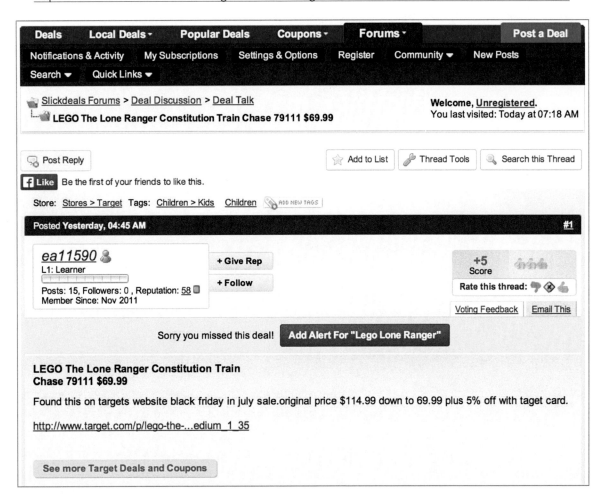

We can see that the Lego set was offered at $69.99. Not exactly an amazing price that I would have expected to see the item sell out, but you can't guess them all right.

The link also shows us the Target product page. It still shows the $69.99 price even though it's not available for purchase.

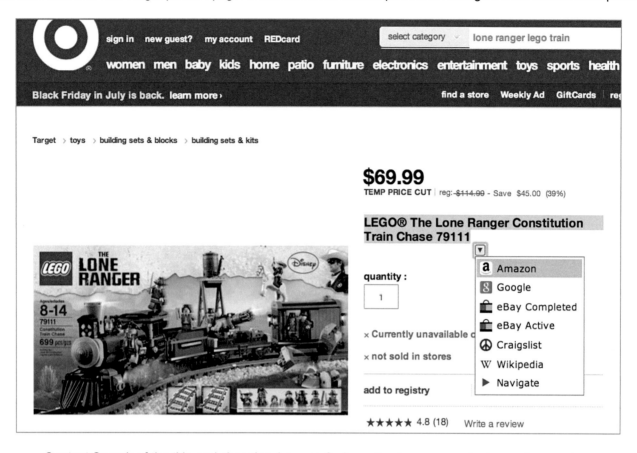

Context Search of the title and choosing Amazon finds us the Amazon product page in one step.

LEGO The Lone Ranger Constitution Train Chase (79111)
by LEGO

★★★★★ ▾   89 customer reviews

| 5 answered questions

Price: **$112.97 & FREE Shipping**. Details

In Stock.
Sold by jr's bookbuyer and Fulfilled by Amazon. Gift-wrap available.

Want it Monday, July 28? Order within **3 hrs 50 mins** and choose **One-Day Shipping** at checkout. Details

http://www.Amazon.com/LEGO-Ranger-Constitution-Train-Chase/dp/B00ATX7JS4/

So the $69.99 price is a good price compared to the market price on Amazon.

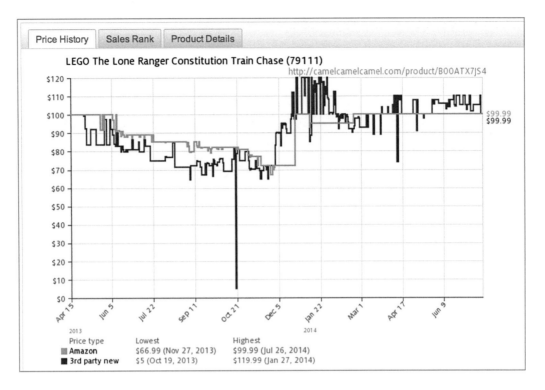

http://camelcamelcamel.com/LEGO-Ranger-Constitution-Train-Chase/product/B00ATX7JS4

CamelCamelCamel shows the price history and you can pretty much guess where Amazon stopped carrying this product. If you couldn't guess, it's when all of the third party seller's price start going up and staying up.

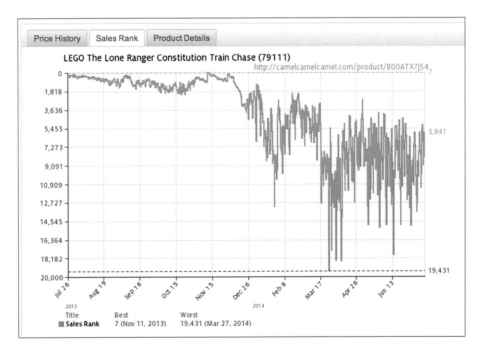

The CamelCamelCamel sales rank graph shows a strong correlation to a drop in sales velocity as price increases from third party sellers.

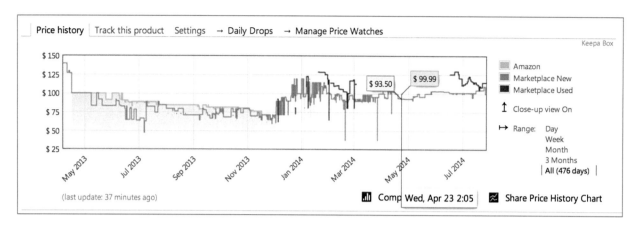

The Keepa graph definitively shows when Amazon was in and out of stock and at what prices.

Bonus Tip: Did you know that Target also sells on eBay?

http://www.ebay.com/sch/targetstores/m.html

The following deal hit FatWallet: http://www.fatwallet.com/forums/expired-deals/1346938/

I received an email for my FatWallet Topic Alert for keyword: Lego

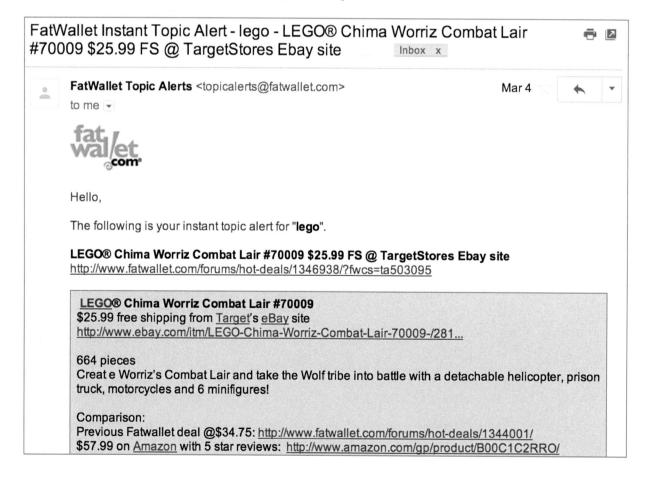

This listing was ended by the seller because the item is no longer available.

LEGO® Chima Worriz Combat Lair 70009 See original listing

Item condition:	**New**
Ended:	Mar 05, 2014 01:34:01 PST
Price:	**US $25.99** [4,060 sold]
Shipping:	**FREE** Standard Shipping
Item location:	Ontario, California, United States
Seller:	**targetstores** (59186 ⭐)	Seller's other items

Target's eBay account sold 4,060 of these items in early March, 2014.

LEGO Chima 70009 Worriz Combat Lair

by LEGO Chima

⭐⭐⭐⭐⭐ ▾ 32 customer reviews

List Price: ~~$69.99~~
Price: **$56.52 & FREE Shipping**. Details
You Save: $13.47 (19%)

In Stock.

Ships from and sold by Amazon.com. Gift-wrap available.

Want it tomorrow, July 26? Order within **47 mins** and choose **Saturday Delivery** at checkout. Details

http://www.Amazon.com/gp/product/B00C1C2RRO/

Here is the Keepa graph highlighting the Amazon price and the third party seller's prices during the same time period.

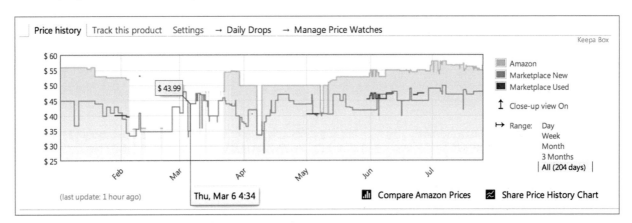

You can see that the price was steady at ~$45 - $50 the entire time despite 4,060 units being sold in a very public and visible way using A FatWallet Topic Alert and promoted by eBay. Remember, the Keepa price does not include shipping from Marketplace New sellers so the blue line prices are actually higher than what you see on the graph.

I shared this deal with the Lego Investing Facebook group and the ScanPower Facebook Group:

https://www.facebook.com/groups/legoinvesting/permalink/360879610716638/

Lego Investing	Members	Events	Photos	Files

 Chris Green
March 4 · Attleboro, MA

Wow! $25.99 with free shipping from Target@ebay!

http://www.ebay.com/itm/LEGO-Chima-Worriz-Combat-Lair-70009-/281269814763

LEGO® Chima Worriz Combat Lair 70009

US $25.99 New in Toys & Hobbies, Building Toys, LEGO

EBAY.COM

Like · Comment · Share

👍 Duane Malek, Rob Salmeron, Livia Forester Wright and 12 others like this.

 Chris Green $57.99 on Amazon: http://www.amazon.com/dp/B00C1C2RRO/

 LEGO Chima 70009 Worriz Combat Lair
www.amazon.com

Howl into battle with Worriz's Combat Lair! Go after Grizzam and Eris with a wol... See More

https://www.facebook.com/groups/scanpower/permalink/477255452376386/

 Chris Green
March 4 · Attleboro, MA

This kit sells for $57.99 on Amazon.com. I know where to get it for $25.99 with free shipping. I just posted in the Lego Investing Facebook Group.

http://www.amazon.com/dp/B00C1C2RRO/

LEGO Chima 70009 Worriz Combat Lair

Howl into battle with Worriz's Combat Lair! Go after Grizzam and Eris with a wolf-powered combat creation featuring 6 huge wheels and 5 detachable vehicles! Launch the helicopter with spinning rotors to combat Eris's aerial attack. Then...

AMAZON.COM

Like · Comment · Share

👍 Glinda Harris Jackson, Adam Hazard Wacker, Bill Gray and 7 others like this.

 Chris Green Want to learn more?

https://www.facebook.com/groups/legoinvesting/

https://www.facebook.com/groups/legoinvesting/permalink/374632312674701/

If you are evaluating this product for resale, entering it in the ScanPower WebScout is easily the fastest way to see the market prices and calculate payouts.

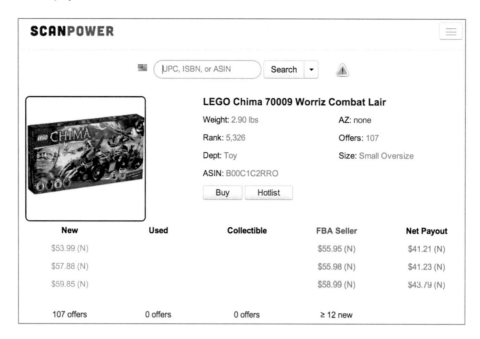

You can also use the Amazon FBA Calculator. Just compare your acquisition cost to your payout.

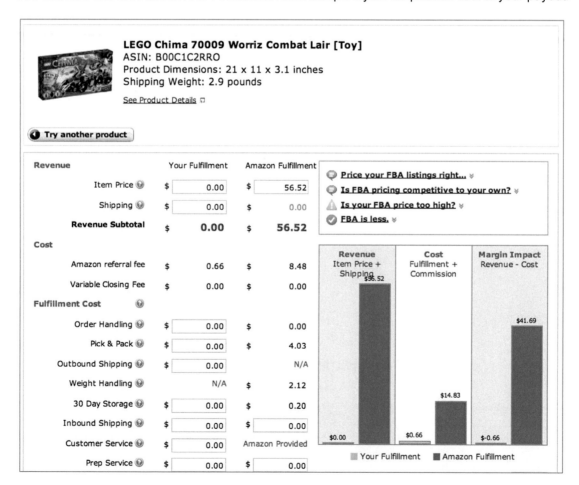

Here is the CamelCamelCamel pricing graph with a highlight of when an additional 4,060 units were sold openly. They were even promoted to multiple groups of Amazon sellers. You can clearly see the price history.

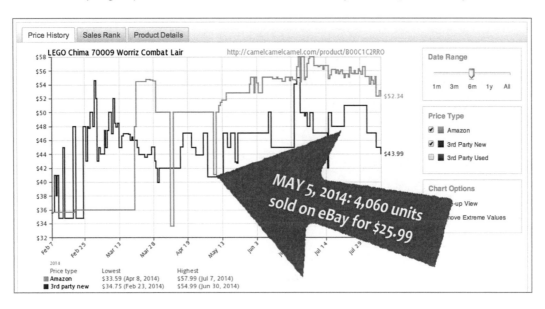

There are three lessons to learn from this example:

First, if you are worried about products 'tanking', or lowering in price, stick to best selling items. Popular sellers. Strong brands.

Second, BUY LOW. Buy below retail. I have never seen a popular, top selling item being sold consistently under retail.

Third, don't buy at retail and expect to sell at over retail prices for very long. Markets come to equilibrium. Prices normalize. More and more people are playing this game. This is serious business. Technology, smartphones, scanners, and apps make this an easy business to try. Competition will come. Be ready. Get in, get paid, get out.

Bonus Tip: USA vs. Canada

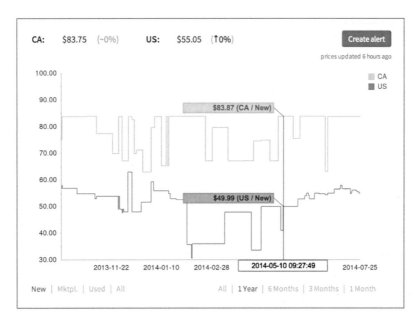

This is the Pricenoia pricing graph showing that this item sells for a higher price in Canada than in the USA.

It's listed for CDN$89.92 or about $84 USD.

LEGO Chima Worriz' Combat Lair
by LEGO

★★★★★ ▾ 1 customer review

List Price: ~~CDN$ 89.99~~

Price: **CDN$ 89.82** & **FREE Shipping**. Details

You Save: CDN$ 0.17

In Stock.

Ships from and sold by Amazon.ca. Gift-wrap available.

Want it delivered Tuesday, July 29? Order it in the next **71 hours and 22 minutes** and choose **One-Day Shipping** at checkout.

9 new from CDN$ 88.95

http://www.Amazon.ca/dp/B00C1C2RRO

On Amazon.com, there are 130 sellers but in Canada there are only nine sellers.

While many Amazon sellers are familiar with sales rank on Amazon.com, they may be unfamiliar with what a corresponding sales rank would be on Amazon.ca.

Thankfully, CamelCamelCamel has a Canadian version of their site!

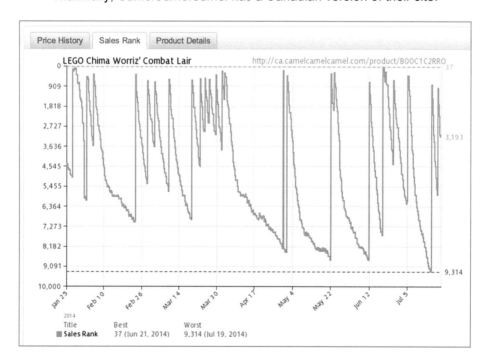

You can see that it definitely sells less frequently, but still sells pretty consistently.

http://ca.camelcamelcamel.com/LEGO-Chima-Worriz-Combat-Lair/product/B00C1C2RRO

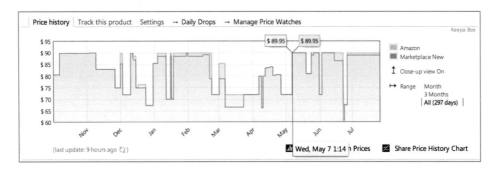

Doing your due diligence, you can check the Keepa pricing history for this item on Amazon.ca.

You can consider the UK and France as well.

Where did my kits end up?

Staying on top of your favorite websites can help you be first to know about future exclusives. Finding Target's business press releases can give you the inside scoop. Back in Chapter 13 we saw how to find this site.

http://ir.viacom.com/releasedetail.cfm?ReleaseID=855392

This press release is about the newest Teenage Mutant Ninja Turtles toys:

Target will be the official destination for exclusive Teenage Mutant Ninja Turtles movie toys beginning July 13 in-store and July 20 on Target.com.

Bonus Tip: To find others, use Google + store names + press release

Bonus Tip: Find their Facebook page and Get Notifications
https://www.facebook.com/target

Target REDcard & Cartwheel

http://www.target.com/redcard/main

Target Cartwheel

http://cartwheel.target.com/

Bonus Tip: LIVE CHAT

I love using the live chat that is built into many websites. If you see an item that you like or want more information on, you can chat with someone right through the website. You can ask about stock levels, store availability, or even ask for a coupon code or a discount. I save THOUSANDS of dollars on HomeDepot.com purchases by clicking the live chat help button before making large purchases. I would ask for a 10% off code and they would always give it to me.

Here you can see how easy it is to use the Toys R Us Live Chat widget.

Bonus Tip: Use the online Live Chat to ask for price matches from other stores or websites.

Bonus Tip: SOLD OUT ITEMS indicate popularity

Maybe you've found a product that is OUT OF STOCK on another website. This can indicate that it's either popular or it's no longer in production (even thought there may still be demand for the product at over-retail price). Here is a quick way to find the product on Amazon (even if it's also SOLD OUT on Amazon).

Highlight the TITLE or main product keywords using Context Search and choose Amazon from the drop down menu.

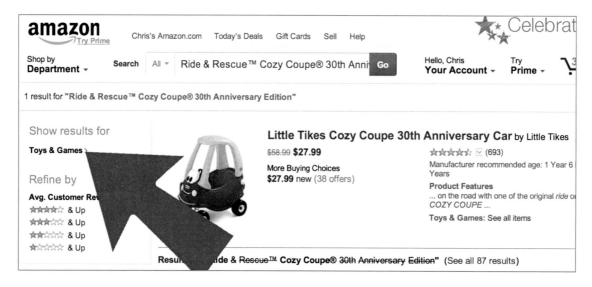

Enable SORT by choosing the Toys & Games Department.

Scroll all the way down until you see the option to "Include Out of Stock".

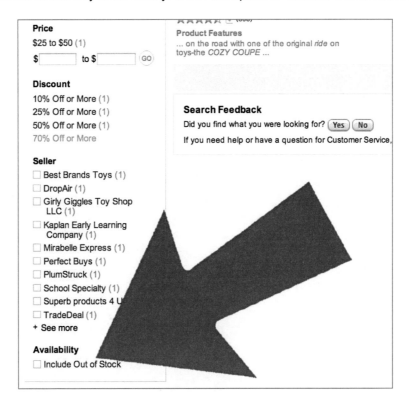

Since Amazon's website is designed for buyers, they sometimes do not show items that are not available for sale since customers would not be able to buy them. As a seller, you still want to be able to find the product page so that you can use the information and data available to decide if you want to purchase an item to sell on Amazon or just to make a list of items that you want to be looking for to resell.

Here you can find the exact product match on Amazon.

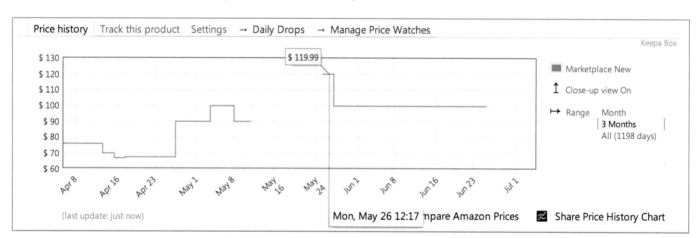

Looking at the Keepa graph, you can see the last times that it was offered and at what price. You could also look at the CamelCamelCamel Sales Rank graph to estimate recent sales (when and how many).

Bonus Tip: If a store exclusive is only available in the retail stores, add it to your BOLO shopping list.

Bonus Tip:

Wal-Mart Savings Catcher: https://savingscatcher.walmart.com

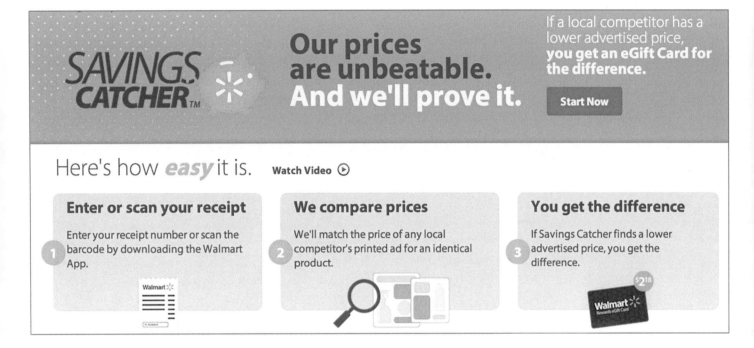

Chapter 17 – Email Lists & Clearance Sections

I highly recommend signing up for email newsletters from your favorite online retailers. If you've ordered from them before, you may be on them already (whether you like it or not). For the most part, these emails are not going to be full of profitable deals to buy and resell online, but getting them and checking them is so easy and quick that it's worth the time to do so. Remember that Full Deal Revealed from DisneyStore.com? That entire deal started from an email that they sent to me.

You may want to set up a new, separate email address (I suggest Gmail for their search and sort ability).

Just make sure the emails aren't going to your spam or promotions folder if you use Gmail.

Here is an example of an email alert that I received from Toys R Us. One simple check of my email shows me that they are offering Comic Convention Exclusives on their retail website for a limited time. They even tell me the exact time that the items will go on sale.

I can look a little closer at the items offered and make a decision if these are items that I'm interested in or not. If I'm interested, I could set a reminder alarm to make my purchases. If not, I just delete the email.

To get on the Toys R Us email list, just go to their website and find the sign up page.

Pretty much every online retail website is going to have an email signup. Here is the one from Wal-Mart:

And here is the one for Target:

What else does every online retail website have? A clearance section! They are usually pretty easy to find. Here is the one from Toys R Us:

Find them. Bookmark them. Here is the one from Wal-Mart.

Target has a clearance section as well.

Create a master list of bookmarks to save your favorite website clearance sections. Open them all up at one time and go through them on a schedule so that you don't miss new additions to the clearance sections.

Chapter 18 – Timing the Market

Sell early, buy late.

http://www.amazon.com/Monster-Lagoona-Hydration-Station-Playset/dp/B004SN4T16/

Timing is incredibly important in the world of Online Arbitrage. Prices come to equilibrium on items being sold at over-retail prices. You want to sell long before this happens. You want to get in, get paid, and get out.

Take a look at this example. How excited would you be to find an item like this?

This was from July 25, 2014. An item with a sales rank under 3,000 in Toys & Games selling for over $70 that can be found at Wal-Mart and Target for about $13.

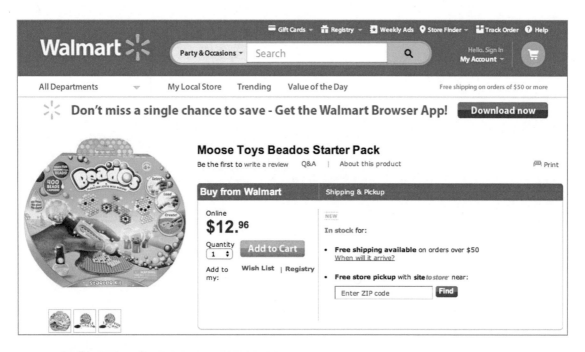

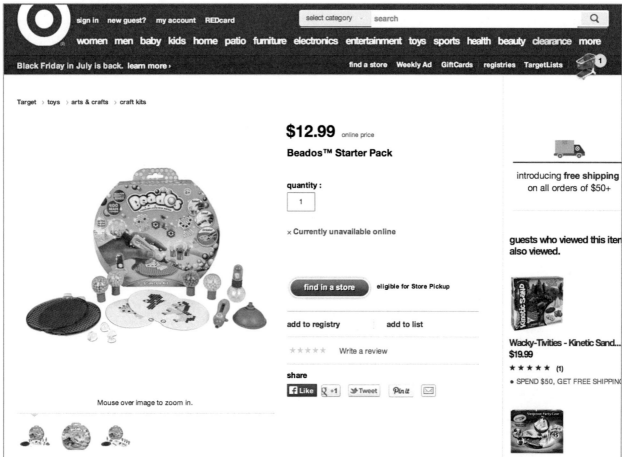

But here is the same item on August 14, 2014. This was a short window of time where supply and demand were way out of sync. CamelCamelCamel shows the prices history here:

Beados Starter Pack
by Beados

★★★☆☆ ▼ 4 customer reviews

Price: **$19.60** ✓*Prime*

Only 13 left in stock.
Sold by SupplyShelf and Fulfilled by Amazon. Gift-wrap available.

Want it tomorrow, Aug. 15? Order within **4 hrs 50 mins** and choose **One-Day Shipping** at checkout. Details

- Comes with everything you need to get started!
- Comes with an easy-to-use Pod Pen to swap Beados colors, over 500 Beados, water bottle, design templates, special accessories
- Imagination comes to life as kids can play and display their characters

Roll over image to zoom in

82 new from $16.99

When you are selling a $13 toy made of cheap plastic for $70+ on Amazon, you should do the happy dance and **SELL AS FAST AS YOU CAN**. Understand the timing of the market. Toys like this don't stay this way forever. Prices will return to normal. Don't wait until it's too late. Get in, get paid, and get out. Always be ready to find the next deal and don't fall in love with your inventory.

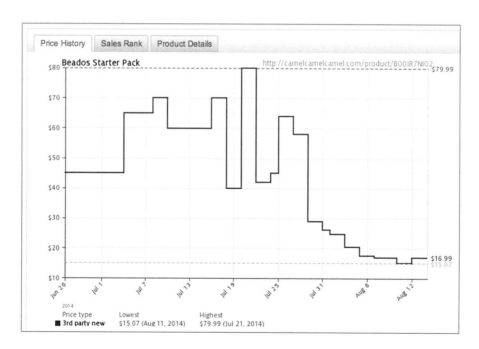

As well as the sales rank history here:

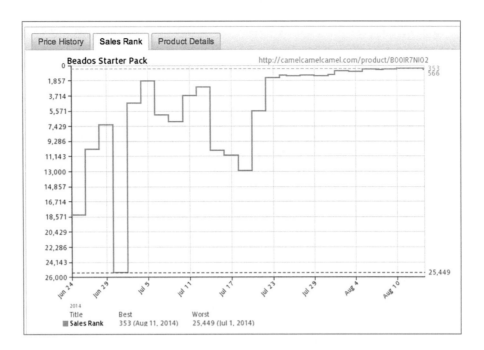

You can see how the sales rank went way up once the prices came back down to normal. Price goes down, sales go up. This is Econ 101 and it happens every time. This is a very clear example of the market coming to equilibrium. This is NOT "tanking" of a product unless the model being discussed is over-retail selling.

When you check the Amazon Movers & Shakers pages everyday for a month, you will start to notice items. You'll notice items that are there a lot and also NEW items. Explore them. Learn about them. Search, Google, and set alerts

Movers & Shakers lists can give you great info about what is suddenly hot, but the key is to find them BEFORE they ever hit Movers & Shakers. Use previous Movers & Shakers finds as a guide.

Now how could you have found this BEFORE it hit the Movers & Shakers page? You could be browsing the Toys, NEW, sorted by PRICE, and check them using PriceJump, WebScout, etc. you could be watching the new toys websites like Zoolert.

I would also look at the other items being sold by the sellers who are listing these at an above retail price. You may get product or sourcing ideas for looking at their other items. You may be able to use this info to find items like these that are being sold at Target for MSRP and on Amazon for above retail or for simple product research to help you learn more about what products sell for above retail when released.

Want to go a step further? Go to the manufacturer and look at buying direct as a distributor.

Watch trends. Look at products. Learn, forecast. Extrapolate.

Chapter 19 – Seasonal Sourcing

When I say seasonal sourcing, I mean any type of buying or selling that varies with the time of the year. And I don't just mean seasons like summer and winter. Seasonal sourcing includes products related to sporting events, celebrity news, holidays, movie releases, product launches, and more.

There are two ways to look at seasonal sourcing. What to buy is important, but we want to discuss WHEN to buy it, and WHEN to sell it. What to pick up OUT OF SEASON cheap and when to sell IN SEASON based on historical prices, sales ranks, demands, and trends.

http://www.Amazon.com/Lasko-100-MyHeat-Personal-Ceramic/dp/B003XDTWN2/

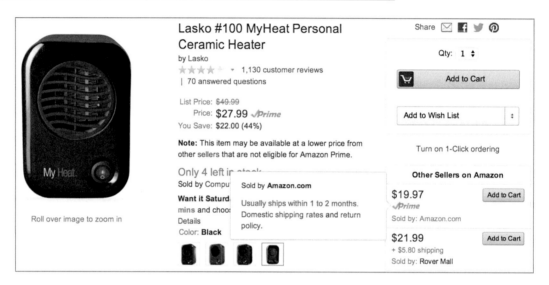

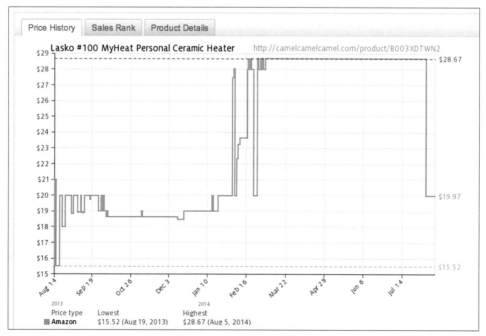

This is why you check the data! Take a look at the prices compared to the time of the year. Higher prices in the summer? Lower prices in the winter? Don't make assumptions. Some items will follow certain patterns but some items will surprise you. Don't assume; rely on the awesome historical data that we have access to.

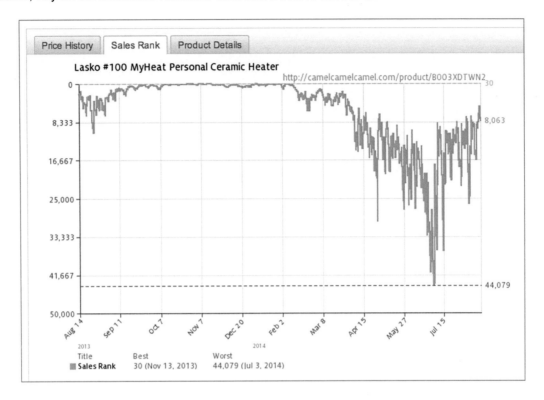

Now the sales rank history graph for this heater should be no surprise. There are certainly more heaters being sold in the winter months than during the summer months. But the prices are very different. There are always random cases where someone somewhere may need a heater in the summer or a fan in the winter.

I found the exact same pattern on fans when comparing summer and winter prices.

You'll see the opposite scenario in retail stores that have to make room on their shelves for seasonal merchandise specific to their location. Keep in mind that different products are in demand in different parts of the country at different times of the year. Never think that all buyers are like you and looking for the same products. If you live in a cold part of the country, the idea of buying fans to resell may sound crazy, but remember that there are other parts of the country where there is a demand for fans all year round.

Bonus Tip: The Wal-Mart Shopper app drops down to show that Wal-Mart also carries this item. They will likely price-match to Amazon. Consider Wal-Mart as a source in the event that you encounter quantity limits from Amazon.

Do Your Homework:

LOOK AT ANY SEASONAL PRODUCT for historic highs and lows. Set up alerts. Make informed buying decisions. Use what you learn to refine your strategies.

Bonus Tip: Google Trends, Keywords

Pick a very seasonal product (a product that you need or don't need based on the time of the year):

http://www.google.com/trends/explore

For example, you could search for a line of toys to see when they first became popular, if they are trending up, or gaining in popularity (possibly predicting the same result for the sale of their merchandise). Or are the products trending down, indicating that the newest hot toy has now become last year's passing fad. This info can help you make good decisions about what to buy, when to buy it, and possibly when it's time to get out.

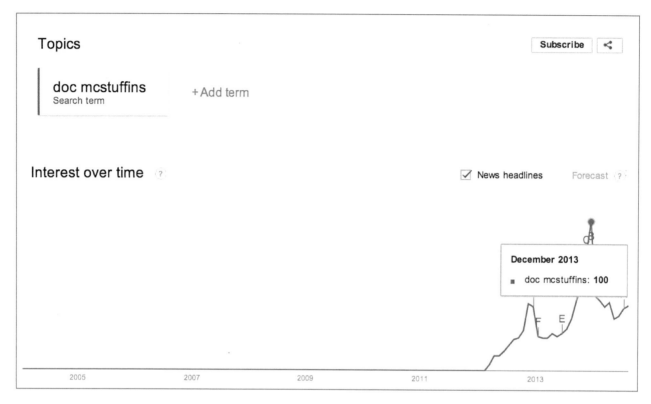

If you are familiar with toys, it should not be a surprise that search interest for Doc McStuffins has no search results in 2011 and clearly peaked in December of 2013. So you can look for a LINE of products to get an idea for trending or expected demand or interest. You could also get more specific and search for individual toys from a product line and compare them to see which ones are getting the most searches. This can help you forecast the potential hot toys from a product line.

But you can get even more specific. Consider checking the Google trends on very specific items and even see what parts of the world are the most interested. In this example for keyword FURBY, you can see that an incredible amount of interest is from Thailand of all places. I have no idea why, but if I received a lot of orders for Furbies from Thailand, I would not be surprised.

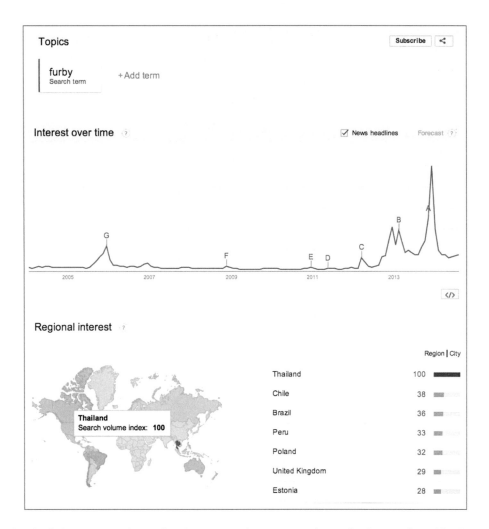

Of course you can also look for seasonal trending items, not just new and popular items. Consider items that people need in cold climates and hot climates like heaters, shovels, sunscreen, and pool toys.

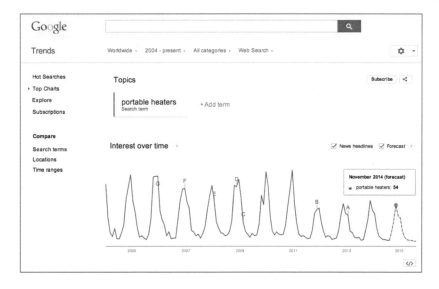

When you're out of season, search for item keywords of products that will be low priced to BUY.

When you're in season, search for item keywords of products that will be low priced to SELL.

Example: Easter-themed products

During a seasonal event like Easter, consider tracking some of the most popular items. Find these items on the Amazon Best Sellers lists. Then look at their price histories on CamelCamelCamel and see if their prices were a lot lower six months ago. You may find a product that you could buy during one part of the year to turn around and sell during another part of the year. Take a look at this item:

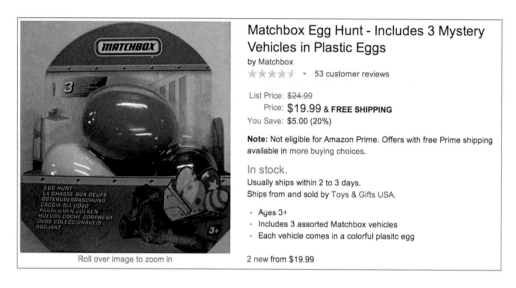

http://www.Amazon.com/Matchbox-Egg-Hunt-Includes-Vehicles/dp/B0041BWVBA

It's currently being sold for $19.99, but what does CamelCamelCamel show?

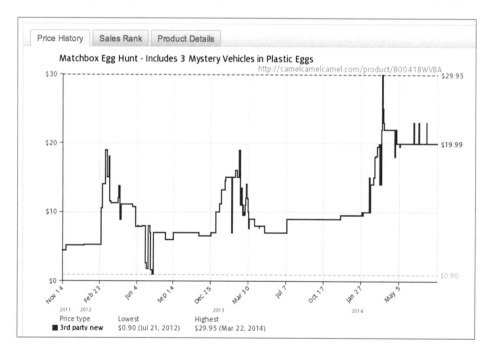

CamelCamelCamel shows no Amazon competition, a high price right at Easter of $29.96, and a low price around July of $0.90! This would be a great item to set up a price alert in the $5 - $7 range and buy them up throughout the year with the plan of selling them at Easter.

http://camelcamelcamel.com/Matchbox-Egg-Hunt-Includes-Vehicles/product/B0041BWVBA

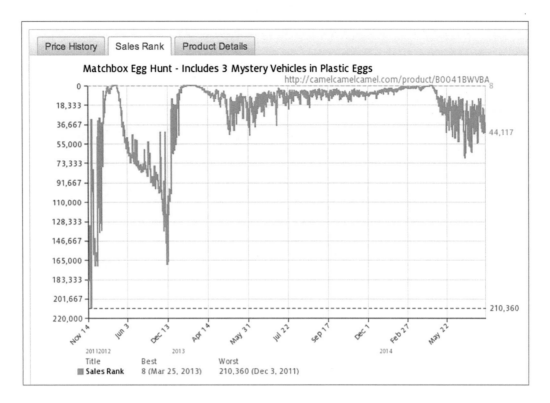

While this product does sell all year long, you can clearly see amazing sales rank spikes during Easter as customers buy this item as a gift.

So keep it simple. Just match up the prices with the time of the year. Look for patterns. Set up alerts. Make buying decisions.

Then find other items and other sites that may have the product and want to MOVE it. Buy in bulk. Wait patiently for seasonal opportunities

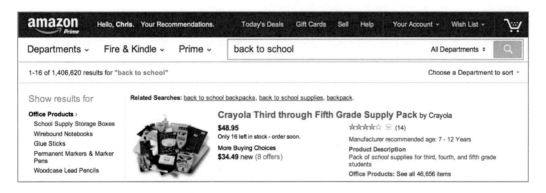

http://www.Amazon.com/Crayola-Third-through-Fifth-Supply/dp/B003UYV1ME

Take a look at this item. Clearly a Back to School item. When do we expect it to see a surge in sales? Maybe you don't have kids. Maybe you do have kids but your kids start school much later than other parts of the country. So when do other parents start their big back to school shopping on Amazon? Well, it's easy to find out by using CamelCamelCamel's historical sales rank graphs.

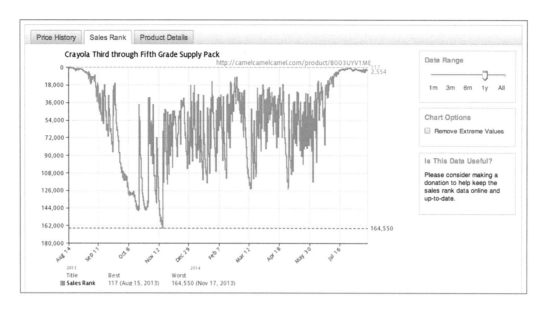

http://camelcamelcamel.com/Crayola-Third-through-Fifth-Supply/product/B003UYV1ME

I was surprised at the Winter back to school. Summer is crazy strong but winter was not. I checked this on several back to school items and the graphs were all similar.

So whether you want to sell sunscreen and pool toys or snow shovels and rock salt, use all of the tools at your disposal to help you buy at the right time and sell at the right time. The timing makes all the difference.

Find a seasonal product, check it on CamelCamelCamel and set the Date Range on the sales rank history graph to ONE YEAR. If a pattern exists, you will see it clearly on this graph. You should also compare this one year graph to the one year graph of prices.

Sell early, sell late

Bonus Tip: Remember, different stores get inventory at different times. Amazon is often not the first to get new products. How can you find these types of products? Well, one thing that you can do is identify previous items or product lines where this was the case. How can you tell? Easy! Look at the Keepa graphs for items on Amazon. Change the date range to show All Prices. Do you see BLUE Marketplace offers being in stock on Amazon BEFORE the orange prices from Amazon show up? That means that third party sellers brought those items to Amazon before Amazon had the items. Sometimes items like this are sold for over-retail profits. Seeing what items did this in the past can be a great clue as to what items and what product lines will have these opportunities in the future.

Sell Fast Example:

Take a look at this example. This was a limited edition exclusive figure for Disney's new Infinity system. It was limited to 5,000 pieces and was given out at the D23 Expo. At the time, you could not buy it. It even says on the package that this item will not be available in stores until 2014 (great reason to SELL NOW!) Some players and collectors wanted this one and paid a hefty premium to have it early.

http://www.Amazon.com/Sorcerers-Apprentice-Xbox-Wii-WiiU-PS3/dp/B00EH9G16W

The CamelCamelCamel price history graph shows prices in the $200 - $300 range. But suddenly the prices stopped changing. What happened?

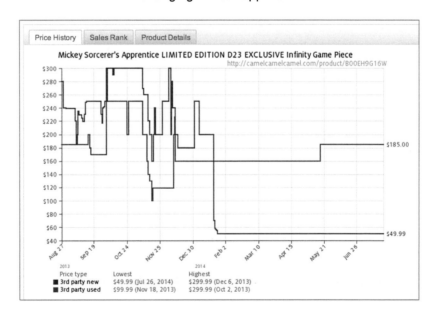

http://camelcamelcamel.com/Sorcerers-Apprentice-Xbox-Wii-WiiU-PS3/product/B00EH9G16W

The sales rank history graph shows that the item was actually selling at those $200 - $300 prices, but then dropped off significantly. What happened?

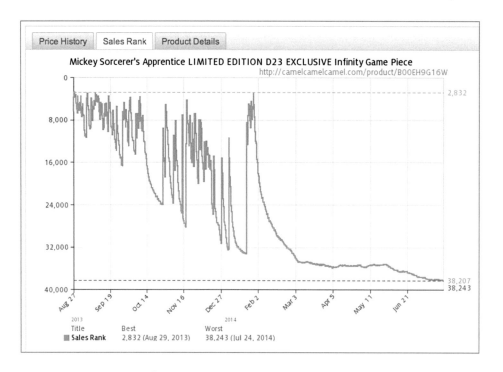

Simple: you can get it now for $12:

http://www.Amazon.com/INFINITY-Sorcerers-Apprentice-Not-Machine-Specific/dp/B00H8YW996/

Should it be any surprise that it started selling 6 months ago:

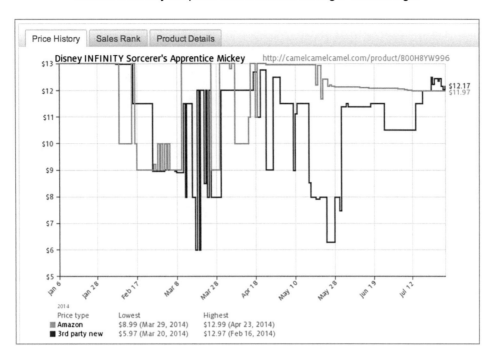

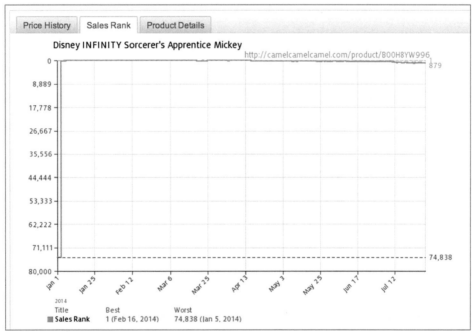

And took over all the sales? People wanted it early and paid more for it.

Bonus Tip:

Remember that sales rank history graph dropping off? There is a lot of information that we can gather here. You can see exactly what happens to an item's sales rank I the Video Game category when it doesn't sell for six months. It will have a sales rank of around 40,000.

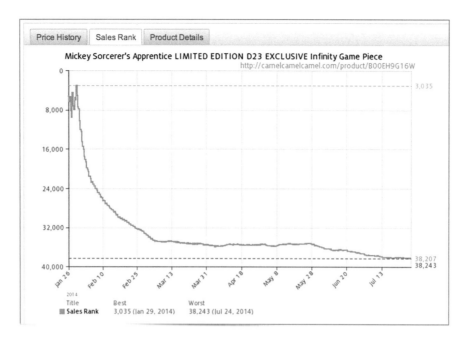

So, based on what we saw with this Disney Infinity figure, when I see things like this, I pay attention:

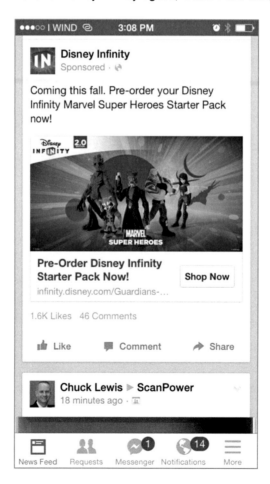

You are following them on Facebook, right?

https://www.facebook.com/DisneyInfinity

It's so easy to LIKE pages and Get Notifications about products and new releases that you are interested in for your Online Arbitrage business. It's so easy to find out about new products and then hop over to Amazon and check for pre-orders:

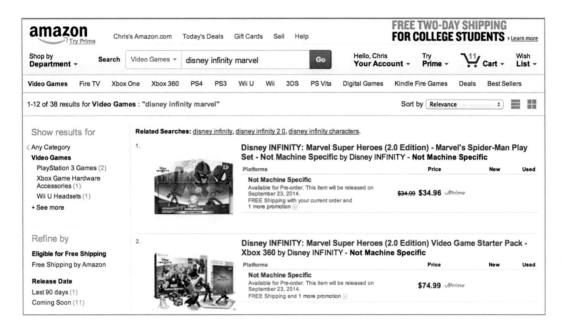

Especially considering that some places, even other sites or local retail stores, may get these before Amazon. They may also end up on eBay before Amazon.

This was a FatWallet Topic Alert for a Christmas product that I received in July:

http://www.Amazon.com/Kids-Preferred-Disney-Baby-Holiday/dp/B00DPK0M00

I shared it in our Facebook group:

https://www.facebook.com/groups/scanpower/permalink/517507688351162/

At the $3.67 price from Amazon, can you buy and hold until Christmas?

Religious & Holiday Products:

Again the Amazon Movers & Shakers page helps to reveal products that warrant a closer look. Let's take a look at the #2 item: KidKraft Rosh Hashanah Set.

http://www.amazon.com/KidKraft-62906-Rosh-Hashanah-Set/dp/B0009EVZ8I

It's obviously seeing a surge in sales to push it up to number two on the Movers & Shakers page. If you don't know what Rosh Hashanah is, you could do a quick Google search:

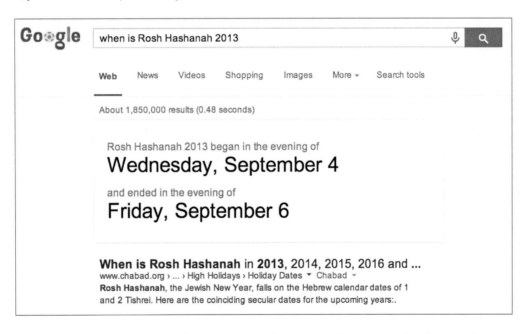

It should start to make sense what to do next. Compare sales throughout the year and look for patterns.

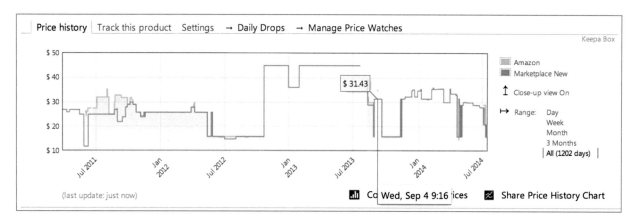

Keepa shows lots of price variations and lots of times where Amazon was not in stock. You can check the prices offered on the exact dates as well as leading right up to them.

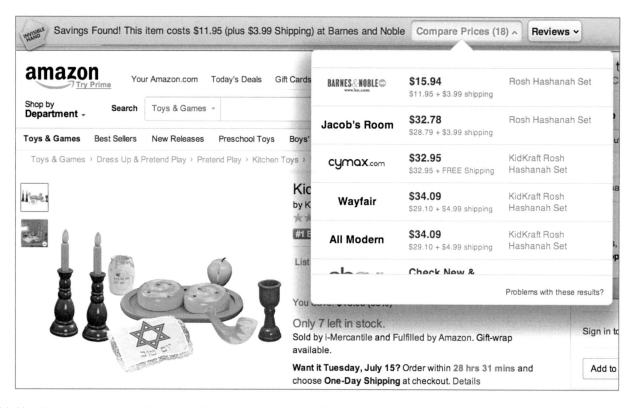

InvisibleHand gives us some other sites that sell this product. Barnes & Noble have this for $11.95 + shipping.

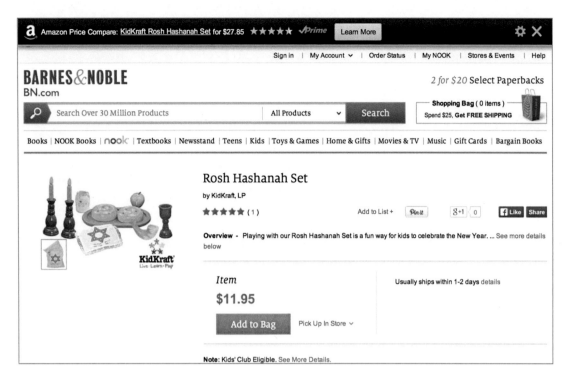

http://www.barnesandnoble.com/p/toys-games-rosh-hashanah-set/22555019

And on the Barnes & Noble website, we see that Amazon 1Button App showing us the Amazon price.

If you want to buy this item from Amazon at the Barnes & Noble price, you can report the lower price to Amazon (shown in Chapter 10). You may encounter purchase limits form Amazon or Barnes & Noble so consider them when deciding where to purchase.

Take a look at the CamelCamelCamel sales rank history:

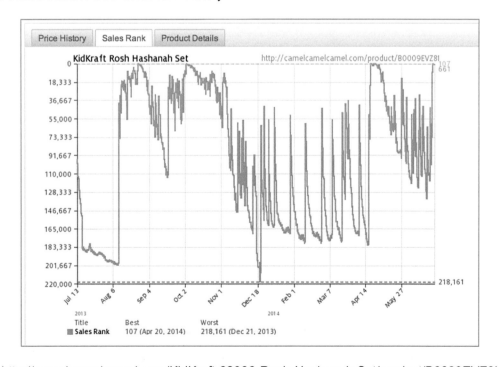

http://camelcamelcamel.com/KidKraft-62906-Rosh-Hashanah-Set/product/B0009EVZ8I

You can see the spike in sales rank leading into September, but then it clearly spiked again in October and then in April. Why? I think its natural to have Jewish holiday items on Amazon spike in popularity and sales for Jewish holidays, even if they are technically the wrong holiday item.

I asked a Jewish friend of mine, Aryeh Sheinbein, about what he thought was happening on this item. He wrote to me, "The May spike is probably for the holiday that is in late May/ early June called Shavuot, and while this toy set is for Rosh Hashanah, it can be used for many Jewish holidays but practically makes the most sense for Rosh Hashanah given what is in the set."

We saw in Chapter 19 about selling products from popular, current movies. Let's take a look on some historical pricing histories from movies that came out a while ago. What happens to the prices of the movie-themed merchandise after the movie is no longer in theaters?

Kids watch movies at home and on Netflix that are no longer in theaters. These kids still want the toys from the movie but they are not on shelves anymore due to limited space.

Take a look at the prices on this item:

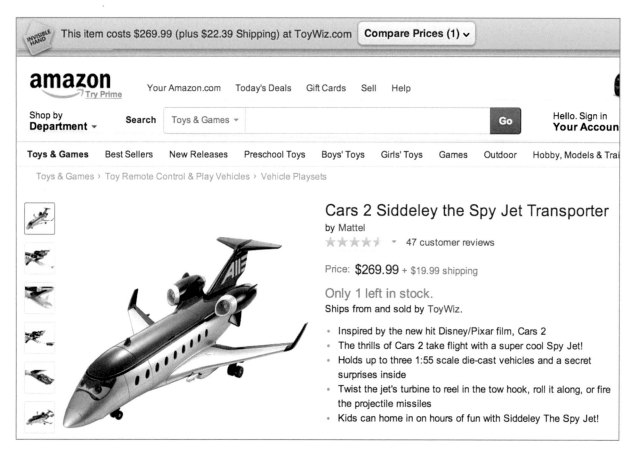

http://www.Amazon.com/dp/B004H4XLR4

CamelCamelCamel price history for the past year shows a steady increase in the prices listed on Amazon.

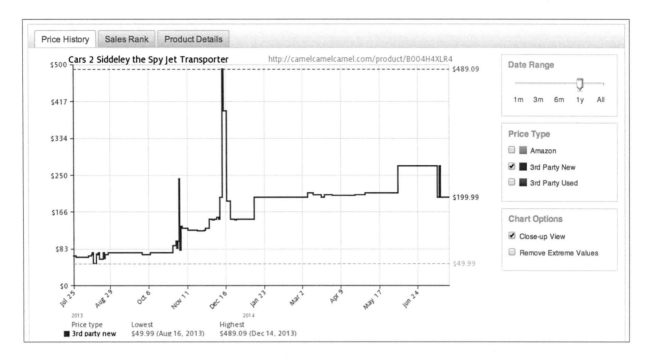

Looking at the CamelCamelCamel sales rank history shows that sales have dropped off significantly, but that the item does still sell consistently. This is what is expected to happen to sales as prices rise.

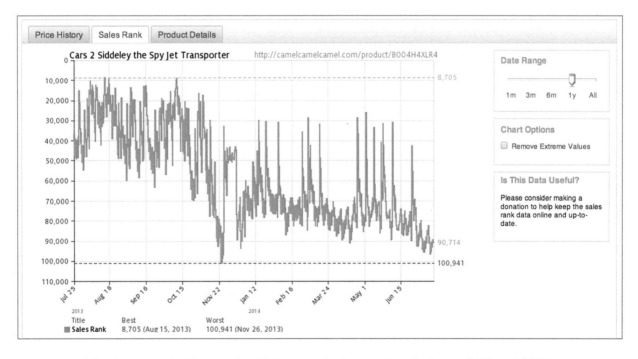

The three-month Keepa price history graph shows prices between $200 and $270.

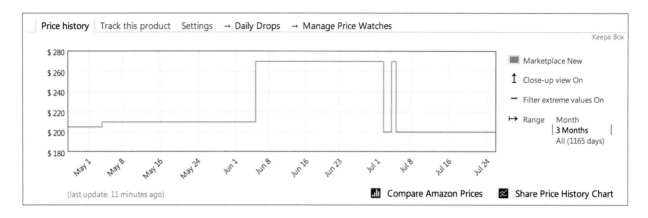

A simple Google will show you the original release date of pretty much any movie:

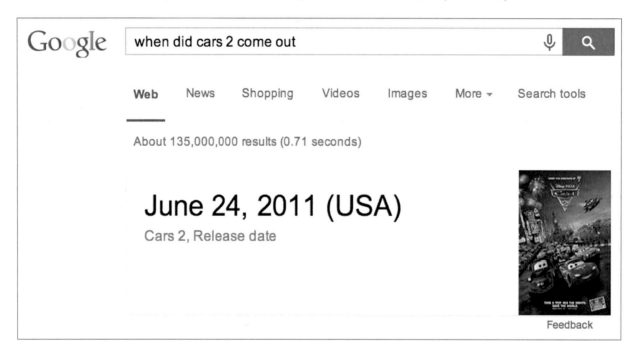

If you stumbled onto this item, you may want to go back and do some research. What can you learn from this item? What is it about this item that lead to the rise in price? Why are customers willing to pay so much for this particular toy?

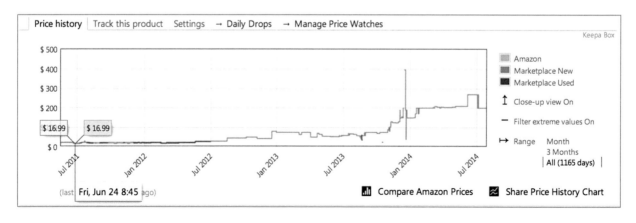

Going back to the full Keepa price history, we can find the price on the date that the movie was released. At the time, Amazon was selling this item for $16.99

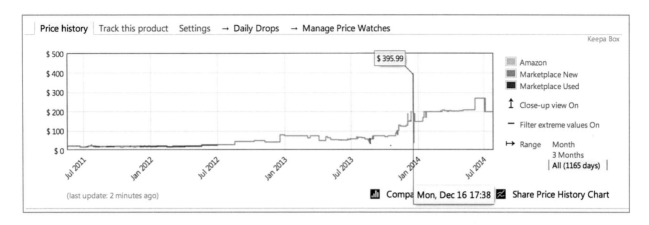

Heading into fourth quarter, you can see this item was at an all-time high price of $395.99.

San Diego Comic Con: http://www.comic-con.org/

San Diego Comic Con (SDCC) is a convention that offers many exclusive toys that collectors are often willing to pay premium prices for. Marking your calendars around this event can help you prepare to profit from this event.

To do some product research, you can do an Amazon search for keyword SDCC.

You can see some of the related searches that are suggested by Amazon. These can be great clues as to what collectors are searching for.

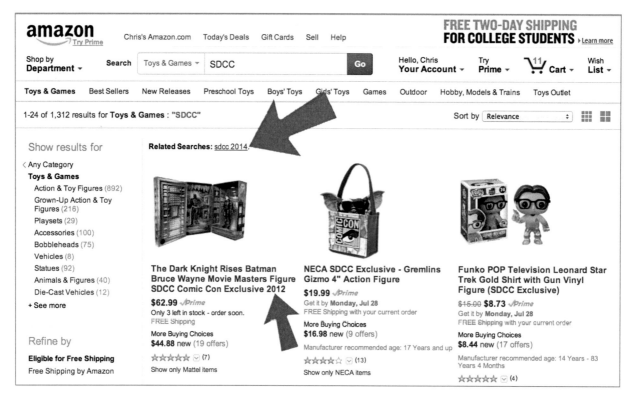

Searching for 'SDCC' shows all kinds of results including results from 2012. Amazon also clearly suggests SDCC 2014 as a search.

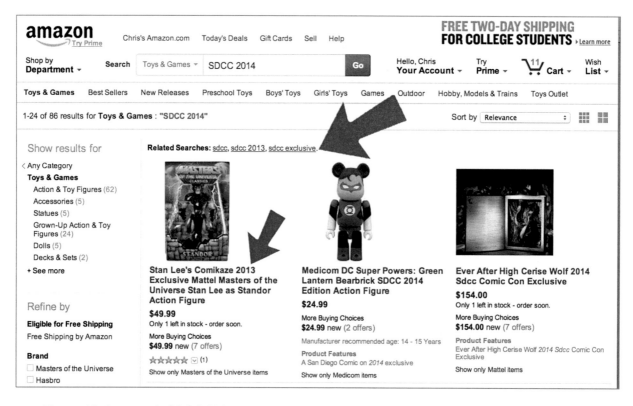

Even with the search SDCC 2014, we are still getting 2013 exclusive items in the search results.

Bonus Tip:

You can EXCLUDE certain search terms by using the minus or dash sign.

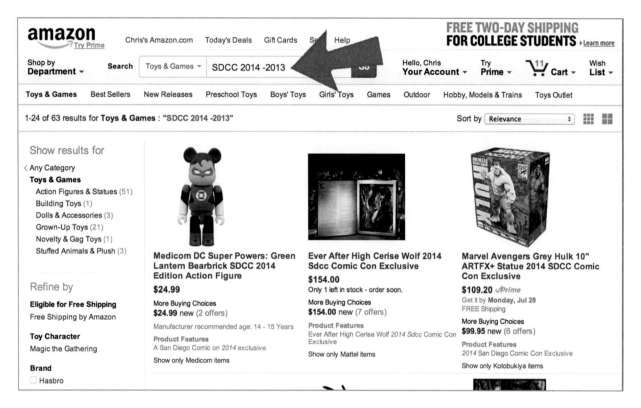

Doing the search SDCC 2014 -2013 will give you the above results for 2014 SDCC items on Amazon.

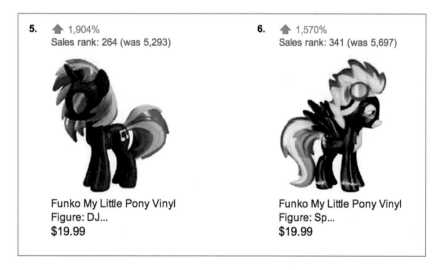

You can spot new SDCC items on Amazon as they shoot up the Amazon Movers & Shakers page. Here you can see two items that hit #5 and #6 at the same time.

A closer look shows the item priced at $19.99 from Amazon but not currently shipping with a future in stock date. You can see from the product details that this is the limited edition San Diego Comic Con version.

Funko My Little Pony Vinyl Figure: DJ Pon 3 Dash- Black Version
by FunKo
Be the first to review this item

Price: **$19.99** & **FREE Shipping** on orders over $35.
Details

In stock on July 28, 2014.
Order it now.
Ships from and sold by Amazon.com. Gift-wrap available.

- Limited Edition!
- San Diego Comic Con Versions!
- Check out the other My Little Pony items from Funko!

http://www.Amazon.com/Funko-Little-Pony-Vinyl-Figure/dp/B00KDHT2NG

Funko My Little Pony Vinyl Figure: Spitfire- Black Version
by FunKo
Be the first to review this item

Price: **$19.99** & **FREE Shipping** on orders over $35.
Details

In stock on July 28, 2014.
Order it now.
Ships from and sold by Amazon.com. Gift-wrap available.

- Limited Edition!
- San Diego Comic Con Versions!
- Check out the other My Little Pony items from Funko!

http://www.Amazon.com/Funko-Little-Pony-Vinyl-Figure/dp/B00KDHT560

There are a few things going for these items in terms of collectability. It's a strong brand (My Little Pony) and it's a limited edition exclusive.

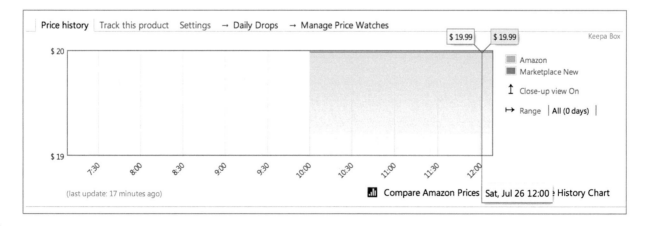

You can see that at the time of these screenshots the items had only been tracked by Keepa for a couple of hours. So by checking the Movers & Shakers pages, you can be one of the first to find new products.

Frequently Bought Together

Price for both: **$39.98**

(Add both to Cart)   (Add both to Wish List)

Show availability and shipping details

☑ **This item:** Funko My Little Pony Vinyl Figure: Spitfire- Black Version $19.99

☑ Funko My Little Pony Vinyl Figure: DJ Pon 3 Dash- Black Version $19.99

Amazon also shows these items as being Frequently Bought Together. This can be very useful in the event that both of these items were not on the Movers & Shakers page. If only one had shot up in sales rank, you could easily find the other one this way. How many other SDCC 2014 exclusive items can you find?

Sporting Events:

Sporting events can dramatically affect the market prices of related merchandise. Even if you are not a sports nut, keeping up to date with the major sporting events can help you spot trends that you can capitalize on. Even if you don't care about the Super Bowl, it's a good idea to know when it is in the event that you are sourcing products related to the teams in the game. How about knowing when the Olympics are starting? Or the World Cup, for soccer?

You could get all that you need by checking www.espn.com a few times a week.

Deal Phenomenon: LeBron James jerseys

Take a look at these two eBay listings:

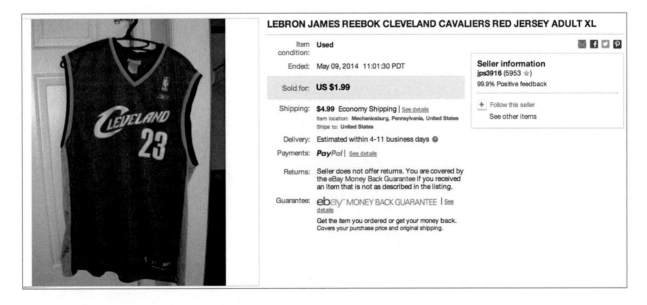

LEBRON JAMES REEBOK CLEVELAND CAVALIERS RED JERSEY ADULT XL

Item condition:	Used
Ended:	May 09, 2014 11:01:30 PDT
Sold for:	**US $1.99**
Shipping:	**$4.99** Economy Shipping | See details
	Item location: Mechanicsburg, Pennsylvania, United States
	Ships to: United States
Delivery:	Estimated within 4-11 business days ⓘ
Payments:	*PayPal* | See details
Returns:	Seller does not offer returns. You are covered by the eBay Money Back Guarantee if you received an item that is not as described in the listing.
Guarantee:	ebay™ MONEY BACK GUARANTEE | See details
	Get the item you ordered or get your money back. Covers your purchase price and original shipping.

Seller information
jps3916 (5953 ⭐)
99.9% Positive feedback

\+ Follow this seller
See other items

On May 9, 2014, this jersey was listed for $1.99 with $4.99 shipping and ended without a single bidder.

http://www.ebay.com/itm/Lebron-James-Cleveland-Cavaliers-Jersey-Adult-XL-Reebok-/291183005282

This jersey ended on July 10, 2014 with a Best Offer accepted under $14.98 with free shipping. What is significant about July 10, 2014?

On July 11, 2014, LeBron James announced that he was returning to the Cleveland Cavaliers after four years playing for the Miami Heat. This was a big announcement because four years earlier LeBron James left Cleveland for Miami is a very public way.

http://www.nytimes.com/2014/07/12/sports/basketball/lebron-james-to-return-to-cleveland-cavaliers-leaving-miami-heat.html

This announcement of returning to Cleveland was all over the news. When something is all over the news, it puts in the forefront of people's minds and generally leads to an increase in demand for related products.

Take a look at the next item that sold on July 11, 2014, one day later. Same jersey sold for $150 + $12 shipping.

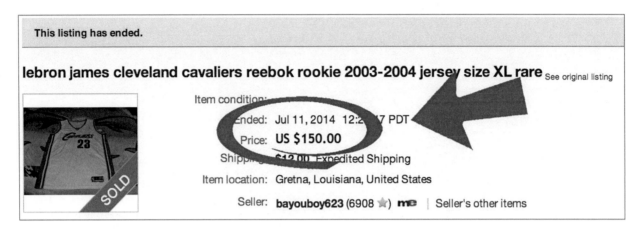

This listing has ended.

lebron james cleveland cavaliers reebok rookie 2003-2004 jersey size XL rare See original listing

Item condition:

Ended: Jul 11, 2014 12:2 7 PDT

Price: **US $150.00**

Shipping: $12.00 Expedited Shipping

Item location: Gretna, Louisiana, United States

Seller: **bayouboy623** (6908 ⭐) me | Seller's other items

http://www.ebay.com/itm/lebron-james-cleveland-cavaliers-reebok-rookie-2003-2004-jersey-size-XL-rare-/160758394742

Maybe you couldn't predict it fully, but if you have LeBron James jerseys during the summertime that he is in free agency, maybe it would be a smart move to wait and see. It's not like the jerseys were selling for good prices anyway.

Lesson: Don't sell LeBron stuff cheap the summer he is a free agent.

Time the market when it's hot, popular, on the news, being talked about. You know there will be demand for all things LeBron (or whatever else is in the news).

What else can you do to stay ahead of the curve of topical sports news? Read some articles and think through to the retail side of things.

Take a look at this article about LeBron James returning to wearing the #23 jersey (he was #6 with Miami). It takes time to make jerseys in China and get them shipped over to the US market. As the beginning of the NBA season approaches, there will very likely be increased demand for LeBron #23 jerseys, especially in and around Cleveland. The NBA will try to forecast demand as closely as they can in order to supply enough merchandise, but there may be an opportunity as items sell out to sell them for an even higher price online.

Here is an article from ESPN about the #23 jersey announcement:

http://espn.go.com/nba/story/_/id/11271524/lebron-james-go-back-no-23-cleveland-cavaliers-return

What else? How about buying tickets for the first Cleveland Cavaliers home game of the season? Buy them online and resell them to the highest bidder. The key is thinking ahead on these. As soon as LeBron makes the announcement that he's returning to Cleveland, you should be thinking about that first home game.

Celebrities in the News:

Robin Williams & Celebrity News Affecting the Arbitrage

http://youtu.be/_u7lNa7jM2E
http://bit.ly/robinwilliamsnews

Some people choose to remember their favorite celebrities in unusual ways. Take a look at what items were at #1 and #2 on the Toys Movers & Shakers list:

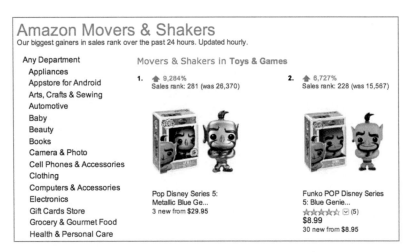

Here is an eBay listing for a Robin Williams autographed picture.

http://www.ebay.com/itm/Mork-And-Mindy-Autograph-Reprint-Robin-Williams-Pam-Dawber-Conrad-Janis-/161175269169

You can see that all of the purchases and Best Offers are from August 11, 2014.

Purchase history

User ID	Buy It Now Price	Quantity	Date of Purchase
g***t (238 ⭐)	US $24.99	1	Aug-11-14 17:35:47 PDT
e***e (2)	US $24.99	1	Aug-11-14 16:38:22 PDT
k***k (50 ⭐)	US $24.99	1	Aug-11-14 16:34:52 PDT
6***g (561 ⭐)	US $24.99	1	Aug-11-14 16:34:46 PDT
6***q (561 ⭐)	US $24.99	1	Aug-11-14 16:33:46 PDT

Offer history

User ID	Offer Status	Quantity	Date of Offer
n***6 (210 ⭐)	Accepted	1	Aug-11-14 18:55:44 PDT
i***e (194 ⭐)	Accepted	1	Aug-11-14 17:15:01 PDT
a***e (1899 ⭐)	Accepted	1	Aug-11-14 16:24:25 PDT
4***p (1004 ⭐)	Pending	1	Aug-11-14 16:55:03 PDT

http://offer.ebay.com/ws/eBayISAPI.dll?ViewBidsLogin&item=111099986262

This high priced item received all of its Offers on August 11th, 12th, and 13th.

Bonus Tip:

Online retailers (where many people PREFER to shop) often run their lead times as short as possible on replenishable products. If an event like this causes a surge in demand, they could be out of stock for days or even weeks. This is a good time to consider looking for products locally at retail stores to sell online. Check products on Amazon for popular items and out of stock items.

.

Chapter 20 – Deals, Tracking, & Discussion

As you look through the deal sites listed in this chapter and gauge their usefulness to your Online Arbitrage business, also be sure to find and follow their Facebook pages and Twitter accounts using the methods outlined in Chapter 8.

The Internet has brought people together. No matter what your interests are, you can find others who share them. This is true even for people who like to save money when shopping (seriously, who doesn't like to save money?).

Many of the online deal sites are geared towards consumers. While they are not specifically for resellers, you'll find that some of the deals are hot enough to buy and resell for a profit. You can find out about many of these types of deals by monitoring these deal sites yourself or using their built in alert systems.

While some sites have full-time staff to create content and post consumer deals, most of them are community driven. This means that members are the ones creating posts and sharing information.

Here are some sites to take a look at:

Ben's Bargains

http://bensbargains.net/

Be sure to Like them and Get Notifications on Facebook:

https://www.facebook.com/bensbargains

Also sign up for mobile notifications from their Twitter account and see who else you should be following.

https://twitter.com/bensbargains

Here is an example of what they share on Facebook and Twitter. The post even says that it's $20 cheaper than Amazon with a bonus $10 Wal-Mart gift card. They make it too easy to qualify deals.

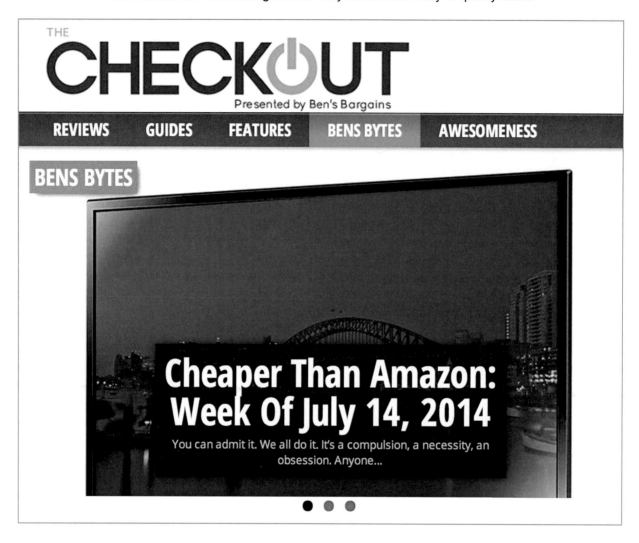

http://bensbargains.net/thecheckout/bens-bytes/cheaper-Amazon-week-july-14-2014/

Could they make it any easier? They have an entire section of items that you can purchase cheaper than on Amazon. That's EXACTLY what you are looking for! This is tailor made for people reselling on Amazon.

Ben's Bargains Guides:

http://bensbargains.net/thecheckout/category/guides/

Free market research to use year after year:

http://bensbargains.net/thecheckout/guides/best-july-4th-sales-year/

Ben's Bytes:

http://bensbargains.net/thecheckout/category/bens-bytes/

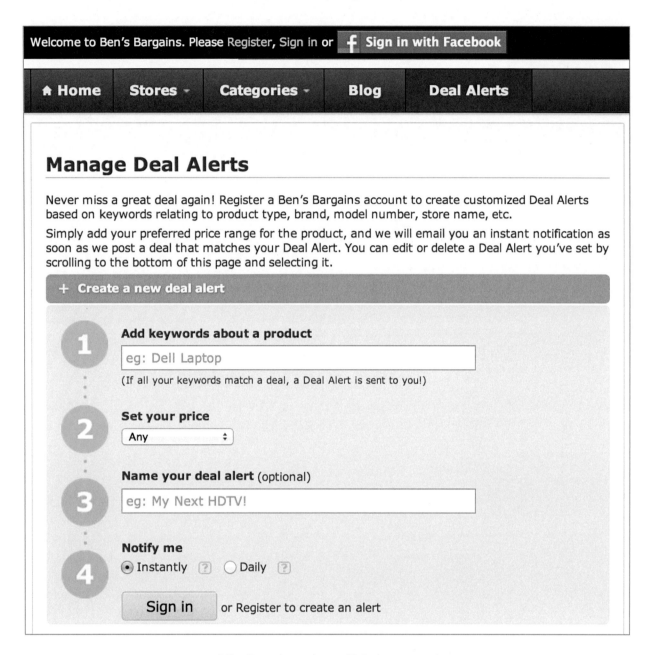

🏠 Home   **Stores ▾**   **Categories ▾**   **Blog**   **Deal Alerts**

Manage Deal Alerts

Never miss a great deal again! Register a Ben's Bargains account to create customized Deal Alerts based on keywords relating to product type, brand, model number, store name, etc.

Simply add your preferred price range for the product, and we will email you an instant notification as soon as we post a deal that matches your Deal Alert. You can edit or delete a Deal Alert you've set by scrolling to the bottom of this page and selecting it.

+ Create a new deal alert

1 **Add keywords about a product**

eg: Dell Laptop

(If all your keywords match a deal, a Deal Alert is sent to you!)

2 **Set your price**

Any ▾

3 **Name your deal alert** (optional)

eg: My Next HDTV!

4 **Notify me**
⦿ Instantly ⍰   ◯ Daily ⍰

Sign in   or Register to create an alert

http://bensbargains.net/alert-manager/

305

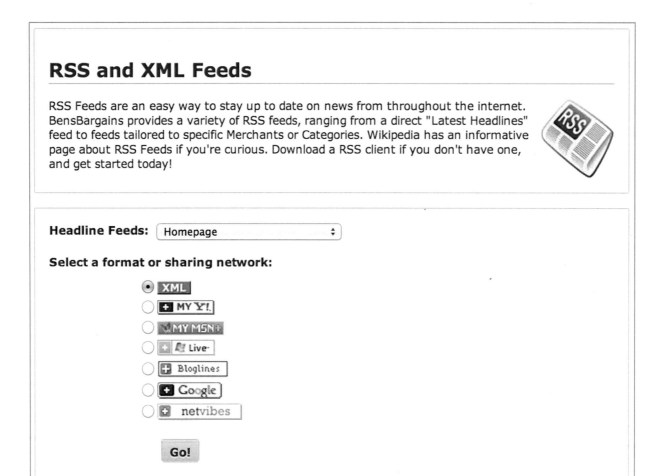

http://bensbargains.net/rss-feeds/

They have some awesome RSS feeds from more than just their homepage. They also have category feeds, store feeds, and other feeds, like: most clicked, most discussed, most bookmarked, and most viewed.

ScanPower has recently developed an advanced RSS Reader specifically designed for online resellers. More information about the ScanPower RSS Reader can be found at the end of this book.

A QUICK GUIDE TO USING BEN'S BARGAINS

Welcome to Ben's Bargains! Even the most seasoned deal hunters need a little help navigating through all of our deals. If you're new to Ben's Bargains or simply haven't been here in a while, here's an overview of our Dealbox as well as an in-depth rundown on helpful tools that include Deal Filters, Price History and Deal Alerts.

BREAKING DOWN THE BEN'S DEALBOX

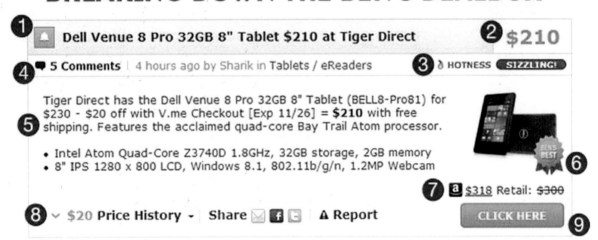

1. Click the bell icon to activate a Deal Alert (requires registration). Title includes product and store information.

2. Sale price of the product in orange.

3. Hotness meter rates deals based on popularity among the community.

4. Clicking comments will let you read and post comments about the deal (requires registration).

5. Deal description includes details about the product, coupon codes, links to reviews and other important information.

6. Ben's Best medals (Silver and Gold) indicate our Editors' Picks for the top deals.

7. Amazon price with link to Amazon as well as the Retail Price of the product.

8. Clicking Price History will show previous deals on the product. Use the Report Link when the deal is no longer active.

9. Click the Green button to see the Deal!

http://bensbargains.net/guide-to-using-bens-bargains/

WHAT'S THE PRICE HISTORY?

Assuming a Ben's expert deal editor has posted the product at least once before, you will see a Price History notification in the bottom left corner of the deal post. This is designed to help you understand price movement over the last several months.

We have included symbols and colors to indicate how the newly posted price relates to the last deal post. They include:

- **Lower Price**: Green Color / Down Symbol
- **Higher Price**: Red Color / Up Symbol
- **Equal Price**: Blue Color / Equal Symbol

If you click on the Price History link, an overlay that details the last five deal posts will appear. You can also click on "See All History" to be taken to a page that lists all previous prices on the product as well as the stores that offered the deals.

WHAT'S A DEAL ALERT?

Don't you just hate missing out on an awesome deal? If you are interested in a specific product, we can send you an automatic deal alert email the second that product is posted on Ben's. You can also set a specific price point for said product in order to filter those notifications even more.

Of course, you need to register for a Ben's account before setting a Deal Alert. After you register and log into your account, there are two ways to set a Deal Alert, Simple and Advanced.

Simple Deal Alert

We have set up a one-click process for you! See the little Bell icon in the top left corner of the Deal box? Click it once to turn it orange and you have set a Deal Alert for that specific product. The next time the product is posted on Ben's, you will receive an instant notification.

Don't want to receive that Deal Alert anymore? Click the Bell icon again to turn it gray and the alert is turned off. You can also turn the alert off on the Alert Manager page.

Brad's Deals: http://www.bradsdeals.com

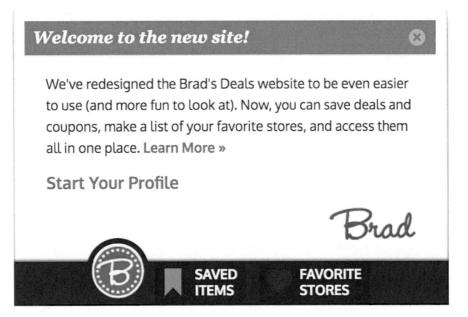

TheFind: http://www.thefind.com

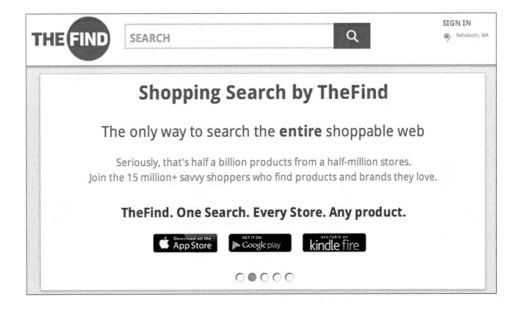

PriceGrabber: http://www.pricegrabber.com/

DealNews: http://dealnews.com/

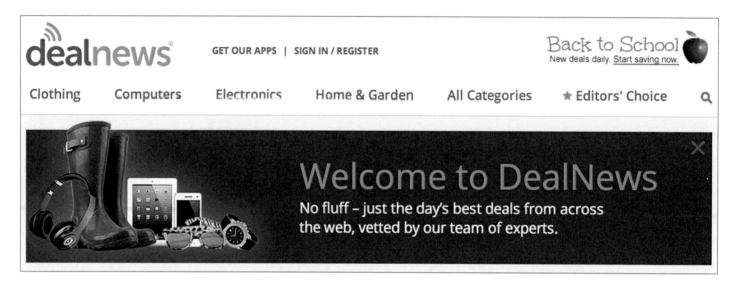

Amazon Seller Forums (Amazon seller account required):
https://sellercentral.amazon.com/forums/index.jspa

Reddit Flipping: http://www.reddit.com/r/Flipping/

ScanPower Facebook Group: http://facebook.com/groups/scanpower

Chapter 21 – Deal Website Spotlight: FatWallet.com

FatWallet is a community-based deal site designed to save consumers money. They also have dedicated, full-time staff that work with retailers to maximize cash back offers, post deals in the forums, and provide value to their members. FatWallet is 100% free to use. Some features like setting up Topic Alerts do require an account.

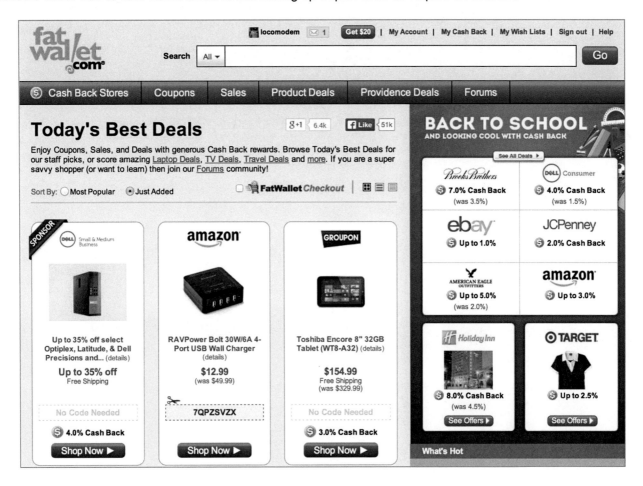

https://www.fatwallet.com/

FatWallet does have a referral program.
If you're new to FatWallet, you can use this link and you'll be sending me a cool $5!
http://www.fatwallet.com/?referral=locomodem

If you want to refer people to FatWallet yourself, use this link:
https://www.fatwallet.com/account/tell-a-friend/

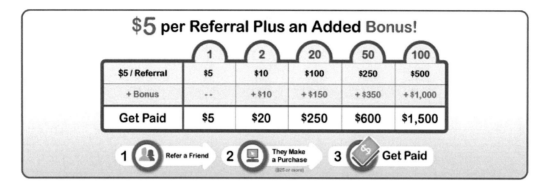

http://www.fatwallet.com/cash-back-shopping/

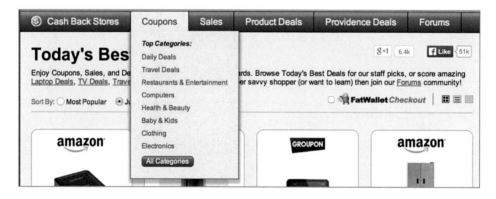

http://www.fatwallet.com/coupons/

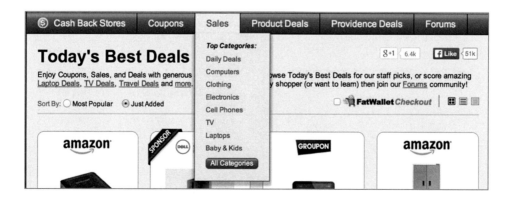

http://www.fatwallet.com/sales/

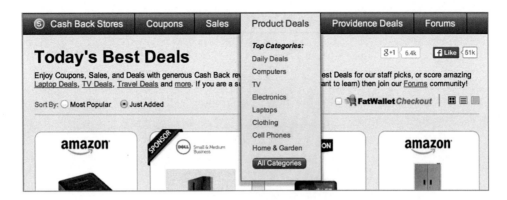

http://www.fatwallet.com/product-deals/

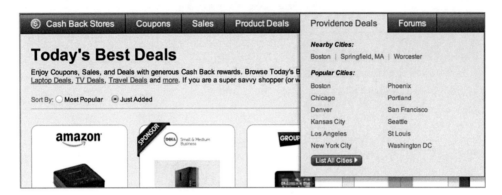

You have to log in to see your local deals: http://www.fatwallet.com/local-deals/

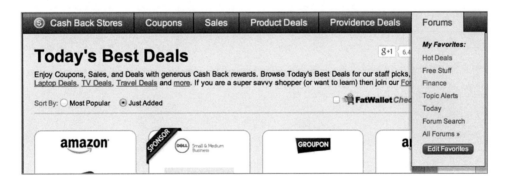

FatWallet Forums: http://www.fatwallet.com/forums/

They also have a whole section for Coupons and Cash Back: http://www.fatwallet.com/cash-back-shopping/

Here is an example of a post in the Hot Deals Forum on FatWallet:

FatWallet members can VOTE on deals by giving them POSITIVE (green) or NEGATIVE (red) ratings. The net rating will show near the top of the post where it says rated. This deal has been voted GREEN. You can see the title, summary, and link to purchase the deal. One awesome thing about FatWallet is that FatWallet staff will 'clean up' the posts and make sure that the titles have the relevant information like title, price, and retailer. The rest of the post will have an image and a link to purchase the product.

Be Careful: I have seen members vote awesome deals down with RED in order to hide the fact that the deal is awesome. They do this hoping that some people who only view the deals that are voted the highest will then miss the deals. It is unfortunate behavior but there's nothing you can really do about it other than simply be aware that it could happen. When you look at Hot Deals on FatWallet, be sure to do your own homework and evaluate the deals yourself. It is useful to look at the top rated deals (posts with the most GREEN), but if you only look at those, you'll miss some other good deals.

So how does FatWallet Cash Back work?

1. Shop

We partner with your favorite merchants to create **Cash Back** stores.
When you log into FatWallet, we document what you earn.
We make sure you get your money.

Click on a special offer or coupon deal. Your online purchases earn **Cash Back** rebates that grow in your FatWallet account. The more you buy, the more you earn. You're earning cold, hard **Cash Back**.

2. Get Paid

Any time you want, you can see your **Cash Back** balance. When you want your money, we can send you a check or transfer the money to your PayPal account. Just tell us.

3. How we make our money

FatWallet earns commissions on the purchases you make through **Cash Back** stores.
We share part of our commission with you.

Date	Merchant	Purchase Amount	Cash Back	Status
10/30/2005	Home Depot	$4,462.50	$133.88	Reported

Here is a nice $133.88 check that FatWallet sent to me for buying something from HomeDepot.com that I would have bought anyway.

FatWallet Topic Alerts: https://www.fatwallet.com/account/tools/

This is easily one of the BEST and EASIEST ways to get alerted of potential deals from the FatWallet Hot Deals Forums. In your FatWallet account, go to Tools & Alerts, and then find Topic Alerts.

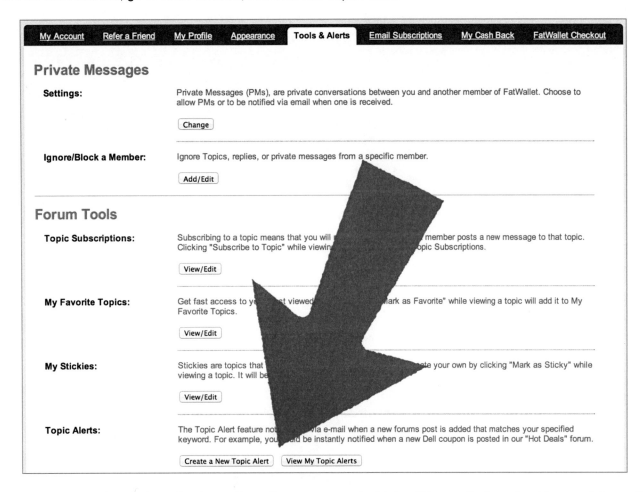

Here are some examples of alerts that I use. Sometimes you have to think a little creatively and put in search terms that you might not normally think of, like 'price mistake' AND 'pricing mistake' because different FatWallet members may post similar types of deals but with different keywords. Think about how other people may be posting. FatWallet Topic Alerts are 100% free so you can set up as many variations as you like.

https://www.fatwallet.com/account/change_topic_alerts.php

Add your own. Consider DISNEY; you may want to use both "disney store" and "disneystore"

Some extra advice? Do NOT use keyword 'Amazon' (but try it if you want; you can always turn it off later). You'll get so many alerts that you'll get tired of reading them all. People post small discounts and deals from Amazon all the time. Refine your FatWallet Topic Alerts so that a higher percentage of your alerts are things to take action on.

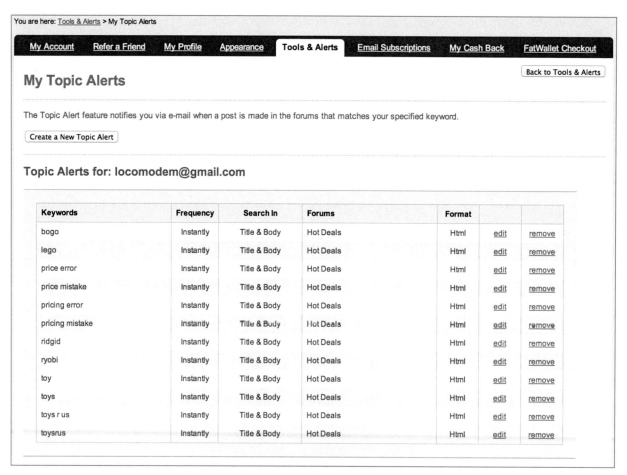

FatWallet has a mobile app:

iPhone/iPad:

https://itunes.apple.com/us/app/black-friday/id295358197?mt=8

Android:

https://play.google.com/store/apps/developer?id=Fatwallet.com&hl=en

FatWallet has an entire section dedicated to saving money and getting the best deals on Black Friday.

Be sure to check it every year: http://www.fatwallet.com/black-friday/

Black Friday 2014

Find the Best Black Friday Deals!

2013 Black Friday Ads

Black Friday Ads
- Original store advertisements.
- See the rumors well before they are released!

See Ads

2013 Black Friday Deals

Use FatWallet's ultimate deal finding tool!
- Filter Deals by store, category, price & more!
- Save deals for later viewing by making them favorites.

Find a Deal

Black Friday Mobile App

Take the Black Friday Deal Finder with you & have all the Black Friday Deals in the palm of your hand.

iPhone / iPad   **Android**

BLACK FRIDAY ALERTS!

Subscribe   We'll email you when Black Friday Deals are leaked from your favorite stores.

Black Friday Forum

Our members consolidate as many deals as they can for Black Friday sales.

View Forum

Black Friday Twitter Feed

Get deals fast by subscribing to the FatWallet Black Friday Twitter feed!

Subscribe

317

Topic Alert Example:

Here is a FatWallet Topic Alert that I received for keyword 'toys':

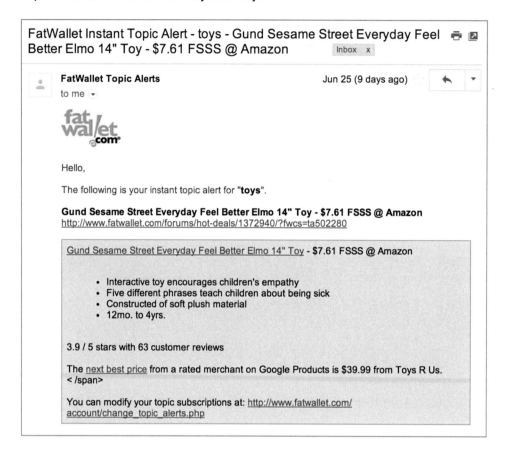

The email provides a link to view the deal details on FatWallet.com where we can gather more information to see if it's an item that we want to take a closer look at.

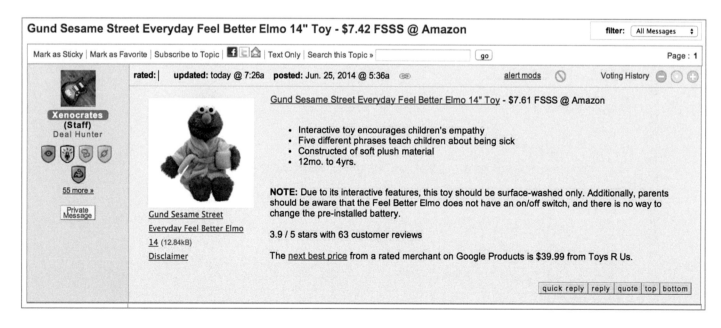

By the time we get to the Amazon product page to look at the data, we see that the item is no longer available from Amazon for $7.61 (or $7.42).

Gund Sesame Street Everyday Feel Better Elmo 14" Toy
by Gund
★★★★☆ ▼ 63 customer reviews

List Price: ~~$34.99~~
      Price: $19.52 & **FREE Shipping** on orders over $35.
      Details
You Save: $15.47 (44%)

In Stock.
Ships from and sold by Amazon.com. Gift-wrap available.

Want it tomorrow, June 26? Order within **8 hrs 40 mins** and choose **One-Day Shipping** at checkout. Details

- Imported
- The world's most huggable since 1898
- Surface washable
- Meets and exceeds all manufacturing guidelines

27 new from $18.10

http://www.amazon.com/dp/B008CNPIAE/

We can look at the Keepa price history and see that the item really was available from Amazon (because the price is in orange) and at $7.61. Looks like we may have missed this one, right?

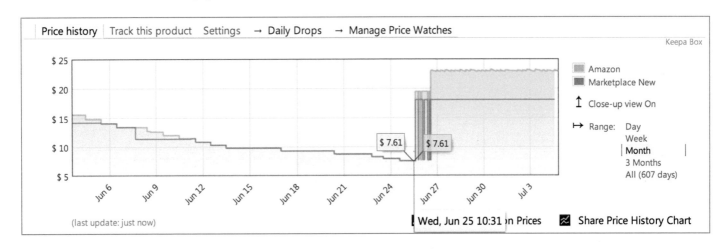

Because it's so easy, we set up a Keepa price alert. Do we set it at $7.61? We could, but let's set it at $8 in case it comes back at a price above $7.61. A $7.61 alert would only trigger at $7.61 or lower.

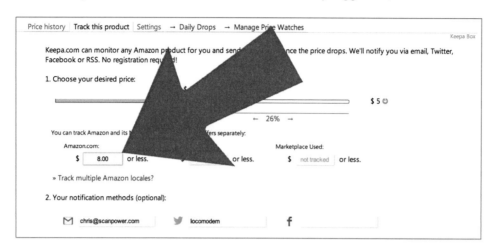

This is a great example of why you should set up price alerts at prices just a little higher than what you're expecting because this product did come back in stock from Amazon a short while later but at $7.79. I have no idea why Amazon is pricing this item this way, but they are.

Because I have the Keepa Chrome extension installed, I get the notification right on my desktop as well as a Tweet.

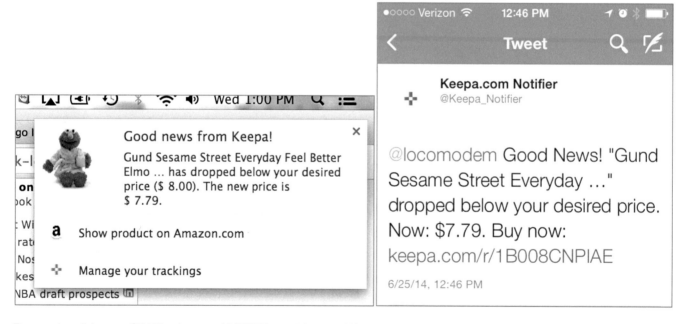

Remember this new $7.79 price would NOT have triggered if my alert was set for $7.61 (previous low price) from the FatWallet Topic Alert email.

FatWallet really has your back when it comes to getting you your cash back. They even monitor potential purchases to make sure that you are getting what's yours. I recently received this email from them:

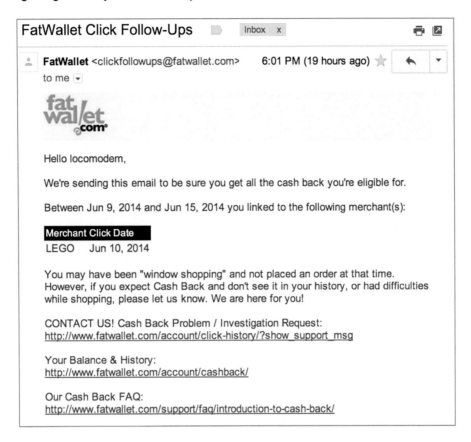

Check out this craziness: You can even use FatWallet Topic Alerts to monitor your own products!

I have a FatWallet Topic Alert set up for keyword RIDGID, a popular brand of tools sold at Home Depot. I received an alert one day about an 18 volt kit being sold for $49.95 on Amazon with the code FSSS which stands for Free Super Saver Shipping. This indicates that it's being sold by Amazon but it can also mean it's a third party seller using FBA (many online buyers don't know the difference).

http://www.fatwallet.com/forums/expired-deals/1006330

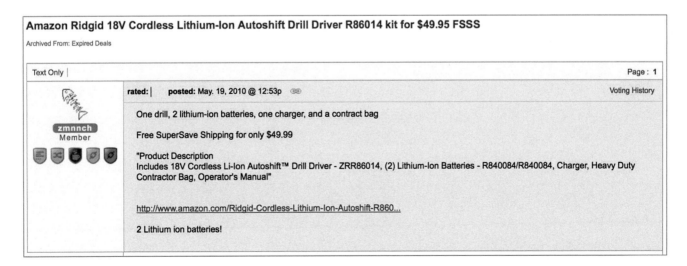

The original poster shared the product description as including the drill, two batteries, charger, and tool bag. This would have been an awesome deal except that because RIDGID is a Home Depot exclusive brand, I knew that it was not Amazon selling these kits. So who was selling these? It was ME! I was the one selling Ridgid drills for $49.95 on Amazon!

locomodem
Happy Member

posted: May. 19, 2010 @ 1:52p

Good find but this is an Amazon error. We created this product page and it is indeed for just the bare drill only. Amazon pulls portions for the product page for more than one seller and occasionally something like this happens when another seller incorrectly adds information on their page. I suspect CPO Ridgid listed their refurbished 'kit' under this listing by mistake. This happened once before. I raised the price to prevent orders while I contact Amazon to have them fix it.

If you ordered this (from us or any other seller), it would be best to just refuse the shipment or cancel your order. A printout or screenshot is not going to be able to make a seller produce something that was not included.

People were buying them up quickly, hoping to catch a price mistake. This FatWallet Topic Alert saved me a lot of trouble by being able to catch this quickly and respond to the situation (I raised price to prevent sales). It would have been a lot more work to correct all of the orders that would have gone out and resulted in the need for customer service and potentially receiving negative feedback from buyers.

So what happened? Another seller uploaded product info that changed the Amazon product details. This was unintentional but could have resulted in many incorrect orders. This particular case would not have been that bad as the customers would have received LESS than they expected and would therefore likely return the items. However, it's possible that the same scenario could happen where savvy customers were purchasing items and receiving MORE than the seller was expecting to fulfill. These scenarios can be more difficult to process returns if customers are looking to take advantage of sellers.

Bonus Tip: You can consider posting deals on FatWallet that you want to sell out. Consider a website that has 500 of a product in stock at a price that can be resold for a profit. You buy 300 either because of limited inventory funds or just a quantity comfort level. You'd rather not have the other 200 units be purchased by another reseller (potential competitor). You could post the deal on FatWallet and hope that the buyer community snatches up the inventory for personal use. Of course, this also runs the risk of another seller seeing the Hot Deal post in the FatWallet forums and learning about a deal thanks to you. Just things to consider. You could also offer those other 200 units to a member of your own mastermind group. More information on mastermind groups in Chapter 29. You can use this same strategy on other deal website like SlickDeals.net, (discussed in the next chapter).

Chapter 22 – Deal Website Spotlight: SlickDeals.net

SlickDeals is similar to FatWallet in that it is a community-based site designed to help users save money. Some of the deals posted are so good they can be bought and resold for a profit. Most deals posted are not that good, so you have to be able to sort and evaluate posts quickly and efficiently. Thankfully, SlickDeals has a lot of useful tools to do just that.

http://slickdeals.net/

SlickDeals has a new page called SlickDeals Live. This page auto-updates with deals. It's worth checking out and bookmarking: http://slickdeals.net/live/

SlickDeals has their own price tracker: http://slickdeals.net/pricetracker/
Read about how it works here: http://slickdeals.net/f/7066882-price-tracker-is-here?v=1

Supported Stores

6PM	Columbia Sportswear	JCPenney	REI
Abercrombie & Fitch	CowBoom	Kohls	Staples
Adorama	Diesel	Lands End	Steam
Amazon	Eastbay	Lego	Sunglass Hut
American Eagle Outfitters	Express	Macys	Target
Apple iTunes	Forever 21	Newegg	Toys R Us
Ashford	GameStop	Nordstrom	Urban Outfitters
Barnes & Noble	GNC	PacSun	Vera Bradley
Bed Bath & Beyond	Home Depot	Petco	Walgreens
Cabelas	HSN	QVC	Walmart
Canon	IKEA	Rakuten	

Here you can see a list of all of the stores that they track.

Be sure to follow their social media accounts:

https://www.facebook.com/slickdeals   https://twitter.com/slickdeals   https://plus.google.com/+slickdeals

In my experience, the most valuable sections of a community-based deal site are the forums.

SlickDeals forums: http://slickdeals.net/forums/

SlickDeals Hot Deals forum: http://slickdeals.net/forums/forumdisplay.php?f=9

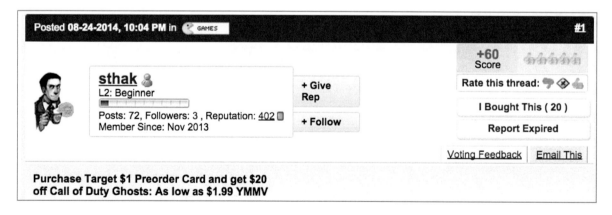

Here is an example of a deal and how you can quickly read it to decide if it's worth a closer look. The +60 at the top means that 60 more people voted this deal UP than DOWN. The better the deal, the more UP VOTES a deal will have from the community. You can also see how many people clicked that they bought the deal (the more the better). You can see the experience level of the original poster (sometimes referred to as the OP). You can give them 'Rep' if they post something useful so that others will know that this person posts quality deals based on their total Rep. You can also choose to follow people who consistently post quality deals.

Be careful to not be fooled by the Score or 'thumbs ups' on a deal. If a deal is absolutely incredible, I have seen community members intentionally vote it DOWN in order to hide it or deter other people from seeing how awesome it is. Always do your own homework and decide for yourself if a deal is a deal or not. Use the visible information to help you browse and sort deals quickly, but be careful to not miss the best ones.

Android:

https://play.google.com/store/apps/details?id=net.slickdeals.android&hl=en

iPhone/iPad:

https://itunes.apple.com/us/app/1-deals-coupons-shopping-app/id584632814?mt=8

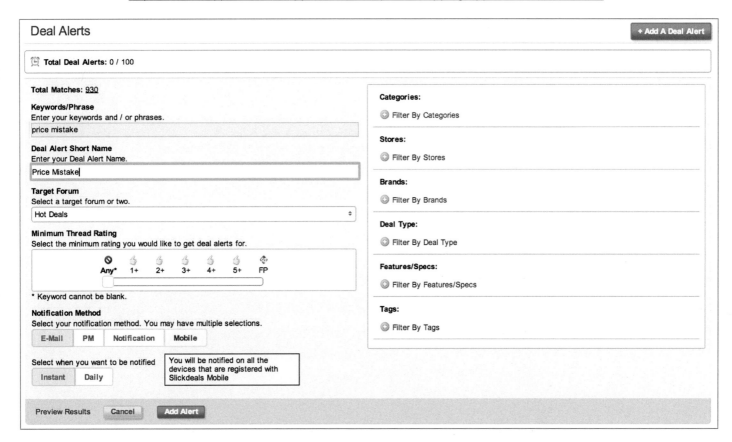

If you want to add MOBILE as your notification setting, you have to download their mobile app and log in with your SlickDeals account. This is very easy to do and totally worth it.

Here you can see some examples of my SlickDeals keyword search for 'price mistake'.

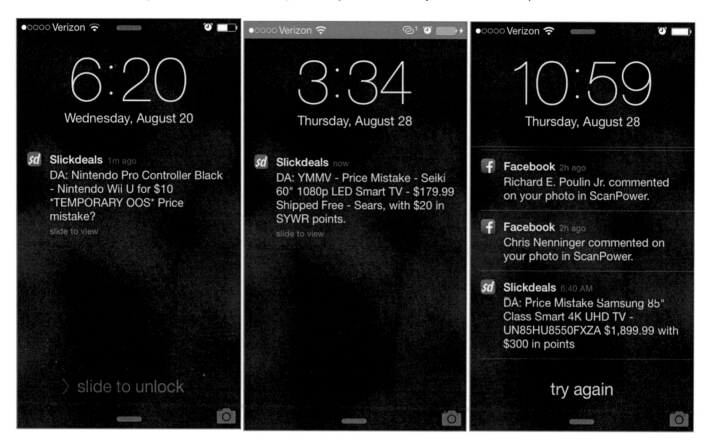

Chapter 23 – Deal Apps

There are so many apps out there and they all do something different. Instead of trying to make a list of apps for you, I'd rather show you how to find the best apps yourself. Consider these searches for "black Friday" in the Apple App Store. You can see which ones are popular/relevant search results and which ones have great user reviews. More reviews indicate more downloads and more users, and that can often indicate that an app is actually providing VALUE and UTILITY.

Consider searching for terms like SHOPPING, DEALS, COUPONS, REBATES:

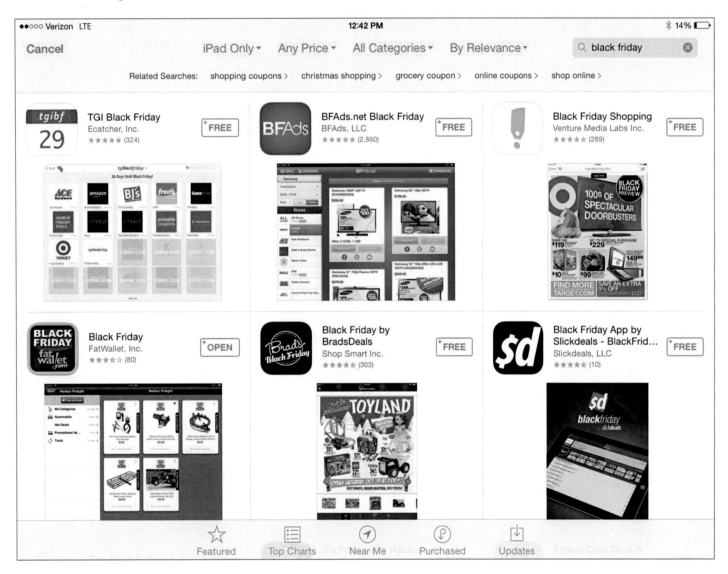

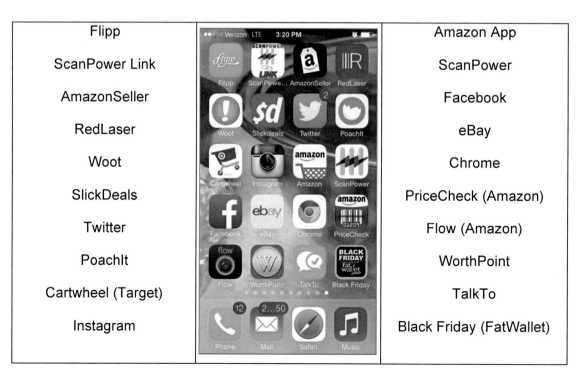

Flipp		Amazon App
ScanPower Link		ScanPower
AmazonSeller		Facebook
RedLaser		eBay
Woot		Chrome
SlickDeals		PriceCheck (Amazon)
Twitter		Flow (Amazon)
PoachIt		WorthPoint
Cartwheel (Target)		TalkTo
Instagram		Black Friday (FatWallet)

Chapter 24 – Get the Best Price COUPONS

Everyone is familiar with coupons at retail stores, but there are also tons of ways to use coupons online to get the best deals for your Online Arbitrage business.

RetailMeNot even has Amazon.com coupons: http://www.retailmenot.com

RatherBeShopping: http://www.rather-be-shopping.com

PoachIt: https://www.poachit.com

CouponCabin: http://couponcabin.com

Chrome Extension: Honey

http://www.joinhoney.com

honey

Effortlessly get the best coupons for thousands of stores

Stop searching for coupon codes and sales.

Click on the Honey button on a supported online store and instantly see all the coupons and sales available for the store.

Click on the Honey button during checkout and Honey will automatically apply coupon codes to your shopping cart.

15 savings found on macys.com

CODES (15) SALES (coming soon)

20% Off Regular, Sale, & Clearance + Free Shipping On $99
CODE: SPINWIN EXPIRES: Mar 30, 2014

Extra 20% Off Private VIP Event
CODE: VIP EXPIRES: Tomorrow

Up To 20% Off Select Categories
CODE: FIVE

25% Off 2+ Handbags
CODE: BAGS EXPIRES: Tomorrow

https://chrome.google.com/webstore/detail/honey/bmnlcjabgnpnenekpadlanbbkooimhnj?hl=en-US

EASY LINK: http://bit.ly/honeyextension

Take a look at all of the other Chrome extensions related to Honey:

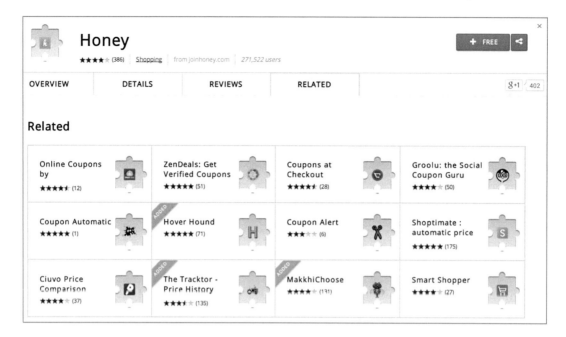

Ibotta: https://ibotta.com

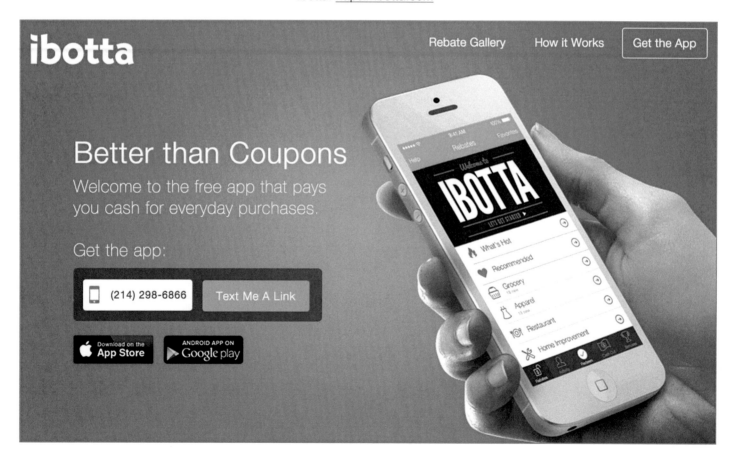

There is also a Facebook group and page set up and run by professional couponer Katherine Cauley.

Katherine was on TLC's Extreme Couponing Season Two. You can watch it Amazon Video here:

http://www.amazon.com/Katherine-Joel/dp/B00601IAKK

Facebook Group: https://www.facebook.com/groups/couponeducation

Facebook Page: https://www.facebook.com/couponeducation

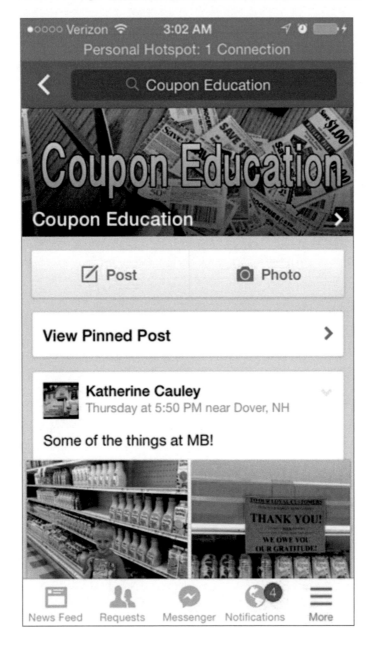

Chapter 25 – Get the Best Price REBATES/CASH BACK

Rebates and cash back are great ways to save money when you're making Online Arbitrage purchases. There are a bunch of different sites. Some will offer higher cash back rates on different stores. Rebates and cash back work by tracking your sales through different sites. These sites earn a referral or affiliate payout for directling the traffic and sales to different sites. These sites then share that payout with you. Some of them send paper checks in the mail and some deposit into your PayPal account.

The only thing to really remember with online rebates and cash back is to actually use them. If you are not in the habit of clicking through one of these sites, it can be difficult to change your behavior. You just have to retrain yourself. You're spending the money anyway, so you might as well get your rebates and cash back!

Ebates: http://www.ebates.com

FatWallet: http://www.fatwallet.com/learn-more/what-is-cash-back

Currently FatWallet has the EXCLUSIVE on cash back for purchases from Amazon and on eBay! Take advantage of this!

http://www.fatwallet.com/Amazon-coupons   http://www.fatwallet.com/eBay-coupons

BigCrumbs: http://www.bigcrumbs.com

CashBackMonitor: http://www.cashbackmonitor.com

Mr.Rebates: http://www.mrrebates.com

CashBackHolic: http://www.cashbackholic.com

SavingStar: https://savingstar.com

UPromise: http://www.upromise.com

ShopDiscover: https://www.discover.com/credit-cards/cashback-bonus/shopdiscover.html

TopCashBack: http://www.topcashback.com

EVReward: http://evreward.com

BeFrugal: http://www.befrugal.com/

Chapter 26 – Get the Best Price PAYMENT

You can't really pay cash for Online Arbitrage purchases, so for the most part you'll be using credit cards or debit cards.

There are two things to consider when it comes to making your payment for Online Arbitrage purchases. First is maximizing Points, Rewards, Perks, Miles, etc.

Amazon Chase Credit Card https://www.Amazon.com/rewards

Get 3% cash back on your Amazon purchases

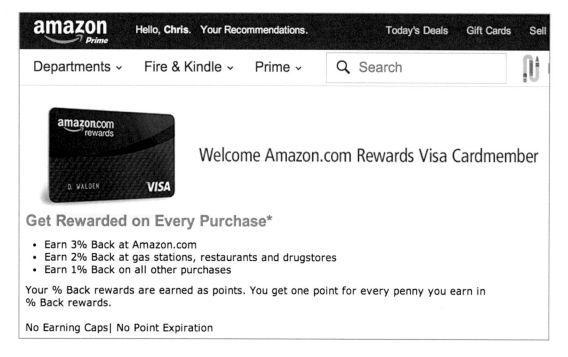

Discover Card has some generous cashback incentives for using their credit card.

https://www.discover.com/credit-cards/cashback-bonus/shopdiscover.html

The second way involves using discounted gift cards. There are many sites that offer these. Here are a couple:

http://www.giftcardgranny.com/

And be sure to LIKE them on Facebook and Get Notifications to see all of their posts.

https://www.facebook.com/GiftCardGranny

Same for their Twitter account. Follow them and turn on mobile notifications.

https://twitter.com/GiftCardGranny

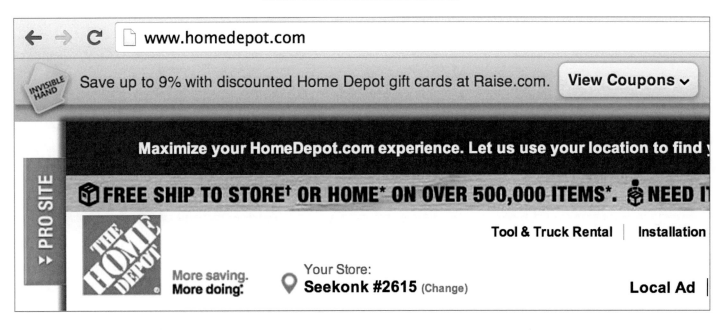

Simply visit HomeDepot.com and InvisibleHand will pop up and let you know that you can buy Home Depot gift cards at a 9% discount from http://www.raise.com

Another one to consider: http://www.thegiftcardfans.com

How Raise Works

Buy Discount Gift Cards

Before you shop online or in stores, check out the Raise marketplace to find discounted gift cards to brands such as Target, The Home Depot, and Macy's. Search by brand, category, or value, and simply add to your shopping cart. With free shipping on all gift cards, it's easy to boost your purchase power and give yourself a raise. Step by Step

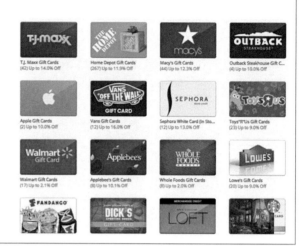

You can even buy them on eBay. Here is a seller selling $100 Toys R Us gift cards for $85, a 15% discount.

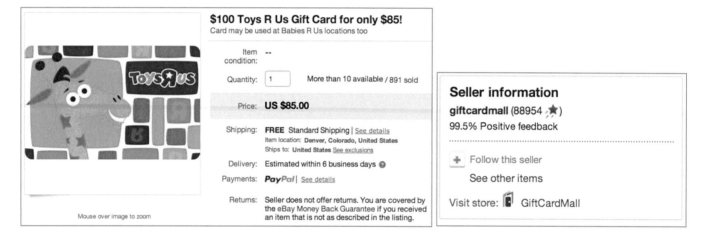

They have great feedback.

http://www.ebay.com/sch/giftcardmall/m.html

Keepa has started to offer Amazon gift cards at discounted rates. This only shows on the Keepa graph sometimes when you're looking at products on Amazon. I have not figured out which products it shows for, but if you look at enough products, you'll notice the little additional tab with the title "New Keepa Special Offer." You can save up to 7% on Amazon gift cards this way which means you can lower your acquisition cost by up to 7% when you use this method to buy gift cards that you'll then use to buy inventory.

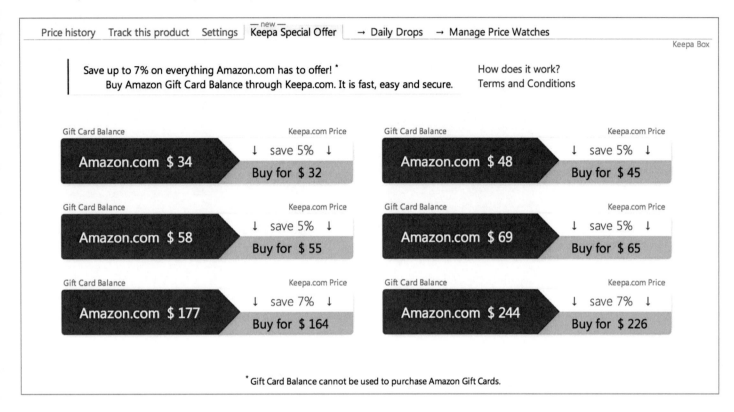

Chapter 27 – Advanced Alerts IFTTT

IFTTT stands for If This Then That: IFTTT.com

This is one of the most underutilized tools right now. IFTTT enables you to create what they call 'recipes' that will trigger an action based on some other occurrence. For example, I can create a recipe to copy a photo to my Dropbox every time I post the photo on Facebook. These recipes can also be used for setting up alerts for different deals.

Time is money so use your time wisely. IFTTT helps you find more deals and get your alerts FASTER.

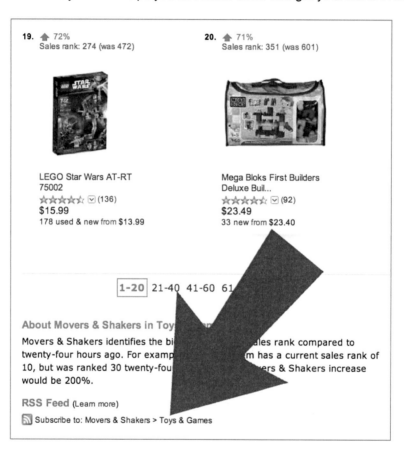

Every Amazon Movers & Shakers page has a corresponding RSS feeds.
Clicking on a feed link will open up a page that will pretty much look like nonsense.
Don't worry about what it looks like. Just copy the address (URL):

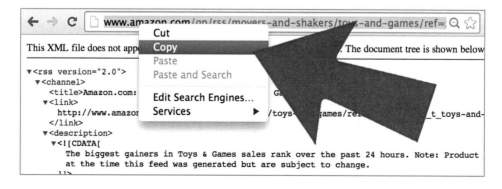

Now we're ready to go over to IFTTT.com

We want to start by creating a new recipe, but this time choose the RSS for your THIS:

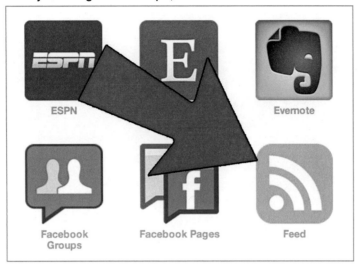

You want to choose "New feed item:"

This is where you want to PASTE in the RSS URL from the Amazon Movers & Shakers page:

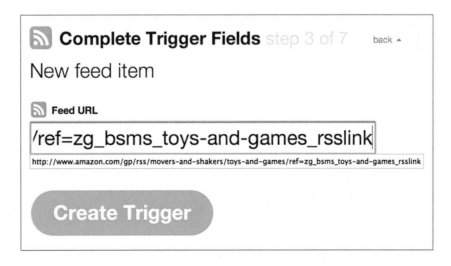

Click on 'Create Trigger.'

Next, choose Gmail as your 'THAT' (this example uses Gmail; experiment and use whatever you want to use, like "add to Evernote" to make a list):

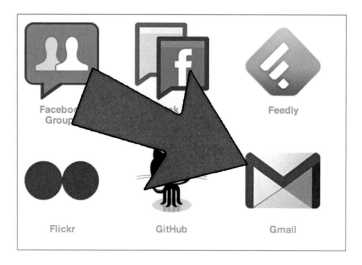

Next, choose Send an email:

Enter your preferred email address. Maybe you set up a new one just for product sourcing.

Preview your new recipe and then click on Create Recipe:

New feed item from
http://www.amazon.c
om/gp/rss/movers-
and-shakers/toys-
and-
games/ref=zg_bsms_
toys-and-
games_rsslink

Send an email from
chris@scanpower.co
m

You can set up this IFTTT recipe for every Movers & Shakers category RSS feed on Amazon.

And if you prefer, there are RSS feeds for: Best Sellers, New Releases, Most Wished For, and others.

You can easily go overkill on these types of alerts, which is why I try to narrow it down to the top items--top three or so. Experiment and see what works for you.

Now maybe you only want to know when there is a new toy on the Movers & Shakers page that is in the top three ranked spots. You may find that it's only the items ranked one, two, and three that have really big jumps that are worth investigating. So consider setting up an alert system for Gmail keywords IFTTT AND #1, #2, or #3 to be sent as SMS text message. Or just search Gmail a few times daily via SORT to only look at the top 3.

IFTTT has lists of other people's recipes. Take a look at what other people are doing to get ideas. Copy the good ones.

https://ifttt.com/recipes

Just remember that your recipes aren't secret either.

Advice: Be specific so that you don't get overwhelmed. You want alerts that you want to act on, not just a ton of stuff that you still have to browse through and sort.

Setting up an alert through IFTTT from an RSS feed - Online Arbitrage

http://youtu.be/djul_CItAEE
http://bit.ly/iftttvideo1

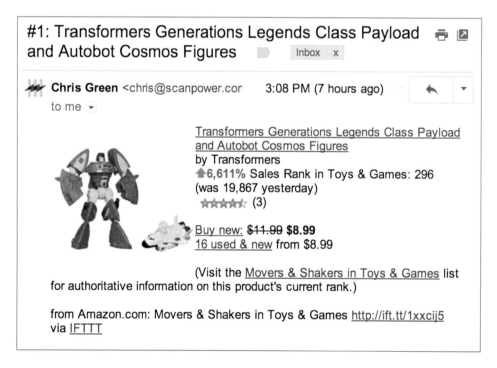

This is the email you get from IFTTT when you have RSS alerts for Movers & Shakers in Toys. You can see this is a new #1 (up 6,611%, ranked 296, was 19,867). The best part about this is that you can see the recorded price that was listed at the time that it was sent to the M&S list. It's possible that an item's price might change from the time of an original price drop to the time that it's posted, but more often than not, you'll have a record of the price that sent the sales rank soaring. You can consider using this price to set up a price tracker alert.

Why is this important? Because you won't always see every price drop. Some are very small windows of time and sometimes even the price trackers won't catch a temporary price drop.

Let's quickly look at the AZ product page for this item that was #1 on the Movers & Shakers list seven hours ago.

You see that it's now listed at a Buy Box price of $19.99. Pricenoia and Keepa caught the drop but Unimerc and TheTracktor did not.

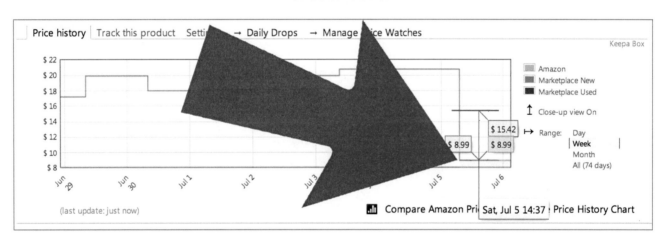

Why does this matter? Because now we know that we can set up an Amazon price alert for $8.99.

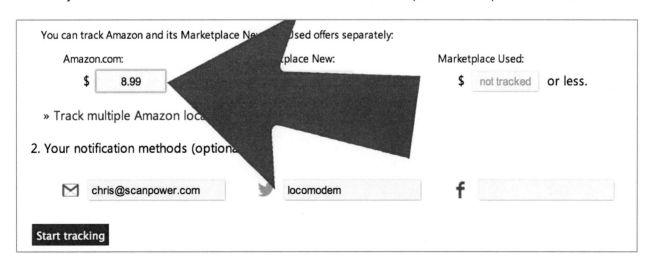

And while we are looking at this item, let's not forget to follow the rabbit trails and check the frequently bought together items:

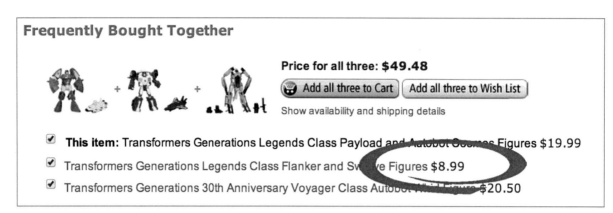

We can see that there is a very similar item for the same low price of $8.99. You can also see this item in the Customers Who Bought This Item Also Bought list:

This one is also selling for $8.99.

But everyone else is selling for ~$20.

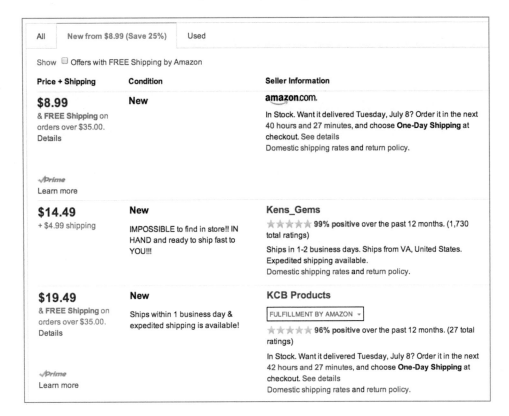

Checking the historical Keepa graph shows a history of Amazon being out of stock, a previous low price of $8.99, and a high price in the past of ~$25.

And in some perfectly timed coincidence, this item just landed in my Gmail as #2 on the Movers & Shakers list:

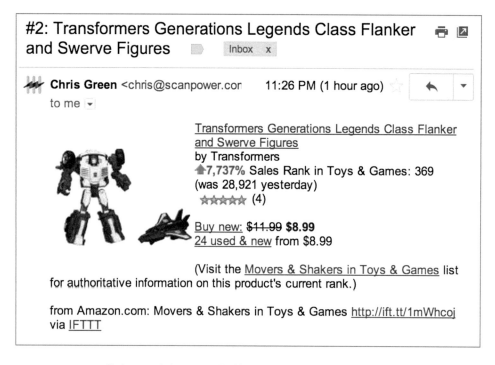

Sales rank is up 7,737% ranked 369, was 28.921.

Here they are at #1 & #2. You can see that Cosmos is still at #1.

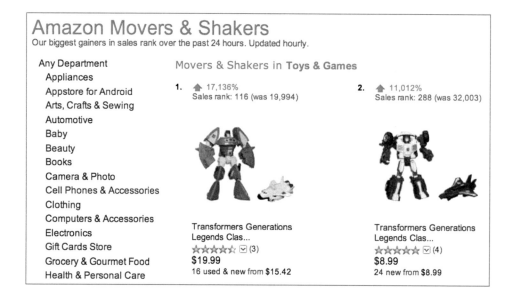

There is a Facebook group just for using IFTTT for online sellers. It's run by professional online seller, Brian Freifelder and it's the best place to learn more about IFTTT. There's also a ton of great info about using IFTTT for things outside of the world of online selling.

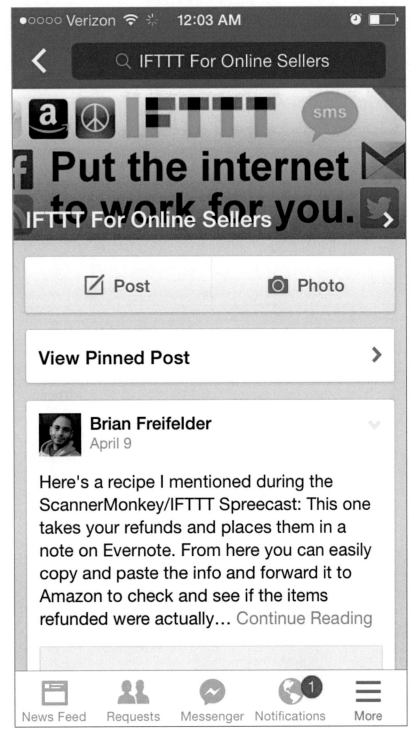

https://www.facebook.com/groups/IFTTTforOnlineSellers/

IFTTT and Craigslist: LEGO FERRARI

Doing any type of search on Craigslist will give you a search result page that can be monitored by IFTTT. This means that you can set up an IFTTT recipe to monitor the Craigslist search results page for new matches. Take a look at this example: **Lego Ferrari**

Why 'Lego Ferrari'? Because the keyword 'Lego' by itself would provide too many matches, with many of them being false positives. The idea of using services like IFTTT is to narrow down your searches to actionable alerts, not just a new funnel to send you a bunch of alerts that you'll still have to sort and sift through. I strongly suggest making these types of searches very narrow and specific. Set up tons of different alerts, but make them all specific so that when you do get an alert, it's something that you really want to act on.

First, to figure out what kinds of searches we want to monitor, we can look up the sales prices of search results. Take a look at the highest prices items sold on eBay for keywords 'Lego Ferrari'.

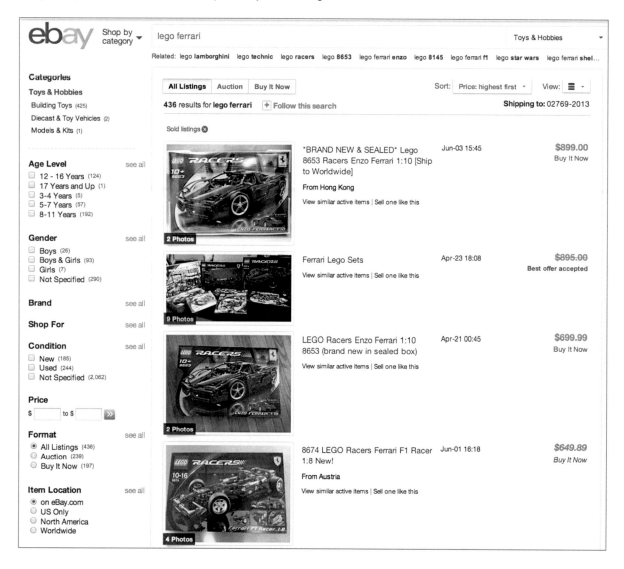

http://www.ebay.com/sch/Toys-Hobbies-/220/i.html?_from=R40&_sop=3&_nkw=lego+ferrari&LH_Complete=1&LH_Sold=1&rt=nc

I like these prices and I would definitely be interested to know when any new listings that match 'Lego Ferrari' are posted on my local Craigslist.

If you have an idea of what you want to be alerted for, you can then check current Craigslist items for those search terms. In this case, 'Lego Ferrari' gives this result:

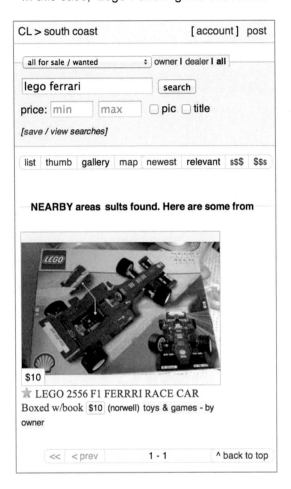

We can quickly find the Amazon product page by using Context Search to highlight the title and choosing Amazon from the drop down menu.

http://www.Amazon.com/dp/B001CKQNIU/

> **Product Details**
> **Shipping Weight:** 4 pounds (View shipping rates and policies)
> **ASIN:** B001CKQNIU
> **Item model number:** 2556
> **Manufacturer recommended age:** 10 years and up
> **Amazon Best Sellers Rank:** #187,253 in Toys & Games (See Top 100 in Toys & Games)
> **Average Customer Review:** Be the first to review this item
> **Discontinued by manufacturer:** Yes

The sales rank isn't great, but it's not too terrible. At the right price, this deal makes sense.

So here is the Craigslist search URL: http://southcoast.craigslist.org/search/sss?query=lego%20ferrari&sort=rel

To use this search yourself, just change 'southcoast' to your local Craigslist location.

You'll need this URL to create the IFTTT recipe.

This time you want to choose Craigslist as your Trigger Channel.

Choose a Trigger   step 2 of 7

New post from search
Copy and paste the URL from the
results page of any search on
Craigslist and this Trigger fires every
time someone adds a new post that
meets the search criteria.

Complete Trigger Fields   step 3 of 7

New post from search

Search results URL

ch/sss?query=lego%20ferrari&sort=rel

http://southcoast.craigslist.org/search/sss?query=lego%20ferrari&sort=rel

Create Trigger

Here is where you'll enter your Craigslist search URL:
http://southcoast.craigslist.org/search/sss?query=lego%20ferrari&sort=rel

Now you have to choose what to do when there is a new match to your Craigslist search.

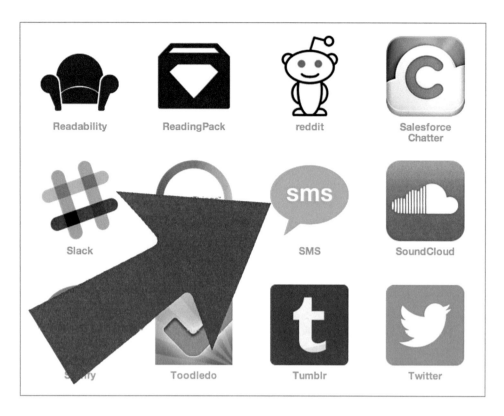

SMS is the same as sending a text message.

Definition: SMS stands for *short message service*. SMS is also often referred to as texting, sending text messages or text messaging. The service allows for short text messages to be sent from one cell phone to another cell phone or from the Web to another cell phone.

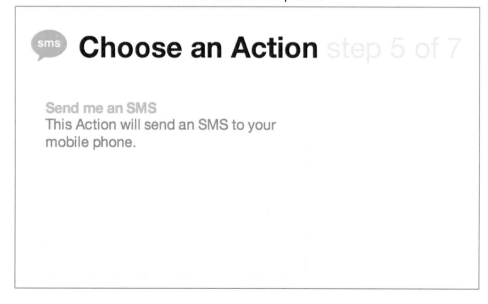

Continue setting up the recipe by choosing "Send me an SMS."

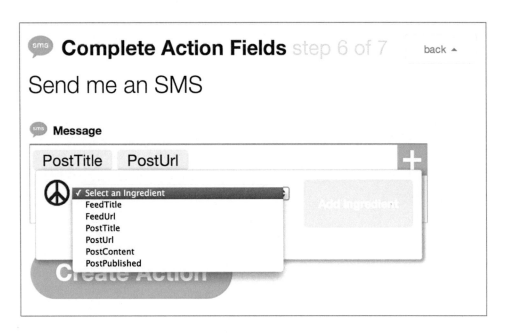

You can choose different 'ingredients' here for more customized alerts. If you keep your searches narrow, you can avoid getting a bunch of 'false positive' alerts for items that are too common. For this reason, the different ingredients here don't really matter.

Finalize your recipe here and then sit back and wait for it to trigger!

LEGO Racers Ferrari 430 Spider
by LEGO

★★★★☆ ▾ 7 customer reviews

Price: $224.99 + $5.49 shipping

Only 2 left in stock.
Ships from and sold by Out-Of-Print-Collectibles LLC.

- 1:17 scale model
- Step-by-step building diagrams
- Spider measures more than 10 inches long
- Features fully detailed engine, adjustable mirrors, and Ferrari decals
- 559 pieces

Click to open expanded view

12 new from $170.00   6 collectible from $72.95

How would you like to get an IFTTT text message about this Lego Ferrari being sold on your local Craigslist?

Here the kids are saying, "Oooooooooo". We kept this one. $25 cash and it was literally 0.2 miles from the office.

If you want more info on Lego Investing, there is a group for that:
https://www.facebook.com/groups/legoinvesting/

Online Arbitrage - LEGO Ferrari, Product Searches, EBay, Amazon, IFTTT, Craigslist

http://youtu.be/r9cJXUo5prY
http://bit.ly/iftttvideo2

Spend too much time on Facebook? Are you a member of too many Facebook Groups? Consider this IFTTT recipe to get a daily digest version of your favorite groups sent to your email:
https://ifttt.com/recipes/181228-facebook-group-email-digest

So say that you want to get the Amazon Movers & Shakers RSS feed sent to you by SMS text message. Or say you want to only see the top three items from the Amazon Movers & Shakers RSS feed by SMS text message and the others can just get archived.

There are two ways to do this. Either filter out the ones you want or archive the ones that you don't want. From my experience, you will end up getting way more alerts that are not actionable so you want to auto-archive as many messages as possible. This first filter will auto-archive everything from the Movers & Shakers RSS feed set up through IFTTT to send to my Gmail that DO NOT contain #1, #2, or #3:

In Gmail, go to settings, Filters, Create New

"From" doesn't really matter. I chose to use '**Has the words**'

"Visit the Movers & Shakers in Toys & Games list"
(this block of text is present in every email from IFTTT about the RSS feed)

I then added #1, #2, #3 under '**Doesn't have**'.

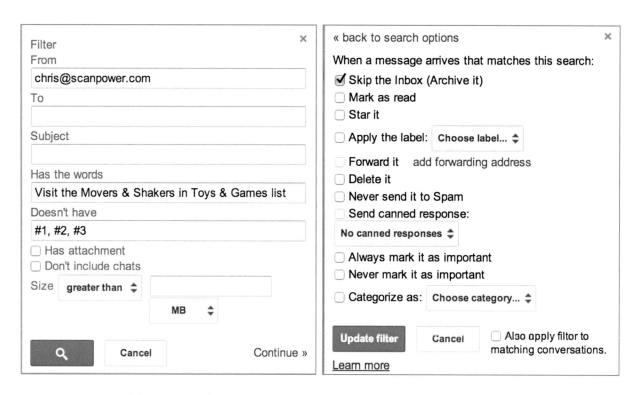

I then check "Skip the inbox (Archive it)." I don't want to see it at all.

This way you will only end up with emails in your Gmail inbox when there are new items on the Amazon Movers & Shakers pages ranked #1, #2, or #3.

An alternative method would be to change 'Has the words' to include #1, #2, or #3 (you may have to set up three different filters). Then choose the checkbox for 'Always mark it as important'. You could then use that filter with an IFTTT recipe to send you an SMS text message every time you receive a new starred message in Gmail.

You should experiment with that works for you here. Maybe you want more than just 1-3. Find whatever works for you.

There is no one right way to use IFTTT. This is why I strongly recommend joining the IFTTT Facebook group and working with others to see what works for them and to improve and refine your own recipes.

https://www.facebook.com/groups/IFTTTforOnlineSellers/

Chapter 28 – Advanced Alerts HTML Monitors

This was one of our most profitable deals I ever did (this is just one receipt from multiple purchases). I was able to act on it quickly because of an HTML alert that I set up. I had found the HomeDepot.com product pages for their Ridgid 24-volt three-piece cordless combo kit as well as their 24-volt drill. The price on the kit was $199 and the price on the drill was $129. They were not available to purchase but at those prices I wanted to know as soon as possible if/when they went in stock. I bookmarked and refreshed the link many times a day, but that wasn't efficient. And what if they came in stock at night? So I used Google to find a service that would monitor the website for ANY changes to the HTML. Why would anyone really need to do this? For the most part, these services are designed to help companies keep track of their competition. A business may want to know as soon a direct competitor releases a new product so that they can react and address any concerns of their customers. But for our purposes, we just want to know if the item has come in stock.

This was a few years ago and I happily PAID for the service that I used. There are many free ones today. Here are a few that I found with a simple Google search for 'monitor a website for changes':

Page Monitor:

http://max99x.com/chrome-extensions/page-monitor

https://chrome.google.com/webstore/detail/page-monitor/pemhgklkefakciniebenbfclihhmmfcd?hl=en

EASY LINK: http://bit.ly/pagemonitorapp

I really like the idea of using this one in Chrome and having multiple tabs open with pages like Amazon Movers & Shakers getting alerts every time they are updated through the day. Or specific CamelCamelCamel pages like Most Recent Top Price Drops – 50% or more.

Change Detection

https://www.changedetection.com/

Change Detect

http://www.changedetect.com/

10 free ways to keep track of changes to any website, without an RSS reader

http://downloadsquad.switched.com/2010/02/08/10-free-ways-to-keep-track-of-changes-to-any-website-without-rss/

A Word About Screen Scraping

What is screen scraping (sometimes called web scraping or data scraping)?

Normally, data transfer between programs is accomplished using data structures suited for automated processing by computers, not people. Such interchange formats and protocols are typically rigidly structured, well documented, easily parsed, and designed to keep ambiguity to a minimum. Very often, these transmissions are not human-readable at all.

Thus, the key element that distinguishes data scraping from regular parsing is that the output being scraped is intended for display to an end-user, rather than as input to another program, and is therefore usually neither documented nor structured for convenient parsing. Data scraping often involves ignoring binary data (usually images or multimedia data), display formatting, redundant labels, superfluous commentary, and other information which is either irrelevant or hinders automated processing.

Data scraping is most often done to either interface to a legacy system, which has no other mechanism that is compatible with current hardware, or to interface to a third-party system, which does not provide a more convenient API. In the second case, the operator of the third-party system will often see screen scraping as unwanted, due to reasons such as increased system load, the loss of advertisement revenue, or the loss of control of the information content.

Data scraping is generally considered an ad hoc, inelegant technique, often used only as a "last resort" when no other mechanism for data interchange is available. Aside from the higher programming and processing overhead, output displays intended for human consumption often change structure frequently. Humans can cope with this easily, but computer programs will often crash or produce incorrect results.

http://en.wikipedia.org/wiki/Data_scraping

For the most part, businesses and websites do not like screen scraping because of the additional load required compared to scrape. In general, scraping would be against the Terms Of Service of many sites.

All that being said, if would fall on each person to decide how they want to run their business. I've included this info about what screen scraping is and how people can use it to try to find deals online, but I do not recommend doing so. I also include it here so that people know what it is and realize that other sellers (their competitors) may be using screen scraping to source their own inventory.

Outsourcing Programming

Like I've said a few times, Online Arbitrage is not hard. It's actually quite easy once you've figured out what you want to look for. I'm including two sites here for sellers who want to go to the next level and look for their own custom solutions to any bottlenecks that they discover in their own businesses that could be solved with the use of some creative programming.

If you can't find a page monitor that you like or you want an additional feature specific just to your Online Arbitrage needs, consider looking for a programmer online and hiring them to make you exactly what you need. Maybe it's just a bulk refresh tool or other kind of timesaving process. Outsource and automate what you can because your time is very valuable.

Elance

Elance.com

If you remember, Paul Retherford and I (ScanPower co-founders) originally met on Elance when I posted a job about printing individual FBA labels. The site has since expanded to include pretty much any service you can imagine. Want to write a children's book? Hire an artist from Elance.

Odesk

Odesk.com

There are sites where you can post specific jobs and find people who have earned a positive reputation for their work. If you wanted to build your own website monitoring program or compile lists of ASINs from Amazon, these might be good places to start. Find someone who is good at what they are good at and you keep focusing on what you are good at.

Want to make a list of every item from a specific website? Consider hiring a programmer to tackle this task with technology. It's all just data. You just have to compile the right data and know what to do with it.

Chapter 29 – Scaling

So Online Arbitrage is pretty easy, right? Truth is, it's almost too easy. Once you learn a few tricks and know what sites to check (and when), and get good at following rabbit trails, you may start to get bored. You may also decide that you want to really GROW this business into something BIG. So how to you SCALE Online Arbitrage?

Well, there's good news and there's bad news. The good news is that, for the most part, you can train and outsource someone to find deals for you. You can still make the ultimate purchase decisions, but making a list with 80% winners should be pretty easy to do. And before anyone starts saying that that's a terrible idea because you'd just be training a future competitor, I'll tell you right now that I've never seen that happen. If you're an online seller, you know that this business is NOT for everyone. So find someone you trust who would love to have a cushy desk job of surfing the Internet all day and put that person to work! You can find someone local or even consider a virtual assistant (more information on virtual assistants in the next chapter).

And seriously, if you don't trust someone enough because you are afraid that they will straight-up stab you in the back after learning some Online Arbitrage tricks, then I wouldn't hire them in the first place. In fact, I'd wonder why you have people like that in your life at all. **#HonestCommentary**

Sorry that this chapter isn't longer, but scaling a business like Online Arbitrage just isn't a huge topic. Take a look at your daily tasks and see what you can replicate or outsource. Look at your products and see what it would take to get more of them. Some parts of Online Arbitrage are limited and can't be scaled.

The Problems with Scaling

A lot of the strategies laid out in this book help you find either products that have limited quantities being sold at UNDER-RETAIL prices, or items at the regular prices that are being sold for a limited time at OVER-RETAIL prices. The thing that both of these practices have in common is that they are limited--either limited in quantity or limited in time. You can't control either of these things. The markets will repeatedly be inefficient and present these types of profitable opportunities, but they cannot be forced or created. You are reliant on way too many outside factors like spikes in demand or product shortages.

Markets always come to equilibrium because time never stops. Demand changes over time and demand directly affects price. The market price is simply set by supply and demand. As supply and demand change, price will follow along. This is why I strongly recommend buying at the lowest possible price (other than all the obvious reasons). When you buy low, you have room to make money even if prices drop. Pay full retail and hope that prices go up over time? That's a risk with no certainties.

Limited quantities

To really grow into a truly sustainable business you need to find replenishable products and/or exclusive products. Exclusive products may include private label products or products that you have an exclusivity agreement with. You may have your own patented and branded product. You can also get into wholesale products (not covered in this book) where the margins may be lower but they can be fast turning and easy to re-order. Having products that are easier to process is another advantage to wholesale.

Outsourcing Research

Learn more at ScanPower.com/VAs

VAs (Virtual Assistants) are people that you can hire to do tasks that you don't want to spend time on. You are outsourcing your daily routine. With computers and the Internet, many of these tasks can be done by anyone, anywhere in the world.

This is all pretty easy when you stop and think about it. Train someone to scour the Internet for deals. Have them focus on your favorite stores or product lines. Have them send you lists that you then decide on what to buy. Give them your cell phone for texts when something is hot and requires immediate attention.

Sounds easy right?

Now, hiring a VA is a pretty big step. You're now on the hook for giving someone tasks and monitoring/managing them. For many online sellers, this is NOT what they ever thought they'd be doing, but you have to look at the benefits to this set up. Low cost and it should free up your time from smaller tasks that pretty much anyone can do. Let's be honest, refreshing Keepa Deals is NOT hard, OK. ☺

But what if you've had some success and you want to try hiring a VA, but you don't know where to start? Well here's a list of people who not only use VAs, but also help people find, hire, and train VAs for themselves. Let them know that you heard about them from this book!

Eric Hardwick: TrainedVAs.com

Brad DeGraw: VAHotlist.com

Tedric Paulk: OnlineResaleDeals.com

John Jonas: http://www.jonasblog.com/my-process-for-hiring-a-filipino-va

You could also hire a team of VAs to compile lists or databases of products from any number of sites, including Amazon. Remember, Online Arbitrage is not hard. We're just comparing products from different marketplaces and looking for pricing inefficiencies.

A VA could use sites like Yoopsie.com to reverse-lookup UPCs from title or keyword searches. They could then match them up to Amazon Product Pages or ASINs. Cross-reference these items yourself or have your VA do it a few times a day. You could compile a list of UPCs or ASINs and run them through the ScanPower Inventory Evaluator*, a tool that can bulk evaluate thousands of products and show you the lowest price, Amazon price, sales rank, payouts, FBA offers (or no FBA offers) and much more.

If you have a list of sites or products that you want to keep close eyes on, hire a VA to do that for you.

Set up some social media search terms for someone to check daily and compile lists of potential products for resale. Take it to the next step and have them also look online for the product pages to see if the product is also marked down online. Give them your zip code, have them check in-store stock levels, and make a list of products that are available at your local stores. You can even have them call the stores to confirm in-store availability.

Seriously, any Online Arbitrage task can likely be done by a trained virtual assistant. Sitting in front of a computer with a well-outlined list of processes can provide you with enough product leads.

*More information about the ScanPower services can be found at the end of this book.

Outsourcing Shipments

Featured business: MyInventoryTeam

This is what makes this business really attractive: the ability to now outsource the entire process of prepping items for FBA. You can have Toys R Us ship items to your house where you have to open, re-label, and then send to Amazon, or you can have those same Online Arbitrage orders shipped to a place that will do all of that for you (for a fee of course).

This makes Online Arbitrage a truly international opportunity. Retail Arbitrage and Online Arbitrage are great businesses, but they still required a physical presence to really grow. When you're doing Online Arbitrage with a service like MyInventoryTeam, you can place orders and build your business from anywhere with a computer and an Internet connection. You place the orders, enter their address for shipment, and they'll do the rest.

https://www.MyInventoryTeam.com

John Bullard Sr. and John Bullard Jr. run MyInventoryTeam. They are both very accessible and would be happy to answer any questions about how their services can help your business. Tell them you heard about them in Chris Green's book, *Online Arbitrage*!

There will likely be other sites popping up that will offer similar services.

You can also try to work with websites or suppliers to ship directly to Amazon's warehouse. They would have to use your inbound shipping labels but as long as they can tell you how many boxes and their weights, you could produce the entire FBA shipment from your computer and email them PDFs of the UPS labels. Some may even put FBA labels on your items (not likely, though). Thankfully, Amazon has its own labeling service as well as prep service (like poly-bagging). So you may have to get creative but there are many ways to get your products purchased, prepped, and on their way to Amazon's warehouses without having to do all of that work yourself.

Mastermind Groups

Did you ever think of this? If you are a member of a small mastermind, get together and hire and train one VA for all of you. Set up a small, private Facebook group where information is shared. Not every deal will suit every member of the mastermind group.

Those VAs that you hired to make databases of all of the products from online retailers or even Amazon categories? Why does that have to be done by just one seller? Spread the job and the cost amongst your mastermind group.

Have your VA monitor the private Twitter feed that you set up following the deal sites. Train them to sort out the best potential deals and send them to you hourly for review.

Easy to say, right? So how do you form a mastermind group? Well, there is no set way to do this, but after being in this business as long as I have, I can give you my feedback based on what I've seen work and what I've seen not work.

I believe that true mastermind groups are formed organically. You'll end up forming your own groups by either networking with other people or being asked to join one by others. Paying to be in a mastermind rarely works. The biggest thing that makes any mastermind truly work is TRUST. If you can find other people to work with that you truly trust, then you can build great things. Those types of relationships don't require membership fees other than providing value by being a part of the mastermind group. Don't get me wrong; all groups have a cost of entry. The ones that I have seen that actually work are the ones whose cost of entry is trust and providing value to the group. Simply paying a membership fee to be part of a mastermind group just doesn't work. The other members won't really know who the other members are nor necessarily trust them (and rightfully so). This lack of 100% trust leads group members to not be 100% committed to the group and that leads to members only sharing things of marginal value.

Here is my advice for getting invited to join mastermind groups: Join existing online communities like ScanPower and ScannerMonkey®. Participate and help other people. Answer questions and share useful information. Show others that you want to help them and that you are also knowledgeable about the subject matter at hand. Once you have a good online reputation, you may find yourself being invited to join existing mastermind groups. You can even offer yourself up as someone looking to join a mastermind group.

By participating in these online groups, you'll start to meet other people. You may find some people who live nearby or source the same stores that you do. Or maybe they source stores that you want to learn more about. Post your Zip Code or area code to let people know where you live without giving away too much private information. Ask others where they are from.

Go to local meetups of online sellers if you have any near you. You can visit www.meetup.com and search for eBay, Amazon, online sellers or other search terms. Networking with other sellers in person is probably the best way to get to really know somebody to see if they are someone that you would want to be in a mastermind group with.

The point is that you have to put yourself out there and offer up some kind of value. Give people a reason to ask you to join.

Alternately, you can just form your own mastermind group and invite the people that you want. Keep in mind that some people may already be in mastermind groups and that this may serve as a conflict of interest.

It's good to have friends in the biz of Online Arbitrage. You can exchange deals or pass along deals that aren't right for you but work for someone else. In turn, they give you good info and deals. Here is an example from a friend of mine, Cheri Smith.

DYMO 1755120 LabelWriter 4XL Handheld Thermal Label Printer
by DYMO

★★★☆☆ ▾ • 104 customer reviews
| 32 answered questions

List Price: $279.00
Price: **$191.88** & **FREE Shipping**. Details
You Save: $87.12 (31%)

In Stock.
Ships from and sold by Amazon.com. Gift-wrap available.

Want it Tuesday, July 8? Order within **40 hrs 16 mins** and choose **One-Day Shipping** at checkout. Details

Cheri sent me a message about buying these @ $115.99. They had 90 in stock. I tried to buy them all buy was limited to three. She later posted it in the ScanPower Facebook group.

https://www.facebook.com/groups/scanpower/permalink/508993912535873/

Even expired deals have value because you can learn about patterns and previous price drops. History often repeats itself or maybe even Amazon sells out at the low price but keeps the price low when they restock. This is why you need to set up your price alerts and in stock alerts.

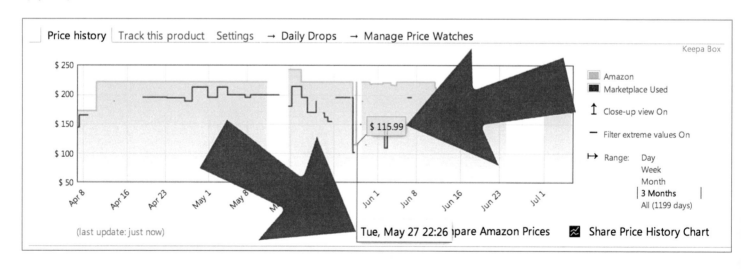

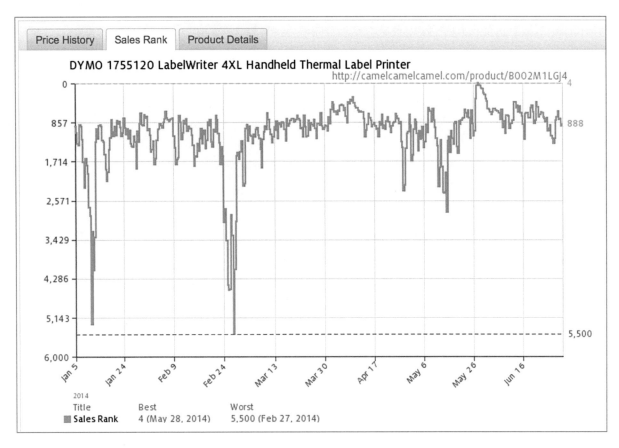

http://camelcamelcamel.com/DYMO-1755120-LabelWriter-Thermal-Printer/product/B002M1LGJ4

This item has a great sales rank, but what if that sales rank is only because of the recent drop in sales price? It's possible, so that's why you check the CamelCamelCamel sales rank history graph. You can see here that it does have a great sales rank over time, making this a great item to buy and resell.

All of the Amazon price trackers missed this drop except Keepa and CamelCamelCamel.

Online Arbitrage - Dymo 450 XL from Amazon $116, Finding, Friends

http://youtu.be/R5ieiQME034
http://bit.ly/dymodeal

Bonus Mastermind Tip: http://www.room.co

There is a new service from the creators of SpreeCast called Room. It's sort of like an alternative to Skype. Four people at a time can join a room. Each room is completely private unless you share the link with others. You can do video calls and voice calls, and it also includes chat. You can share your screen with others as well.

I love the idea of using Room.com for mastermind groups. Just create a room and leave it open. Pop in when you have a question and see who is there. The link never changes and it's not recorded. It's kind of like a portal to four other people.

Chapter 30 – Daily Deal Sites – Highlight WOOT.com

There are many "Daily Deal" sites out there that basically sell one product every day (or until they are sold out). Sites like this try to sell items at a hot price. Sometimes these deals can be resold for a profit.

You can do a quick Google search to find many of them: https://www.google.com/#q=daily%20deal

Pros: low prices, ignored by many sellers, short windows of opportunity (when sold out, no more competitors)

Cons: quantity limits, time-sensitive (have to pay attention), very visible to other resellers

Depending on your Online Arbitrage experience level, you may want to buy and hold some of these items. If they end up on the daily deal sites, they might be products at the end of their retail life cycle. As supply dries up, there may be a market for the products at over-retail prices if there is still demand for the products. I accidentally did a long-term hold on a wooden Thomas the Train set with Jeremy the airplane.

http://www.Amazon.com/Thomas-Friends-Wooden-Railway-Airfield/dp/B000J52AIG/

At the time of this writing, it's not available on Amazon but Keepa and CamelCamelCamel show the last listed price at $259.99. I bought mine for $49.99 from WOOT. I forgot about the item until my son found it and wanted to open it. I scanned it first and it was listed for $159.95 on Amazon at the time. I told him that we'd find something else as a gift and to let daddy sell this one.

The first and arguably most popular of the daily-deal sites is WOOT: www.woot.com

WOOT originally listed one product per day, but now they list several products from different categories. They still do one primary product that sells on their homepage for 24 hours or until it's sold out. In June 2010, Amazon purchased WOOT.

WOOT also does something called the WOOT-OFF. This is where they offer another product after the first product sells out. This continues all day long, sometimes for multiple days. A WOOT-OFF can be over at any time. Some items will only be available for minutes or even seconds depending on the quantity available and how good the deal is.

They even made a song about the WOOT-OFF: http://d1f1o3nyf7spcy.cloudfront.net/wootoff.mp3

Online Arbitrage from Daily Deal Sites like WOOT.com

http://youtu.be/-e8xkD-_wLg
http://bit.ly/wootdealvideo

Get the WOOT app to get WOOT OFF alerts!

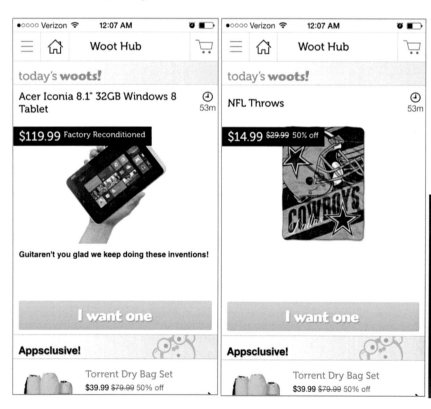 

These pictures are specifically here for Dalton Teeny Man Tyson.

And as you can see, WOOT is now sending out EXCLUSIVE deals through their app. They are calling them Appsclusive Deals. I have not had time to look at many of them yet, but I like the idea of being early on something because there are certainly going to be fewer people (and potentially fewer competitors) viewing the Appsclusive Deals on the WOOT app compared to the WOOT website. You'll also get alerts during a WOOT-OFF when new items are offered. This is an easy way to get the jump on your competition that may be manually refreshing their browsers during a WOOT-OFF.

The founder of WOOT recently launched a new deal site called MEH: https://meh.com

At the time of this writing, they are selling this item for $30 (in refurbished condition):

http://www.Amazon.com/Philips-HSB2313A-Soundbar-Discontinued-Manufacturer/dp/B003TXFK4Q

The price on Amazon is $89.95 Used and $149.95 refurbished. So, yeah, you probably want to keep an eye on MEH.

Chapter 31 – Amazon Warehouse Deals

Amazon Warehouse Deals is where Amazon returns (as well as all your damaged FBA inventory) go to die--I mean, be resold.

This is the direct link to Amazon Warehouse Deals storefront:

http://www.Amazon.com/gp/node/index.html?ie=UTF8&marketplaceID=ATVPDKIKX0DER&me=A2L77EE7U53NWQ

You can use the same sorting techniques described in the previous chapters. Choose a department, choose a percentage discount, and then sort by price: high to low or low to high.

BONUS TIP: the price tracking graphs like Keepa will return the pricing information for the overall Amazon ASIN, even if you are focused in and viewing an offer from a specific seller like Amazon Warehouse Deals. This can be an easy way to check the Buy Box or market price and compare it to the Amazon Warehouse Deals price to see if they are selling at a price low enough to be interesting.

Here is an example of something that I bought for my wife from Amazon Warehouse Deals. I stumbled onto it when I was searching the Sports & Outdoors category during their crazy 80% off sale.

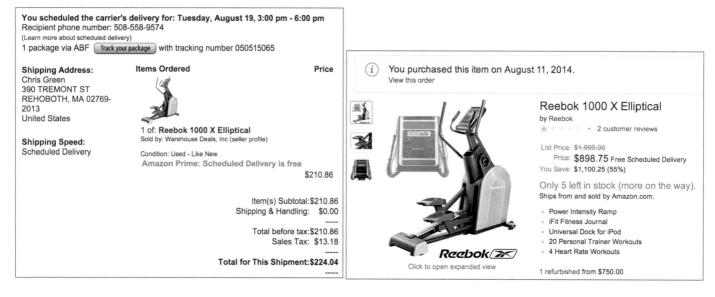

Look at the Keepa graph. See how that BLACK Marketplace Used line just got lower and lower? The bigger the distance between that line and the top of the orange line the better. This means it's a larger percentage (relative) discount.

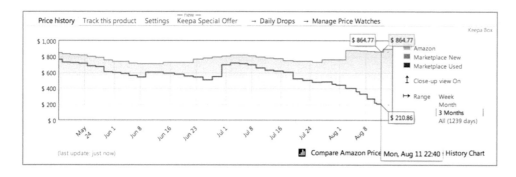

At this price, I didn't even ask if she wanted this item. If she didn't want it or even if she decided later that she didn't want it, we could also sell it locally on Craigslist for an easy profit. A quick check for the going prices for elliptical machines confirmed that this was a low risk purchase.

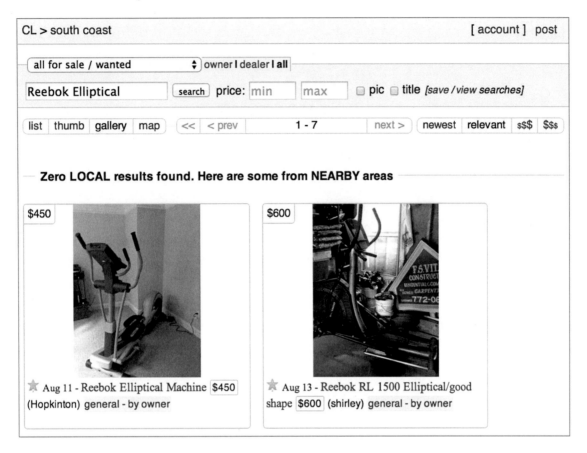

BONUS TIP:

To be honest, I am completely fascinated with the idea of monitoring Amazon Warehouse Deals for items like this and then selling them locally on Craigslist. Most resellers do not have this model on their radar either because they haven't thought of it, they aren't interested in the model, or they don't have the capacity for it. If you could flip one product per day for $200 profit like this elliptical? Yeah, I can handle that. Just need more time in a day. Maybe that will be another book.

Bookmark this page and see what you can come up with:

http://www.Amazon.com/gp/node/index.html?ie=UTF8&marketplaceID=ATVPDKIKX0DER&me=A2L77EE7U53NWQ

Chapter 32 – Liquidation

The largest and most popular network of sites dealing with liquidation merchandise is http://www.liquidityservicesinc.com/

Some of these sites are for large, industrial production equipment and machinery. Feel free to check them out, but they are not going to be the places to find inventory to resell online in the same sense as the scope of this book.

Consider all costs when sourcing products from liquidation service such as shipping and compensate for the fact that you may be buying items with no inspection.

The three that we will take a closer look at are www.liquidation.com www.govdeals.com and www.secondipity.com

My first piece of advice is to not just go for the interesting and/or popular lots. Everyone goes after the sexy products. You'll have more competition and more competition means that people will compete for lower overall profit. Consider looking at the lots that no one wants. Sometimes no one wants them because they are junk, but sometimes it's just because they are not sexy products. Lower competition means that you can get lower prices when you buy, thus yielding better profits. **Remember, don't fall in love with products; fall in love with profits.**

When considering sources like these, you may want to start small. Start with a lot that you are OK losing money on. Learning the process has value in itself. Maybe start with lots that you can physically inspect or pickup to save shipping costs.

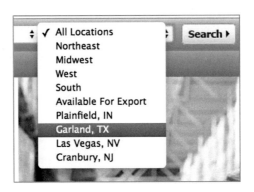

http://www.liquidation.com/c/about/index.html

Liquidation.com is a Liquidity Services, Inc. marketplace where professional buyers can source commercial surplus inventory and government surplus assets in an online environment. Bulk lots are sold by the truckload, pallet, or small package, and conditions range from new in a box to customer returns and used. Their wide variety of product categories includes apparel, computers, electronics, housewares, industrial equipment, vehicles, and much more.

Use their search function and filter down by LOCATION.

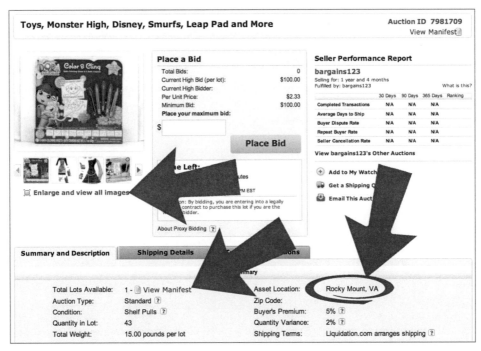

When you find a listing that looks interesting, look at the pictures and the manifest. Consider ALL additional fees like buyer's premiums, taxes, shipping, etc. Check to see if it is pickup only or if you have to arrange shipping yourself (and if you have to use a carrier and be able to receive pallets). Remember that not all carriers will provide a lift-gate. If you are receiving pallets at your home or apartment, be sure that you have a plan to receive the shipment.

Some of the listings even take PayPal.

Do your homework and avoid getting burned. Do a quick search for keyword LEGO and you'll see a few listings that are obvious bootlegs. Reselling bootleg, fake, or counterfeit merchandise is BIG TROUBLE. You can lose your selling privileges permanently on Amazon for a single infraction.

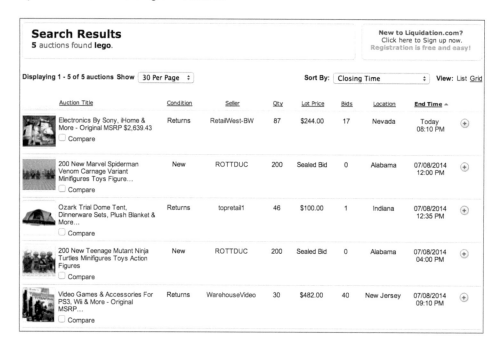

The listing details make it painfully obvious that they are not real: Quote "NOT LEGO BUT SAME QUALITY "

http://www.govdeals.com/

GovDeals provides services to various government agencies that allow them to sell surplus and confiscated items via the Internet. Each participating agency has its own auction rules and regulations and may be subject to government ordinances.

Inventory List- Apple Products

Inventory ID	Name	Description	Quantity in Stock
06214-195s		Part Number--Model Number	
	iPhone 4s 64GB	MD270LL/A--A1387	1
	iPad Mini 16GB	MD531LL/A--A1432	2
	iPad Mini 32GB	MF080LL/A--A1490	1
		ME277LL/A--A1489	1
	iPad Mini 64GB	MD539LL/A--A1454	1
		MD542LL/A--A1455	1
	iPad 64GB	MD524LL/A--A1460	1
		ME197LL/A--A1460	1
		MD527LL/A--A1460	3
	iPad 128GB	ME411LL/A--A1460	6
		ME407LL/A--A1460	1
	iPad 16GB	MC773LL/A--A1458	1
		MD510LL/A--A1458	2
	iPad Air 16GB	MD788LL/A--A1474	1
	iPad Air 64GB	MD787LL/A--A1474	1
	iPad Air 128GB	ME906LL/A--A1475	1
		ME898LL/A--A1474	1
	Apple TV	MD199LL/A--A1469	2
	iMac 27"	ME088LL/A--A1490	1
	iMac 24"	ZFQ0014L--A1225	1

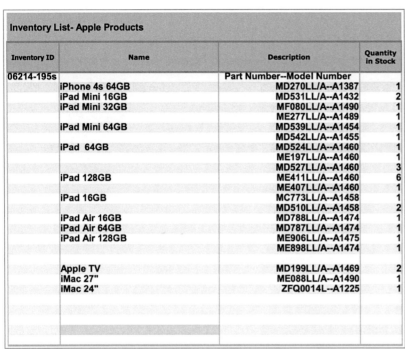

http://www.govdeals.com/photos/4703/Attachments/4703_7591_0.pdf

How would you evaluate this lot? It's simple, really. Just start with an Excel file and go one by one. Or even go retro and use pen and paper. Find exact matches on Amazon and eBay. Even consider Craigslist. It's too easy since they give model numbers.

When sourcing this way, also consider additional expenses such as buyer's premiums, shipping, transport costs, etc. All costs must be considered. Also take into account the fact that boxes or packages may not be in the exact condition that you expect. If you can inspect, great; but if not, factor in some room for 'buying blind'. If you buy from the same place or companies repeatedly, you'll start to know more closely what you're going to expect.

Here is the auction page, where you can see what it ended at:

http://www.govdeals.com/index.cfm?fa=Main.Item&itemid=7591&acctid=4703

Auction Closed

High Bidder: d****************************m

Sold Amount:	$12,802.00
Buyer's Premium (5.00%):	$640.10
Total Price:	$13,442.10

View Bid History

Terms and Conditions

146 visitors

At the time of this writing, only 146 people even looked at this listing. That's pretty crazy low in the days of the Internet. Will it always be this way? Sometimes I think yes because it takes a special kind of person to do this business and to buy lots like this. But I also say no because this business is wide open and visible to all who want to try it out so if there is profit to be made, it's inevitable that competition will enter the marketplace.

So now you're familiar with a site and you've found some searches that you like. Bookmark them! The craziest stuff ends up on these sites; you just have to be ready and find it.

http://www.govdeals.com/index.cfm?fa=Main.AdvSearchResultsNew&kWord=lego

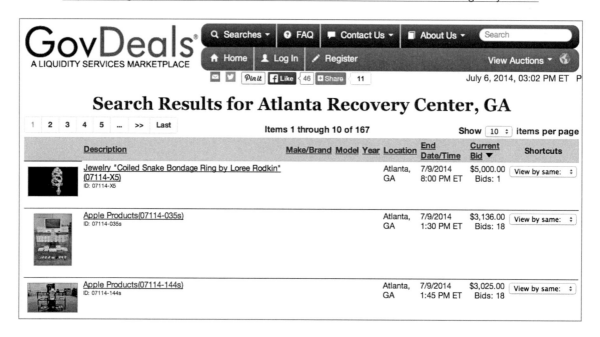

Maybe you've found a seller that consistently has items that fit your business model. Bookmark them! This is the seller that sells these large lots of LEGO and Apple products.

http://www.govdeals.com/index.cfm?fa=Main.AdvSearchResultsNew&agency=4703

This Atlanta Recovery Center is pretty amazing. I don't know exactly where they get their stuff, but I'm suspicious that they are recovered assets from illegal international online purchases that were caught before being shipped out. The large Apple and Lego lots always consist of primarily flagship, high priced items. These are items that can easily be resold for CASH.

Here is another Lego lot that sold with only 282 views.

http://www.govdeals.com/index.cfm?fa=Main.Item&itemid=6707&acctid=4703

Auction Closed

High Bidder: d**********************m

Sold Amount:	$4,425.00
Buyer's Premium (5.00%):	$221.25
Total Price:	$4,646.25

View Bid History

Terms and Conditions

282 visitors

Inventory List			
04214-145s	**Lego's**		
Inventory ID	Description	Model Number:	Quantity in Stock
	Technic	9398	3
	Town Hall	10224	2
	Tower Bridge	10214	1
	The Lego Movie	70810	3
	Creater	10233	4
	Creater	10232	2
	The Simpsons	71006	6
	Volkswagon Camper Van	10220	5
	Star Wars	10240	2
	Star Wars	7965	2
	Star Wars	10221	1
	Star Wars	10236	1

It really couldn't be much easier since they even give you the set numbers.

Look at the final winning bids. Do you agree? Do you think they spent too much or did they get an awesome deal? Would you have bid more? RUN THE NUMBERS yourself and see what you come up with. Seriously, DO THIS; like homework. Consider it a test. If you don't use these easy, completed examples right in front of you, are you really going to be serious about pulling the trigger and placing a bid on an active lot?

Sometimes you may need to get creative or supplement a liquidation buy to complete items to make them saleable. Take a look at this one:

http://www.govdeals.com/index.cfm?fa=Main.Item&itemid=72&acctid=5561

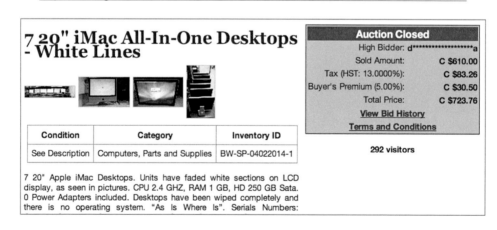

Reading the description, you see no power cords, no operating system. These would be things that you would have to acquire at additional cost. Consider this as you evaluate this particular auction for resale if this type of business is part of your online sales strategy.

The cost for these came in at just over $100 each PLUS the cost to acquire power cords and install the operating system.

378

Then look on your potential sales channels to see the going prices. Calculate the fees, commissions, payment processing fees, etc. when calculating your potential profit. Be sure to also calculate the value of your time to prepare a deal like this. Maybe you have a competitive advantage in an area such as computer refurbishing. Maybe you don't.

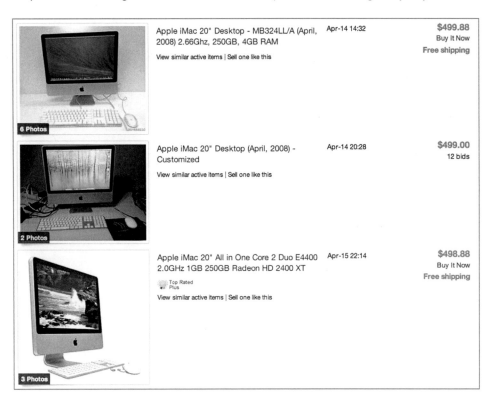

Maybe you can ADD VALUE in other ways. Adding software (people often pay more for simplicity of having things pre-installed). Maybe you use the same strategies in this book to purchase discount software in bulk online so that you have extra copies to install that you then charge full price for and mark up the difference since you bought it at a low price. Take a look at what other sellers are doing. What works? What doesn't? What sells? What doesn't? COPY what works. Don't try to reinvent everything all the time.

If you start doing a lot of this type of thing, it would be very smart to build up a customer base. Keep track of who has purchased from you. What did they purchase? As you acquire more items to sell, maybe you'll be able to sell them direct especially if you sell them locally or on eBay. Going directly to your previous eBay customers to follow up is a great way to boost profits by not having to pay the eBay and PayPal fees.

http://www.secondipity.com/

This is their site for direct to consumer sales. Deals can be had but often there are limited quantities or purchase limits.

Have you ever heard of Secondipity? Most people have NOT, meaning that it's not a site that is on everyone's radar and bookmark lists yet.

They seem to have purchase limits but you can find deals to resell or even to keep for your business.

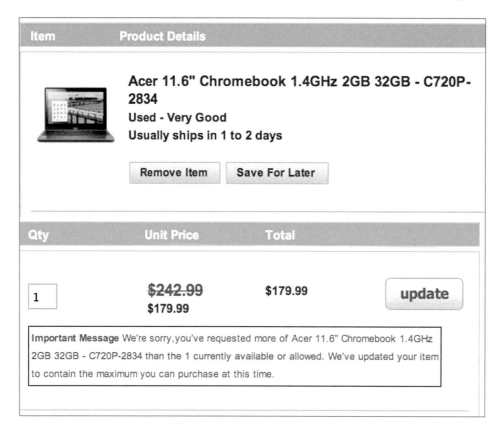

They even have a clearance section:

http://www.secondipity.com/Clearance/b/2399619011

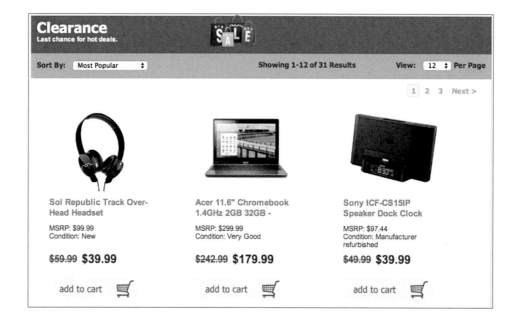

Chapter 33 – Sourcing on eBay.com

EBay is a MARKETPLACE of sellers, not a traditional online retailer. One major advantage that eBay has over Amazon is their Completed and Sold listings. You can go to eBay and actually see what has sold and for how much. You can't do this on Amazon. Unless you are the only seller, the best that you can do is guess based on sales. There are a couple of third-party tools that can provide deeper insight into historical eBay prices (including the very valuable SEASONAL pricing data):

WorthPoint

http://www.worthpoint.com/

Terapeak

http://www.terapeak.com/

EBay Advantages

On eBay, you can have a little more contact with the seller compared to Amazon. You may contact the seller and negotiate a better price or additional quantity. EBay listings have a BEST OFFER option, where you can offer less than the asking price.

Bonus Tip: Apple recently launched two refurbished stores on eBay:

http://www.ebay.com/sch/factory_certified/m.html

http://www.ebay.com/sch/factory_outlet/m.html

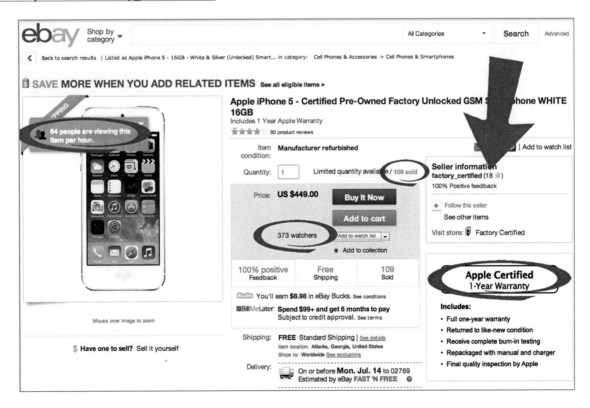

When I am most excited about checking the listings from this seller? Easy, when it's close to the release of the new iPhone. At the time of this writing, the iPhone 6 is scheduled to come out soon. No surprise they are moving iPhone 5 inventory. It's also a good time to check INTERNATIONAL prices.

EBAY CAUTION: Supply chain issues, Fakes, Counterfeits

If you plan to resell product purchased from eBay on Amazon.com, you better be able to prove the supply chain in the event that you have to defend yourself against an accusation of counterfeits. Be very sure that you are buying from a trusted, reputable source when buying from eBay, especially when buying a large quantity of something.

Just like liquidation listings (or any site for that matter), be careful buying from eBay for resale.

Red flags: ships from China, no retail packaging, spelling errors in the listing, pictures show items that are not available from anywhere else, description details:

Manufactured in China. New, so they may have minor imperfections or scratches, since there is no box.

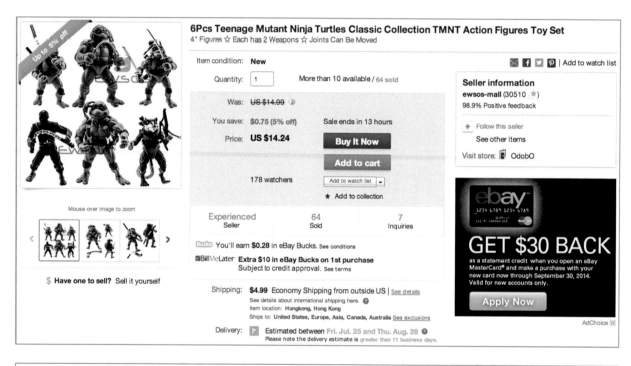

**Set of 6pcs TMNT Teenage Mutant Ninja Turtles
Classic Collection 4" LOOSE Figure**

Manufactured in China. New, so they may have minor inperfections or scraches, since no box.

Condition : Brand new, without box.
Quantity: 6 pcs / pack
Material: PVC
Anime/Movie: Teenage Mutant Ninja Turtles
Weight: 0.5 KG
Size: approx. 4inch (Tall)
Packing: pp bag with bubble wrap, will pack it carefully before sending.

I don't know how this seller is getting away with it on eBay, but this would not fly on Amazon.

Do your due diligence and avoid potentially risky purchases to protect yourself.

How do I know what to search for/sell?

Just start searching and eBay will tell you the rest! They will give you search suggestions and these suggestions will be popular searches. If the searches are popular, you can bet that the search results will be popular products. You can see here in the Action Figure category that eBay suggests TEN different search terms. If you're unsure where to start, start with those.

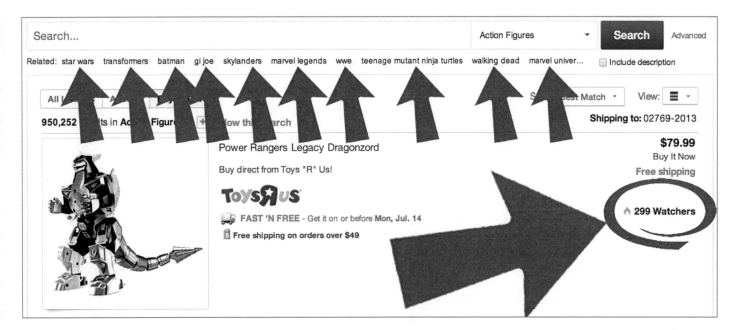

EBay even shows you how many people are watching specific listings. This can be a great way to get a sense for how popular an item is. You may add the item to a list of products that you expect to go out of stock due to high demand. When they are out of stock from everyone else, that's when you can set the market price on your products.

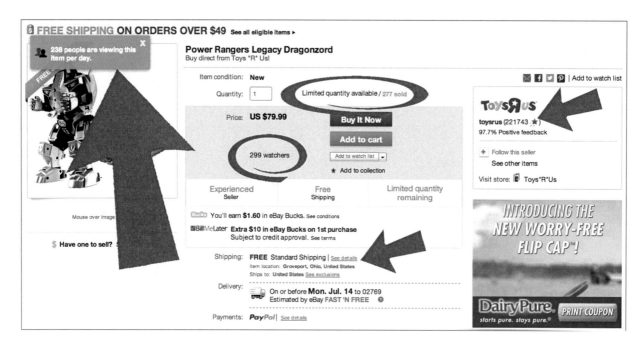

The eBay detail pages gives even more information such as how many people are viewing the item per day as well as the number of units sold (information you would never get from Amazon).

To quickly compare the eBay prices to Amazon prices, you can use Context Search to highlight the text on eBay and then choose Amazon from the drop down menu.

And in one step you are at the Amazon listing.

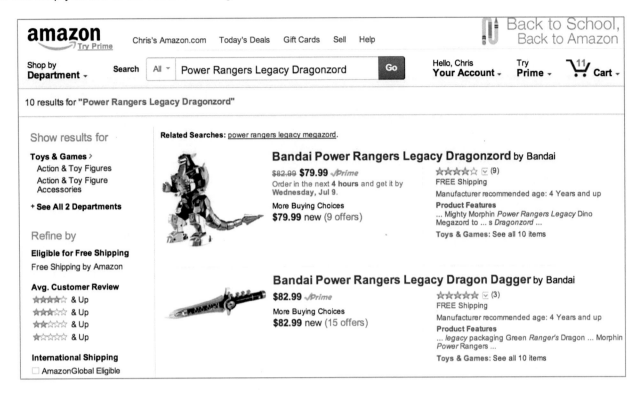

http://www.Amazon.com/Bandai-Power-Rangers-Legacy-Dragonzord/dp/B00I8OSDUE

Looking at the Keepa data, you can see that Amazon did go out of stock and that the price peaked at $106.13 + shipping during that time. Not enough room for a profit if purchased at $79.99, but useful information nonetheless.

So while this item did not have a huge margin, you can quickly see how easy it is to go from eBay to Amazon and check for potential opportunities. If the price when Amazon is out of stock was higher, you could consider setting up a Keepa alert or other tracker.

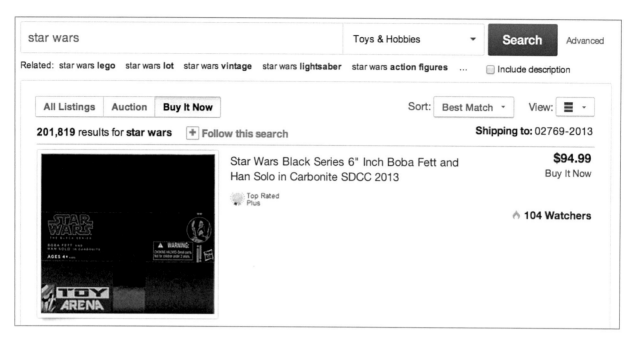

Here is a popular result for eBay search 'star wars'.

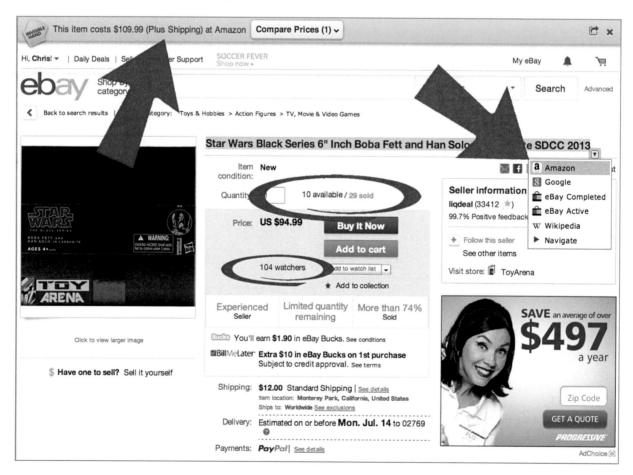

You can see how many have sold, as well as how many eBay buyers are watching the item. In this case, InvisibleHand helps us out and tells us that the item sells for more ($109.99 + shipping) at Amazon.com. So we use Context Search to highlight the title and choose Amazon from the drop down menu.

http://www.Amazon.com/dp/B00E18HTE2

First, you can quickly find the Amazon product page and see the Buy Box price has an additional $12 shipping. InvisibleHand is still kicking; this time telling us that the item is cheaper on eBay! This is one reason that I really like InvisibleHand; it works both ways instead of just on one site.

If the price difference between eBay and Amazon was greater, what would be the next steps in evaluating this deal?

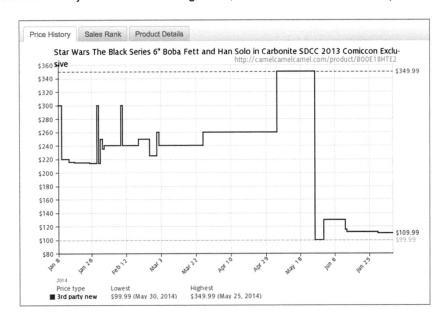

http://camelcamelcamel.com/Black-Series-Carbonite-Comiccon-Exclusive/product/B00E18HTE2

Looking back at the prices using CamelCamelCamel, you can see that this item used to sell for a much higher price. This is evidence that sometimes selling when the prices are high is the best move to make. Sell items when they are hot.

We would also want to check the historical sales rank history through CamelCamelCamel to see if sales are trending up or down. High priced offers on Amazon can look good, but if they aren't selling it's a waste of your time and money.

I put the CamelCamelCamel graphs in here to demonstrate how a drop in price increases sales. A six-month history on both shows how the item was selling sporadically at the higher prices and more frequently at the lower prices.

You saw earlier in Chapter 16 how even major online retailers use eBay to sell products. You may want to find the eBay account of the major retailers. Two examples:

Toys R Us: http://www.ebay.com/usr/toysrus

Target: http://www.ebay.com/sch/targetstores/m.html

Use Google to find others.

Here is an example of an item that is now on my radar because it originally came up on TheTracktor Movers page:

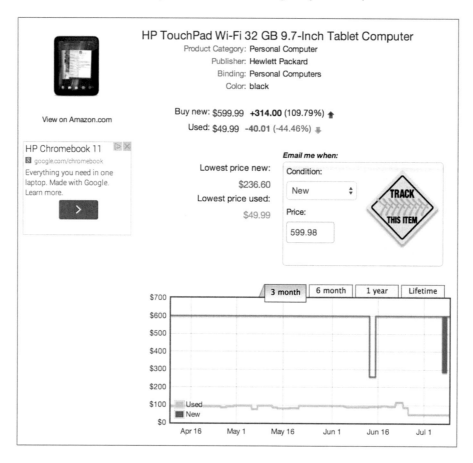

You can see a pretty strong price on Amazon for this item in New condition with a couple of recent price drops. Used prices are much lower and may be what more buyers are purchasing, but some buyers will pay a premium for New.

http://www.amazon.com/HP-TouchPad-9-7-Inch-Tablet-Computer/dp/B0055D66V4

Here you can see the Amazon Buy Box for this item in new condition is $289.99.

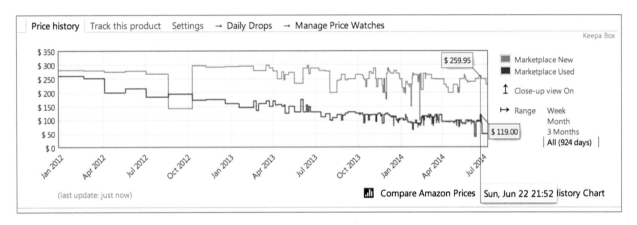

Keepa shows no Amazon competition in the past 924 days (discontinued item) and pretty consistent prices from Marketplace New and Used sellers (I like this).

Additional Information

ASIN	B0055D66V4
Customer Reviews	★★★★☆ ☑ 1,243 reviews 3.9 out of 5 stars
Best Sellers Rank	#2,236 in Computers & Accessories (See top 100)
Shipping Weight	3.3 pounds (View shipping rates and policies)
Shipping	Currently, item can be shipped only within the U.S.
Date First Available	June 19, 2011

The sales rank is good.

Using Context Search, we highlight the title and choose eBay Completed from the drop down menu.

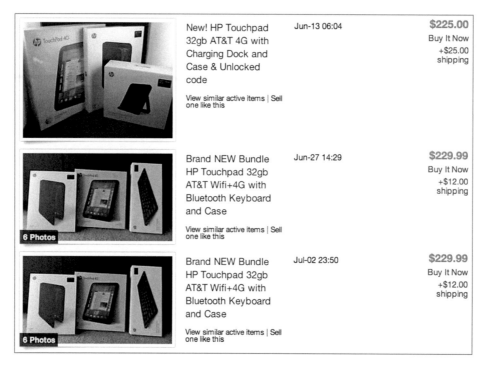

We find several listings that have sold in the $230 range that include additional accessories (items that could potentially be resold separately if these bundles were purchased).

At the right price, these look to be an easy moneymaker to buy from eBay and sell on Amazon. But let's simplify and automate this as much as possible by using eBay's **Follow This Search**.

When you set up the search that you want to follow, be sure that you SORT the results the way that you want BEFORE following the search. If you choose Completed, Sold Listings, Price: Highest First, etc., they will carry over to your search results.

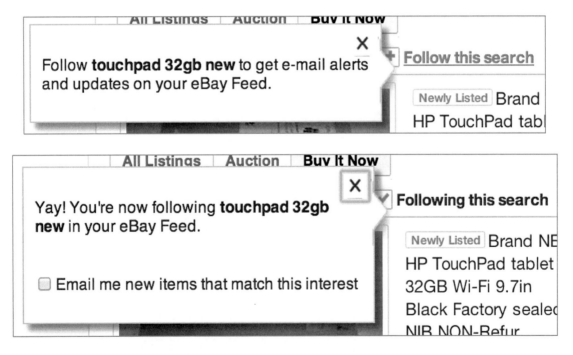

In addition to following this search in your eBay feed, you also want to check the box to receive emails when new items match your search interest.

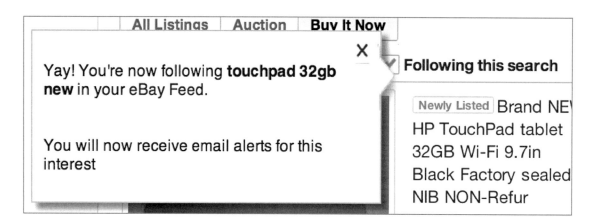

You'll be getting new item alerts right in your email inbox.

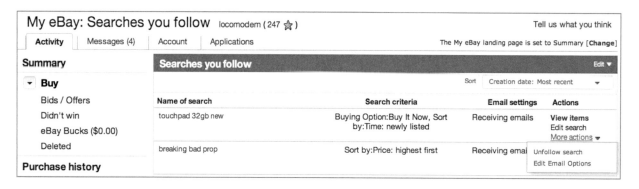

You can manage your followed searches in your eBay account.

Here is an example that was sent to my email. $165 Buy It Now price with $15.55 shipping. Seller has 100% feedback and over 1,000 positive ratings.

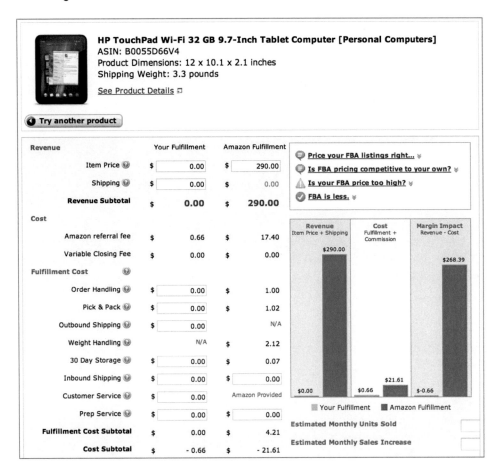

Using the Amazon FBA Calculator to see the payout at the current Buy Box price of $290, you see that you'd receive a payout of $268.39. Subtract your acquisition costs of $165 + $15.55 shipping and you're looking at profit of $87.84 on a single transaction. One box in, one box out; almost $90 in your pocket.

A faster way to evaluate potential deals and see the new FBA payout is to use our ScanPower WebScout program. It's web-based so it works from any browser with an Internet connection. You'll see the payout amount for several different offers all on one screen.

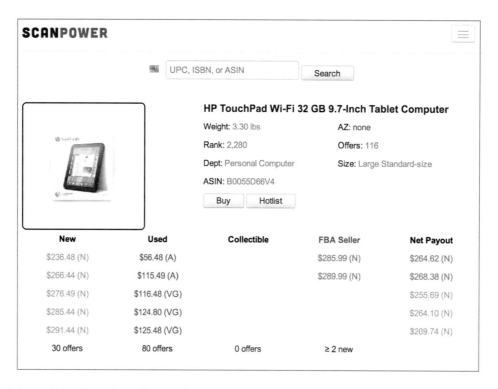

You can find more information about ScanPower WebScout at the end of this book under Vendor Spotlight: ScanPower.

Sometimes you'll want to go to eBay to try to find items that you stumble upon on Amazon. You'll often find pages for high priced items on Amazon when you're researching a new product line. You can then consider trying to find that item on eBay.

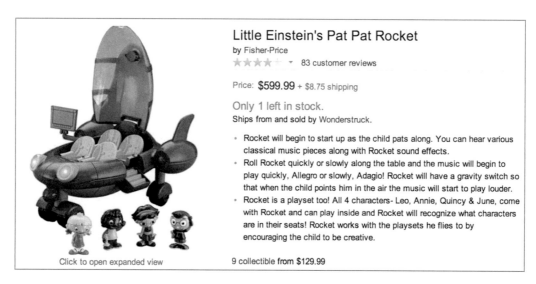

http://www.Amazon.com/Little-Einsteins-Pat-Rocket/dp/B000NVW07M/

Here's an example of a toy with very high prices in both New and Collectible conditions. Like other searches, highlight the title text using Context Search and choose eBay Completed form the drop down menu.

In one step, you'll be taken to the eBay results where you can see the prices that the items ended for.

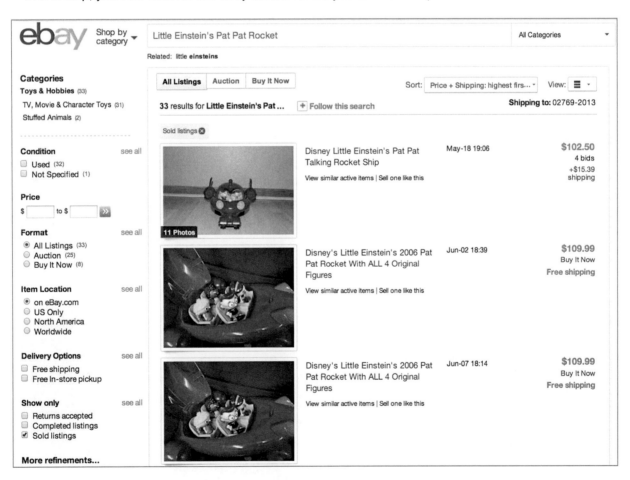

If the prices show a possible opportunity, set up eBay keyword alerts and followed searches and try to catch items with good BIN prices.

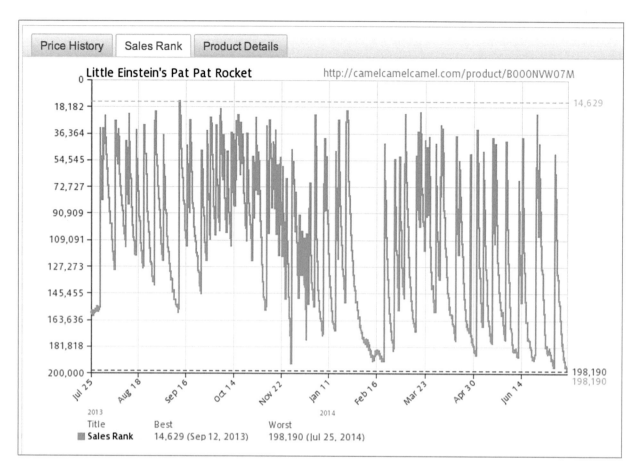

Title   Best   Worst
■ Sales Rank   14,629 (Sep 12, 2013)   198,190 (Jul 25, 2014)

http://camelcamelcamel.com/Little-Einsteins-Pat-Rocket/product/B000NVW07M

Even if you think it's crazy that anyone would pay such high prices for items, always check the data. Here you can see the CamelCamelCamel sales rank history showing that while it may not sell frequently, it does sell consistently.

Most of this book is about selling on Amazon but don't forget other channels. I'd find it hard to believe that items that are this popular (due to number of watchers) on eBay couldn't be flipped for a quick profit locally on Craigslist.

CRAIGSLIST HUSTLE

I'm convinced that you could be buying up hot technology deals on eBay and selling them locally on Craigslist. Run the numbers and decide if that makes sense for you. There are plenty of people out there who will look to Craigslist first for a laptop or cell phone. They want something today, not tomorrow. If they have cash, you could flip some products from eBay to Craigslist each day and earn some cash flow. This is a much different model than selling on Amazon, but it's easy enough to run the numbers from the comfort of your couch and computer to see if you think it would work in your area.

Take a look at the $300+ laptops listed on my local Craigslist site. Looking more closely, I think some people are doing this with items sourced on Amazon already. Sneaky and smart!

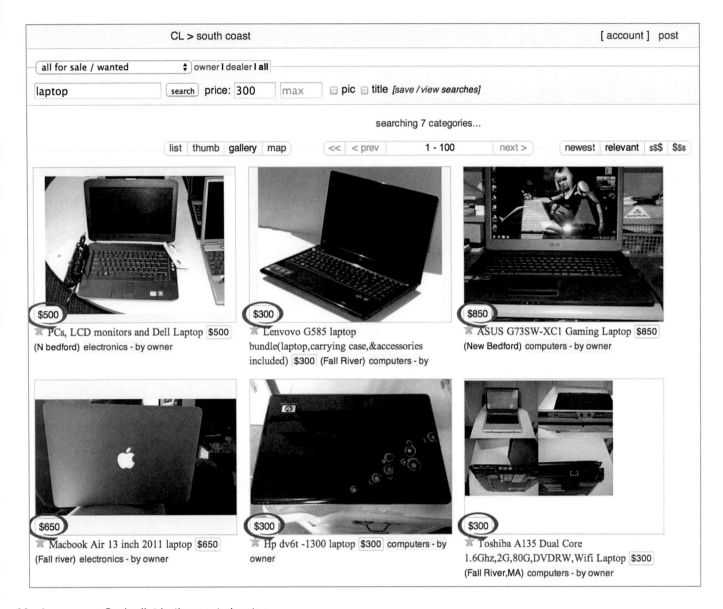

Much more on Craigslist in the next chapter.

EBay Typos:

There are a ton of sites that let you search eBay for items with typos. The idea is that those items will not come up for customer searches and therefore get less exposure and end for lower prices.

Find some of the more popular ones here: https://www.google.com/#q=ebay+typos

This is not my preferred method of eBay search because you'll likely be limited to onesie-twosie items for your efforts.

Chapter 34 – Sourcing from Craigslist

Craigslist may not be the first place that you think of for Online Arbitrage but you can sit at home on the computer and look for profitable inventory to resell on Craigslist. You'll likely have to go and get it, but if the deals are good enough, it can be really worth it.

This BuzzFeed article has some really good tips for getting the best deals and running the best searches:

http://www.buzzfeed.com/peggy/useful-tips-every-craigslist-user-should-know

Tips like using these search term phrases: "My wife/husband is making me"
"My wife/husband doesn't like"
"My wife/husband won't let me"
"But now we have kids"
"Leaving country"
"Liquidation"
"End of lease"
"Must go"
"No reasonable offer refused"
"Everything must go"
"ASAP"

When sellers on Craigslist use terms like this, it's very likely that they are desperate or have room to negotiate on price.

Another suggestion is to set your minimum price to $2 to filter out spam and service posts.

Craigslist can be a great place to meet other people locally, but do be cautious and put your personal safety first when considering meeting people. Meet in public spaces. Once you've met someone and made a deal on something, you may decide to ask if they have more products or similar products. By being open and friendly (tell them that you sell online), you may find that they open up about some opportunities that you would have completely missed. I know several people who have made connections with large lots of inventory from friends and family members of people that they met on Craigslist.

Tip: Ask sellers ahead of time if they smoke and avoid items that may smell of smoke. In general, it's just not worth messing with.

For the most part, Craigslist is for local pickup only. You can try to get sellers to ship products to you. If you do this, I suggest using PayPal for payment protection. If the deal is good enough and you're desperate that they ship it to you, consider offering them more than their asking price. Money talks.

Search Tool: Cubix Solutions

http://www.cubixsolutions.com/

Cubix Solutions offers a powerful program called Classified Searcher.

From their website:

Classified Searcher is an **automated Craigslist search software** that delivers filtered Craigslist results, based on your specific and personal preferences.

Simply install **Classifieds Searcher** on your computer (it takes less than a minute), log into your account (only if you have the POWER version - the FREE version doesn't require login) and start exploring a whole new world of classified ads. Based on your criteria, the software will deliver results from all the supported sites. Using Classifieds Searcher you can:

Search **multiple Craigslist cities and categories** at the same time.

Set up **alerts** and **forward new results** by email and/or SMS. **Automatic searching!**

Send mass email replies using multiple accounts. Set up **auto-reply** for **newly found ads**!

Embedded browser, map and timeline previews!

Thumbnail preview for ads with images!

Multiple searches supported! All searches are saved locally for future use!

Export your result in CSV format for use in external systems!

Once your searches are created you can let it run in the background and gather results for you. Configure **email and/or SMS forwarding** and you won't even have to be in front of the computer. This software product doesn't just save your time - it helps you find deals that you would otherwise miss.

Using search tools, you'll want to set up keyword alerts. But what if you're just starting out and you don't know what search terms to use? Well, start looking at what's listed and what the prices are. Remember, we want to keep your average sales price up. Messing with cheap stuff from Craigslist makes even less sense because of the potential additional work to acquire products. Find some items and compare them to the matching Amazon product pages using Context Search. Make a list of interesting matches.

Here are a couple of easy examples:

Apple Hi Fi – this was an iPad dock produced by Apple that is no longer made. Some people still want this item and will pay a premium price for it. It turns up frequently on Craigslist.

Check the Amazon product page for current prices:

http://www.Amazon.com/Apple-Hi-Fi-Stereo-Discontinued-Manufacturer/dp/B000BKBYY0/

You can see that the lowest Amazon price at the time I took this picture is $184.99, which doesn't leave much room for a profit. This is another reason why having access to historical Amazon pricing info is so valuable. Pulling up TheTracktor, you can see the lowest listed price for the past three months is right around the $400 level. Offers come and go, so don't worry about single offers at low prices. Someone will buy them and the offer will no longer be there. Sometimes the offer may be low enough that you want to buy it yourself to relist at a higher price!

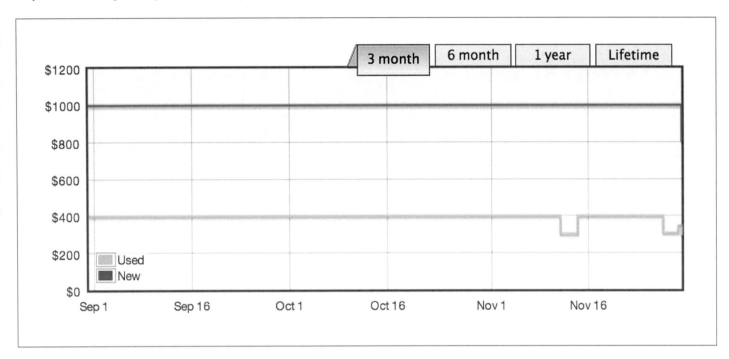

Searching for keyword LEGO on Craigslist is an easy one.

When you find something that looks interesting, check it out on Amazon using the Context Search extension.

Find the Amazon product page and compare the prices.

IRIS LEGO 6-Case Workstation and Storage Unit with 2 Base Plates

by IRIS USA, Inc.

★★★★⯨ ▾ 375 customer reviews | 28 answered questions

Note: This item is only available from third-party sellers (see all offers.)

Available from these sellers.

- Workstation, storage and display unit all in one - creative play chest.
- Includes two building base plates.
- Building base plates fit on top of unit and inside portable project cases.
- Raised edges of top keep base plate secure for building or displaying creations.
- Portable project cases serve as filing system for sets or grab 'n go solution.

6 new from $239.99   2 used from $269.99

http://www.Amazon.com/IRIS-6-Case-Workstation-Storage-Plates/dp/B0031P85VC

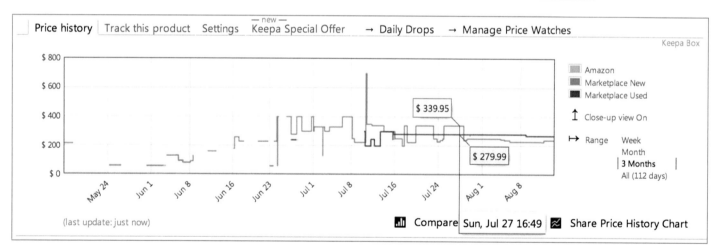

Use Keepa to look at historical prices to be sure that you aren't looking at non-competitive outlier prices.

Here are another THREE Craigslist search tools and TWO Chrome extensions to try out:

Search Tool: Search Tempest

http://www.searchtempest.com/

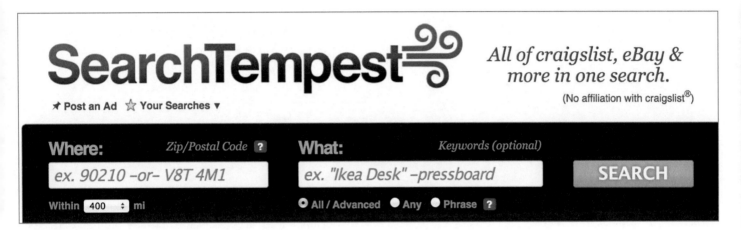

Search Tool: ZoomTheList

http://zoomthelist.com/

✔ Like Share You and 421 others like this.   ៩+1 +42 Recommend this on Google

Two fast and easy ways to search Craigslist like never before...

1. ALL of Craigslist: Easily search ALL of Craigslist at once by keyword, or search state-by-state by keyword

(this is the top section of the left hand column)

2. Local Craigslist Search: Effortlessly browse and search Craigslist by keyword and category, going city-by-city.

Search Tool: Craigslist Buddy

http://craigslistbuddy.com

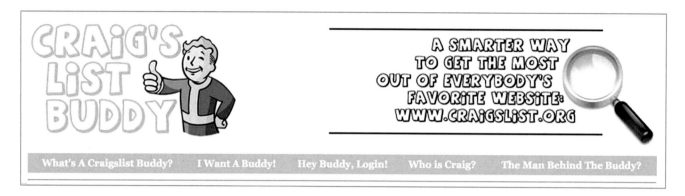

What's a Craigslist Buddy?

Craigslist Buddy (CLB) is a cool tool that lets you keep track of your favorite Craigslist listings as they happen. Craigslist Buddy checks the last 10 entries of your favorite Craigslist category every 5 minutes (24 hours a day, 7 days a week) and drops you an email and/or text message if it finds what you're looking for. It also lets you track the number of people that check out any postings you listed!

Extension: CraigsHunter

Checks Craigslist every 5 minutes for your saved queries. Shows number of new Craigslist posts in the Chrome Toolbar. Shows system tray popup notifications. Detects and ignores re-posts.

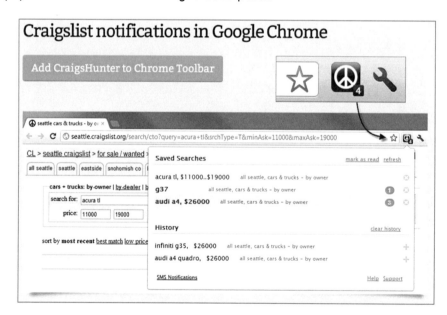

https://chrome.google.com/webstore/detail/craigslist-notification/aenadocogjnkbmchfnkpipdinoleakbj

EASY LINK: http://bit.ly/craigshunter

www.craigshunter.com

Extension: Craigslist POP

Become a Craigslist Power User and instantly view Craigslist ads and images without a single click!

Mouse over Craigslist postings to view them instantly!

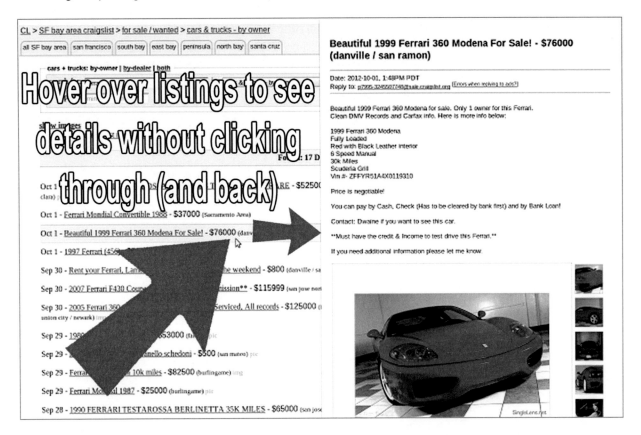

Download now and save hours -- works for all Craigslist sections -- simple, clean, & fast.

https://chrome.google.com/webstore/detail/craigslist-pop-for-power/aikbdokcmcbbeaadpdbhlcdcgghdkhja

EASY LINK: http://bit.ly/craigslistpop

Bonus Tip:

Amazon Electronics Trade-In Program

http://www.Amazon.com/gp/b/ref=ipr_tcg_ti2?ie=UTF8&ie=UTF8&node=2226766011

Source products from eBay or Craigslist that will net you positive cash flow through this program.

Chapter 35 – Shopgoodwill.com sourcing

http://www.shopgoodwill.com/

This may be a chapter that you didn't expect to find, but the fact remains that you can sit at home and even find products from thrift stores and have them delivered to your house these days. You likely won't find replenishable inventory or even mass quantities of identical products, but if you know what you're looking for and you're there at the right time, you can pick up some big money makers.

Consider this search from what we saw in Chapter 14: Lego

Some very high-end Lego kits have shown up on the Goodwill auction site. Kits like the Eiffel Tower that sells for over $2,000:

http://www.Amazon.com/LEGO-Make-Create-Eiffel-Tower/dp/B000P0Z9KQ

http://www.shopgoodwill.com/search/searchKey.asp?itemTitle=lego&showthumbs=on&sortBy=itemCurrentPrice&sortOrder=d

This search will show you the highest priced Lego auctions on the Goodwill auction site.

It's worth checking on every now and again. Maybe you'll stumble onto a great item that everyone else misses.

If you're into eBay and the 'thrill of the hunt' of thrift stores, be sure to join the Thrifting With The Boys Facebook group run by Jason T Smith and Bryan Goodman, stars of television's Thrift Hunters. You can find it here:

https://www.facebook.com/groups/ThriftingWithTheBoys/

This is the largest thrifting group on Facebook and offers 100% free help to thrifters of all experience levels.

Here's a picture of us jamming at our local Meetup in Massachusetts.

If you're in the area (MA, NH, RI, CT) and you'd like to see when our next Meetup is, please visit:

http://www.meetup.com/MAsellers/

You can find the latest information about the Thrift Hunters TV show on Spike TV at:

http://www.spike.com/shows/thrift-hunters and http://www.thrifthunters.com/

Chapter 36 – Facebook

More and more people are spending more and more time on Facebook. There are groups for discussing Amazon and FBA, groups for sharing deals and BOLOs, and even groups for selling products (yard sale and garage sale groups).

To search for a term in a Facebook group, use this link:

https://www.facebook.com/groups/scanpower/search/?query=ABC where ABC is your search term and scanpower is your group name/ID. This will only work for closed groups if you are a member of the group.

Maybe you want to make a bookmark for all the recent posts in ScannerMonkey® that have the keyword BOLO. You'd use:

https://www.facebook.com/groups/ScannerMonkey®/search/?query=BOLO

The more traditional way to search Facebook groups is use the magnifying glass at the top right corner of the group:

At the time of this writing, this search is normally not very good. It will often not return relevant results. Use with caution. I do not believe there is a similar search method for MOBILE.

Facebook yard sales are becoming very popular places where people can list stuff for sale and find local buyers.

To find new, local groups, use this link: https://www.facebook.com/browsegroups/

Open Facebook groups have an RSS feed that you can use to monitor for keywords. Find out if your Facebook groups have RSS feeds here: https://apps.facebook.com/groups_to_rss/

For closed Facebook groups, there is a service called Wallflux that will create an RSS feed even for closed groups.

An admin of a closed Facebook group would need to add this capability (not a free service): http://www.wallflux.com/

Alternately, turn Notifications ON for the closed groups that you want to monitor. Then use Gmail filters to sort and identify posts of interest for free.

To see the groups that you are a member of and to change your notification settings, go here:

https://www.facebook.com/browsegroups/?category=membership

408

You can toggle your favorites ON and OFF here. Your favorite groups will stick to the top of your Facebook Newsfeed page while your other groups will mostly be hidden.

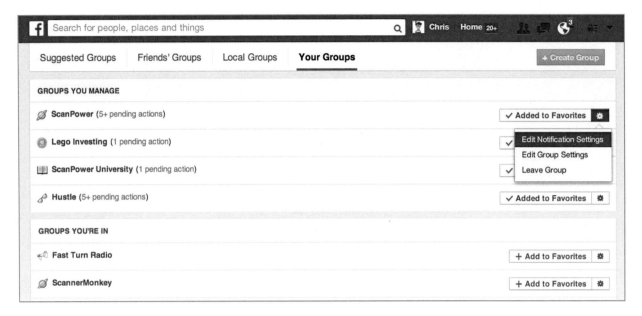

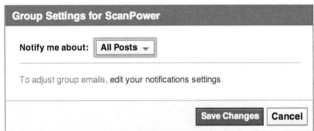

Clicking on 'edit your notification settings' will take you here:

https://www.facebook.com/settings?tab=notifications&section=Groups

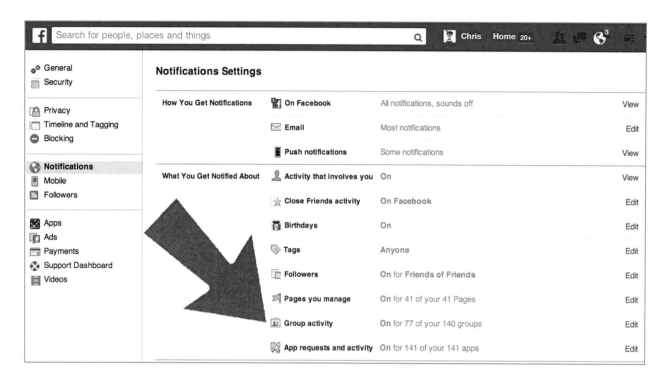

You can also get here from your homepage by clicking the settings at the top right:

Then choose notifications from the left hand side like you see in the previous picture.

Once you're on the page, you can change them all in bulk:

410

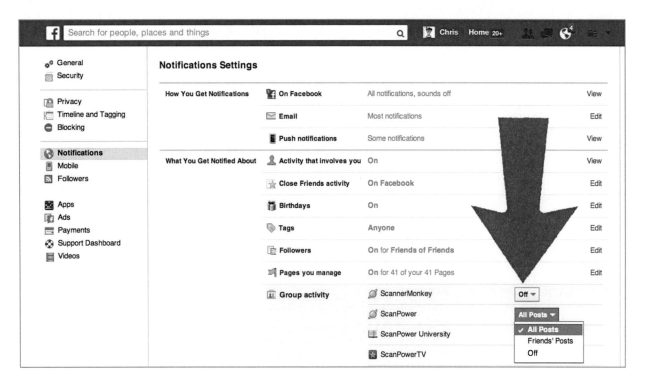

Once completed, scroll down and click CLOSE.

To get individual post notifications you can LIKE or COMMENT on the post in the group. You can also choose the drop down menu and choose Get Notifications if you want to follow the thread. This is useful because all of the comments will be copied to your email so you'll have a record of the thread even if the thread or comments are later deleted.

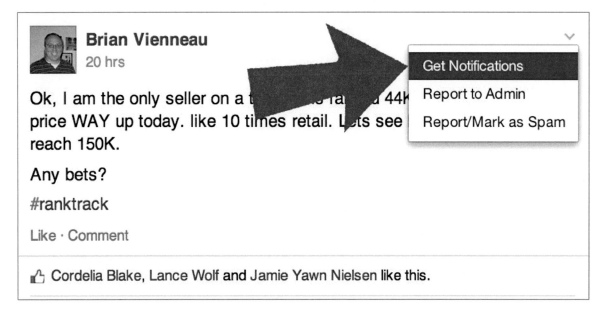

Let's see how that works on MOBILE (iPhone example):

You can click on Get Notifications to get updates and emails for every comment made on this thread. This is very helpful not just to stay up to date with active threads in your groups, but also to ARCHIVE the entire thread (all posts, even ones that get deleted or edited) in Gmail, which is much easier to search than traditional Facebook search.

If you visit one of your groups using the Facebook mobile app (or facebook.com in a mobile browser), you'll see the group info and options. One of these options near the bottom is Edit Notification Settings. This allows you to edit your notification settings from your mobile device.

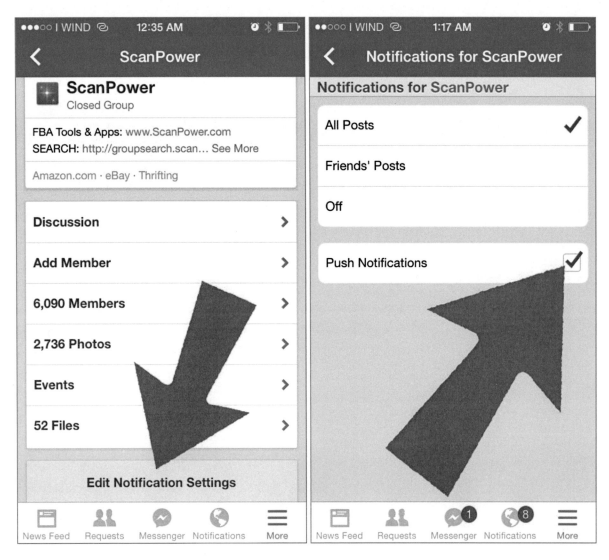

This is a big deal (at least at the time of this writing) as this is the only place that I have found where you can turn on PUSH notifications for groups. This means that you will get an alert for every new post (or friends' posts depending on your notification settings) for groups that you are monitoring: BOLO groups, masterminds, yard sales, etc. For any group where timely action is vital, this is what you want to have turned on. Remember, it's a game of who gets the deals first. You want to use any and all methods to get the right information delivered the right way so that you can be the one to capitalize.

So now that you have the notifications coming to your Gmail account, you have to sort, filter, and get the ones that you want to see and possibly take action on.

You can enter this text search in the Gmail search bar at the top:

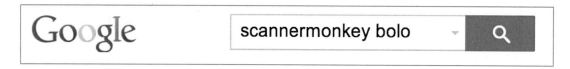

You can search for GROUP NAME plus a keyword. Example: ScannerMonkey® bolo

Or a group name plus a poster's name if someone always posts good info or deals. Or keywords for yard sale groups like NIB (New In Box), MISB (mint in sealed box) or whatever other keywords you find are included in posts that you find relevant and profitable to your business.

Setting up a search and filter would look like this:

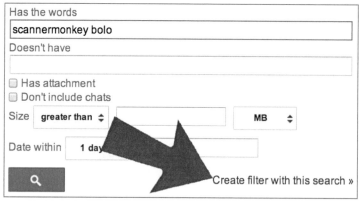

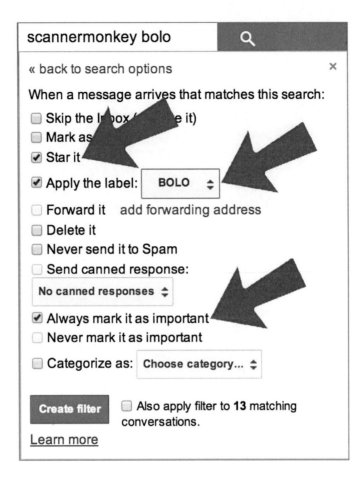

Maybe you view your Gmail using labels so you label it BOLO, or maybe you filter all your important messages. I like to STAR them and then use IFTTT to get a text every time a new email is starred.

See Chapter 27 for more information about Gmail and IFTTT.

Bonus Tip:

There are tons of sites out there with tips and tricks for using Gmail optimally and creatively. This Google search will bring up some of the best ones:

http://www.google.com/search?q=gmail+tricks+tips

Chapter 37 – Bonus Tips & Tricks

This chapter includes some bonus tips and tricks that didn't really fit into the other chapters.

You know those Chinese sellers that sell low-priced items with free shipping on Amazon and eBay? Guess what? Lots of buyers don't like waiting for slow shipping. Sounds like you just found some potential suppliers of products. I know this goes against what I've been saying about low price points, but you don't have to sell single items. Maybe it's an item that can be sold as a 6-pack or 12-pack. Think creatively. One of the biggest hurdles to sourcing from China is finding a supplier and shipping overseas. It's all right in front of you. Just find the products that are selling from these Chinese sellers, contact them, order in bulk, then turn around and sell it yourself. Better yet, get some to FBA and sell to the Prime buyers that are definitely not waiting on Chinese shipping speeds.

Deal Commentary Video:

I put together this video showing you two moneymaking deals with commentary on how they were found and some creative ways that you can profit from them.

Items mentioned:

TRENDnet Wireless AC1200 Dual Band Gigabit Router - $80 item being sold for $29.99
http://www.Amazon.com/gp/product/B00BKFYLFO

Dove Beauty Bar, Shea Butter 4 ounce – 4 pack - $10 soap being sold for $1.49
http://www.Amazon.com/gp/product/B003YOON0C

Tools mentioned: Keepa, TheTracktor, CamelCamelCamel

Online Arbitrage - Commentary on TWO Easy Money Making Deals

http://youtu.be/f_PnBXcpakk
http://bit.ly/dealcommentary

Keywords Outside of Category

You've already seen how you have to choose an Amazon department or category in order to get additional sort options, but this can also be limiting. If you are doing research on a toy line and you're in the Toy category on Amazon, you'll miss relevant keyword matches from OTHER Amazon categories.

For example, this is the #1 best selling towel on all of Amazon, but if you were in the Amazon Toy category when you searched for keywords 'frozen' or 'frozen towel', you would completely miss this item. Sometimes the strategy is just to sell those items from other categories because there will be less competition. Sometimes it may be an item that should be listed in the Toy category that you can bring over and capitalize on the high search volume of those keywords in the Toy category.

Manage UPS Shipments with Text Messages

Here is the Amazon page to get alerts for your Amazon shipments:

http://www.Amazon.com/gp/help/customer/display.html?ie=UTF8&nodeId=468530

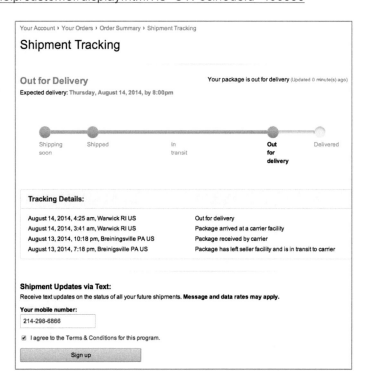

Here is the UPS page to set up SMS text alerts for your UPS shipments:

http://www.ups.com/content/us/en/bussol/browse/wireless.html

Getting price matching from Amazon

Amazon used to be very liberal about adjusting prices on your Amazon purchases for up to 30 days after purchase. There were even websites set up to track items and alert you to price drops so that you could ask Amazon for a price refund or adjustment. Amazon did away with this practice near the beginning of the launch of the FBA program, possibly because customers would not differentiate Amazon purchases and purchases from third party sellers using FBA.

I bought two items from Amazon recently. Each one was $293.77 as you can see.

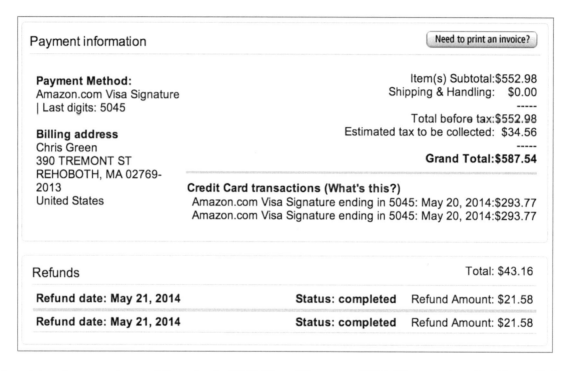

Just a few days later, Amazon dropped the price to $272.19, a difference of $21.58 on each order. Normally I would not send a message to Amazon customer service about a price difference like this (if I would even notice), but it was within such a small time period and added up to over $40. Here is their response:

I don't know if this is official Amazon policy, but the Amazon customer service representative mentions, "within seven days of the delivery of your order." That seems fair to me. If it was a longer period of time, I would not have asked for a price adjustment.

This was an easy price-matching situation because the item was still showing the new, lower Amazon price when I emailed Amazon customer service. Sometimes these price adjustments from Amazon are very short lived. An aggressive low price from Amazon may only be available for a few minutes. When this happens (or when you think that the new, lower price may not last very long), **TAKE A SCREEN SHOT AS PROOF.** Amazon customer service may not have access to historical Amazon prices and if the new, lower price that you saw is no longer active, you may have a difficult time getting Amazon to honor that price adjustment. You can submit a screenshot to Amazon customer service to help make your case and get your price adjustment.

Amazon FLOW

Amazon FLOW is incredible. Let's just leave it at that. Download it, try it out, and you'll agree that Amazon FLOW is just flat-out incredible.

https://itunes.apple.com/us/app/flow-powered-by-Amazon/id474664425?mt=8

http://bit.ly/flowiphone

https://play.google.com/store/apps/details?id=com.a9.flow&hl=en

http://bit.ly/flowandroid

Amazon FLOW works by image recognition, but it doesn't take a picture like Google Goggles or Image Search. You simply open the FLOW app and hover the camera over an item (works best on retail packages and book covers). When the app detects a match, it pulls up the Amazon product page and shows you the pricing information.

Woot.com's product titles are images so you can't copy and paste them to search. But you can hold up Amazon FLOW on your iPhone or Android device and pull up the listing on Amazon by just pointing the camera at the screen:

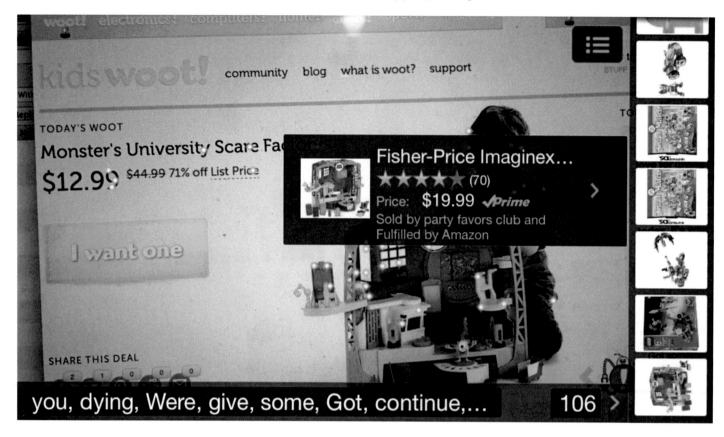

You can use this on ANY SITE. Go to www.target.com, find their clearance section and just hover your phone over each and every item instead of highlighting text and doing a Context search or copy & pasting into an Amazon search.

Remember that Ziploc Vacuum Sealer System that was posted on Instagram as a Target clearance buy for $20 from Chapter 8? Scan it with FLOW for a quick way to find the Amazon listing and price without having to search or type:

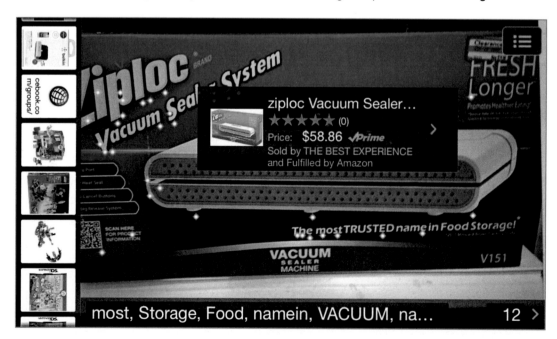

420

Awesome App: Flipp

Flipp is the easiest way to browse retail flyers and save money. Quickly browse the brands you love, clip items straight to your shopping list, and highlight top deals across flyers. http://www.flipp.com/

I love Flipp because you can get flyers from all of the major retailers digitally. You can choose a store and then choose your desired discount (percentage off) using a simple sliding feature to see all of the matching items. It takes literally a few seconds to see all of the items in the Wal-Mart flyer that are 70% off or more. This is powerful stuff!

I like to use Flipp on my iPad for the bigger screen and then use Amazon FLOW on my iPhone to pull up the Amazon listings. Some items will also be on sale from the store's websites, but some may be in store specials only.

BONUS TIP: find the discounts that are the most attractive for resale and then PRICE MATCH. Try to price match online as well.

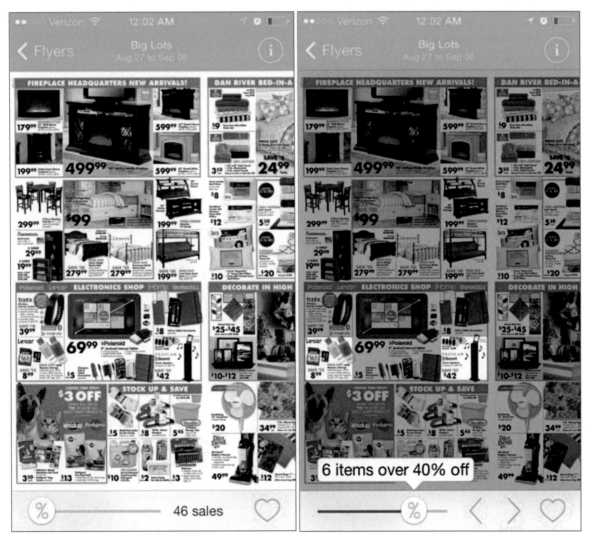

Check out this magical app! It pulls up local store flyers and you can slide the % over to see how many items are at different discounts. In less than a second, I can see that there are six items listed at 40%+ discounts in the Big Lots flyer. The app even highlights the items to find them easily. Next step? Use Flipp on an iPad or other tablet and use Amazon FLOW to do image search. You can save items to a shopping list and save your favorite stores as well.

Amazon Exclusive Search

http://www.Amazon.com/s/ref=nb_sb_ss_i_0_16?url=search-alias%3Daps&field-keywords=Amazon%20exclusive

Making a profit on Amazon Exclusives requires patience as well as a few scenarios playing out. First, you have to hope that Amazon goes out of stock at some point and that demand continues to exist at a price above your purchase price. While they are still available from Amazon, they may not be great for resale on Amazon.com, but many buyers go to other sites first (like eBay). So consider listing/selling Amazon exclusives on eBay. Example:

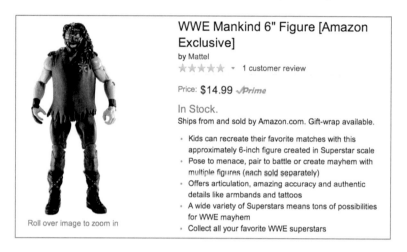

http://www.Amazon.com/WWE-Mankind-Figure-Amazon-Exclusive/dp/B00L62VCV2/

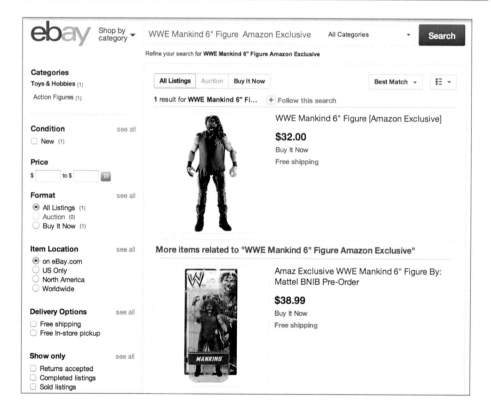

You can see that even while it is still available on Amazon for $14.99, it's being listed on eBay for $32.00 and $38.99. They had not sold at the time of this writing.

My advice on Amazon Exclusives

Are they memorable? Do they stand out? I don't like the Mankind example for this reason. It does not appear to be a figure that has any significance to warrant an over-retail price other than to collectors who want every figure or to Mankind fans who want this figure over another, lower-priced figure. Also, look at what has happened historically on other Amazon Exclusives using CamelCamelCamel and Keepa. What happened to the price when Amazon stopped carrying the item? How was sales rank affected? Has the item sold on eBay after Amazon went out of stock? At what prices? Look at the sellers of the item; are they new or experienced? You know that they decided to buy and resell the item so what can you learn from them?

Sometimes crazy pop-culture references can lead to Online Arbitrage opportunities:

http://www.buzzfeed.com/adamdavis/Amazon-reviews

Playmobil Security Check Point
by PLAYMOBIL®

★★★★★ ▾ 218 customer reviews
| 13 answered questions

Price: **$199.99** & **FREE Shipping**. Details

Only 1 left in stock.
Sold by MY-TOY-SALE-LLC and Fulfilled by Amazon. Gift-wrap available.

Want it Monday, July 28? Order within **27 hrs 4 mins** and choose **One-Day Shipping** at checkout. Details

5 new from $199.99   1 collectible from $295.00

This item often shows up on lists of Amazon products with hilarious customer reviews. A little publicity and all of a sudden some people will actually want to buy this set.

http://www.Amazon.com/dp/B0002CYTL2

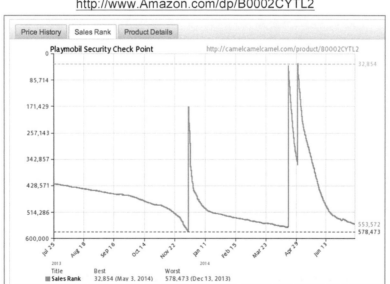

You can see that it sells very infrequently, although it does actually sell. Always be sure to check CamelCamelCamel sales rank histories before buying products like this.

http://camelcamelcamel.com/PLAYMOBIL%C2%AE-36138-Playmobil-Security-Check/product/B0002CYTL2

The one-step way to take a look at the eBay marketplace is to highlight the title with Context Search and choose eBay Completed from the drop down menu.

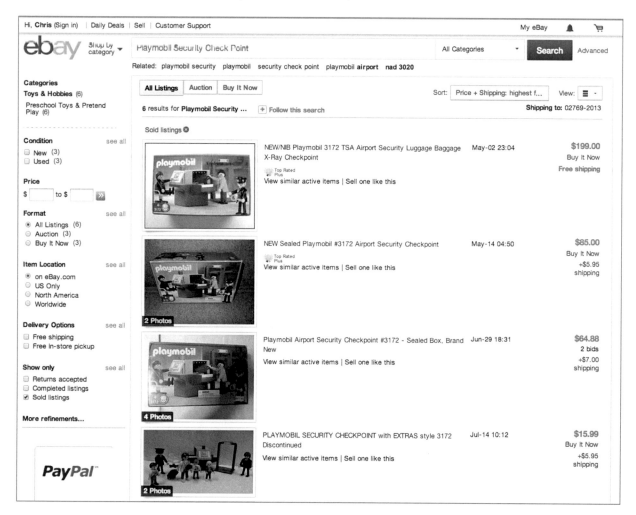

You'll see that the item actually sells on eBay as well: sometimes at high prices, and sometimes at low prices. If the margins are right, you might even consider getting into Used/Collectible items

Chapter 38 – Sharing Deals & BOLOs - Commentary

It should be very obvious by now, but Online Arbitrage deals have VALUE. Finding them makes you money, but only if you actually execute on the deal. What if there was a way to get value from finding an Online Arbitrage deal without ever having to spend a dime or process inventory?

A good friend of mine, Jay Bayne, runs a membership site called ScannerMonkey®. It's an online community of sellers who help each other and share deals. Some deals they share will be hard to find and some will be more actionable. Jay compiles a list of **BOLOs** (**B**e **O**n the **L**ook **O**ut) from every retailer for ScannerMonkey® members.

In addition to a closed Facebook group for ScannerMonkey® members, Jay also runs something called the BOLO Exchange. This is a Facebook group for people to meet and trade information on their own terms. For example, someone could post that they have a BOLO from Toys R Us stores that is ranked in the top 20,000 in Toys, costs $12, sells for $48 and gives an FBA payout of $39. They can also say that they are looking for other Toys R Us BOLOs or that they want some Online Arbitrage deals. People can send messages privately and network with each other for mutual benefit. As relationships are formed, they can exchange deals and information directly or even form their own mastermind group!

More information can be found at www.ScannerMonkey®.com. Tell Jay you heard about ScannerMonkey® from this book!

Online Arbitrage - Deals, BOLOs, VALUE, ScannerMonkey®, BOLO Exchange

http://youtu.be/MgAwU3AeqMY
http://bit.ly/boloexchange

Have you ever found a deal on Amazon for a specific seller like Amazon retail but the deal either wasn't for you or you just wanted to show it to someone else? If you just send them the ASIN or the Amazon product link, it will show them the Buy Box price, which may not be the price that you want to share with them. For example, when Amazon is at a hot price and they run out of stock, sometimes they will still take orders with future in-stock and delivery dates. When this happens, Amazon's offer will be listed in the other offers section. You can still share a specific URL with this offer by adding the Amazon offer to your cart, then editing your cart, and clicking on the item. Here is a short video about how to do this:

Online Arbitrage - Sharing Individual Offers from Amazon

http://youtu.be/-bJOp5iwEek
http://bit.ly/sharingoffers

Making Tax Exempt Purchases – Online

Quick question: Who is responsible for paying sales tax on retail items?

The buyer? Well, sort of. The correct answer is the END USER. The end user is the buyer who buys the item to use. There may be other buyers along the way, but it is only that last buyer, the end user, who pays the sales tax. When Wal-Mart purchases its inventory from a vendor or manufacturer, they do not pay sales tax.

As you are likely well aware, end users who buy online only pay sales tax on in-state purchases or on online purchases where the website has an in-state presence, or 'nexus'. This is one reason (out of many) that Amazon was able to become so powerful. By not having to collect sales tax on interstate purchases, their prices have been lower than if buyers purchased the same items in-state and had to pay sales tax. A lot of this is changing on Amazon as I write this book so be sure to check with the current tax laws both in your state and on Amazon.com for the most accurate and up-to-date information. Amazon is charging sales tax on more and more orders. As Amazon pushes towards same-day delivery options, it's very likely that pretty much all Amazon orders will be subject to sales tax.

When you buy items at retail or online that you intend to resell, you are not the end user. You are a reseller. Resellers do not pay sales tax on items that are destined for resale. Instead, they collect and remit sales tax just like any other retailer. If you want to act like a 'real' retailer, you have to play by the same rules.

Resellers who resell to in-state buyers are required to collect and remit sales tax on those in-state purchases. In a simplified example where you sell to all 50 states equally, you would only be collecting taxes on 2% of your sales, or from one out of fifty states. The other 49 states, or 98% of your sales, are sales on which you are not required to collect or remit sales tax. These rules change when you use Amazon's FBA program, as you will now have inventory in many different states. Amazon seller support can help you with how to properly set up your tax settings in your account. Amazon will then collect the sales tax for you, but you will be responsible for remitting it to the government.

The rules around sales tax are changing dramatically as I wrote this book. Instead of giving all of the current possible scenarios around sales tax collection on Amazon, I'm going to refer you to ask questions in our Facebook group. I also recommend you contact the guys at TaxJar. They have great sales tax solutions for Amazon sellers and it's their job to stay up to date with online sales tax rules. http://www.taxjar.com

This is not cheating or tax evasion; this is knowing and following the law. Knowing the law and the rules of resale will allow you to work smarter than your competition. Remember, knowledge is power! People who buy and sell retail products who don't follow this one simple rule will have product costs that are much higher than yours. This means your margins are bigger and you make more money. Over the long run, your business will thrive while they will be working too hard for less.

Here's how it works:

Every state will be a little different, but they will all be very similar. Google your local comptroller's office. They likely have their own website. You can call or email and explain what you want to do. Tell them you are a reseller and you want to know what your state requires to purchase tax exempt for resale. They will know exactly what you are talking about and will be able to help you. You may be able to do the entire thing online. When I first started, I had to actually go to the comptroller's office to fill out paperwork. Now the process in Texas is completely online.

Once you have your state tax ID number, you have to know how to use it. Some states will have a form that you can print out and present to the retailer. Some stores will just want the number for their records. Some stores will want to see the actual tax ID certificate so you may have to carry it with you. Some stores, like Home Depot, require you to set up a tax-exempt account in their computer system. This can be more difficult to initially set up, but it is actually the easiest to use.

Once your account is set up, you just have to tell them the purchase is tax exempt and give them your phone number, and they can pull up your account.

You may find some retail stores that will not sell to you tax-exempt for resale. This may be because they are a discount store that does not want their competition buying and reselling their products. If the margin is good enough, there is no reason to not still buy their inventory (and pay the sales tax) and resell the products online for a profit. Almost all of the major retailers will give you absolutely no trouble when purchasing tax-exempt for resale. If they do, politely ask to talk to a manager so that you can learn their rules for tax-exempt purchasing.

If you do this enough, you will run into lazy cashiers who just don't want to bother with the additional steps at checkout. Just be polite, but firm. You are running a business and you need to be diligent about lowering your costs and protecting your margins.

Some stores may do tax-exempt purchases so infrequently that they look at you like you are speaking a foreign language when you present your tax-exempt information. Always be polite and explain what you want to do. You may have to help them through the process or even have a manager come over to assist. It can sometimes take longer to check out with your purchases when doing tax-exempt in these situations, so use discernment when deciding to wait it out. If it takes 30 minutes to process and you're saving $200 in tax, definitely see it through. If it is a small purchase and you're only saving $3 in tax, just pay it and move on. Your time is a precious commodity that you cannot get back!

You may be asking if purchasing tax-exempt is only for local retailer purchases or can online deals be purchased tax-exempt? The answer is that anything you buy online for resale can also be purchased tax-exempt. It can be a little more complex, but here's how to do it:

Many websites that you can buy from will already be tax-free so don't worry about those. Let's use an example of a site that has a local presence in every state: HomeDepot.com. There is no way to check out at HomeDepot.com without paying sales tax. They may change this at some point, which would be awesome, but currently you have to pay the sales tax on all online orders. After you purchase, you contact HomeDepot.com customer support and explain that you are a reseller and that the items that you purchased are for resale. They will send you the paperwork to file for a refund of the sales tax. You fill it all out and include copies of all relevant documents such as your tax ID form and fax it back to them. They will then refund the sales tax that they charged back to your credit card. Not as easy as just not paying it at checkout, but still very worthwhile to process.

Another option is to claim sales tax credit when filing and remitting your sales tax records. Each state may vary, but when you file your sales tax records each month, there should be an option for entering an amount for purchases on which you were claiming sales tax credits. So even if you pay tax at checkout because you didn't have your sales tax ID or just checked out and paid sales tax in the interest of expediency, you can still claim the sales tax credit so that your purchases net out as tax free.

In my experience, it is a much better idea to not pay the sales tax when you purchase than to pay it and then try to get it back. Keep your business as simple as possible!

This is all a method of lowering your costs. The lower your costs are, the higher your margins will be. Simply knowing the rules allows you to have lower costs than your competitors. It's awesome.

If you live in an area where you will be purchasing tax free for resale from several different states, be sure to talk to your accountant or tax professional to be sure that you are following the rules for each state and filing any required reports properly.

As with all laws, tax laws can change. This information is accurate at the time of this writing. Be sure to check online for the current rules to be sure that you are following them correctly.

SETTING UP AMAZON TAX FREE

https://www.Amazon.com/gp/taxExemption? (Amazon Seller Central account login required)

With the Amazon Tax Exemption Program (ATEP), you may be eligible to use your tax exemptions on future purchases from either Amazon.com LLC or Amazon Digital Services, Inc. In order to establish and maintain your ATEP enrollment, we require that you provide us with a valid tax exemption certificate for the state(s) where you are located, and that you update your certificate on a periodic basis, in accordance with state laws and our Terms & Conditions.
Submit files online or email auto-exempt@Amazon.com

Example: Kmart

http://www.kmart.com/cstax/nb-100000000000012

http://bit.ly/kmarttax

Request Tax Exemption
We are required by law to collect all taxes based on where your order is being shipped or delivered. When you review your order total during the checkout process, you'll see the estimated sales tax. The actual charge to your credit card will reflect the applicable state and local taxes.
Tax Exemptions
If you're a tax-exempt entity, you can take advantage of your tax-exempt status for qualifying purchases made on Kmart.com. You simply place your order as usual and send us a copy of your certificate or other required documentation along with your Kmart.com order number to taxexempt@customerservice.sears.com or fax a copy to 1-847-645-6493. We will process the tax credit within 2 business days.
Although we keep a record of your tax-exempt status, you must follow the steps above with each tax-exempt Kmart.com purchase to receive the applicable tax credit.

Example: Wal-Mart

http://help.walmart.com/app/answers/detail/a_id/37

http://bit.ly/walmarttax

I am a retailer. What can I purchase tax exempt?

State law exempts items that are resold in the normal course of business. Items not normally resold in your business but purchased by special request may be taxed by our website. For these items, you may contact your state's Department of Revenue to request a refund of tax paid. Items or supplies used to run your business are taxable.

How do I submit my exemption information?

For Items Purchased from Walmart.com
Please call your state department of revenue or visit their website to determine the proper form you'll need to complete for your state. See our list of state department of revenue phone numbers and websites to locate the appropriate phone number.

Then fax your completed documents to our Tax Exemption Team at 1-877-971-5965 or email them to wmcserve@wal-mart.com.

Your request will be reviewed by one of our tax specialists. You will be notified by email once your tax exemption request has been processed.

- If approved, you will receive an email with instructions on how to request a refund on the eligible purchases made online and your exemption expiration date. We are unable to automatically exempt taxes during the online checkout process, and can only refund you the exempt taxes after you've made your purchase.
- If your request is denied, we will provide the reason why and may request additional information.

For Items Purchased from a Wal-Mart Marketplace Retailer
If your Order Details page in My Account shows the seller of your item to be anyone other than "Walmart.com," then you have purchased that item from one of our Marketplace Retailers.

If you have tax-exempt status, you will need to contact the Marketplace Retailer directly and have your order manually adjusted. Please visit the Marketplace Retailer Information Page for Marketplace Retailer details and contact information.

Once tax is credited, how can I get an updated invoice?

You may log into our site and check the status of your order through Track Your Orders. The Order Details, which can be used as an invoice, will show the credit as an adjustment to your order.

I have tax-exempt status at a Wal-Mart store. Do I have to file again?

Yes, you have to set up a new information file at Walmart.com or with the Wal-Mart Marketplace Retailer you are purchasing from. The Wal-Mart Stores information does not link with the Walmart.com information.

Are there limitations on payment methods for tax-exempt purchases?

Yes, many states require organizations, schools, churches and hospitals to use organizational funds. This means the credit card or checking account must be issued to the organization.

Who can I call to find the proper tax form for my state?

Please find your state below:

State	Phone Number	Website
Alabama	334-242-1490	www.ador.alabama.gov
Alaska	907-586-5205	www.dor.alaska.gov
Arkansas	501-682-7104	www.dfa.arkansas.gov
Arizona	800-843-7196	www.azdor.gov
California	800-400-7115	www.boe.ca.gov
Colorado	303-238-7378	www.colorado.gov/revenue
Connecticut	800-382-9463	www.ct.gov/drs
Delaware	302-577-8205	www.revenue.delaware.gov
District of Columbia	202-727-2476	www.otr.cfo.dc.gov
Florida	800-352-3671	www.myflorida.com/dor
Georgia	404-417-3209	www.etax.dor.ga.gov
Hawaii	800-222-3229	www.state.hi.us/tax
Idaho	800-972-7660	www.tax.idaho.gov
Illinois	800-732-8866	www.revenue.state.il.us
Indiana	317-233-4015	www.in.gov/dor
Iowa	800-367-3388	www.iowa.gov/tax
Kansas	785-368-8222	www.ksrevenue.org
Kentucky	502-564-4581	www.revenue.ky.gov
Louisiana	225-219-7462	www.rev.state.la.us
Maine	207-624-9693	www.maine.gov/revenue
Maryland	410-767-1300	www.comp.state.md.us
Massachusetts	800-392-6089	www.mass.gov/dor
Michigan	517-636-4230	www.michigan.gov/treasury
Minnesota	651-296-6181	www.revenue.state.mn.us

Who can I call to find the proper tax form for my state?

Please find your state below:

State	Phone Number	Website
Mississippi	601-923-7015	www.dor.ms.gov
Missouri	573-751-2836	www.dor.mo.gov
Nebraska	402-471-2971	www.revenue.ne.gov
Nevada	775 684-2000	www.tax.state.nv.us
New Jersey	609-292-6400	www.state.nj.us/treasury/taxation
New Mexico	505-827-0832	www.tax.newmexico.gov
New York	800-462-8100	www.tax.ny.gov
North Carolina	877-252-3052	www.dornc.com
North Dakota	701-328-3470	www.nd.gov/tax
Ohio	888-405-4089	www.tax.ohio.gov
Oklahoma	405-521-3160	www.tax.ok.gov
Pennsylvania	717-787-1064	www.revenue.state.pa.us
Rhode Island	401-222-2950	www.tax.ri.gov
South Carolina	803-898-5788	www.sctax.org
South Dakota	800-829-9188	www.dor.sd.gov
Tennessee	800-342-1003	www.tn.gov/revenue
Texas	800-252-5555	www.window.state.tx.us/taxes
Utah	800-662-4335	www.tax.utah.gov
Virginia	804-367-8037	www.tax.virginia.gov
Vermont	802-828-2551	www.state.vt.us/tax
Washington	800-647-7706	www.dor.wa.gov
West Virginia	800-982-8297	www.revenue.wv.gov
Wisconsin	608-266-2776	www.revenue.wi.gov
Wyoming	307-777-5200	www.revenue.wyo.gov

Vendor Spotlight - ScanPower

In the summer of 2010, Chris Green and Paul Retherford launched a service called FBAPower. It was the first third-party program designed specifically for FBA sellers. Innovative features such as displaying competitive FBA offers, differentiating Amazon's price, calculating 'price + shipping' (FBA net), and individual FBA label printing were introduced to the world of online selling. It's fun to be the first!

They later introduced FBAScout, the world's first live scouting service for iPhone and Android devices. Using the phone's camera or a wireless Bluetooth scanner, any seller now had unlimited access to marketplace pricing information. They could scan and sell pretty much ANYTHING. It included never-before-seen features like full product title, multiple UPC matches, product image, and FBA payout calculations.

It was a perfect combination of the pairing of Amazon's FBA program and the widespread adoption of smartphones with 3G and 4G wireless data speeds that ushered in a new era of product sourcing. No longer were sellers bound to the physical limitations of warehouse space or order processing and no longer were they limited in potential product knowledge. With a smartphone any seller, anywhere, could access Amazon pricing data and make sourcing decisions. And with FBA, they could send their entire inventory to Amazon and no longer spend their time picking orders and packing boxes. This was a turning point, and it was revolutionary.

Expanding outside of "just FBA," FBAPower was renamed ScanPower. They continued to release new and innovative programs and apps including ScanPower Repricing to help keep sellers' listings competitively priced and ScanPower Inventory Evaluator to bulk evaluate thousands of products at a time to quickly find the money makers.

The most popular ScanPower package is the Power Pack. It includes unlimited ScanPower Mobile Scouting using the ScanPower app for iPhone and Android, bundled with unlimited listing, labeling, and repricing using the ScanPower Listing & Repricing programs. These are web-based and work on Mac and PC.

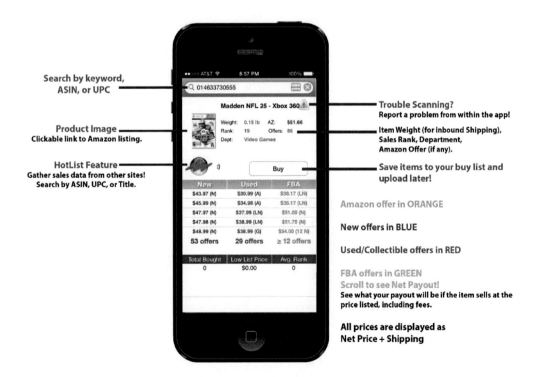

Use special signup code AMAZONBOOK to get a free one-month, full-featured trial of the entire ScanPower suite of tools.

Sign up here: https://unity.scanpower.com/register

Two new services that fall right in line with the strategies laid out in this book are:

ScanPower WebScout

A web-based tracking tool for serious Online Arbitrage sellers. Set up tracking on Amazon items or from other online retailers. Set triggers, get alerts, follow trends, and make better buying decisions. Online Arbitrage is not difficult. Streamlining and automating item tracking allows you to not only spend more time on the most profitable parts of your business, but also helps you get the jump on your competition and get to the best deals before the other sellers even know they exist.

For more information on ScanPower WebScout, please visit: ScanPower.com/WebScout

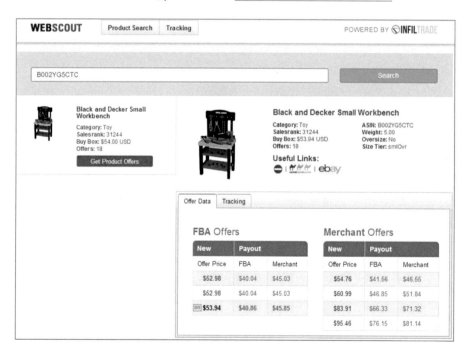

The new ScanPower WebScout takes Online Arbitrage to a whole new level. Enter a UPC or ASIN and get the complete pricing picture on one screen. Prices, sales rank, Buy Box, and payouts allow you to quickly see if it's an item with potential profits.

And whether you buy the item now or decide to pass, you can now start TRACKING the item for future profitability. And we're not just talking about tracking the Amazon price. We're talking about tracking the sales rank as well as the price and availability from OTHER WEBSITES!

What does this mean? Well, take a look at the graph. You can see the trends in price and sales rank from Amazon as well as the price and availability being tracked from Kohls.com.

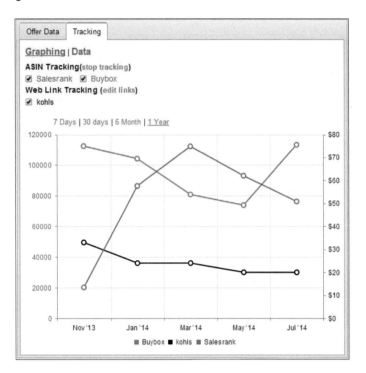

Do you see what you're able to do here? You can start tracking items and get alerts when the price on Amazon rises to a price that meets your margin goals. Sit back and wait until a product can be bought for $20 and sold for $70 while at the same time having a sales rank under 100,000.

The markets are always fluctuation and in equilibrium. Maybe not at the point in time of scanning a product, so start tracking them and be the first to know when market conditions meet your desired business goals.

This really takes all of the guesswork and risk out of the equation. Using the new ScanPower WebScout to monitor and track items takes Online Arbitrage to a whole new level.

In addition to the new Amazon ASIN tracking, the new ScanPower WebScout includes Web Tracking. You can choose which items and which websites to TRACK and then you'll have the ability to SORT.

This is incredible. Start tracking items and let the computers do the work for you. Say you want to see the items from Target with a minimum 40% margin that are ranked under 40,000 in the Toy category on Amazon. BOOM; here's your list. You can choose to sort by PROFIT or MARGIN. You can also watch the TRENDS of sales rank and price. Has the price been going up lately? Has the sales rank been going down? It's fun to find a product with great margin and profit, but if the sales rank is getting worse and worse, you may not want to buy too many of them.

Maybe you have some Wal-Mart gift cards to burn and you want to see the Amazon items that can be sourced from Wal-Mart with the best sales rank (for a quick turnaround) and minimum 10% margin. You'll get a list of those products.

It's all about having the best, most relevant data in order to make buying decisions. Online Arbitrage is easy when you really think about it. Anyone can do it, but the sellers with the best tools are the ones who get to the best deals first.

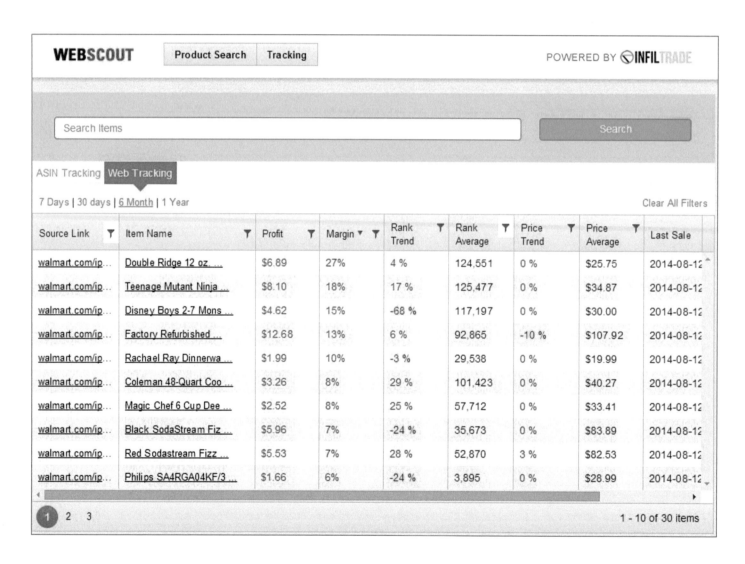

Source Link	Item Name	Profit	Margin	Rank Trend	Rank Average	Price Trend	Price Average	Last Sale
walmart.com/ip...	Double Ridge 12 oz. ...	$6.89	27%	4 %	124,551	0 %	$25.75	2014-08-12
walmart.com/ip...	Teenage Mutant Ninja ...	$8.10	18%	17 %	125,477	0 %	$34.87	2014-08-12
walmart.com/ip...	Disney Boys 2-7 Mons ...	$4.62	15%	-68 %	117,197	0 %	$30.00	2014-08-12
walmart.com/ip...	Factory Refurbished ...	$12.68	13%	6 %	92,865	-10 %	$107.92	2014-08-12
walmart.com/ip...	Rachael Ray Dinnerwa ...	$1.99	10%	-3 %	29,538	0 %	$19.99	2014-08-12
walmart.com/ip...	Coleman 48-Quart Coo ...	$3.26	8%	29 %	101,423	0 %	$40.27	2014-08-12
walmart.com/ip...	Magic Chef 6 Cup Dee ...	$2.52	8%	25 %	57,712	0 %	$33.41	2014-08-12
walmart.com/ip...	Black SodaStream Fiz ...	$5.96	7%	-24 %	35,673	0 %	$83.89	2014-08-12
walmart.com/ip...	Red Sodastream Fizz ...	$5.53	7%	28 %	52,870	3 %	$82.53	2014-08-12
walmart.com/ip...	Philips SA4RGA04KF/3 ...	$1.66	6%	-24 %	3,895	0 %	$28.99	2014-08-12

1 2 3   1 - 10 of 30 items

ScanPower RSS Reader

Earlier we saw how to use RSS feeds to work with IFTTT alerts (Chapter 27). Here we will expand on the use of RSS feeds for Online Arbitrage.

What is RSS? (from http://www.whatisrss.com)

RSS (Rich Site Summary or Really Simple Syndication) is a format for delivering regularly changing web content. Many news-related sites, weblogs and other online publishers syndicate their content as an RSS Feed to whoever wants it.

Why RSS? Benefits and Reasons for using RSS

RSS solves a problem for people who regularly use the web. It allows you to easily stay informed by retrieving the latest content from the sites you are interested in. You save time by not needing to visit each site individually.

Some important sites that have RSS feeds available to online sellers:

Amazon Movers & Shakers, Best Sellers, New Releases, Most Wished For, Top Rated, and Gift Ideas

The RSS feed is at the bottom of each of these Amazon pages:

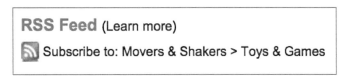

CamelCamelCamel has RSS feeds for any Top Price Drop sort that defines crazy-powerful:

Wal-Mart: http://www.walmart.com/cp/RSS-Feeds/621119

Ben's Bargains from Chapter 20: http://bensbargains.net/rss-feeds/

FatWallet from Chapter 21: http://www.fatwallet.com/rssinfo.php

Many other sites have RSS feeds as well. Just Google the site name + RSS to find them.

You read earlier about using RSS feeds to monitor sites and set up ales. With the ScanPower RSS Reader, you're able to automate this process, quickly view the newest price changes, and compare them to historical pricing and graphing sites like Keepa and CamelCamelCamel all on one screen. When you can evaluate more deals and do it faster than your competition, you'll be the one scooping up all of the best inventory while your competitors wonder where all the deals went.

Take your Online Arbitrage to the next level by automating searches and getting all relevant information all in one place for quick product evaluation. The more products that you can evaluate and the faster that you can evaluate them, the more profitable deals you're going to find.

For more information on ScanPower RSS Reader, please visit: ScanPower.com/RSSReader

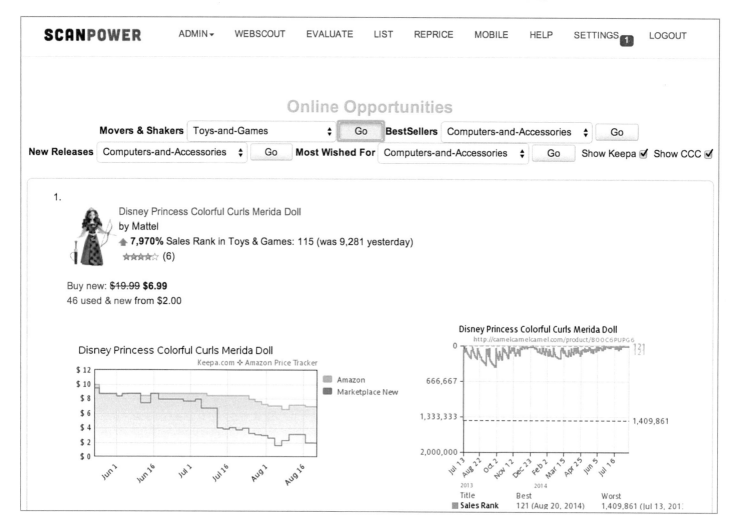

That's it. Phew. You made it to the end. THANK YOU for buying the book! I truly hope that you enjoyed reading it as much as I enjoyed creating it. Please visit www.OnlineArbitrage.com for the latest updates. This business keeps changing so that's the best way to stay up to date with any changes to this book.

Let's connect! Please find me online at facebook.com/chris and join our group at facebook.com/groups/scanpower

Or email me at chris@scanpower.com. You can even call or text me at 214-298-6866

Video Checklist

60-Minute FAST TRACK to becoming an AWESOME Amazon seller! http://www.scanpower.com/fbavideos

Getting 94 UPS Delivery Notification Emails at one time from Disney Store Online Arbitrage http://bit.ly/upsemails

Online Arbitrage - Finding Deals on the Homepage of CamelCamelCamel iPad Keyboard & Case http://bit.ly/cccipadcase

Online Arbitrage - Amazon Sports & Outdoors 80% Clearance Buys http://bit.ly/80percentdeals

Online Arbitrage - Dino Zoomer - Fourth Quarter 2014 Breakout Hot Toy? http://bit.ly/zoomerdino

INTRODUCTION

Online Arbitrage - Be Aware of Your Amazon Browsing History http://bit.ly/shoppinghistory

Chapter 2

RAW Online Arbitrage - Entire Process, Rabbit Trails, Research, Deals http://bit.ly/entireprocess

Chapter 3

Online Price Tracker and Mobile App - PoachIt.com http://bit.ly/poachitvideo

Chapter 4

Online Arbitrage - Example of using KEEPA.com to quickly find and evaluate deals http://bit.ly/keepavideo

How to use www.keepa.com to identify Online Arbitrage opportunities on Amazon.com http://bit.ly/keepavideo2

Chapter 5

Online Arbitrage - CamelCamelCamel walkthrough for resellers, tracking http://bit.ly/camelvideo

Chapter 7

Online Arbitrage - TheTracktor.com, finding deals, quickly evaluating them, setting up alerts http://bit.ly/tracktorvideo

Chapter 9

Learning more about My Little Pony toys from Toys R Us, Target, Amazon, and Hasbro http://bit.ly/ponyvideo

Chapter 10

Online Arbitrage - Amazon Suppressed Buy Box http://bit.ly/suppressedbuybox

Movers & Shakers, Keepa, Alerts, Frustration Free Packaging, Oversize, and MORE http://bit.ly/dealexample

Online Arbitrage - Quickly evaluating items from the Amazon Movers & Shakers list – TOYS http://bit.ly/quicktoys

Amazon Movers & Shakers - NERF Toys on sale http://bit.ly/nerfsale

Paw Patrol Research and Alerts from Amazon Movers & Shakers Pages http://bit.ly/pawpatrolvideo

Searching for Out Of Stock (OOS) Paw Patrol Toys on Amazon.com for Online Arbitrage http://bit.ly/pawpatrolvideo2

Online Arbitrage - Finding the Amazon Listing for Sold Out Amazon Items http://bit.ly/soldoutitems

Chapter 11

Online Arbitrage - When a good deal isn't as good as you think http://bit.ly/notadeal

Online Arbitrage Deal Due Diligence - TheTracktor.com http://bit.ly/tracktordeal

Chapter 12

Online Arbitrage Rabbit Trails - TheTracktor Almond Joy Candy Replenishables http://bit.ly/rabbittrail1

Online Arbitrage Rabbit Trail - CamelCamelCamel Dog Treats http://bit.ly/rabbittrail2

Online Arbitrage Rabbit Trail - Keepa Deals to Wal-Mart Starburst Candy http://bit.ly/rabbittrail3

Amazon Movers & Shakers Rabbit Trail to eBay - NERF GUNS http://bit.ly/rabbittrail4

Online Arbitrage - BOLO Hunting with Pricenoia, Keepa, CamelCamelCamel, Google, and ToyWiz http://bit.ly/rabbittrail5

Online Arbitrage - Rabbit Trail Deals, Lawn Mowers, and $1,000 American Flags http://bit.ly/rabbittrail6

Chapter 13

Online Arbitrage - TMNT April O'Neil, Google Searches, and Rabbit Trails http://bit.ly/rabbittrail7

Chapter 19

Robin Williams & Celebrity News Affecting the Arbitrage http://bit.ly/robinwilliamsnews

Chapter 27

Setting up an alert through IFTTT from an RSS feed - Online Arbitrage http://bit.ly/iftttvideo1

Online Arbitrage - LEGO Ferrari, Product Searches, EBay, Amazon, IFTTT, Craigslist http://bit.ly/iftttvideo2

Chapter 29

Online Arbitrage - Dymo 450 XL from Amazon $116, Finding, Friends http://bit.ly/dymodeal

Chapter 30

Online Arbitrage from Daily Deal Sites like WOOT.com http://bit.ly/wootdealvideo

Chapter 37

Online Arbitrage - Commentary on TWO Easy Money Making Deals http://bit.ly/dealcommentary

Chapter 38

Online Arbitrage - Deals, BOLOs, VALUE, ScannerMonkey®, BOLO Exchange http://bit.ly/boloexchange

Online Arbitrage - Sharing Individual Offers from Amazon http://bit.ly/sharingoffers

Made in the USA
Middletown, DE
11 November 2014